EVERYBODY
WAS
KUNG-FU
DANCING

Other books by Chet Flippo:

Your Cheatin' Heart: A Biography of Hank Williams
On the Road With the Rolling Stones
Yesterday: The Unauthorized Biography of Paul McCartney

EVERYBODY WAS KUNG-FU DANCING

Chronicles of the Lionized and the Notorious

Chet Flippo

St. Martin's Press   New York

"The Lionized and the Dead: A Murder and a Literary Star Turns Fugitive" from *New York* magazine, August 10, 1981. Reprinted with permission from the author.

"The Mysterious Rhinestone Cowboy" from *Gallery* magazine, December 1989. Reprinted with permission from the author.

"John Lennon vs. Albert Goldman" from *TV Guide,* March 4, 1989. Reprinted with permission from the author.

"The Very Reverend Al Green." Printed with permission of *Tennessee Illustrated* and Whittle Communications.

"The Private Years of John Lennon" by Chet Flippo from *Rolling Stone* issue 380. Straight Arrow Publishers Inc. © 1982. All rights reserved. Reprinted by permission.

"On the Town With Tony Bennett" from *New York* magazine, May 11, 1981. Reprinted with permission from the author.

"I Sing the Solid Body Electric: An Interview With Les Paul" from *Texas Monthly,* August 1974. Reprinted with permission from the author.

(Credits continued on page 293)

EVERYBODY WAS KUNG-FU DANCING: CHRONICLES OF THE LIONIZED AND THE NOTORIOUS. Copyright © 1991 by Chet Flippo. All rights reserved. Printed in the United States of America. No part of this book may be used or reproduced in any manner whatsoever without written permission except in the case of brief quotations embodied in critical articles or reviews. For information, address St. Martin's Press, 175 Fifth Avenue, New York, N.Y. 10010.

Design by Karin Batten

Library of Congress Cataloging-in-Publication Data

Flippo, Chet.
    Everybody was Kung-Fu dancing : chronicles of the lionized and the notorious / Chet Flippo.
        p. cm.
    ISBN 0-312-06349-0
    1. Rock music—United States—History and criticism.   2. United States—Popular culture.   I. Title.
    ML3534.F63 1991
    781.64′0973—dc20
                                                                91-18105
                                                                CIP

First Edition: October 1991
10 9 8 7 6 5 4 3 2 1

MAY 2 6 1992

For Doug Sahm,
a.k.a. Sir Douglas

Contents

Preface

People often ask me, "Chet, just exactly what have you learned from twenty years of magazine work?" I seldom answer them, but when I do, I tell them that magazine writing is not too dissimilar from the job of being a sweeper behind a circus parade. You surely know the story of the sweeper who was complaining about all the elephant manure he had to sweep up. When asked why he didn't just quit, he said indignantly, 'What? And leave show business?''

Not to put too fine a point on it, magazine writing can be enervating. It can be degrading. It can also be one hell of a lot of fun. In some ways it reminds me of the military: You get to travel and see the world and meet lots of interesting people. You also have to follow the rules and put in your time before they'll let you out to do what you really want to.

In my case, I started magazine writing twenty-one years ago for the plain and simple reason that there was one particular magazine that I liked very much. That magazine was *Rolling Stone* and I decided that I wanted to work for it and went on to do so. It was enormous fun and incredible hard work for several years. Then it wasn't so much fun anymore but it was still very hard work. So I left. That was also about the time that a lot of magazines in this country decided that their proper function was to serve as a cheerleader for the rich and famous, a function that some of them are still performing.

That's one reason that I was long resistant to the idea of publishing a book containing some of my magazine pieces. Those books are generally just full of a bunch of profiles of rich and famous people. That stuff is hard enough to read once, in the magazine itself, let alone twice.

But my editor, Jim Fitzgerald, and my agent, Jim Stein, convinced me that there was a way to make an anthology a cohesive work that might even make a point or otherwise serve some useful purpose. I am grateful to them for that.

I am also grateful to editors of the following publications: *Rolling Stone, New York, TV Guide, Playboy, Texas Monthly, Fame, GQ, Q*

Magazine of London, Special Report: Personalities, and *Tennessee Illustrated.*
Special thanks go to the Country Music Foundation.

The pieces herein represent a cross-section of two decades' worth of
toiling behind this old Smith–Corona. May you read them in peace.

Chet Flippo
Malibu, California
March 3, 1991

Part One

THE LIONIZED

Chapter 1

Justice

The Lionized and the Dead: A Murder and a Literary Star Turns Fugitive

At 5:00 A.M., Saturday, July 18, 1981, twenty-two-year-old Richard Adan decided to call Ritchie, his bride of five months. Adan, a Cuban-born actor-dancer-playwright, was working the lobster shift as a waiter in his father-in-law's restaurant, the Bini-Bon, at 79 Second Avenue, on Manhattan's Lower East Side. It's a popular twenty-four-hour spot in the middle of a neighborhood of artists, actors, musicians—and criminals—where rents are low and a small-town, look-after-your-neighbor atmosphere still prevails. Some people persist in calling the area the "East Village." Just up Second Avenue, what used to be the Fillmore East is now the Saint, a gay disco of moneyed elegance. Outside, wandering mental patients relieve themselves in the gutter next to glittering limousines.

The Bini-Bon, though, is home to neighborhood artists who linger for hours over fifty-cent cups of Lapsang souchong tea and leave messages for one another on the overflowing bulletin board by the pay phone up front.

At 5:00 A.M. that Saturday, however, business was slow—just a guy and two women having breakfast together. A good time to call Ritchie, thought Adan. They both were so busy with classes and work that they didn't see each other enough. They were happy, though. Just recently they'd finally been able to afford to move out of Ritchie's stepfather's place, on East 10th Street, and rent their first apartment, up on 17th. And Richard had written a play, a drama about his neighborhood, which

the La Mama Experimental Theatre Club, a block away from the Bini-Bon on East 4th, had decided to produce.

He called Ritchie; she answered sleepily. She said she had a rehearsal scheduled and what did he want? They joked a while, then said good-bye. Richard, who was wearing black chino pants, a black T-shirt, and a short, dark-blue waiter's apron, went back to his station, between the bar (a misnomer, since the Bini-Bon has no beer or liquor license) and the kitchen.

The pale, gaunt man who was sitting with the two young women at the fourth table in from the door got up from his wrought-iron ice-cream-parlor chair and walked four paces across the white-tiled floor toward Richard Adan. The man was wearing steel-rimmed glasses, a tan shirt, black pants, and brown shoes, and had a stubbly walrus mustache. He had dined at the Bini-Bon many times before and was known there. That night, he and the two young women, who told a waitress they were students at Barnard and Vassar, had been drinking their way through the Lower East Side, passing through the Berlin Bar on Broadway. One report said they had ended up at Night Birds, a dim, raucous dive across the street. The pale, gaunt man, by official accounts, asked Richard Adan where the men's room was. The Bini-Bon, Adan told him, has no public rest rooms, mainly to discourage mental patients in the area from using the place. Authorities say that the pale, gaunt man refused to believe Adan and in fact took his answer as a personal insult. The two spoke in measured tones. There was no pushing or shoving. Then the pale, gaunt man invited Richard Adan outside, and they went.

What they said outside is not known. They walked to the corner of Second Avenue and 5th Street. Something happened. In a blur, the two figures passed in front of the restaurant, and outside a liquor store next door, the pale, gaunt man drew a knife and expertly penetrated Richard Adan's heart with a single thrust. Adan staggered backward and collapsed on the grimy sidewalk. He bled profusely. A doctor later said that he had died exactly eight seconds after the stabbing. He died with his eyes stark wide open. The last convulsions of pierced heart sent blood pumping out both ears. Even so, dozens of people gathered and tried to give him mouth-to-mouth resuscitation.

The 911 call from the Bini-Bon brought two cops immediately from the 9th Precinct, a stone fortress half a block east on 5th. (The station house was used for the exteriors in "Kojak.") The pale, gaunt man rushed back into the Bini-Bon to get the women, and the three ran west on 5th Street. Police quickly captured the women. The man got away. The women said that the man who had escaped the cops was one Jack Henry Abbott, author. The women have since been unavailable to the press. The ambulance responding to the 911 call arrived thirty minutes after the 911 call—29 minutes and 52 seconds too late.

Jack Henry Abbott, thirty-seven years old, was an unlikely figure to become simultaneously a literary celebrity and a wanted man. Born in Oscoda, Michigan, on January 21, 1944, half-Irish, half-Chinese, Abbott was ousted early from a broken family and deposited in foster homes. He dropped out of school in sixth grade. At nine he was first sent, for antisocial behavior, to a juvenile-detention center. At twelve, he went to the Utah State Industrial School for Boys. Released when he was eighteen, he soon landed in the Utah State Penitentiary, in Draper, for stealing and cashing checks. Three years later, he killed a fellow inmate with a knife and injured another in a fight, drawing an additional three-to-twenty-year sentence. In 1971, he escaped. He robbed a savings bank in Denver and lived in Montreal before being caught. The bank robbery earned him a nineteen-year sentence. By his own admission, he was more than a problem prisoner. He claims he spent between fourteen and fifteen years in solitary confinement, eventually getting to the point where he ate cockroaches.

It has been said that long-term convicts become either jailhouse lawyers, to win a retrial, or jailhouse writers, to win some high-toned literary giant as a patron or supporter. Eldridge Cleaver wrote his way out. Kate Millett sponsored a convict in California. William Buckley helped spring Edgar Smith from prison in New Jersey. Buckley immediately put him on his TV show, "Firing Line," and for a while Smith was a kind of sideshow for Buckley. Until Smith was arrested and re-incarcerated for kidnapping and attempted murder. Buckley wasn't around when Smith went back to prison.

Prison groupies are nothing new—though the French were always better than Americans at spotting up-and-coming jailhouse writers. Some of Norman Mailer's friends began worrying about his prison fixation years ago. They felt that Mailer—whose literary output deals largely with violent conflict or sex, or both—had become some sort of chip-on-the-shoulder Hemingway without a war to knock the chip off.

Then came Gary Gilmore. Even before Mailer latched onto him and started writing *The Executioner's Song* about him, Gary Gilmore was already Jack Henry Abbott's hero. (Gilmore was in fact the idol of serious prisoners everywhere because of his spit-in-the-face-of-the-firing-squad attitude.) Abbott, a voracious reader who had long been firing off letters to literary giants (Jerzy Kosinski was severely scolded by Abbott for not being a Communist), wrote to Mailer. Abbott told him he couldn't possibly write a prison book without knowing what prison was like for someone who grew up behind bars. Mailer agreed, and they corresponded. Mailer got Bob Silvers, editor of *The New York Review of Books,* to publish some of the letters in the June 26, 1980, issue. Erroll McDonald, an editor at Random House, thought the letters might be the basis of a book. Random House editor-in-chief Jason Epstein agreed.

McDonald got in touch with Mailer's agent, Scott Meredith, and a deal was made for Abbott to write a book. The advance was for $12,500, most of which went for legal fees to help Abbott earn parole. McDonald visited Abbott in the federal penitentiary in Marion, Illinois, and brought back reams of letters.

In August 1980, Abbott's request for a federal parole was denied: He had a record as a chronic troublemaker, and, moreover, he had no job offers or job possibilities on the outside. In the next few months, Abbott suddenly became a cooperative prisoner and was offered work as Mailer's researcher. In January, his federal parole request was approved, and he was transferred to a Utah prison to serve out his state sentence there. At that point, Mailer, McDonald, Silvers, and Meredith (but not Epstein) wrote glowing letters to the Utah State Board of Pardons. Random House was about to publish a collection of Abbott's letters, entitled *In the Belly of the Beast,* with an introduction by Mailer, who was finishing his long-awaited Egyptian novel and said he needed further research, guaranteeing Abbott a job as his research assistant at $150 a week. Utah was sufficiently impressed to terminate his sentence. Federal authorities had told Abbott he'd be officially paroled on August 26. In the meantime, though, he was out of prison. On June 5, Abbott flew from Salt Lake City to JFK, where Mailer met him and took him to the Salvation Army Men's Correctional Facility, a halfway house at 3rd Street and the Bowery.

McDonald said he had to show Abbott how to do things that he had never done as a free adult, like open a bank account and find a doctor. He said he even had to show him how to catch a bus. Having spent most of his life in institutions, Abbott literally did not know what civilian life was like. Yet he had the run of the city—despite still being a federal prisoner. Unfortunately for him, he became a celebrity author as soon as he hit town.

Critics praised his book but mostly glossed over the strong impression it gives that he was probably incapable of instant rehabilitation.

He wrote,

> There is a saying: *The first cut is the deepest.* Do not believe that. The first cut is nothing. You can spit in my face once or twice and it is nothing. You can take something away that belongs to me and I can learn to live without it.
>
> But you cannot spit in my face every day for ten thousand days; you cannot take all that belongs to me, one thing at a time, until you have gotten down to reaching for my eyes, my voice, my hands, my heart. You cannot do this and say it is nothing.
>
> If society has the right to do to me what it has done (and is still doing), which society *does* have, then I have the right, at least, to walk free at some time in my life even if the odds are by now overwhelming that I may not be as other men.

Abbott was obviously uncomfortable with instant stardom. He gave an interview to *Rolling Stone* magazine that was so boring it was killed *after* he became a fugitive. Mailer and Abbott went on the TV show "Good Morning America." It was painful to watch. John Forsythe was substituting for David Hartman, and he and Mailer and Abbott were

obviously lost. Forsythe asked Mailer questions about Abbott, as if
Abbott weren't even there. Abbott broke out in a Richard Nixon–like
sweat and rolled his eyes. When, rarely, he talked, he said only that he
was still "trying to get an attitude" toward freedom, that he thought
he had been manipulated by behavioral psychologists, and that he felt
no fear that "propensities" that had driven him to crime in the past
might return. "I don't even remember what I was sent to prison for,"
he said coldly.

At the Salvation Army facility, five and a half hours after Adan's killing,
the police were furious. A "security guard" who works the door, and
Dennis Banks, Abbott's counselor, had let them into the center, but
they had been denied entry into Abbott's room until they got a warrant,
which takes several hours. Abbott's small room, upstairs, overlooking
the Bowery, was double-locked. None of the other rooms were. Abbott
had installed a dead-bolt lock after complaining that someone had been
coming into his room and "messing with his papers." No one had a
key to the extra lock, so the police had to break in. The room had a
bed, a desk, and a chair. Federal marshals removed Abbott's personal
effects.

A prison official said the facility's attendance records showed that
someone had personally verified Abbott's presence there at midnight
Friday and again at 3:00, 7:00, and 8:00 A.M. Saturday. Witnesses have
placed him elsewhere. The deskman told police that he had faked the
8:00 A.M. check-in. Center staffers initially refused to believe that Abbott
was a suspect in a violent crime.

A source said that the facility had a policy of making a random search
for weapons every four to six weeks. John Dockendorff, the center's
director, said that a regular weekly search is conducted. The residents
of the center are prisoners awaiting parole, so the building is, in effect,
a prison with no bars. One night, after the supposed 11 P.M. curfew, I
sat across the Bowery and watched. In three hours, twenty people went
in and out.

After the disappearance of Abbott, federal prison officials began a
"thorough review" of the halfway house.

As a site for a home to "reorient" hard-core offenders to society, East
3rd Street between the Bowery and Second Avenue seems the worst
place in the world. Derelicts, criminals, dope peddlers, dope addicts,
serious mental cases, you name it, they line the sidewalks night and day.
The Men's Shelter at 8 East 3rd, across the street, deals with about 1,500
men a day. There's even a class of criminals in the area so base that they
prey on the Men's Shelter derelicts.

"Welcome to Bellevue South," Ann Pollon, a sculptor and neighborhood activist, told me on a walking tour of the area.

Besides the Salvation Army and the Men's Shelter, there is Booth House on the Bowery (also run by the Salvation Army, and mostly housing mental patients), the Bowery Mission on Broadway, the Women's Shelter on Lafayette, and the numerous SRO hotels that become homes to mental patients who have been dumped from Manhattan State Hospital. Violent crime is a way of life here. "We should all sue the city," a resident said. "We're being held prisoners in our own homes."

This is the area where life prisoner Jack Abbott was supposed to get back into society.

Very few people in the neighborhood knew that 1 East 3rd was full of prisoners. Said community activist Susan Leelike, "I didn't know those were federal prisoners. Just one more nail in our coffin down here. The Salvation Army has been pious and hides under a cloak of God. It was always very hard to get information out of them."

That it is. I went down to 1 East 3rd the night after Adan was killed, knocked on the locked door, and was buzzed in. In a dark room I could see two Doberman pinschers and a semicircle of men with arms folded silently staring at me. I asked for John Dockendorff, the facility's director. There was a long silence. "Monday morning," one man finally said, and I didn't mind leaving.

Monday, in daylight, the place was a bit cheerier. I was buzzed in and saw the large dayroom in daylight: a tattered couch, pink walls, a desk where tenants sign themselves in and out. Twenty cushioned chairs filled the middle of the room—four orderly rows of five chairs each. On the left was an organ; on the right, a piano. The chairs faced a large glassed-in office that was raised about a foot from the dayroom. Walking toward me was a man I recognized as Dockendorff. He was wearing a dark sport coat, a dark open-necked shirt, black trousers, and sunglasses. I identified myself. He spun on his heels without speaking, took out a set of keys, unlocked the dead-bolt lock on the door to his glassed-in office, went in, and locked the door behind him. He signaled with a finger to a young woman, who asked me to leave immediately. "We have nothing to say to you," she said. "Well, then," I asked, as I was eased out the door, "who does?" "Call Edward Henson . . . Bureau of Prisons," she said.

Many phone calls later, I found an Edward Henson, a "community-programs officer" with the U.S. Bureau of Prisons. He said 1 East 3rd was a Salvation Army facility that was under contract to the Federal Bureau of Prisons and the New York State Division of Parole to provide pre-release services to prisoners about to be released. What were the services? He was not completely sure: "decompression treatment, job situation, community orientation." He said he thought there were nine federal prisoners plus six prisoners serving weekend sentences, and an unknown number of New York State parolees. He said he thought the facility was checked morning and evening to make sure nobody ran away. He said the facility had last seen Jack Abbott at 7:30 A.M. on Saturday, and authorities there didn't know he was missing until the police came around three and a half hours later and asked, Where the hell is this Abbott guy?

"I will *never* go back to prison." Abbott said that to several people (whom police will not identify). In the hours after Adan was killed, he may have beat on Erroll McDonald's apartment door. The Random House editor refused to answer the knocks and has since moved out of his apartment. At 11:00 A.M., as police officers arrived at the Salvation Army facility, Jack Abbott was eighty-four blocks uptown having lunch with writer Jean Malaquais at 87th and York. During the lunch, he didn't say anything about a stabbing. The police might have found him there had they not been waiting for a search warrant.

On the Tuesday before the incident, Abbott had called on agent Scott Meredith and drawn $1,000 against advances of foreign book sales. At the time of his disappearance, he apparently had most of that money. Investigators are still trying to determine if Abbott had reverted to a previous heroin habit.

Norman Mailer has refused to comment. Abbott's other backers have been quicker to point out that they had praised only Abbott's literary talents and had not endorsed him as a person. Meanwhile, some of them are living in fear, dreading a midnight knock on the door by a desperate fugitive holding a knife with a one-inch-wide blade.

Some people still doubt the "bathroom theory" as the motive for murder, but Detective William Majeski, of the Ninth Precinct, is not among them. "Abbott and Adan did not know each other," he said. "According to witnesses, this was an argument over using the bathroom." It was a "macho thing," said one source close to the investigation.

One week after his son-in-law was killed, Henry Howard sat at the same table in the Bini-Bon where Jack Henry Abbott had dined.

He appeared exhausted but he said he wanted to talk. "At first I didn't want to talk to the press at all, but then I saw all these newspaper stories about 'famous author murders waiter.' Famous author murders statistic number fourteen, and I thought, 'Oh, wow, man, he has Random House, Norman Mailer, Jerzy Kosinski behind him.' Well, Richard was *not* just a statistic. He was a talented human being with a positive vision of his future. His writing was poetry; it wasn't based on prison experiences and the bottom line of society, the dregs. He had something to say."

He sipped his coffee and stared at the counter behind which Richard Adan, whom Howard frequently called his son, would normally have been working.

"It was really odd," he continued. "It was a very, very low-key discussion about using the bathroom. I say low-key because otherwise someone would have called the police. All the staff here has been warned a hundred times to not confront any customers, just call nine-one-one if they won't leave, and that's it. I think that Richard saw the guy was upset. He was very quiet, and he said, 'Let's go outside and we'll settle it out there.' And Richard went, thinking there would be no violence."

Had he been approached by federal agents?

"Yes," he said angrily. "I threw them out of here. They killed my son. Jack Abbott's a loaded gun. You don't put him out on the street. You don't take somebody with twenty-five years in a garbage camp, in a horror camp, and suddenly throw him in the streets of the Lower East Side. Are you kidding? I mean, *we're* not equipped to live down here. Let them try him out on Fifth Avenue at Fifty-seventh. If jail is the belly of the beast, then what is the Bowery? And it's not over, 'cause he's still out there. And when you've graduated from the belly of the beast, and you've killed before and you're terrified . . . It's like what my daughter said: 'He killed my husband, but I don't want him killed. I just want to make sure that he never ever kills anybody's husband again.' And the only way that can happen is to take him off the streets and take him off *forever*. Don't experiment with our lives."

The Mysterious Rhinestone Cowboy

Marvin Gammage, who rides herd over the tiny orange-and-white Texas Hatters shop on South Lamar, in Austin, Texas, gets a regular trade of celebrities who want custom-made hats. He has autographed pictures on the wall of Charlie Rich and Willie Nelson, Jerry Jeff Walker and University of Texas football coach Darrell Royal, governors and senators and ambassadors, all giving off the old 100-watt grin for being important enough for Marvin to make them a hat. If you're just the usual off-the-street trade with an old fedora to be cleaned and blocked, you can count on a two-month wait. Big shots mean nothing to Marvin either; what he sees in a man is his hat size and if the hat size happens to belong to a Mideast potentate, that won't speed up the service.

He's seen everything and met everybody and makes the best hats in the world, so he seldom pays any attention when someone who acts important stalks into the six-by-twenty waiting room.

Therefore, it was an event of great import when, one Saturday afternoon, Marvin looked twice and actually blinked once at a customer coming through the door. The patron walked with the lurching sideways gait of a biker, and other customers cleared a path for him and wondered if they should grab the kids and run. This looked like a tough cookie for sure. He was big and confident, you could tell, and was wearing spurs and rhinestones and an eight-inch-wide leather belt with silver studs and giant letters proclaiming that the owner was DAVID ALLAN COE. This David Allan Coe jingled up to the counter and announced in a soft voice that he'd maybe like to see about getting a hat. Ever anxious to please, Marvin pointed to the models on display. Coe shook his head, silver earring dangling, and looked for something else. "Jerry Jeff said y'all had *big* hats."

Ralph Anderson, Marvin's young apprentice, nodded knowingly. "*I* know what you want. C'mere." Ralph reached under the counter and pulled out a dog-eared copy of the 1941 Stockman's Catalog. "Look at these here hats," said Anderson.

Coe looked. Eight pages on, his eyes lighted up. "This's it!" What he'd found was the old "Montana Dick" hat, a close relative of the models that Tom Mix and Gene Autry popularized, with a seven-inch crown and a five-inch rolled brim. "You just cain't find these no more"—Ralph winked—"but we bought up the last supply." Coe wanted one, immediately, the bigger the better. "I'll tell you what," Ralph confided. "I know you're playin' at the Opry House tonight. I'll just make you up a black Montana Dick and you can wear it on stage tonight."

Ralph went to work, submerging himself in a cloud of steam in the back room, and four hours later he emerged with an enormous black hat, the only known Montana Dick extant. Ralph had found an inch-wide rhinestone hatband, which pleased Coe no end. He scrambled to his feet from the corner, where he had sat writing a song, his mere presence upsetting the customers. Coe sat the Montana Dick on his tumble of brown hair, backed away from the mirror, scrutinized his image from every angle, and allowed himself a rare smile of approval. "This's *it*."

He ambled outside, oblivious to the stares of passersby, and tried various poses in the Montana Dick until he found the cowboy slouch that fitted him. "Jerry Jeff's gonna be jealous of *this* hat," he said, laughing.

Not many people, in or out of show business, can get away with walking the streets in a glitter suit, patent leather boots, cascades of jewelry, self-administered tattoos, and the biggest hat this side of central casting, but with David Allan Coe it all seems natural. He's a born magnet, it seems, for attention. "Even when I don't have my rhinestone suit on," he says, "I still really attract people. They look at me like I'm *somebody* but they don't know *who*. But they *know* I'm not just the average guy walkin' down the street."

That's the last thing anyone would accuse Coe of being. He's suddenly the hottest item, the most valuable property in country music, and it's one of the unlikeliest stories to ever come out of Nashville, a town which has harbored more than its share of curious inhabitants. His life reads like the kind of film American-International would like to make about country music. He was born in 1939 in Wheeling, West Virginia, and his childhood ended when he was nine years old: he was nabbed acting as a lookout while his father pulled off an armed robbery. Young Coe went off to reform school. His "ornery" nature, said an acquaintance, combined with the nature of such institutions, conspired to keep him locked up until he legally became an adult. Four months after his release, he went to prison for armed robbery.

In state prison in Ohio, he says he killed an inmate. Coe was showering one day when a man walked in and told him, "You're gonna suck my dick." Coe replied, "You got the wrong guy." The man persisted. Coe grabbed the wringer off a mop bucket and hit him twice. For that, he says, he went to Death Row for three months, until the state abolished capital punishment. Coe was finally released on parole when he was twenty-seven. (He seems totally unfazed when I later tell him that Ohio prison authorities can confirm neither the death nor the fact that he was on Death Row. "I killed him, Chet, I swear to you.")

Eighteen straight years of confinement would break many people; it only strengthened Coe's determination to succeed. He listened to the music of Johnny Cash and Merle Haggard and decided that he, too, could be a country star. After a year on parole in Wheeling, he took off for Nashville in high gear.

"I'd always been singing and writing, mostly in prison, but I'd also made a couple of little records in Ohio on a little label where they press you up a thousand records. But I always wanted to go to Nashville, and I quit my job and left my wife and kids—*everything*. The first thing I did when I got there, when I pulled into town I had twenty cents in my pocket and I had gotten a phone number from a guy in Ohio. I called this fellow on the phone. He had a pressing plant and he told me I could just pull my car up behind his plant and sleep there and he'd meet me in the morning. I helped out around his plant, sweepin' floors and carryin' stuff, like a stockboy. He would do a lot of custom sessions and I would play rhythm guitar and make money that way. And I rewrote people's songs and then I sold some songs, sort of the standard story, I think. Willie Nelson sold 'Family Bible' for fifty dollars to get started and I sold a song called 'Road Map to Heaven' for fifty dollars.''

Coe laughed sardonically. He was sitting in a motel room roughly the size of a four-man cell, and he got up periodically to pace and to open the door a little wider. Besides leaving him branded with spidery, pale blue tattoos, prison has left Coe with an aversion to closed doors. He does not like to talk about prison, but sometimes does. "The biggest thing about prison, man, is the tension. You never know from one minute to the next when some motherfucker is gonna lose his mind and try to fuck you or start stabbin' people for no reason at all. You might be one of them people, just because this guy couldn't handle it. It's just a very intense, uptight situation. All the time. Constantly." Prison left him very watchful, and he said he awakens at the slightest sound, ready for . . . whatever.

In the motel room, Coe left the prison memory and returned to Nashville. "I was living in the back of my hearse, Kristofferson was living over the top of Combine Music in a little room, and Mickey Newbury was living in an old fishing boat. Buzz Rabin was playing at a place called the Wheel, and I met him the second night I was there. He brought me up on stage and we passed the hat around and got a little money."

He told Rabin he was sleeping in his hearse, so Rabin invited Coe to share his sunken houseboat. Coe painted his name on the side of the hearse and got up early every Saturday to drive down and park in front of Ryman Auditorium. He stood beside his car all day so that anyone attending the Grand Ole Opry would see his name. Finally, a reporter, Jack Hurst of the Nashville *Tennessean,* asked him what the game was.

"I told him I'd been in prison and wrote songs," said Coe, "so he wrote a big story in the Nashville paper called 'Dave Coe Sings, Writes and Hopes,' and it was really a good story. At the end, he said, 'Will David Allan Coe be just another drifter who comes to town for a matter of a few months and leaves discouraged or will David Allan Coe be one of the future superstars? Only time will tell.' " Coe grinned slyly. When he'd gotten out of prison, he'd promised himself he would be a millionaire before he was forty, and his grin said that he was ahead of his timetable by a few months.

After a couple of years in Nashville, Coe got a recording contract with Shelby Singleton, a flamboyant independent operator who got his start by signing the Big Bopper to Mercury back in the Fifties and later struck it rich with "Harper Valley PTA" and not so rich with a ballad about William Calley. Singleton bought out Sun Records and attempted to revive the legendary label—which had launched Johnny Cash, Elvis, Charlie Rich, and others—as SSS (for Shelby Singleton's Sun). He was not successful, but he did produce two albums for Coe, which are now collectors' items: *Penitentiary Blues* and *Requiem for a Harlequin*.

The prison influence showed in those early albums; it does not now to any great extent. "Every now and then I do go back and write a prison song like 'River.' I want to stay away from that mainly because Haggard's already exploited that whole thing and the best thing that could happen if I wrote the greatest prison song in the world is that people would say I was copyin' Merle.

"Prison *did* make me bitter," he replied to a question. "I just don't show it. I just accept the fact that there's no sense in banging your head against a stone wall. Instead of being bitter, *hostile* bitter, I'm bitter to the sense that I'm tryin' to improve things, like I've got a publishing company for convicts and ex-convicts called Aliases Inc. And I've brought the Seven-Steps Foundation into the state of Tennessee, to try to motivate ex-convicts. It's sort of a personal fight against the system, the prison system. Prisons— When you go into prison, you got so much time to do, they expect you to do your time and they don't really care how you do it. They don't really care whether you come back to prison or don't come back to prison. If nobody came back to prison, they'd be out of a job, so they're not really into rehabilitation. They *have* improved in the past ten years, I have to give 'em some credit, but it's because of organizations like the Seven-Steps Foundation."

After cutting his albums, Coe landed a tour with Grand Funk Railroad, which was just beginning to make its name touring in the South. Grand Funk went on to cut a string of gold albums, and David Coe went back to living by his wits in Music City. C&W star Mel Tillis presented him with a cast-off rhinestone suit and Coe decided he'd never wear anything else. Nashville was full of singers who were forsaking their Nudie outfits for more conservative dress, so Coe went around town buying up the surplus outfits, and soon people took to calling him the "Rhinestone Cowboy." Except for the songwriters who heard and admired his work, he was regarded as a colorful eccentric. He found an identity by joining the Outlaws, a notorious Southern biker group, and is still loyal to them. At the same time, he was considered part of Nashville's outlaw cowboys, a loose-knit contingent of songwriters that has included Willie Nelson, Waylon Jennings, Guy Clark, Kristofferson, Tompall Glaser, and others who were bucking the status quo and fighting the feudal aspects of Nashville's music structure. By and large, Nashville proper—the established producers and publishers and wheeler-dealers—did not take them seriously, since the situation in Nashville had been stable for two decades and there was no reason to think things would change. The "new breed" of songwriters was dismissed as being "underground" or "hippie" country musicians. That makes David Coe hot under his rhinestone collar.

"Let me explain *why* we were labeled underground country," he said, the words tumbling out. "I mean that's like callin' someone a hippie or a nigger. It's like the establishment sayin' these are not country people and don't accept them because it's just hippies tryin' to capitalize on the country-music scene and don't accept them as bein' Nashville country music. That's because we *are* the real country music now. We're writin' truth and that's what country is; it's not crewcuts and white buck shoes, all-American Mom's-apple-pie bullshit. Like 'Hee Haw.' I wouldn't play on that fuckin' show if they gave me a *million dollars*. I wouldn't do it because it's not real.

"One of these days these good songwriters and good singers are gonna bust loose and change this whole world, and I like to think that I'm gonna be one of the first ones to make it, because there's never been a true third-generation superstar yet. Kris went so far and then got involved in actin' and other things. Merle Haggard was the last real country superstar."

Coe finally started on his personal road to stardom only recently. After years of trying to break into the C&W hierarchy, he finally cracked it wide open when he wrote "Would You Lay With Me (In a Field of Stone)," which became a number-one country hit for Tanya Tucker.

Suddenly, he was accepted in Nashville. "It was really strange," said Coe. "They have to accept you when you write a number-one song, but there're people in Nashville who've written hit song after hit song and you never hear anything about them. But when 'Would You Lay With Me' was number one, there was more press about David Allan Coe and people comin' up to me and sayin', man, that's a great song. All because they really never thought, they never took me seriously, they never thought I could write a hit song. That's when they started callin' me the *Mysterious* Rhinestone Cowboy."

Record companies began courting him and he settled on Columbia, cut an album, and began touring. First stop was Max's Kansas City, the durable rock emporium in New York City. There, his blend of traditional, shirtsleeve C&W and progressive, "underground" country won him an acceptance that startled Coe at first. "Max's was like standing room only *every* night. I was surprised, but I loved it. That's *my* club in New York. What was strange, there was a lot of transvestites there and people with glitter on and stuff and they were lookin' at me like, 'Who is this guy?' "

In Austin, at the Texas Opry House, Coe faced a mixed crowd: a strange combination of straight, down-the-line C&W fans who had come out to drink and dance, and a sprinkling of curious young listeners.

At first, he managed to alienate all of them. Young people disliked the crude jokes; the old folks didn't understand such songs as "I'd Like to Kick the Shit Out of You." After the first set, he sensed the needs of the crowd and settled into a hybrid C&W that had just enough of what everyone wanted: impersonations of Haggard and George Jones and Hank Snow shifting into ass-kicking, rocking country. What was satire to one group was good, solid C&W to the other, as when he improvised the "perfect" country song, which contained the essential ingredients of Mother, prison, trucks, trains, and alcohol:

> I was drunk the day my mom got out of prison
> And I went to pick her up in the rain
> But before I could get to the station in my pickup truck
> She got run over by a goddamn train.

He came off stage with a tight grin that let you know he had faced a tough audience and won. "Usually," he said, "when I'm headlining a show I get like eighty percent freaks and twenty percent rednecks, but this crowd tonight was strange. But they all get along, I've never seen no trouble. We're tryin' to turn young people on to country music because young people buy records, old people don't. Of all the types of music, country is the only one that has really never had its day and I think it's gonna be a national thing soon. People in Nashville were surprised when Tom T. Hall packed Carnegie Hall. I wasn't surprised. There's a perfect example: I played a benefit at Rahweh Prison and there was a guy who looked just like Johnny Cash—he sounded more like Cash than Cash does—but they booed him off the stage. If they had wanted to see Johnny Cash, they wanted to see Johnny Cash, they didn't wanta see some motherfucker who acts like Johnny Cash. They want the real thing."

Was there a danger, I wondered, that success would transform David Coe into something other than the real thing, as it has to other performers? He already had a custom-built Cadillac El Dorado with a rhinestone interior and Bob Dylan had made a special trip to Columbia's offices in New York to pick up a copy of his album. What was left?

Coe laughed a strangely mirthless laugh. "The only difference success would make to me would be in my life-style. I am *really* into being comfortable. I mean I don't give a fuck if they call me a hippie capitalist or whatever they want to call me. I'm into having a big Southern mansion with fifty rooms in it if I can afford it and a swimming pool, because, man, I've wasted twenty years in prison and I just wanta live now. I'm *tired* of dying."

Obviously, success hasn't changed him yet: Coe made sure before leaving town that he had sent autographed pictures over to Marvin and Ralph at Texas Hatters, thanking them for the Montana Dick.

John Lennon vs. Albert Goldman

The first time I saw *Imagine: John Lennon* it was on a double bill in a Southern shopping mall and I was pleased by the irony of the marquee: John was sharing it with *The Last Temptation of Christ*. Even in death, John couldn't entirely escape one of the many controversies of his storied and regrettably brief life.

I refer, of course, to John's infamous remark in 1966 that the Beatles were more popular than Jesus. That little offhanded pearl dropped in an interview—and quoted "out of context," naturally—almost sank the good ship Beatles. Their records stoked a great many bonfires, the KKK marched against the Fab Four, they received numerous death threats, and radio stations across the United States began to ban their music. To ensure the physical safety of the group, which was then touring the U.S. for the last time, John had to make a public apology. It went against his grain to do so, for he really had been quoted out of context.

"I was right, but I was wrong," John later told me. And that was emblematic of his whole outspoken life and career. He was seldom, if ever, afraid to speak his mind about any issue under the sun—regardless of whether he knew anything about it or not. But he was also quick to confess his sins, to admit he was wrong, and his mix of naïveté, shrewd instinctual intelligence, and brutal honesty certainly made him unique among rock stars, if not among all pop stars. His accessibility, his humanness, his vulnerability all made him a virtual folk hero to an entire generation.

I first met him through my editorial assistant, whom John was pursuing while he was on the loose from Yoko in the early 1970s. I was the New York bureau chief of *Rolling Stone* magazine and was therefore someone John—with his keen nose for the news (especially being in it)—wanted to know. After I later took an active interest in his struggle to avoid deportation by the INS (Immigration and Naturalization Service) at the direction of the Nixon Administration, we talked frequently. And when I was able to obtain—and publish—a secret memo from Sen. Strom Thurmond to Attorney General John Mitchell proving that the deportation effort was politically motivated, John and I spent more time together. At the time, his career was actually on the wane and he was able to walk the streets of New York undisturbed. In the wake of the Beatles' bitter breakup, not everyone was willing to accept John's erratic solo records or his eccentric life with Yoko, and he became, as he laughingly put it, "a walking footnote to history."

As ever, though (as I quickly discovered), John's mind never stopped. He was constantly examining and reexamining his life and spilling the results out in public to the point where sometimes you wanted to tell him to shut up, that you were sick and tired of hearing about his latest peccadilloes, detailed lists of his drug trips, passionate amours, falls off the wagon, bouts with heroin, fights with Yoko, descents into the gutter, and other such tidbits fit for a seamy soap opera.

All of which makes me think he would have appreciated the brouhaha over his life and times, as recited in a growing number of video, film, and print productions. And he would certainly relish the fact that most of them fall into one of two sharply divided camps. One camp asks, "John Lennon: Saint or Godhead?" The other leans toward, "John Lennon: Ogre or Demon?"

The John Lennon I knew very much had a foot in each camp—and fully realized it and sometimes agonized over it and often reveled in the fact. But at least he admitted it, unlike the run-of-the-mill rock star, who hides behind a carefully crafted public relations smokescreen. John, bless him, was a real piece of work. To say he elicited strong opinions in all he met is an understatement, and one that goes far to explain the passion with which his life is being reexamined. As the best and the brightest of a gifted generation of rock 'n' rollers, John shouldered the burden of millions of fans' expectations. I'm still surprised he did as well as he did with that kind of baggage to carry.

The burden of those expectations came from everywhere and everyone: no exceptions, least of all his second wife, Yoko Ono, who was chiefly responsible for the material that makes up *Imagine: John Lennon* the movie, the book, and the soundtrack album. (His first wife, Cynthia, wrote her book some years ago.)

Yoko and John shared an incredibly tumultuous relationship over the years, much of it lived out in public. Yoko is still greatly resented—unjustly, I think—as the dragon lady who broke up the Beatles and ruined John Lennon. The truth, for many people, is harder to accept: no one ever forced John Lennon to do anything he didn't want to do. One day when I was in court with John in lower Manhattan (he was fighting a monster lawsuit by the since-indicted mob-linked record executive Morris Levy), we went out to lunch in nearby Chinatown. John was in obvious heaven as we ordered and young, giggly Chinese women hovered around him. "See these girls?" John said. "Any one is mine. But Mother [his term of endearment for Yoko] is here for the long haul."

With the benefit of hindsight, it's easy to see why John was attracted to someone like Yoko. Her empathy for the melodramatic life of the tortured, sensitive artiste matched and even exceeded his own. Each dawn brought fresh challenges in the battle against boredom. What do you do, after all, when you've been the Head Beatle and had the whole world at your feet? Only John and Paul had been accorded that kind of universal celebrityhood. Paul's reaction to it had been a withdrawal into a normality so stunningly banal that John never forgave him for it. (Paul's musical birthright turned into a mess of pot arrests.) John himself furiously plunged into what would always be the Next New Thing, whether it was the antiwar movement, the avant-garde, trepanning, macrobiotics, primal scream therapy, high-definition TV—whatever, as long as it was out there on the cutting edge. Boredom was the only real sin, as far as he was concerned. (John once confessed to me that the only reason he and Paul had fired Pete Best and replaced him with Ringo was that they had become bored with Pete.) Not an admirable quality, perhaps, but then the sheer enormity of Beatlemania and its effects on these untutored, fairly naïve young men erased or altered many of their "normal" qualities.

Imagine is not the sort of sugar-coated pill a lot of critics expected from Yoko: it's fairly evenhanded in allowing John to present himself. But then, he was very good at that.

Another surprise in the years since his death has been the string of parasitic, would-be tell-all books about John. Since, as I've said, John was pretty much an open book himself, there didn't seem to be much call for further amplification of his life. What all these books have ended up being about, of course, is John and Yoko, with the emphasis on Yoko. There were (minor) revelations from her tarot card reader; there was her assistant who claimed Yoko pushed her into having an affair with John; and then there was Albert Goldman, whose *The Lives of John Lennon* promised to reveal as many bombshells as had his previous book, *Elvis,* which was a virtual catalog of the King's binges on food, drugs, and sex.

What a disappointment. From every standpoint. As with *Elvis,* Goldman clearly loathed his subject, refused to admit the importance of his music or what it stood for, and recited litanies of real—and in Lennon's case imagined—atrocities against decency. As for revelations, about the only thing I didn't already know was the meaningless fact that Yoko sometimes would ambush John in the morning before he had his coffee by strewing little gifts from the cat box onto the kitchen floor in his (barefoot) path.

There are numerous other little vignettes of their turbulent domestic life, none of them exceptionally revealing or surprising, given John and Yoko's volcanic personalities. Much of the detail of their life together in the Dakota is glimpsed in helter-skelter verbal snapshots offered up by a personal assistant and a visiting neighbor. Much of it is highly contradictory. John comes off as a Howard Hughes–like recluse who lay about nude in the dark—except on those frequent occasions when he went out. Or: He was a reluctant father who was afraid to touch his little boy Sean—except when he spent all his time with him. Or: He was afraid of and manipulated by Yoko—except when he wasn't. Pure junk, as far as I know. John was a difficult person, but he also became a caring friend and a loving father and husband.

A major problem with the book is that Goldman identifies his two principal Dakota sources but doesn't bother to add that his main source was a trusted Lennon employee who was later arrested and convicted of stealing John's notebooks, journals, stereo equipment, and even his clothing. The other source is described as Yoko's "only close friend," though Goldman doesn't mention that she sued Yoko for a million and a half dollars, claiming her child was hurt in an accident at Yoko's apartment, and collected a settlement.

Goldman claims that John and Yoko were responsible for having Paul busted for drug possession in Japan and that John and Brian Epstein had a homosexual relationship for years. Wishful thinking on Goldman's part.

The shopping list goes on and on: most of it is pure speculation. Goldman has used his fevered imagination to piece together fragments of fact and utterly fails to flesh out a remarkable life.

John was certainly no angel. Most of the time he was worse. Which is to say, he was perfectly human. And much more fragile, vulnerable than you might think. Much of his public bravado covered up a lack of self-confidence. Think of it: In his entire adult life he trusted only two people completely: Paul McCartney and Yoko Ono. Paul, he felt, betrayed him. Goldman would have us believe Yoko, too, let him down. I don't think so. Goldman also ignores the main reason people loved John Lennon, apart from his razor-sharp sense of humor, his bouts of compassion and social conscience, and his total frankness: his music. That'll be around for a long time.

I'll always remember the last time I saw him. We had gone to a fortune-teller in Little Italy. Even though Yoko was heavily into Magick and the supernatural, John was fairly skeptical about the whole business. Even so, he was always curious. When he came out of the teller's booth, he was roaring with laughter. "What'd she say?" I wanted to know. John wiped his eyes and said, "She told me the Beatles would never get back together."

Chapter 2

Prudence

The Very Reverend Al Green

At one time, Al Green was mentioned in the same breath as Elvis and the Beatles. He was the next Otis Redding, the next Sam Cooke. He was gonna have it all. Then he walked away from guaranteed superstardom to pursue what he said was a higher calling.

Al Green's whereabouts these days, at least on most Sunday mornings, is a thousand light-years away from the spotlights and fleshpots of show business. To find Al Green these days—the Reverend Al Green, that is—head south on Memphis's Elvis Presley Boulevard, now a street of fast food and slow dreams. After you pass the Elvis-Mart strip across the street from Graceland, slow down and start looking for Hale Road on the right. It's fittingly incongruous that Al Green, superstar, should have re-emerged as Al Green, preacher, in the very shadow of Elvis and in the same vaguely white-trash part of town called, with an envious nod to Caucasian gentility, Whitehaven. But this is where Al landed when he shunned the temptations of sinful show business and turned to serving the Lord.

Hale Road is an unlikely looking haven for Al Green's temple to God: a narrow lane of lower-middle-class ranch houses, several of which seem to be up for sale every time I come through. Black church in a white neighborhood, don't you know.

The church, up ahead there at number 787, is a surprise. It looks like what it was when Al impulsively bought it after his conversion: a modest, unprepossessing little Assembly of God church for white folks. Respectable looking in a Southern suburban sort of way. The main part of the church, the sanctuary, is a little rotunda of dark wood. Out in

front, a sign proclaims that this is the FULL GOSPEL TABERNACLE, REV. AL GREEN, PASTOR. A little portable billboard, the kind with plastic letters that slide into slots, stands just inside the parking lot and proclaims: ALL IS WORTHLESS COMPARED TO KNOWING CHRIST. A pithy saying from Reverend Al.

At a quarter to eleven on this brilliant Memphis Sunday morning there are perhaps a dozen cars already in the parking lot and not a solitary BMW or Saab or Jaguar among them. Nothing but working-class Detroit iron and the occasional Japanese compact. Everything's on a much smaller scale than public speculation about Green's Christian enterprise would have you imagine. This is understandable. After all, when the reigning "Prince of Love" took his spectacular talents off the secular auction block and went into the Jesus business, a lot of folks naturally expected him to shine into it on the dazzling order of a Father Divine or Daddy Grace, complete with a huge golden-domed tabernacle, acres of parking for the faithful, rows and rows of dapper deacons and sensual sisters in the choir, and satellite transmitters out back to beam the message of faith and love to the four corners.

Not a chance. Al Green and his tabernacle are merely life-sized. Walk through the double doors into the sanctuary and a sister demurely clad in white bids you "Good morning" and "God bless you" and ushers you past the one piece of religious art in the sanctuary to a pew. It's a mural of the Rapture, the moment when the faithful are called up to heaven, and it always stops the tourists who have sought out Al's church. The tourists, in the main, are European or Oriental Al Green fanatics who have never seen a graphic depiction of the Rapture: this one realistically shows airliners crashing against a city's skyline and entire freeways full of smashed-up cars disgorging their cargo of dead and mangled and sinful bodies, along with the Clorox-white heavenly souls of the saved wafting their way heavenward from the carnage below.

You take your seat on a hard wooden pew, underneath the beamed white ceiling of the rotunda. There are no more than fifty or so people gathered for the 11:00 A.M. service. All are black, most are women, and all are dressed in their elegant Sunday morning best, crisp white outfits and dashing hats and seamed white stockings and two-toned pumps. There's no talking and all eyes are directed to the vestry, where the two dozen members of the robed choir are filing in. Above them is a hand-painted red-and-white scroll exhorting, "Let God Be Magnified."

In the space between the pews, which are arranged in a semicircle, and the choir loft are an altar, a platform and podium, and, at stage left, an orchestra consisting of an electric bass, drums, piano, and organ. The players start noodling a tune as the choir files in: nobody is in any kind of hurry. Obviously, praising God is an all-day affair. The choir members start clapping and swaying and launch into what becomes a fifteen-minute version of "We're Gonna Make It." The walls are already shaking and this is only a warm-up. More and more people filter in until there're maybe a hundred by 11:30. It's still mostly women, and they're rocking and clapping along with the choir.

At about ten minutes to noon an obvious thrill of electricity runs through the sanctuary as the reverend himself emerges on the scene. He bounds onto the platform from the vestry door. At age forty-three, and in spite of his flowing black robe and white collar, Reverend Green looks no older than and just like his pop persona from years past. The "Prince of Love" has lost none of his luster, I'll wager, judging from the mostly ecstatic reaction of his parishioners. He pretends not to notice and instead concentrates on his immediate objective: a large goblet of what appears to be orange juice sitting on his podium-cum-pulpit. He takes a long draught from the goblet, his trademark ruby-red eyeglasses catching and reflecting the filtered sunlight in the church as he tilts his head to drink.

There is complete silence as he lowers the goblet and looks around the room, establishing eye contact with most. Then he puts the goblet down. The sound is like a pistol shot, and galvanizes everyone's attention. Green leans over the pulpit, points an index finger toward the congregation in general, and calls out liltingly, "I don't know what you came to do, but I came to praise the Lord!" He laughs the throaty, rolling laugh of almost self-congratulatory triumph that seems to be peculiar to evangelists. "Glory! Repeat after me: I am what God says I am." The congregation, by now swollen to perhaps a hundred and twenty-five or so, does so, standing. "I have what God says I have. I can do what God says I can do!" There's to be no hellfire-and-damnation here: Al Green's church is clearly a church of joy.

Green warms to the task at hand. In the Southern gospel tradition, he is clearly in no hurry. The service, church members tell me, may last two hours or it may last five. Depending on how the spirit moves, they say. It is not uncommon for Green to preach and sing for hours on end with a stamina that you don't find on the rock circuit anymore. He's only forty-three now, but he's been doing this—in one form or another—since he was nine years old. He came from a family of share-croppers in Forrest City, Arkansas, and he and three of his brothers began performing as the Green Brothers when he was nine. Three years later the family moved to Grand Rapids, Michigan, and Al's gospel career continued until he was sixteen. Which is when his father discovered that Al was paying more attention to the devil's music—especially the rock and roll of Jackie Wilson—than he was to serving the Lord. So he was exiled into the secular world of rock and pop, although those early years obviously influenced him enormously. Even after he entered the pop music world full-tilt, Green's vocal attack never strayed far from the pure gospel sound, nor did his basic message, which never got too far away from the text of love.

On this Sunday morning in Memphis, Al shmoozes along comfortably, basically making everyone feel welcome and good and happy. He exudes joy and confidence and well-being. "God is blessing our little church," he says as he pauses to introduce all the visitors in the church. It is a warm feeling to stand and be applauded by the congregation, I must admit. "I want to welcome all of you," he rambles on. "It's a little warm in here, so you can start fanning yourselves. If your shoes are too tight, take 'em off!" He laughs genially, as do the worshipers. "God wants you to be happy! He wants you to rejoice and be exceedingly glad. Amen! Can somebody say amen!" The last is not a question: it is a call for a response, which he enthusiastically gets. The call-and-response is one of the oldest traditions in gospel and blues, and a very effective one. "Can somebody say praise the Lord!"

(At about this point, I have to confess, I am visited by a terrible vision of Madison Avenue discovering this little corner of faith and joy and turning it into some kind of stomach-churning Chevrolet or Coca-Cola commercial. When I later mention it to Green, he is not surprised. "You would be amazed," he says, "at the number of people who show up here to get ideas for songs and things. Oh, yeah, I can spot 'em. I'm thinking about half-seriously putting a copyright sign up at the door: 'All rights reserved. Anything you hear in this church cannot be used outside of these confines.' ")

All this time, the drummer and organist watch him closely and augment everything he says: a swelling tide of organ chords for him to ride on and emphatic drumming to emphasize what he has just said or to punctuate a sentence. Story and song, preaching and singing, are so wedded in the black gospel tradition that sometimes it's difficult to tell where one leaves off and the other begins. Almost as an exercise in just that tradition, Green almost offhandedly mentions the blessings being accorded the church. "I thank God for these last twelve years of this ministry. I haven't regretted one day of preaching the gospel. I thank God for that." Then, with the briefest pause—but one that registers dramatic effect—he begins singing the late-nineteenth-century hymn "Near the Cross," and the band members don't miss a beat. The words are familiar to any sometime-churchgoer, but Green gives them a new reading with his utterly unpredictable phrasing and attack: *"In the cross, in the cross, be my glory ever, till my raptured soul shall find, rest beyond the river."*

His voice is so achingly sweet that goosebumps involuntarily rise on my arms. This is *incredible* singing; this is so far beyond what Al Green does at his occasional public concerts these days as to be . . . as to be . . . *incredible*. Is that really an inner light coming from his face as he throws his head back exultantly and begins a false ending to the hymn? I don't know, but I quickly realize that I am witnessing one of the best performances by a performer that I have ever seen, anywhere. He's screaming over the organ and drums as the first false ending comes up. The band shifts to what seems to be a slow fade-out as Green exhorts, "Hallelujah! I don't know about you, but when trials and tribulations come, I wanna be near the cross. Can you say amen somebody?! Near the cross!" In a minute he's singing it again, and then he slows to a chant, "Glory to God! Stand up on your feet, will you?!" In another minute the song seems to be over but the music continues; Green will slide in and out of singing and preaching for the next couple of hours. He's moving like the superstar he is: never still, exhorting, prancing, jumping, running. He is a man possessed, and he's matched move for move by the congregation. There's no turning this vehicle back now.

After barely an hour into the service, it's very easy to see graphically just how all of rock and roll came in one form or another out of the black church: the beat, the rhythm, the moves, the call-and-response, the false endings, the drama, the emotional buildup and release, the dancing—in a word, the catharsis. Obviously Al Green learned all this as a child and it is now second nature to him. He practiced it for the Lord as a child; he says he took it over to the other side to serve Mammon, and now he's back in God's corner, working the boards as well as or better than any performer who ever lived. Mick Jagger doesn't have this kind of crowd control or these moves. Neither does Al Green—except when he's in church.

You would have to go back to Al's real idol—Sam Cooke—to find a singer with this kind of direct wiring to an audience. Cooke, whose troubled secular and spiritual musical identity crisis was very close to Green's own, was killed in a tawdry shooting uncomfortably like an episode in Green's life. Comparisons to Cooke are unavoidable: both were the premier gospel and then secular soul voices of their time, both were very private men, both attracted women followers on a phenomenal scale, both were strong and independent and proud black men. Cooke was shot to death, supposedly after attacking a woman companion in a cheap motel. Green was badly burned by a spurned lover (Mary Woodson, who was married to someone else, though Green claimed to not know that), who threw hot Cream of Wheat (not grits, as the popular legend has it) on him in his bath and then killed herself with his gun. There are, however, other unspoken comparisons. Cooke was the first black performer to attempt to control his own business and become an independent record business entrepreneur. There are still whispered rumors in the music business that Cooke was silenced just because of that; that an industry that at the time was heavily corrupt had no need or desire or room for a black crusader and business rival. Green withdrew from the pop music field into the less-than-lucrative gospel music area just when he was peaking in his popularity and could have become the predominant music figure in Memphis, if not in all of the South in the record business. By all indications, music has not made him a rich man. Green will not comment on his own history in the record business, though he did tell me that Sam Cooke's death affected him "Very, very much."

*   *   *

By half past noon, Reverend Al is just getting warmed up. My jacket is off and I'm starting to wipe the sweat off my face. "It's not important," he is saying, "how you go about the program. What's important is how you worship God. Amen. I guess it's time for me to do mine now, the choir has been wonderful." He launches into a breathtaking *a capella* version of "Love Lifted Me," his voice growling and crooning and swooping and diving, and the spirit level in the place is starting to edge off the dial. Now and then one of the faithful will catch the spirit and start dancing in place, hands held heavenward. And then start dancing *out* of place, pirouetting and jackknifing all through the place, bouncing off pews, sometimes sprinting up and down the aisles. The women ushers start to hover at the back, each holding a large folded-up white cloth, which, it turns out, is a lap robe of sorts. Whenever one of the women faithful crashes to the floor in the throes of the spirit, an usher modestly drapes a lap robe over the woman's lower extremities in case her dress hikes up. It saves a lot of emotional wear and tear on the children, not to mention the men.

Everyone today is shaking with the spirit, even before Reverend Al gets into his sermon, which is based on Exodus 14: all of it. Reverend Al teasingly lifts his black robe a few inches and starts stamping his shiny black loafers. "Whoa!" he exclaims. "I want all you visitors to know that if I stomp my feet—don't run off. That's how we worship the Lord! Glory! Our topic today is Exodus fourteen: when your back is to the wall! We are going to eat the Word today, we are going to eat the Word and feast on the Word, glory to God!"

He starts preaching, and he preaches it for nigh onto two hours, swooping in and out of songs and parables. He runs wild through the aisles; he mock-swoons as elegantly as James Brown ever did; he high-steps higher than O.J.; he stalks the pews as sinuously as any panther; he howls and struts and jukes like a broken-field runner. He tosses his microphone, crouches, and then sprints and dances his way to the back. He staggers, falters, seems stunned, and then—miraculously—he recovers! But the truly remarkable thing is that he is not just riffing for two hours—the sermon is well thought out and organized, even though it's delivered without benefit of notes or outline. And it's delivered full-bore; Reverend Green is a spiritual runaway ride. The emotional level in the tabernacle is unmeasurable: no one will escape today without being emotionally wrung-out, one way or another.

The faithful are fully caught up in the spirit. A largish woman running headlong at full speed hits the double doors like Dick Butkus and crashes through to the sunlit parking lot: an usher chases after her. Bodies slam to the carpeted floor; an elegant black leather pump sails off a falling woman's foot and arcs through the air, missing my head by a scant inch. An elegantly dressed grandmother is caught in the throes of what seems to be whiplash. Lap robes are laid down over collapsing women all over the place. Reverend Al is ecstatic, the band is pumping, and the floors are shaking. The altar call begins and, one by one, the sinful wind their tearful way down to be cleansed. "That's two God has called," Reverend Al yells. He places his hand on a young woman's head and proclaims, "God has already healed you! He has healed you today! Let me give you a good Southern hug!"

When it's finally over, more than three hours later, he stands by the pulpit to congratulate the converted and to greet any well-wishers. He also signs more than one autograph for comely young fans. Sweat is pouring off him. His tired, triumphant smile is not that of a rock superstar who has just dazzled the masses—the kind of smile I've seen enough times to grow weary of. Reverend Al seems to be sincere about what he's doing. Is he for real or what?

The next morning, while I'm waiting to meet Reverend Green for lunch, I ponder again the incongruities of his life and career. For all his considerable talents, his pop career was as brief as it was spectacular. Willie Mitchell started him out covering the Temptations, the Doors, and the Bee Gees. Then he got into his own thing, with the likes of "Tired of Being Alone," "Let's Stay Together," and "I'm Still in Love With You." Remember back to 1973, when he was everybody's star of the year and this was part of the spoken introduction to his shows on his first big tour: "It's showtime! Here's a young man's got to be solid gold! The prince of peace! The god of love and happiness. . . . Four gold singles! Two gold albums! That makes you the world's greatest superstar! Here he is: Al Green!"

It would not surprise me later to hear Reverend Al Green speak of that earlier, worldlier Al Green as some kind of alien being: He has distanced himself so much that he refers to that early incarnation in the third person. Even so, I reflect, Al's oft-discussed rejection of the pop-music world is perhaps not quite as clear-cut and evenly demarcated as it seems on first blush. To begin with, there's the fact he's continued to do concerts in pop venues over the years. And that he's dallying a bit with that world with his latest single, an Al B. Sure mix of "As Long as We're Together" that's as funkified as anything he's ever done. His long-distance duet with Annie Lennox on "Put a Little Love in Your Heart" was ambiguous enough to qualify as a religious song, to be sure. He's on A&M Records now, after years on a small gospel label. He's hinting these days that he may expand his musical horizons a bit without compromising his spiritual principles.

With all this in mind, I reflect on his adult musical career, which certainly has been an unusual one. After his father exiled Al from the family quartet, he started a pop group called Al Green and the Creations, later becoming Al Green and the Soul Mates. They had a top-ten hit with "Back Up Train" in 1967, but the group broke up and Al ended up touring as a solo act on the chitlin' circuit. His unlikely break came the next year in a joint in Midland, Texas, where he was the opening act for a Memphis musician named Willie Mitchell. Mitchell, who was beginning to make waves as a producer, liked what he heard and invited Al to come to Memphis to be turned into a star. Al asked how long it would take. Year and a half, Willie told him. Can't wait that long, Al said. Even so, he turned up in Memphis a few weeks later, and Willie indeed made him a star. The combination of Green's sensuous, free-floating, gospel-style vocals over Mitchell's rock-bottom rhythm resulted in a string of hits, ranging from 1971's "Let's Stay Together" to 1975's "L-O-V-E."

Meanwhile, tragedy struck his private life. A friend, Mary Woodson, felt rejected by Green and killed herself in his house after throwing boiling cereal on him in his bath. This caused him to rethink priorities. He was re-converted to the Lord in an Orange County motel room epiphany. He bought the church on Hale Road and became Reverend Al three years later. He was preaching and still trying to tour pop. He dropped Willie Mitchell and started producing himself, creating in the process what surely is his masterpiece: *The Belle Album* (1977), which graphically deals with his struggles with Satan. He followed that effort with undistinguished records in 1978 and 1979, although they were not pure gospel. It was obvious he was not writing much anymore. In 1979 he toppled off the stage during a pop concert in Cincinnati and heeded God's warning to straighten up and serve only Him.

Since then, that's exactly what he's done, in the process winning— to his chagrin, since he didn't get any as a pop star—lots of gospel Grammies and sticking to the straight and narrow. But you get the feeling he's getting a little itchy for some action. One clue: Why do ministers of the Lord (who also sing) need public relations agents? Another sign: Green reunited with Willie Mitchell for 1986's much-heralded A&M album *He Is the Light,* an album that disappeared unceremoniously. Now Mitchell is gone again and the trendy Al B. Sure is his new musical helpmate. All of that, of course, is fine: The Lord helps those who help themselves. And the Lord certainly doesn't want or need second-rate help out there on the firing line.

Al Green is such a pure musical talent he doesn't have to explain anything. On the other hand, I'd love to have lunch with him and talk over a few things. I'm delighted he feels the same way. His niece Tina telephones and says he will meet me in the lobby of my hotel, the Peabody, shortly. She is carrying a buzzing walkie-talkie when I rendezvous with her in the lobby; she reports that Al is running a little late.

When he arrives, it is of course a major event. A second young woman from the church carrying another walkie-talkie precedes him, the hotel staff expects him, and he strides in grinning and waving like a Presidential candidate. As he *should*. He looks splendid in a tailored dark suit with a subdued silk tie and a red carnation in his lapel. And the trademark red-frame glasses. He greets me effusively, as if he really remembers me (preachers and politicians do that automatically), and in two shakes of his silk tie he has us all seated at a fine table in the Peabody's Dux Restaurant, two waitpersons hovering tableside.

His charm is infectious: everyone in the place is smiling. We get our big glasses of iced tea and talk small talk. He is fascinated to learn that crosstown Memphis rocker Jerry Lee Lewis was once a fundamentalist preacher, and Jerry Lee's feuding with his preacher-cousin Jimmy Lee Swaggart reminds Al of his little brother Lionel, who apparently is a lapsed preacher. And then the soup arrives.

"Reverend Green," I ask, "what about this Al B. Sure single. Isn't that quite a departure for you?"

He puts down his spoon and laughs. I've been warned by other writers that Green is a quirky interview. "Ah, ha-ha. I don't know if it's a departure or an arrival! It's one for sure! We just shot the video for that in L.A.; it's gonna be kind of a wild video." He goes on and on about what a nice video it probably is. "So it's gonna be an arrival, yeah, or a revival for Al." He laughs. "Everybody's excited about it. It looks like the good Lord has blessed us for so long till we're kinda expecting him to do it. I got a card the other day, a lady sent me a birthday card. It said, 'I hope you live to get to be a ripe old age,' and then when you open the card it says, 'Another year should do it!' Isn't that funny!"

He laughs again and passes me some cheese bread. "You'll love it."

I try some. It *is* quite good. "Reverend Green," I say, "can you talk about your conversion and how you left rock 'n' roll?"

"Oh, yeah," he says with vigor, buttering some cheese bread. "I was in a trauma, man, I was in a *trauma*. I don't know. I could of did three or four different things. I could of jumped off a building. I could of— Oh, I could of did a number of different things—I was in such a turmoil. This was in '73, '74, with 'Sha La La (Make Me Happy),' uhm, we had like seven straight top singles there, besides the albums they came out of and, uhm, I don't know, when I was born again in '73, uhm, I'll never forget that day."

"That was the start of your big tour, wasn't it?"

"Yes. I was working the Cow Palace in San Francisco and we flew down that night to Anaheim and I did two shows that night at Disneyland and I was born again that same morning. About four-thirty that morning I was born again, I was renewed, I was cleansed, I was healed. Yeah [in response to my question], I was alone, although I hadn't planned to be alone. But I was so tired after three shows in one night I was alone when the Lord came to me."

Green starts toying with a pepper mill and seems absorbed with getting it to work right.

"Did you," I ask, "want to leave pop music because of the pressure or was it primarily a spiritual thing?"

"Well," he says, idling the pepper mill, "a lot of it was pressure, trying to meet the demands of what people think you oughta be. I mean, I sold a lot of records. *We* sold a lot of records. We did real good, the Lord blessed us to do well, but, see, there is a great demand on you to keep that up and sometimes I didn't want to keep it up. I had a farm out in Oakland, Tennessee, and I liked to go out there and sit by the lake and read Genesis or something. And people would call from L.A. out to the farm and say, 'What's Al doin'?' And my man Curtis would say, 'Oh, he's readin' the Bible.' Curtis would tell 'em that. I said, 'Curtis, don't tell 'em what I'm doin', just tell 'em I'm not available.' But he says, 'Oh, yeah, Al's out there readin' the Bible.' People thought I was *nuts*. But I enjoyed it. I thought it was wonderful. But there are those demands on you. *Mmm,* this is good soup! You got to taste this, it's souper! This is downright down-home. Oh, look! I dropped my bread in it! He knew that was what he wanted to do!"

Green laughs and sops up some soup. No fool he.

We talk about Sam Cooke a little between courses. Green shakes his head. "His death bothered me a great deal. Very, very much. I couldn't understand it, couldn't understand *her,* couldn't understand *them,* I just couldn't understand it."

Tina clears her throat loudly and says, "Uncle Albert, not so much pepper on your potato, now. You won't be able to taste it, now will you, Uncle?"

Green doesn't look up, saying, "Oh, I'm sorry. I wasn't raised in this fashion." A waitress appears and asks, "How's everything?" Green holds up the pepper mill and asks, "Is this thing working? Twist it around and see if it's going." She says, "You want me to try it on yours?" Green recoils in mock horror. "Try it on mine? What're you doing? I love it! Isn't it working? Try it! Now do it! Give me another one. There you go. That little one wouldn't do it. Now, screw it around! Ooh, yeah! Now, that will work! That's working! Good God a mighty! It's just sproutin' pepper here now! This is cookin'! Ooh, this is strong!

"Sam Cooke," he says to me. "I couldn't understand any of that. He was too talented. But why is it that talented people like him, or a lot of other stars or artists, wind up with terrible home lives? Why is that? You tell me!"

I venture guesses as to self-punishment, *nostalgie de la boue,* and so on.

"Uhm, yeah, yeah. Like when I started the promotional tour, they said, 'Now, no upside-down stuff!' " He laughs uproariously.

His omelet arrives. We discuss James Brown's problems. He suggests that Brown's plight may be a blessing in disguise, since his prison stay is obviously getting him off drugs. "Because I hear that James was seriously on the Stuff."

"Was that," I ask, "ever a problem for you?"

"The Stuff? Naw. Not really. Tried it a few times, you know, but I figured I had to do my work. If I couldn't concentrate well, I didn't want it, that simple." Tina interrupts sharply. "Is your omelet good, Al?" He pushes it around on his plate. "I'm tryin' first to see if it's friendly."

"Is there," I ask, "a fundamental conflict between your performing for the public and for the church?"

He answers easily. "Nope! No conflict. It don't bother me. Somebody called out a request the other night for 'Let's Stay Together,' so I sang it. Then some lady calls, says she's from the church, is outraged, so I had to sit her down, tell her, when I say 'Let's Stay Together,' that's serving Him. Then she's singing, 'Oh, good, praise the Lord, bless you.' Oh, no, I don't find any—Some kids in North Carolina thought there may be some conflict in my doing a song with Al B. Sure. Who is a secular artist and me being a gospel preacher, minister at that, and that would be, you know, questionable, but I don't think so. So we did the eleven o'clock news the other night and the phone started ringing and they said, 'I just saw you on the news.' I said, 'How was it?' They said, 'Fabulous!' Sooo . . ."

"But surely," I say, "you must have caught some criticism for the song with Annie Lennox."

He pushes aside his omelet and answers sharply. "Oh, yeah. But I'm made to be different. I'm not made to be everyone else. I didn't come out here to do what I'm told to do, except by God. I didn't come out here to do what people suggest I oughta do. I'm gonna come out here and be led by the spirit of the Lord to do as I plea—not as I please so much as what I'm instructed to do. And that's to me important. Not someone else's opinion of me. Yeah. So if they wanta complain, let 'em complain. . . . I think that the love that we're talking about is truly getting to be more universal. It's not just me and my little group, you know? If you get a secular artist like Annie Lennox, like Al B. Sure, or like Reverend Green, if you will, and put them together and they want to do something for the Lord, then I don't think we should point a finger and judge these people when they're trying to do good; if they're talking about love, L-O-V-E, it's good. It's good."

"I can't argue with that," I say, "but have you ever been tempted to do a TV ministry?"

Green gets excited. "Oh. No. *No*. Never. Nope. No. I don't want to. It's too *demanding*. [He furiously stirs a fresh glass of iced tea.] Too much preparation. Smile for the camera. Get your makeup right. See, at the tabernacle, you don't have to worry about that. You go out just the way you are. [He claps his hands.] You slip your robe on, you go straight out, you have prayer, you go straight out [claps again], and you go, 'This is a day that the Lord has made! All rejoice!' And everybody goes 'Yeahh!' [Claps hands.] And be glad. Weelll. I *like* that. I like the freedom. I don't wanta have some guy sayin', 'Tape!', somebody sayin', 'Dry him off!' "

Green stops to study his audience, which includes everyone within the sound of his voice. Pleased, he continues. "Then again, I *know* that I could make too much money. I know that I could, you see. I could make tons of money and I don't want—I just don't want it. I would trade that, just to be happy. I want to be happy. And I wanta do what I do, like what you saw yesterday in the tabernacle. That's all I want. I don't want diamonds and expensive cars. I have an old '83 Cadillac out there you can borrow with about a hundred thousand miles on it. I'm not questing for anything that's out of reach. I just reach for—Like when I started the sermon yesterday, I *believe* the promises that have been made to me. I want that and I'm going for it. Yeah. You were there yesterday, you saw it, you saw those people responding and rejoicing and you saw the joy. The Lord is my strength, I mean, how can you trade that? Now, there's other ministers I've heard that make a hundred and forty, a hundred and fifty million a year, but I don't, that's not what I'm after—in religion. I could sing rock and roll and make that kind of money. But I don't want to. I think we got our thing going, uhm-uhm."

Reverend Green accepts a cup of coffee, spoons it around, and volunteers that he thinks his next music project may be "more controversial and more questionable! But not out of line to what our beliefs are. And it's gonna be exciting." Is it, I ask, controversial as in secular?

"Well, I'm just finishing putting the lyrics down. I've written four songs, five songs of the new stuff that I haven't cut yet. I did 'The Message of Love,' which is coming out next. I might cut these in New

York or L.A. Al B. Sure wanted me to come and mess around in his studio at the house. Because his mom is an evangelist. So I might try it."

I get more coffee and ask him about *The Belle Album,* of which he's obviously proud. "Well, Belle is about a girl. It was, if you will, a pivotal point of the career. To me it is. Some guy tried to tap it down to the point of where you say, 'Belle, it's you that I want but it's Him that I need.' Yeah, that's it. Belle was a woman. *Belle* is about a girl and it's about being in love and it's about that struggle that you're talking about between God, I love you, honey, and I need you God. [He repeats both lines loudly, bringing the waitress on a dead run.] But that was it. I'm two people, I'm spirit and I'm carnal. I'm mortal, I'm human, I'm, you see? And I need both to be full. That album, that was when we were struggling with *self.* That's why in that same album, at the end of 'Georgia Boy,' Al hits the gi-tar and says, 'The hell with it!' Well, that is his struggle. . . . I was struggling with everything. It's so hard to go out on stage and try to sing rock and roll and wind up quotin' scriptures outta the Bible. People in front of you are trying to drink their champagne and date their neighbors' wives and, man, you ain't no fun! I remember one time I took the Bible out on stage in Chicago and started reading scriptures. I mean, there's a struggle within yourself to try to balance things. Amazing, but He brought us through."

He sits back and beams the contented smile of a man who—if not on top of the world—has at last and at least come to grips with who and what he is.

The Private Years of John Lennon

John Lennon pursued his career of being a non-performing ex-Beatle private person with the same intensity that he had always brought to his music. He returned to Yoko in March 1975, after a year and a half of separation. After Yoko took him back and—as important or more so—after Sean Ono Lennon was born on October 9th (John's birthday as well) of that year, he did not so much become a different person as he became the adult man he had always wanted to be. The reason was Yoko. She gave—nay, *imposed,* upon him—the direction he felt he needed. And she gave him Sean Ono, whom both viewed as a perfect child capable of being reared under ideal conditions to become an ideal human being: one free of sexism and racism and all the other *isms* that John and Yoko felt were branded upon helpless children. During the

pregnancy, John and Yoko were fanatically health conscious. They went to classes and studied natural childbirth. But Yoko had a difficult delivery. When labor began, she went into convulsions. John called for a doctor, but when the doctor entered the delivery room, he allegedly ignored Yoko and raced over to John and said, "You know, I always loved your music as a Beatle, and I always wanted to shake your hand!"

"Fuck *off!*" John screamed. "Save Yoko's *life!*"

They sedated Yoko and delivered Sean by Caesarean section.

While he was in the hospital nursery, John studied the behavior of the nurses and noticed that the black nurses turned on disco radio and the white nurses turned on country and western. John wanted Sean to be a bit freer musically, and prepared his own collection for Sean at the Dakota. He stocked a jukebox for Sean's room with everything from Elvis Presley to Donna Summer.

Yoko, even while pregnant, had gradually taken on the duties of running Lenono (John and Yoko's corporation) and assuming the role that rock managers Allen Klein and Brian Epstein had played earlier in

John's career. John was happy to turn all of that over to someone he fully trusted; trusted to buy dairy cows or Florida real estate all day in Lenono's office on the ground floor of the Dakota, while he raised Sean on the seventh floor with the aid of a large domestic staff.

During John's legal battles, John and Yoko made a swift trip to Egypt and spent a night in the Great Pyramid. Yoko, besides being a psychic, loves Egyptology and came back to New York City with a big collection of ancient Egyptian regalia. She had already confounded the many record-company attorneys at legal meetings by showing up as John's only representative (a non-attorney Japanese feminist artist). Now, she turned up for legal conferences garbed in ancient Egyptian robe and headdress. John said he loved that, as he sat at home and learned to bake bread in the wilds of Central Park West's most famous address.

John seriously thought of himself as a house husband. He agreed with Yoko's sentiment that carrying a child for nine months was an enormous obligation for a woman and that, after delivery, either the father or society ought to tend to the child for a while. John not only did that, he gladly submerged his will to Yoko's and turned his attention to his son.

Elliot Mintz, an intimate of John and Yoko's for years, recalls John saying, after he saw Lenono staffers giving Sean a chocolate bar to keep him quiet: "*Screw* these people. Sean is not gonna eat sugar, and Sean is not gonna watch TV commercials and people shooting each other, and he's not gonna have the TV as a baby-sitter, and he's not gonna go to school, and he's not gonna be ignored, and he's not gonna have his questions unanswered."

Says Mintz, "He'd be bathed at night by John, with John in the same tub, and flesh would touch flesh, and he'd be kissed good night, and if he had a question, he'd be answered. And if John went out for a walk, Sean would go with him; Sean would not be put off onto someone else. Although John and Yoko had all the money in the world, they had no baby-sitters.

"So John did that and prepared food and baked bread. Then, when Yoko came back from a day's work and talked about some big deal that she'd put together, John would say, 'I don't want to hear about that. Sean has a pimple—somebody must be slipping him sugar. So get twenty copies of *Sugar Blues* and distribute it to the staff and tell them that shouldn't happen.' "

John's new life—once he had renounced his coking and drinking and carousing in Los Angeles—became surprisingly ascetic. Except for a passion for multimegatar cigarettes called Gitanes (which are to France as Luckies are to the U.S.) and a constant thirst for down-and-dirty black, *black* coffee, John was one of the most detoxed rock stars. He and Yoko had been on heroin together (Yoko would later ill-advisedly say that they had done smack to celebrate their talents as artists) and had gotten off it together.

John was quite serious; life with Sean and Yoko in the Dakota was all that mattered to him. One night, late, he called Mintz in Los Angeles. "He said, 'An incredible thing happened to me today, Elliot,' " recalls Mintz. "And he said it with such reverence that I thought he was going to divulge a really significant spiritual experience. I propped myself up and said, 'Yes?'

"He said, 'I baked my first loaf of bread, and you can't believe how perfectly it rose. I've taken a Polaroid photo of it, and I think I can get it out to you by messenger tonight.' "

They used a courier service instead of the mail, because people collected souvenirs when they saw Yoko or John's name on something. So someone would pick up the communication, get on an airplane and fly with the communication to the person it was going to. "It's the same as the mail," explains Mintz, "except instead of an eighteen-cent stamp, it's a four-hundred-and-thirty-dollar plane ticket."

Elliot Mintz met John and Yoko when he did a phone interview with Yoko for ABC radio in 1972. How he physically met John and Yoko and became one of their few friends says much about the way they lived. It is a story that Mintz himself tells best:

"Yoko was very pleased with the live interview. I called her back the next day to thank her. After we began talking, we found that both of us are telephone freaks. I average six hours a day on the phone; she averages eight. Yoko has a belief that you can achieve a greater level of intimacy over the phone than you can in person. The feeling is that through the veil of anonymity—of not looking into faces, not being conscious of clothing, hair, how you look—all you're dealing with is mouth to ear; it is highly personal. People say things over the phone, even to strangers, that they never would in person. So, Yoko and I talked for a number of hours, and we found that we had much in common—mainly the phone. She knew that I was an insomniac. Yoko herself does not sleep the way most people do: She takes catnaps, she practices autohypnosis, she counted John down to sleep.

"So we talked on the telephone. Three or four weeks after this dialogue had begun, John became curious as to whom his wife was calling at four in the morning—leaving the bedroom and going to the kitchen and calling this radio announcer in Los Angeles. At about the same time, I started doing a syndicated television show, which turned up on channel five in New York at three in the morning. So, for the first time Yoko and John got to see what I look like. Then, Yoko said that I should do an interview with John. We did a live interview over the phone for an hour. After that, John became interested in what Yoko and I talked about, so he started calling me as well. You know how John had difficulty working the telephone and figuring out the numbers. But there was something about the freedom of calling me at all hours of the day or night. He knew that he would never wake me, since I'm an insomniac. So the three of us became phone pals.

"I would get home from my radio show at two in the morning and talk effortlessly to Yoko till four-thirty or five-thirty A.M., and then John would just be waking up and he would call. Neither of them had any friends, because there was enough going on between them that they didn't need to see any other people.

"Some months after this, they decided to drive across the United States and found themselves in Santa Barbara. They called me. Yoko said, 'We've seen America; now we'd like to see you.' They gave me directions as to where to meet. I drove from L.A. to Santa Barbara; they ended up, for reasons I still don't understand, in Century City. So, after three hours of calls on pay phones, we laid eyes on each other for the first time. I pulled up beside a dusty station wagon in this field. I remember how excited John and Yoko looked, because they kept pointing at me and giggling to each other, having recognized me from television. This was a rather bizarre reversal of roles. I got inside their car and John said to Yoko, 'Well, there he is. Go over and give him a hug.'

"They had rented a house in Ojai, near Santa Barbara. It was summertime, and we went to the swimming pool. Yoko changed into a chartreuse one-piece bathing suit. She lay down on the diving board over the pool, with her waist-length jet-black hair hanging perpendicular. I was struck by her extraordinary beauty. I kept hearing movement behind me: John was putting on a bathrobe to take off his pants so he could put on his bathing suit. He just smiled and said, 'I'm English, you know.'

"We talked politics for an hour. They said they had just made this album called *Some Time in New York City* and wanted me to hear it. We went inside, and John took the record and did something that would characterize him for many years. When it came to anything mechanical— from a pair of binoculars to a hi-fi set or a tape recorder—he was thoroughly helpless. He couldn't get a stereo turned on for all the money in the world. He said, 'Wait'll you hear *this*,' and he put the tone arm down on the record and ran back to where Yoko and I were sitting, between the two speakers. *Nothing.* The machine was not plugged in. Yoko continued to stare at the ceiling. Finally, we got the thing playing. John referred to it as one of his 'lost' albums, because it was about

Angela Davis and John Sinclair and Black Panthers. They said, 'Hey, take this acetate back to your radio station and play it. You're the only guy who's got it.' I did. I was tired. I forgot that there were four-letter words and Black Panthers on it, and ABC was not big on those at the time. I played the entire album and held all the commercials and opened the phones for the reaction. John and Yoko came to L.A., and I asked them if they'd heard the show. John said he'd tried to get it but the radio didn't work. Yoko looked at the ceiling. John had tried to get the show on AM, when it was on FM. John asked me how the show had been received.

"I said that it had been received very well, other than that I had been fired for playing the record and that my radio career had come to an end. 'That's fine,' John said. 'That's *fine*. You come with us. We're going to San Francisco tomorrow.' I went with them.

"We found ourselves in the Miyako Hotel in San Francisco for a month—a traditional Japanese hotel with tatami mats on the floor. The first three days, we conversed only by phone. It was more comfortable for me that way. I was still *overwhelmed* by their presence. One day, they invited me to their room. At the time, John and Yoko were in their 'incredibly skinny period,' and I knew that they had not been out of that room and had not eaten for two or three days. They said they wanted to talk to me about some stuff. I said, 'Fine.'

"They led me into the bathroom and turned on the water. The noise was deafening and the heat was overwhelming, and they were talking about seeing Bobby Seale and Huey Newton for an appearance on an upcoming TV show that John and Yoko had been asked to host. I said, 'Excuse me, why are we sitting in the bathroom discussing this when you have a very nice room in there?' Yoko said the likelihood was that the room was bugged. John just looked at the ceiling. [It was later established that John and Yoko were under constant government surveillance.] The one time we left the Miyako, Yoko said, 'Let's try and eat, John.' He said, 'All right, let's try it.' We left the room, got into the car, and started down the Pacific Coast Highway.

"About fifteen miles out, Yoko looked at John and said, 'It's too much, isn't it?' He said, *'Yeah.'* They turned the car around and went back to the hotel. It was too much for them to go out into the real world. When the two of them were together, they were insulated, isolated, protected, and free. If that happened to mean starvation as well, you accepted it as part of that."

It was well known in certain circles that Yoko was very heavily into Magick and made no decisions without consulting one or several of the circle of astrologers, psychics, readers, spiritual consultants, numerologists, direction experts, interpreters of I Ching, seers, and the like who made up Lenono's unofficial cabinet of advisers.

John believed in Yoko and never questioned any decision or command she made. He made many of what came to be called "rounds" or "direction trips" without contesting the wisdom of her commands. He went around the world in two days. He went to South Africa. He went here, he went there. She told him it was something he needed to do.

When Elliot Mintz first asked Lennon about all this, Lennon told him, "She will say things you will not understand. Go with it. She's always right."

Years later, Mintz said he felt that John and Yoko had a Don Juan–Carlos Castaneda sort of relationship. "John looked to her as a sorceress, as a high priestess, as a magician. I'm a fairly pragmatic guy and consider myself to be a realist. But I am now a believer in her abilities. She *is* telepathic. I do know that. I do know she reads minds.

"I do know that she is extraordinarily psychic and has extraordinary premonitions. Whenever something would come up, John would look to her and say, 'I'd like you to check it out.' If she were to say, 'I think it's important for you to travel in a northwesterly direction for approximately eighteen thousand miles tomorrow morning,' that would be enough. She has said those things to me, and I have done them. She would say, if you do this, it's going to dramatically alter the next six months of your life in a favorable way. There were direction moves that she gave me that did significantly alter the structure of my life.

"Sometimes, Yoko grew impatient with the necessity to explain it to us. At the same time, John was not a gullible man. He was basically a cynic. He had been burned by some of the best—like the Maharishi, for one. Yoko has been interacting with these people all her life. You've got to run a pretty good scam to get past her for more than four or five readings. So if Yoko buys it, it's good enough."

(The unanswered question remains: With all the psychic and telepathic minds around John Lennon, why did none of them register at least a small alarm about the numbers that made up the day of December 8, 1980? Why was there no warning?)

The Dakota, a forbidding Gothic castle studded with gargoyles, is an appropriate setting for Magick. Its exterior is the one you saw in *Rosemary's Baby;* the Dakota's ruling committee would not allow any filming inside the building. The Dakota has a long history of ghosts, the most famous being a little blond girl wearing silver shoes who bounces her ball down the hallways. Her appearance supposedly signifies death. John apparently never saw her. The only Dakota ghost he acknowledged encountering was the Crying Lady Ghost.

*   *   *

Mintz became a confidant and traveled frequently with John and Yoko. A typical trip went like this: A courier hand-delivered to Mintz a one-way ticket to Japan with accompanying instructions signed by John's distinctive line drawing of himself with glasses and Yoko and Sean. The instructions directed Mintz to fly to Tokyo, where a man would meet him, take him to a train station, and give him a card with Japanese markings to indicate which train to take. He should disembark at the eleventh stop and wait for further instructions.

The day before Mintz left for Japan, Elvis Presley died. John Lennon's hero. Mintz called Lennon in Japan to give him the news. Said Lennon: "Elvis died in the army. The difference between him and us [the Beatles] is that, with us, our manager died and we lived. With Elvis, he died and his manager lives. Come to Japan."

Mintz: "So I flew to Tokyo, and of course there was no one there to meet me. It was a hundred and ten degrees, I was exhausted and had no idea where I was going. This was characteristic of the travel arrangements. Although John and Yoko always traveled first class, it was always bungled. Everywhere I went around the world with them, it was almost a joke. There was *never* anyone to meet them, never a VIP lounge, never a limousine. We'd be out there, looking for taxicabs with everybody else, being shoved aside, baggage always lost. The primary reason for all this, we later learned, was that any reservation for John Lennon was taken as a joke! During those lost years, after 1975, the reason John quit using the phone was that any time he picked up the phone and said, 'Hi, this is John Lennon. I'd like a piece of chocolate cake,' the response would be, *'Sure.'* So he gave up trying.

"At the eleventh stop, at three in the morning, I got off the train and it looked like a ghost town. There was one very old man with a gray beard. I hoped he was the guy. I smiled at him and he bowed. I said, 'John Lennon,' and he smiled. I said, 'Yoko Ono,' and his face lit up and he shook my hand and said, *'Ah so.'* He pointed to two broken-down bicycles, and we peddled off into the night. It had to have been six miles. I thought I was gonna have a coronary. After seven light-years, I saw a lake and a Japanese inn and gardens, and I heard the sound of flute music. I was looking to give the old man a tip, but he was long gone. I stood there alone, worn out, in the rain, but dumbfounded by the smell of cherry blossoms. A shoji screen opened, and a woman led me in. I was given a mineral bath and a kimono gown and a room that was filled with incense and pounds of fresh fruit. In the center of the fruit was a grapefruit, and on top of that was a little handwritten note saying, *We are all together now, just like a family. We'll see you in the morning. John, Yoko and Sean.*

"I fell asleep. The next morning the screen opened, and there they were. John had never looked as high and wonderful. He wore a beautiful antique kimono, and Yoko was next to him in a white silk kimono. They both had hair down past their shoulders, and washed it in magical water that just made it shine and come alive. It was just a *vision*—a sight to behold. We embraced and went down a little lane and had some sushi. Yoko left us. John said, 'Look, you're gonna see and hear a lot of stuff here that you're not gonna understand. Just trust her. Just *trust* her.' I asked, 'Well, what are we gonna do?' He said, 'We're just gonna be, we're just gonna *be*.' I said, 'Well, what do you do here all the time?' John said, 'Well, after you slow down a little, you'll just see it.'

"They would wake up very early and then have a shiatsu massage. Yoko liked to take an ice bath, which she still does in the morning. She fills the bathtub with ice cubes and gets in it. Makes her alert. It's not my idea of how to start a day, but she likes it. Then they would do yoga and go off with Sean for a walk, stop off somewhere for some noodles or something like that. Life just became more and more simple. Less and less input.

"We went out to Kyoto, the ancient city of shrines and temples, and John was into it. We sometimes joked about the paradox of him singing 'God' and 'I don't believe in I Ching, and I don't believe in magic, and I don't believe in Buddha, and I don't believe in Krishna'—but, let me tell you, he believed in *all* of it. John basically read two types of books. His favorite subject was history. He entertained the idea briefly, he told me, of writing a historical text under a pseudonym. His second-favorite reading subject was occult-related material. Even during the primal-scream period, he just went through the rituals. He did not describe himself as a religious guy and didn't go to church every Sunday, but he believed in the Spirit. Yoko was the same, only she was into it further. In many ways, John was a Biblical scholar and could quote scripture at will. When we went to the shrines in Kyoto and John worshiped in front of them, Yoko would get impatient, because she had been through all of that before and she was less impressed with shrines and Buddhas and all that stuff. But John was deeply moved and deeply touched by all of it.

"I think we spent about four months in Japan that trip. They took over the presidential suite in the Hotel Okura. It was so large that there were nine or ten adjoining rooms for assistants. The living room was so big John and Sean played soccer in there, and we set up racing cars down the hallway. The Okura is the equivalent of the Plaza in New York, or the Beverly Hills. The security was very tight.

"We always sang a lot. Yoko, John, and I would spend at least two hours a day singing. It was always songs from the Forties or Fifties, because they never listened to the radio. Yoko had very little knowledge of Elvis or Bill Haley or the Shirelles, except for what John had taught her. John had never learned how to read music and couldn't get the chords right, and I couldn't sing. So the three of us, in hotel rooms around the world, would try to sing. Yoko would say, 'Let's do something that I know this time.' I'd say, 'Yeah, let's do "Silhouettes." ' She would say, 'Hmm, "Silhouettes." ' John would say, 'I think I've got the chords. Let me see—"passed your house. . . ." ' I'd say, 'No, no, *no,* it's "took a walk and passed your house late last night." ' Yoko would say, 'I *can't* stand it!' John would say, 'If you would just stop, I'll get the chords. . . .' Finally, Yoko would say, 'Do the one that I like—do my favorite one.' That was 'The Way We Were' from the Streisand–Redford movie. Gosh! Did they love that movie! John had his hair cut Robert Redford style.

"One night, John and I were sitting in the living room. He was a little bored, a little homesick. He said, 'I would just like to be in my own bed, with my Scott amp and my books next to me.' I said, 'Yeah, I hope that the numbers will be right so we can leave soon.' He was playing acoustic guitar and started playing 'Jealous Guy.' Now, I can't tell you how huge this living room was. All of a sudden, the elevator doors opened and a Japanese couple walked in. They were obviously dressed for dinner. They walked around and looked out at the view of Tokyo, and then sat down. John just kept playing.

"They lit cigarettes and talked. I suddenly realized that they thought they were in the lounge of the restaurant. They took a wrong turn, came into a huge, very dark room where there was a lounge musician playing guitar and singing in a foreign language, and there was one other guest, waiting. They had a cigarette or two, and I guess it was because no waiter had arrived to take their order that they finally looked at John, exchanged some words, and got up and left, obviously displeased. That was John Lennon's last public performance. It wasn't the Madison Square Garden show with Elton John in 1974; it was in the Hotel Okura in Tokyo in 1977. For an audience of three."

Whenever they flew—if there were John and Yoko and Sean and Mintz—they would buy four first-class seats. They would also buy all the seats on their right side or left side and in front of them and in back of them. Which would make it impossible for some stranger to turn to John and ask, 'When will the Beatles get back together?' on a twelve-hour flight. On a Lufthansa flight, they once turned the lounge of the 747 into a playroom for Sean, with electric race-car tracks.

John was an expert flier. One thing he loved was the gift catalogs on planes. He would ponder them very carefully. Yoko was less discriminating. She would just check every square, write down her American Express number and her address, and that would be that. John loved buying attaché cases. He had dozens of them, literally dozens. He collected them. He was very proud of the fact that he could travel around the world with just one attaché case. He was a good traveler, in that sense. Yoko would take twenty-seven bags, with someone to pack and unpack them for her, and then do shopping in various cities, where she had to get more clothes. John believed he could get everything he needed for going around the world into an attaché case. In his case, one very lightweight suit, a couple of pairs of slacks, a couple of shirts, a toilet kit.

Regarding his travels, John said, "All I am doing is changing bedrooms. The outside is not particularly relevant to me. I'm not gonna go sightseeing. It's not like I want to go see Disneyland, and I'm not going to sign up for polo and volleyball." For John, a new hotel meant new room service and different foods and new TV programs, which he loved. In New York, he watched TV constantly. His favorite shows were Tom Snyder's "Tomorrow" and the Johnny Carson show.

When TV bored him, John would turn to radio and tapes. He liked "The Shadow." He would listen to old tapes by Hank Williams, Carl Perkins, and Jerry Lee Lewis, and everything Bing Crosby had ever done. He listened to Sir John Gielgud reading Shakespeare. He had one hundred taped hours of Alan Watts lecturing on Eastern wisdom.

Elliot Mintz gave John some books about Howard Hughes, and they started joking about how Hughes had lived his secret years in hotel rooms, watching movies. As a joke, Mintz started calling John "Mr. Hughes" and wore white gauze gloves and a white face mask when he entered John's bedroom. John loved it. John had already started to refuse to sign autographs, had quit answering the phone, and was refusing to allow his picture to be taken—all apparently as part of his decision to retire from rock 'n' roll.

John Lennon's "white bedroom" in the Dakota became the center of his existence. It was a room barely ten by twenty feet, and its walls were exposed white brick. The room is empty now: Yoko closed it off a few weeks after December 8, 1980, when she discovered that she could hear nothing but thousands of mourners, seven floors beneath her window on 72nd Street, singing "Imagine."

When John Lennon inhabited the room, it was a quiet, dark sanctum. John had always loved bedrooms and sleep. He and Yoko's bed-ins for peace had been famous worldwide, and his love for sleep showed up in such songs as "I'm So Tired."

The bed he loved was just box springs and a mattress resting on two dark, wooden church pews. There was a white, five-button phone on the white wall above the pew that served as a headboard. The phone never rang; its lights flashed, so John never answered it. There were dozens of other phones throughout the Lenono complex in the Dakota. This phone was for outgoing, rather than incoming, messages, as a rule. John liked to sit atop the white-linen-covered bed with its rich brown quilts and read or write or play his red Stratocaster. Beside him on a white bookcase were his beloved old Scott amp-receiver, his favorite earphones, and his cable-TV control box for the giant Sony at the foot of the bed. The fireplace in the room was seldom used; the TV always was. John referred to his TV as his "electronic fireplace."

At times, the TV was not even tuned to a channel. Without his thick-lensed glasses, John was extremely nearsighted, and he liked the constantly changing warm hues of the TV screen. His Gitanes and ashtray were by his side. He liked to wear jeans and a cowboy shirt, or one of his Japanese kimonos. Incense burned twenty-four hours a day.

The room was carpeted in deep white pile. All visitors were expected to remove their shoes, Japanese-style, before entering the room. There was a single white wicker chair on the right side of the bed—Yoko's side—where a visitor might sit. If the visitor were male, he might also be asked to remove his jacket.

John's side of the bed was sacrosanct. It was the one territory he had reserved to himself. It was where he kept his writing and his reading and his music and his cigarettes. John said several times that when he was growing up in his Aunt Mimi's house, he had been confined; when he was grown and rich, he was determined to make up for that. Lenono assistants knew to hand John's tea tray to Yoko, who would then pass it to John. No one walked around John's side of the bed. It was his last retreat.

John's attention span was relatively brief. He would run around the cable channels every few minutes. Yoko would agree or not. But John loved TV and usually picked the channels.

Once, when a visitor from California was there and adjusted the TV, John started laughing and said, "The colors are all wrong. You're from Hollywood. All the people there wear makeup, so you're used to seeing people with pink faces and blue eyes and blue suits and the L.A. tan."

What was probably John's last attempt to stand on his own was the Club Dakota.

John had heard about the Blues Bar, the little private club downtown that John Belushi and Dan Aykroyd kept for themselves and their friends. Even though John didn't go out, the idea of such an intimate boîte appealed to him: a good-time club where he would be ultimately protected from the thousands of fans who would ask, "Where's Paul?" or "When will the Beatles get back together?"

It started when, for his thirty-eighth birthday, Yoko got John a beautiful old bubble-top Wurlitzer jukebox and Elton John sent him an electric Yamaha piano. John found an empty room in the Lenono complex and put both machines in it. He started spending more and more time in that room. The jukebox was full of Frankie Laine, Bing Crosby, Guy Mitchell, and the like. The room was off-limits to everyone but John and Yoko and Mintz.

On Mintz's next trip to New York, John told him, "What we should do with this room is turn it into a very chic, private club. Like an old English club. We'll just get some stuff and surprise Mother."

The two men prowled lower Manhattan and bought cheap overstuffed couches with crocheted doilies, dentist-office standing ashtrays, martini shakers, cheap watercolors of flamingos in flight, and a cheap cigarette machine so club members could buy smokes while waiting in the hallway to be seated. They got a bottle of aged brandy and sneaked brandy snifters out of the pantry. They went to Canal Street and bought moldy black tie and tails for themselves.

The Club Dakota opened on New Year's Eve 1979. Lennon and Mintz were charter members, and Yoko was an honorary member, because John knew she would immediately try to integrate it sexually. They were the only three members. Mintz and Lennon put on their tails and white gloves, and John sent a formal written invitation on a silver serving tray to Yoko to attend the opening.

She put on a simple but elegant black gown and came. She sat down and refused a drink and gaped at the flamingos. The room was candlelit. John was wearing a white T-shirt and his old Liverpool school tie with his tails. The Wurlitzer cast greens and purples and reds around the room. At midnight, the Wurlitzer played "Auld Lang Syne" and John and Yoko danced together. They and Mintz toasted one another and watched fireworks over Central Park. John never seemed happier.

A month later, Mintz returned to New York and found the Club Dakota nonexistent. The beautiful bubble-top Wurlitzer jukebox and the Yamaha piano had been put into storage. The rest of the club—the overstuffed couches and flamingo paintings and the like—had been thrown out. Mintz asked Lennon what had happened to the Club Dakota. John told him that the club had been getting a little too popular. That was all he said about it.

Several months later, Yoko suggested that it was a good time for John to take the sailing trip he had always claimed he wanted to make. She thought Bermuda was a good direction. He agreed. Around this time, he had been hinting that he would not mind creating some rock 'n' roll again but that he was not completely certain he still had the spark within him to do so. (He watched Johnny Carson every night and admired the show, but he was not overly confident that he could go on such a show again.)

When John reached Bermuda in the summer of 1980, he called Yoko and thanked her: "It's *great!*" Life then proceeded placidly. At John's request, Sean and his nanny flew to Bermuda to join him. Yoko had to take care of a few business deals, so she stayed in New York. John and Sean enjoyed swimming and sailing and doing less. One day they toured the botanical garden and admired an orchid named Double Fantasy. Every day at the beach, they ran into a woman artist, who finally summoned her nerve to ask John if she might be allowed to paint John and Sean as a family portrait. He agreed.

Every day John and Sean went to the artist's studio to pose for the portrait. When Yoko called them, the maid was instructed to tell Yoko that John and Sean were out swimming. John and Sean brought back the painting to the Dakota as a surprise gift for Yoko. The painting—about four feet by three feet—now hangs above Yoko's desk in the Dakota.

Lenono assistant Fred Seaman, who was along on the trip, had long ago given John tapes of such new groups as the Pretenders, Madness, the B-52's, and Lene Lovich (whom John referred to as Lenny Lover-itch). John had laid them aside. He started listening to them in Bermuda, and he said he snapped to the fact that what he and Yoko had been doing musically ten years earlier had finally caught on with the new rock bands. He and Yoko had already been there and back, he said, with some satisfaction.

One night, he asked Fred to take him to a disco to check out the latest musical developments. (He had not been to one since going to the Ad Lib in London in the Sixties. He had studiously avoided all discos in New York City, especially Studio 54.) John and Fred club-hopped, and in one of the clubs, John heard "Rock Lobster" by the B-52's and said immediately that they were doing Yoko's act from ten years before. He told Fred, "Jesus, get the axe [guitar] and call Mother. She's finally made it. They do her to a T."

John began writing songs at a furious pace. "Woman" took him perhaps fifteen minutes. Simultaneously, in the Dakota, Yoko had started writing songs. One night, after John had great difficulty reaching Yoko in New York, he got her on the phone and said, "Listen, I just wrote this thing. Let me sing it to you. It's 'Woman.' " Yoko said, "That's good. I wrote a song too. It's called 'Beautiful Boys.' Let me sing it to you."

They sang songs to each other for days. When John finally got back to New York, Yoko asked, "Wanna do it?" John said, "Yep."

They agreed to go into a studio and do an album and even a tour. At the Hit Factory in New York, Yoko forbade drugs and turned one room into an Egyptian temple—with palm trees, an antique white piano, and white phones for her. Session musicians, who were used to coke and cognac, were served sushi and tea instead. John taped a huge photograph of Sean on the studio wall. Yoko put plates of sunflower seeds and raisins before each musician's microphone. Shiatsu masseuses were on call for them.

The evening of December 8, 1980, when they had recorded Yoko's "Walking on Thin Ice" for their next album, John was happy. He said several times that he was gratified to see Yoko finally get the critical acclaim he felt she would have already achieved had she not been a Beatle wife. He was proud of that. In the limousine on the way back to the Dakota, he told her that they had finally become a team and erased the old image of John and Paul.

The only thing John and Yoko ever differed about was the use of limousines. Yoko wanted them on call practically twenty-four hours a day, whereas John often took taxicabs. Both of them loved to walk the streets of New York City, the city they loved because they could walk its streets by themselves and the people were so cool that their coolness protected them more than any twelve bodyguards ever could. He had gotten used to the Dakota groupies—just like the Elvis Presley gate people—who were there all the time but respected his privacy.

Even when John and Yoko took a limo, they would often stop it out on West 72nd Street, then walk into the courtyard like ordinary citizens, saying hello to the fans on the street instead of having the limo drive through the high iron gates to safety. On December 8, 1980, they stopped outside the gate for the last time. When John fell, he was carrying in his right hand a tape of Yoko's song "Walking on Thin Ice."

On the Town With Tony Bennett

"Listen to this," Tony Bennett said as he popped a cassette into his Sony tape player.

Stevie Wonder's voice floated out of the speaker, filling the suite at the Park Lane: "Hello, Tony. I'd like to first apologize and sincerely say I'm sorry for being late with this tape. As you probably heard, we lost the original tape. Nevertheless, I wanted to do it over for you with the synthesizer to give you the basic vibe of the string sound or whatever. Okay? So here we are at four o'clock in the morning in the studio."

After a lush synthesized lead-in, Wonder sang, "This town, old town/ The place I spent my younger years/The house that sheltered me from fears . . ."

"Isn't that something?" said Bennett. "Stevie wrote that song for me. I'm doing a contemporary album now with people like George Benson and Billy Joel and Stevie. That song is fantastic; it's in the Gershwin tradition."

If anyone knows the Gershwin tradition, it's certainly Tony Bennett, who's spent the past thirty years singing nothing but what he calls "good music." He's an interpretive singer whose repertoire has always consisted in the main of work by such stage composers as George Gershwin, Rodgers and Hart, and Irving Berlin. He stubbornly stayed with that music even when rock and Top 40 radio threatened to shove him aside, despite such Bennett hits as "I Left My Heart in San Francisco."

Although he's cut eighty-eight albums, Bennett is without a recording contract at the moment. The main reason is that he's still idealistic enough to wait for a contract that meets his terms. He also performs a great many benefits, the latest of which is a series of concerts this week for New York City's Police Athletic League. He said he is doing it as a tribute to his hometown. The star is almost constantly on the road, and because of that, not many people know that Anthony Dominick Benedetto (Bob Hope dubbed him Tony Bennett long ago when Bennett was going around calling himself "Joe Bari") is a lifelong New Yorker. In fact, just before we met, he had closed a deal on a co-op on 55th Street, a few notes away from Carnegie Hall, where he first knocked 'em dead on June 9, 1962, with a concert that became a legend. His new home is not much farther away from Astoria, where he grew up and worked as a singing waiter.

It was a long way from the obscurity of Astoria to the point where, some time back, Frank Sinatra broke his customary public silence to say of Bennett, "Tony's gonna come out now and he's gonna tear the seats outta the place for you. Because he's my man, this cat. He's the greatest singer in the world today, this man, Tony Bennett."

That's a remarkable claim, and I asked Bennett about that and about whether or not he thinks of himself as Sinatra's successor.

"Well," Bennett said, flashing his famous crinkled smile, "they claim that I'm the heir apparent. I don't even know what that means, because we're two different animals. Frank is ten years my elder, and I still have a way to go yet. There are some strong storm warnings that if I just stay healthy it'll get good, it'll start getting *good*." He delivered a strong wink.

For all Bennett's humility, there is no disputing his standing as the world's best saloon singer. He is a deceptively low-key performer who can make the biggest hall seem intimate. He also has unrivaled taste in song selection: He has long been known as the "standard singer," because any song he does becomes a standard. And, as I quickly discovered when we left the Park Lane and went out for a stroll, his popular appeal cuts across all class lines. I asked Bennett how he handled the public and why he never went in for bodyguards and heavy security and entourages the way some performers do.

"I'll tell you," he said as we turned down Sixth Avenue. "If I walk down the street like this, swaggering, with my shoulders back, everybody will say, 'Hey, Tony, how you doing,' you know, because I'm just walking like a citizen."

On cue, he was stopped by two young men, one black, one white, who wanted his autograph on twenty-dollar bills they pulled out. Bennett's manner with them was so smooth that he left them all but bowing and scraping.

"I see what you mean," I said as a cabdriver stopped his car, jumped out at us, and started singing "I Left My Heart in San Francisco."

"Yeah," Bennett said, "there's a way of creating chaos and there's also a way of *not* creating it. One time—just for a gag—in Vegas, Tom Jones was coming in surrounded by cops and screaming kids, so, just for a joke, I jumped into the middle of the cops and everybody stopped screaming 'Tom Jones' and started screaming 'Tony Bennett.'"

We ran into comedian Jerry Stiller on 57th and Sixth; he and Bennett got each other up-to-date, and then we walked on. "You know," Bennett said, "Sinatra used to have to walk underground through the pipes of New York City just to get out of the Paramount Theater after a show. The only way they could get him past the crowds was through the sewers of Manhattan." Bennett shook his head in wonderment.

At age fifty-four, Tony Bennett could not be in a better position. His type of music—"good music"—is respected again. His place in history is already secure. He was trained as an opera tenor (his voice has deepened in the last thirty years to near-baritone), but his personal crusade has been to keep alive the music of composers such as Richard Rodgers, Harold Arlen, and Jerome Kern, simultaneously retaining some of the fire of such torch singers as Billie Holiday and Lena Horne.

Bennett's most amazing accomplishment, though, has gone largely unrecognized. He was the man who sang the first country-and-western crossover hit—"Cold, Cold Heart." That may not sound like too much these days, when everybody's doing it, but it was a feat at the time. He knocked down the walls between Tin Pan Alley—the songwriting-factory monopoly—and singer-songwriters who wrote for their peer group. In 1951, country songwriters were called "hillbillies," and they could not get as much as a demo tape into the Brill Building, on Broadway, where songwriting was a nine-to-five assembly-line job.

The song that changed all that was written by Hank Williams, a country superstar who was as hillbilly as they came. In 1951, Jerry Wexler (since a partner in Atlantic Records and producer for Aretha Franklin, among others) was a reviewer for *Billboard* magazine. He was already responsible for a country-gone-pop hit, having persuaded Patti Page to record "Tennessee Waltz" on the strength of a recording of it by a black singer, Ace Harris. Wexler was also friends with Mitch Miller, who was head of artists and repertory for Columbia Records. Wexler sought out esoteric records, and after he got Hank Williams's single of "Cold, Cold Heart," he took it out to Mitch Miller's house in Stony Point. After he heard it, Miller got a young Columbia Records singer named Tony Bennett to record it, and the rest is hysteria.

Despite that success, Bennett was still dubious about cutting country songs and never did another one. Part of the reason was Williams himself. "I was just a young kid," Bennett explained, "and Williams called me up, and all he said was, 'What's the idea of ruining my song?' "

Bennett started out wanting to be a painter or a jazz singer. His first public engagement was on July 11, 1936, when the Triborough Bridge was opened. "My mother put me with Mayor LaGuardia cutting a ribbon on the bridge," he said, "and *all* of New York City was walking behind us. Mayor LaGuardia and the whole city walking the length of the bridge. You talk about carnival in Rio or Mardi Gras in New Orleans—those were nothing compared to that day. Maybe it's my own youthful imagination now, looking back at it, but it was a *spectacular* day. Everybody was singing 'Marching Along Together,' the *whole* city was singing and they were *up*. Highly idealistic about the future. And Mayor LaGuardia was patting me on the head and I saw everybody feeling so good and I just said, 'I'd like to do this the rest of my life, make people feel that way.' It really was indelible for me. And then, when I was fourteen, I got my first job, at the Democratic Club in Astoria. They paid me fifteen bucks for singing at a beer party. Then I started working as a singing waiter over at Ricardo's in Astoria Park."

Midway in our walk, Bennett wanted to stop at an American Express office to straighten out a problem with his credit card. In the time it took to travel the four blocks from 57th and Sixth Avenue, Bennett signed thirty-five or forty autographs and said hello to thirty-five or forty other people who just wanted to say "Hello, Tony" and bask in the golden glow of a bona fide international celebrity. (I have to step in here and say that I was surprised by the respect Bennett is accorded by *everyone:* I've walked these same streets with John Lennon and Mick Jagger and not seen so much recognition.)

As we walked into the AmEx office, I announced that "Tony Bennett is ready to do his commercial," and when Bennett was the only one who laughed, I clammed up. It would take forty-five minutes to straighten out his card. One clerk told Bennett that her father had once kissed him on an airplane. He gave his all-purpose chuckle, and we sat down to wait.

One thing that I'd wanted to ask Bennett about for years was his feeling about being put on the shelf by radio stations when Top 40 took over. He was quick to answer the question. "The change came in 1955. No, it wasn't just Elvis. All of a sudden, everybody was impressed by Detroit and the idea of obsolescence. Before, in the days when Goddard Lieberson was running CBS, he had a very ethical philosophy. He told every artist, from the top classical artist to the lowest pop artist, 'If you make a record, make it last, make a record that will last forever.' I would hire—and Mitch Miller would hire—the finest musicians. There were from fifty to seventy men on each record. We really gave full performances, and we never left the studio until the record was just right. As a result of that, the records made the catalogues and they still sell today just like current records. I get the same royalties now as I did in 1950. That's because the albums hold up, they don't sound old-fashioned, they don't sound dated.

"But in 1955 it changed. They started going for this obsolescence idea. They didn't want records that would last, they didn't want lasting artists, they wanted *lots* of artists. It became like a supermarket: Go with the next, the next. So they started discarding people like me and Duke Ellington and Leonard Bernstein. The marketing guys took over. It took a big walk away from melodic music. It suddenly became very unprofessional to be professional. Which was very neurotic."

Bennett was still very young when his kind of music was put on hold.

He smiled wryly. "Well, I started late. I started when I was twenty-seven, having scuffled for seven years just trying to get jobs. I didn't look like any other singers, so they couldn't fit me into a category. They just said I should get a nose job so I would look like Tony Martin. He was big at the time. So they figured all singers had to look like somebody else. This is where perseverance comes in. But there is a trend coming back, a heavy-duty trend, luckily. There was a time when if you got up and did a lindy hop, everybody just laughed you off the floor. Now the young kids—at Carnegie Hall the other night with Count Basie and Sarah Vaughan, I started dancing with Sarah, and she asked,

'Do you lindy? Do you jitterbug?' I said, *'Sure!'* and we started doing it and the place went crazy. Now, that couldn't have happened five years ago. So there is a change for the better, I believe."

AmEx finally got Bennett's card fixed, and we started walking back uptown, stopping every twenty feet or so for the star to sign more autographs. "You know," he said between signatures, "you should go see *Amadeus*. That show taught me a lot about how to survive in this business." What were his influences, the things that got him into the business and that helped him survive all these years?

"Count Basie is one," Bennett said. "I tell you, that's my favorite relationship of any in the music business. There's a warmth between us. He's the *boss* as far as I'm concerned. He and Ellington. Ellington was like the sky, you know, and Basie is like the ground, like the earth. To me, they are the two pillars of jazz. I was always frustrated because when I came out of the service, the big-band business was over with. I was *weaned* on the big bands. I grew up seeing these guys. So, when I became successful and somebody would ask, 'How'd you like to work?' I'd say I'd like to work with Tommy Dorsey or Duke Ellington. These were masters who knew everything about the audience and had this great heritage."

We walked up on Park Avenue, with every sixth person or so doing a double take upon seeing Bennett. "How do you find songs, Tony?" I asked. "A song like 'I Wanna Be Around'?"

Bennett stopped short. "*That* came from a housewife in Youngstown, Ohio. Sadie Vimmerstedt. She wrote a fan letter to Johnny Mercer and she said, 'I just came up with a phrase that sounds like you: "I want to be around to pick up the pieces when somebody breaks your heart." Johnny, that sounds like something you would say. Why don't you write a song with that idea?' Johnny wrote the song and liked it so much he gave her fifty percent of it. He's an honorable guy. The song became an international hit. That was unusual, but once it was put into a pro's hands like Mercer it all worked."

Once back at the Park Lane, we settled down with coffee. Bennett stood for a long time looking out over Central Park. "This is the most beautiful view in the city," he said finally. "Here, here's a drawing I did from this view." (Bennett has had a following as an artist for years and regularly exhibits his work under the name Anthony Benedetto.) Why had he decided to do a week of benefit shows for the PAL here?

"Well," he said, "it's really a salute to New York's nightlife. I'm indebted to New York. It's the greatest city because of its vitalness. You can get that in other cities, but you have to search for it. Here, you just walk up the street and see the best paintings in the world. And there are great teachers sprinkled all over this city. It's the greatest place in the world to learn the ropes, to get streetwise, to get this terrific education. Chicago has transformed itself into a cultural center, and San Francisco is America's Paris. But this one is the *big daddy*. They're always talking about what a tough city this is. What I'm trying to do is dramatize the fact that there's plenty to do here. I hope other artists and cultural centers will celebrate it like I do. I'm just an individual artist, right? But I think everybody should celebrate it."

Bennett fell silent and watched as the setting sun turned Central Park into a green oasis brushed with gold.

As a veteran of eighty-eight albums, how does he feel about the course of American popular music?

"Oh." He stood up and thumped the table to emphasize his point. "I've come to the complete conviction that the songs of the nineteen-twenties and thirties in American music are deep, *very,* very deep. I think that one hundred years from now they will become America's classical music—the Richard Rodgerses, the Gershwins, the Kerns—it was an *era*. We were poor in those days, but there was great hope, and this city was building, skyscrapers were going up, everybody felt we were going toward something great. Those songs will *live*. They might be out of fashion, but what is good *is* good and will always be good. People like Harold Arlen, who was *destined,* you know. He wrote 'Somewhere Over the Rainbow,' 'Black Magic,' 'Stormy Weather,' 'One for My Baby.' It's part of our heritage. And I doubt that it's ever going to go out. You just say, 'They can't take that away from me.' It's hard to beat."

Chapter 3

Temperance

I Sing the Solid Body Electric: An Interview With Les Paul

If you don't step lively, Les Paul is likely to run you down somewhere in the twenty-nine-room mansion he fills to bursting in the woods near Mahwah. He's a genius—he'll tell you so—and his energies and ambitions can't be confined. One minute he's prancing through the large, well-equipped recording studio (still in commercial space), pausing to show you the *first*, the *original* eight-track recorder that he built in 1954 and which has "lasted like a Sherman tank," and a second later—shirttails flapping behind him—he's hurtling up a staircase to rummage through a teetering stack of Les Paul Gibson guitars: 200 guitars that list from $525 to $765 fill several rooms and protrude from closets and bathrooms. Some are being torn apart and rebuilt, the others already have been. "I've completely rebuilt every guitar I ever had," he said, stopping to ransack a closet. He comes up with a spanking new Gibson Oxblood Artist case and opens it. "Look at this." He is amazed. "A brand new Les Paul Custom." He regards it with the clinical air of a mechanic inspecting a trashed Buick transmission: an imperfect object to be rebuilt.

That's why Les Paul may well be the most important figure in popular music in the last two and a half decades. He is *not* interested in music per se; he is an electronics technician and inventor (self-taught) whose mania is music *delivery systems*. True, he and Mary Ford (born Colleen Summers: Her name was completely changed by Paul—whose own real name is Lester Polfus—upon their marriage in 1949) had an incredible list of hit songs that started with "Lover" in 1949 and ran right on through the Fifties with "Nola," "Tennessee Waltz," "Mockin' Bird Hill," "How High the Moon," "The World Is Waiting for the Sunrise,"

"Just One More Chance," "I'm Confessin'," "Smoke Rings," "Bye Bye Blues," "Tiger Rag," "I'm Sitting on Top of the World," "Vaya con Dios," "I Really Don't Want to Know," "I'm a Fool to Care," "Whither Thou Goest," "Hummingbird," "Moritat," "Cinco Robles," "Put a Ring on My Finger," and "Jura." Les Paul's success was largely due to the shimmering spatial quality unique to his recordings, a quality that was the result of his electronic expertise—his pioneering in multitrack recording and overdubbing and his perfection of the solid-body electric guitar, an idea he had been toying with since the thirties. He built the prototype in 1941. He called it "The Log," and it was nothing but a four-by-four wooden log with strings, a pickup, and a plug. It took him several years to convince Gibson that the concept could work and the company finally issued the Les Paul Standard in 1952. By then, however, he had already built and was using the extremely complicated Les Paul Recording Guitar, which he only allowed Gibson to issue in 1971. Les Paul guitars are generally regarded by musicians as the standard and today are played by musicians as diverse as Jimmy Page, Jeff Beck, Leon Russell, Richard Betts, Mick Taylor, Leslie West, and Pete Townshend. The Les Pauls, most musicians agree, have the hottest pickups and the longest "sustain" ability.

Now fifty-eight years old and a bachelor (he and Mary Ford were divorced in 1963), Paul leads the life of an inventor, working from late afternoon till sunrise amidst thousands of tapes, miles of wiring, banks of consoles, stacks of amplifiers, and his guitars and oscillators. During the past year he has played a few concerts, leading Capitol to release *The World Is (Still) Waiting for the Sunrise,* more or less a Les Paul/Mary Ford greatest hits package.

Of medium height and build, he bears an astonishing resemblance to a pale George C. Scott but talks about twice as fast. He's a wisp of a man, with thin, orangeish hair and, his most distinctive feature, piercing eyes. His right arm is permanently bent: After a bad car wreck in 1948 the elbow joint was knocked off, and he told the doctor to set the arm at an angle so he could still play guitar.

As the interview began he seated himself at the kitchen bar, which was covered with stacks of papers and schematic drawings. He offered to make coffee, but once he began talking he forgot all about it and hours later was still holding empty coffee cups before him. If ever there was a single-minded man, Les Paul is he. Interestingly, the only person he compared himself to was Thomas Alva Edison. "He used to," marveled Paul, "when he had something big going, he would move a cot right into the plant and stay there till the project was done."

Les Paul built *his* plant around himself.

What's behind the Les Paul disappearance and recent reappearance onstage?

I retired ten years ago—okay?—and in retiring I went into some of the projects that I'd been wanting to do but had been too busy for. So in those ten years I was busy inventing different items, many of which you know about—guitars and pickups and so on. [He holds patents on a floating bridge pickup and the LP 70 electro-dynamic pickup and was the first person to put two pickups on one guitar, the first to build a guitar with fourteen frets, and he "discovered" the echo effect in recordings.] But I also invented different types of transducers and patented them and sold them and the last one I sold went for half a million dollars. *Highly* successful. Then about a year ago a friend called and said, "Les, can you help me out? I'm in a real bind and I need a guitar player." I hadn't played guitar for ten years and so I was embarrassed because I never practice and rarely do I ever pick up a guitar except when I'm performing, which is unusual.

So you went and played . . .

Let me just explain, give you background to understand what's going on. Now, I said if you're in that much of a bind, I'll come in as long as you don't mention my name, don't say who the hell I am. In no time at *all,* Count Basie was in there and *every* guitar player and musician. God, they came from all over the place and they enjoyed it. Then I got a fan letter from a high school kid out in Hempstead, Long Island, wanting me to play out there. They enjoyed that very much and kept yelling out for "How High the Moon" and things I thought high school kids never heard of and could care less about, so this continued on and I started playing jazz concerts and playing more but still working on my projects here.

Did you ever have any electronics training whatsoever?

None. It all came about because in 1929 a guy was winding turns of wire on an oatmeal box and I said, "Hey, Harry, what are you doing?" He said, "I'm building a crystal set." I said, "What in the world is a crystal set?" So he told me and drew out the schematic, and this phenomenon is that it can actually pick up a radio station. I became so intrigued with it that I built one and at the same time they were putting in sewers in front of my house and this fellow on his lunch hour was playing the harmonica and that intrigued me. I asked him where I could get one and he said, "Here, take this one." So I started playing blues harmonica on it and I became the first guy in Waukesha [Wisconsin] to play a harmonica backwards.

How did you know to do that? Were you just experimenting?

No. I listened to WSM from Nashville and to guys like Sonny Terry. In learning harmonica I figured that I better get a guitar or banjo to go with it. So I got a banjo.

And was that when you made that "shotgun" harmonica holder?

Right, right. Nobody's ever made one better. You can flip the harmonica over with your chin while you're playing. And my mother had an electric piano—not electric, a pump piano—which I made electric; I figured I ain't gonna pump this damned thing all the time. I also went farther ahead than that—I started to do *multiples* [overdubbing] on the piano by punching in my own holes on the rolls.

Didn't you learn music then by watching the keys and marking them?

Yeah, I saw this key go down when that note was played, so I finally figured that was C and this was D-flat and so forth. All this just grew and then inside of a year I was playing a lot of radio stations, singing and playing country music, and I didn't even know there was a Depression.

What kind of guitar were you playing then?

An L5. This was 1929, my first L5. I started out with the finest guitar. No, I gotta retract that. I started out with a Gene Autry guitar, a five-dollar guitar.

Is that old story true that you took the back off that guitar and stuck a phonograph arm . . .

No, no, I didn't take the back off. I just took the phonograph needle and stuck it right in the guitar, so instead of hearing the record, you heard my guitar. Now the reason I did that was because on Friday and Saturday nights they had roadhouses in those days where I would play. And I would play a drive-in hamburger place. Everybody in their cars couldn't hear me, so the first thing I did was build a PA system. They could hear my voice then but not my guitar, so I made an electric guitar.

Was that when you joined that band?

Right. I was making like a hundred dollars a week. Then a cowboy band came to town and they had a guitar player—there just *weren't* any guitar players then—I went nine miles out of town and sneaked in the bathroom window of the roadhouse and listened. He played beyond the third fret and I had thought there was *nothing* up there past the third. He was going up and down the board like a streak of lightning and I said, "My God almighty!" He said, "You play guitar, kid?" I said yeah and he said to play him something, so I did and he said, "Hey, kid, you're all right." So, during the break, he showed me some chords and harmonics and showed me what a diminished was and an augmented. Next, the boss of the band heard me and asked me to join the band. I said I'd have to ask my mother—I have half a year yet to go in high school and I'm thirteen years old. He said, "Well, tell your mother I can pay you eight bucks." She said, "Why would you want to do that for eight dollars?" and I said, "I think I can get nine but mostly I want to because of this guitar player. I could learn so much from him."

This guy should be immortalized for teaching Les Paul. What was his name?

Joe Wolverton. So I joined the band and the first thing I found out was that they paid eight dollars a *night,* not a week. So I was the highest paid guy in the band and who did they let go right away but Wolverton. And I had wanted to be with him, not with the band. But that got me away from home and to Chicago and on the WLS "Barn Dance."

And then at the age of seventeen, you were both the house bandleader and a hillbilly star at WJJD there?

Yeah, but then I stopped being a hillbilly—I was "Rhubarb Red"— because I was being torn between two names. And I wanted to be a jazz artist. Something was pulling me toward progressive music and country music was becoming dull to me. Now, parallel to all this, I had made my third recording machine. The first one was back before I joined this band when I built my PA system. I stared at my mother's radio and I figured if that speaker is putting out that sound, then it would just seem logical that if you took a pickup and put it where the speaker is, you'd feel it with the needle, and I tried it and it worked. It wasn't long before I would take an aluminum disc and gouge out a record and I heard myself—and I still have the record—and this was a great, great step.

Were you also listening to other guitarists on records?

Oh, yeah. I would get records by Nick Lucas and Carson Robison, Gene Autry and the Three Keys. Eddie Lang intrigued me—he ended up with Bing Crosby—and when I heard Bing's radio program for Primo Cigars and I heard this guitar player behind him, of course I had to figure out what he was doing. Now they didn't have picks in my time so I took a piano key, carved it down, and shaped it into a pick. And now, I'm saying to myself, I gotta make an electric guitar—gotta go to electric because in a jazz group you couldn't really hear an acoustic and I'm worried about the guy in that barbecue stand or whatever.

Was this before you built the Log?

The Log came in '41. So the first thing I did was to build a pickup. In building this pickup, it was mighty crude but it evolved from an earphone off my crystal set headphones and I held it over a string and it reproduced the sound and I said, "Well, if it does it with one, it'll do it with six. So, if I can duplicate this under each string I will *have it*." And then I finally made one that went under all six strings and that became the pickup. In 1934 I was broadcasting on NBC on the electric guitar and it was my own contraption and everybody could hear me and in 1937 I was well on my way to New York.

How did you make the transition from country to jazz?

I'll make this story short. I had two guys who had enough nerve, with no money—I had money, they didn't—to go to New York and I said a little lie. I told them I knew Paul Whiteman very well and had a lot of pull in New York. I didn't really know anybody in New York, but I had to get them to go with me, the whole Les Paul trio. So we rehearsed for two years—it was Jimmy Atkins, Chet's brother, singing, and Ernie Newton on bass. After two years, we only knew two numbers good, but we had those two down pat—"After You've Gone" and "Out of Nowhere." So we came to New York and ended up at the Chesterfield Hotel. The other two guys were broke and they said, "So are you gonna call your friend Whiteman?" Whiteman hung up on me, of course, and the two other guys said, "What did he say?" I said he said he wanted to see me right away. We went over there and the secretary slammed the door on me. They're looking at me in amazement and in the meantime there's Fred Waring standing there waiting for the elevator.

So we just started to play and Jimmy was singing. Waring listened and said, "Come on with me." This was in the Ed Sullivan Theater at Fifty-third and Broadway and Paul Whiteman is on the thirteenth floor or something and Fred Waring is on the eleventh. So he takes us into rehearsal and stopped everybody—sixty-two Pennsylvanians or whatever—and said, "If you like this trio as much as I do, I'm gonna hire 'em." And we did the two numbers, and of course the amplifier blew a fuse right in the middle and we had to finish it acoustically. But he said, "You're hired." And we're now in New York with Fred Waring and we stayed with him for five years.

Once you got to New York, did you find other guitar players to jam with, to learn from?

There were probably three or four other guitar players and it was very important that I find them because if there was one that had something that I didn't have I made it a point to find out what it was. Also, I virtually lived up in Harlem. At eleven-fifteen, when that program signed off on NBC, I was in that car in a *flash* and I was right uptown and jamming with all the greats in the music business that you can name. There was *no one* that I wasn't playing with in the after-hours joints: Art Tatum playing the piano, Herman Chittison and Ben Webster, Louis Armstrong and Stuff Smith. At that time there were only two guitar players around in New York that really had their heads together and one was a fellow called Leonard Ware, who played four-string guitar that was very good, and then there was myself.

The rest of them had their heads somewhere else, they weren't into jazz really. Now, there was a guy named Floyd Smith who played good blues with Andy Kirk's orchestra. And it was then—sometime in the late thirties—that in walked a kid named Charlie Christian, and we became very good friends and so he asked me, "What have you got there?" And then he got a guitar like mine and a pickup like mine, but he played his own thing, he had his style of playing. And he went with Benny Goodman. I had more flash, more technique than Charlie had but less drive, and so we used to love to be together because we could pick each other's brains because we were on different wavelengths.

Charlie and I would really battle each other—and we'd battle for *blood*. We'd go up there onstage and chop each other to pieces and then go out to eat together. When I first heard Charlie what amazed me so much was he could play so few notes and really get it across, where I was playing a million notes. His few notes meant more than all mine. He would say, "I've got trouble playing fast." And I would say, "Well, I've got a problem, I need to play slow." And, of course, Charlie had a great influence in straightening my head out *fast*. In playing less notes and meaning *more*. So this skinny kid came walking in and scared the hell out of everybody and I really dug him. I dug him a lot.

How did you then end up in Los Angeles with your own studio?

In '41 I went to Fred Waring and I said my feet are bothering me and I want to leave and go join Bing Crosby. Fred said, "Well, where did you meet him?" I said, "I never met him just like I never met you, but I am going to play with Bing Crosby, that's where I'm heading." And I got as far as Chicago, where they made me musical director of two stations and I stayed a year but only because the money was good and I couldn't get it out of my mind that's where I wanted to go, to L.A., and be in movies and to be with Bing Crosby and others. And sure enough, in 1942, I got out there. But I no more than landed there when they drafted me in the Army and who did I end up with but Meredith Wilson. So there I was with Meredith Wilson in the Armed Forces Radio Service, which is probably the *biggest* break in my whole career, because my job was to do nothing but play for Rudy Vallee, Bing Crosby, Amos and Andy, Fibber McGee and Molly, Johnny Mercer, Kate Smith. Then when I left the Army in '43 I went with Bing Crosby and I went with NBC as a staff musician.

My hooking up with Crosby is a long, long story. But I had to find out just where he was—how he lived and ate and slept and everything else, just to run into him. And he hired me and my trio and he got me my contract with Decca Records. The first thing we did with Bing was a hit—"It's Been a Long, Long Time." He used to come over to my back-yard, to my studio there, and he'd listen to the sound and he leaned against the wall one night and said, "This is the *greatest* sound. I've been all over the world and never heard sound this great in my life." Bing liked good sound. If he hadn't encouraged me, I'd never have built the studio.

In those days you were allowed five programs, and I had my five programs on the staff at NBC and I had others with Frank de Vol, Fibber McGee—so many it's hard to remember them all. Then it was about '44 or '45 that the Andrews Sisters approached me and said they would like to have me travel with *them*. I started to travel with them, which I thought was better than with Bing. I learned an awful lot from them and from Lou Levy, the man who taught the Andrews Sisters. He paid me very well, twenty-five hundred a week, and that was a pretty good salary to be making in those days, and again I wasn't happy. And Crosby had said to me, "Why don't you build your own studio?" And so it was time that I leave the Andrews Sisters and build a recording studio for blood, so to speak, this one is *mine,* for me.

And that's when you took a flywheel out of a Cadillac and made it into a turntable?

That's when I took the flywheel and used it dynamically balanced, and the war was on, so I was called Dr. Paul, and I sent to S.S. White for some dental belt and out of a jukebox I got the motor to run the recording machine. So, I built the studio in my garage and it started to become famous overnight and who is recording in my studio but W.C. Fields and the famous record is "My First Drink of Water" and "Talk on Temperance," and if you'll listen you'll find it's Les Paul playing the guitar and I'm engineering the date and playing the piano.

Was this the beginning of the Les Paul "sound"?

The studio was a *legend* because of its sound. Now, this was the beginning of what we call close mike technique—this had *never* been used, it had been pounded into their heads that you should be three feet away from a microphone, no closer than two feet, if you get within a foot, then the bass is building up, et cetera, et cetera. There was no such thing as an echo chamber or tape-delay echo—what I had made was a record-delay echo, and that was very simple. You put a playback pickup right behind the record head, so you drop the cutting head, put the pickup right behind it, and you now have your echo and you have a feedback loop and you take the source and return it to where it came from, and in no time at all the whole industry was in my backyard. From all of this emerged the idea of multiple recordings, which I had been toying with since my mother's player piano. I had made multiples as far back as 1935 where I wanted a background so that I could practice, so I would put down a couple of guitar parts on my two recording machines that I had in a closet in Chicago. This was disc recording. I'll get to multiple tape later.

What's the history of the Log?

Before I went to the West Coast came about the idea of the Log. I went down to Epiphone on Fourteenth Street in New York and said, "What would it cost me to rent your factory on Sunday?" And they said, "It don't cost you anything." And all they want is to look over my shoulder. And they asked me why I'd want to make a four-by-four guitar. I had my reasons. At the time, way back, there was only *one* pickup on a guitar and I found that *two* pickups were better than one and there were effects you could get. So I asked Gibson to build me a guitar and allow the bracing to be in the proper place so that I could mount a second pickup and they raised their eyebrows. This was 1941. The interesting part about this was when I first approached Gibson with the idea of a solid-body guitar, they as much as said, "Get him *out* of here." There's a story that Mr. Berlin [M. H. Berlin, president of the parent corporation which included Gibson] told me. When they signed me up, I was the "kid with the broom handle." And they didn't want the name Gibson on that guitar: "The name is too valuable and too high class—we make too fine a product to have it on a broom handle." But he was intrigued with the idea and they brought this up with me. "What are we gonna call this guitar?" And I said, "That's very simple—call it the *Les Paul Guitar*." We hemmed and hawed around for several years and finally signed the contract.

When I was working in Chicago, Gibson approached me and gave me their new guitars and let me field test them, tell them what was right or wrong with them. They kept feeding me with guitars. I've been with Gibson now through five of their presidents. I don't get paid for it, but they will call me up and say, "Well, we've got a problem. Can you help us?" And I'll go up there and help them out.

How did the idea for a solid body come to you? Was it just a desire for more sustain in your guitars?

It came about gradually. It came about as far back as putting the phonograph needle in the guitar—I got feedback and so it wasn't until a short time later that I started to tuck towels into the F holes and then I cut a hole in the back of the guitar and I was putting blankets in there. Then I asked Gibson to make a guitar with *no* holes in it so that no sound came out of it at all, and Charlie Christian ordered one like it, and whatever I ordered, Charlie ordered. We had a mutual admiration for each other, but when it came to being an innovator, he just turned on the volume and he chomped away and he put it in his case same as many guitar players I know today. If a wire comes off, God help 'em—they take it to the nearest music store and it's fixed and they don't even ask what was wrong.

To answer your question—gradually we got to a solid body and I realized in the late Thirties that I was now running a piece of steel through that instrument and the guitar just looked like a guitar and actually the bridge was suspended on a piece of steel and it had *nothing* to do with the guitar. I finally said, in the late Thirties, "This is where it's at, and to prove it I want to make the Log," and when I made the Log that was positive proof. I had maybe two hundred guitars in my house in the Forties; I was making guitar after guitar after guitar. Leo Fender and his people would come back there and see what I was doing, and the Log was long before Leo Fender was doing it. I met Leo before he made his first guitar. He gave me a Telecaster and I used his amplifiers for quite a long time. I admire the man because he does a good job. But we're not rivals, because his instrument is nothing like mine and mine is nothing like his. His is a different type of pickup and different neck and different construction.

What changes have there been in the basic Les Paul guitar from its introduction in 1952 until now?

It's identical to the original. We don't make any changes. It's the same instrument. Well, I shouldn't say there are no changes—you may see a change, for instance, in the tuning pegs. The tuning pegs are better now, the old ones used to be open to dust and they weren't as rigid in construction.

What is it that makes the Les Paul such a sought-after guitar?

Two main reasons. The first is the most important. It sustains, and that's because of the construction. The other is the pickups. I won't use the ten-cent ceramic magnets in mine because in a year or less those will stabilize and start demagnetizing and your sound deteriorates.

But you didn't have humbucking pickups at first.

No, the first ones didn't. The humbucking pickups came about after two years. Humbucking means that two coils are wound identical, okay, and by reversing the polarity of them—in other words, when the two are reversed and then connected in series—this will cancel out the hum. It's 180 degrees out of phase and it's a method of knocking out unwanted noises; it reduces the extraneous magnetic field. The guitar is like a mine sweeper, it's a sensing device, not only to pick up the voltage created by the string but it's also wide open to extraneous noises. So the first thing I did was to humbuck the coils and the second thing was to shield what we call the hardware, that being any pieces of metal involved in the pickups. They asked me if it would be okay to make this change and that change so I said, "Well, send it to me and I'll tell you." So, when you say an original Les Paul guitar, there are four or five original Les Paul guitars. But *the* original Les Paul guitar was with the Les Paul tailpiece on it and had the non-humbucking coils and it was gold and black and it had a maple top and if I were to take my first Les Paul guitar and play it for you and then play a Les Paul that came off the line a month ago, I guarantee you couldn't tell the difference. There is no difference.

I was thinking more of the Recording guitar, which is certainly different.

Oh, the Recorder is what I had and this story is simple. I said you cannot have this because this is *the* Les Paul sound and *this* I will not divulge and I am keeping *this* to myself. And I will tell you how to build a guitar and a pickup but it will *not* be the pickup that I use. It wasn't until 1967 that I called Mr. Berlin and said, "Now that I have retired from the business I will give you my secret and you can have the low impedance pickup that I have been using for years and years and I will give you some of the things that I asked to keep to myself," because this made me stand out from the others for the Les Paul sound, which I was making a buck on. Capitol Records spoke of the "new sound— Les Paul and his new sound." This was created mostly because of the instrument and it was so far *advanced*. Now, when I handed it to Gibson . . . Gibson finds this is a rather shocking thing to say, but the kids of the younger generation, and this is not a putdown, but the younger generation took a long time to find out where it was at. And it's going to take them a long time to come up to where it's at now because we constantly stay ahead. If a player is just now getting to know how to handle the one that came out in 1952, we throw something at him that is more sophisticated and harder to understand because it has so many controls on it and so many functions.

So, it doesn't sell like the old original because technically it has less level—let's start out here. It's common knowledge that for every action there's a reaction and if you want high level you sacrifice frequency response. If you want extended response, if you want true reproduction, you're going to have less output but which you have *plenty* of, and by making my pickup in the Recorder, you have less level but a better sound, an extended sound, expanded, wider frequency range. You can run cable from here to New York City and will notice no loss whatsoever in the frequency response. But if you take a high impedance guitar and you run cable from here to that TV set, you're gonna lose x amount of dB of highs and it's going to increase until finally you don't have a guitar, you have a muffled *bass*. Now, I have a hundred feet of cable when I go out onstage. I *leave* my amplifier, I say good-bye to it. I can change everything right at the guitar. I have a microphone built in my guitar. This all came out by Gibson and was not accepted by the player. But—going to the amplifier, it's a cop-out. That's when I know a player is in trouble, he's back there turning knobs.

This control system of yours, that's the Les Paulverizer?

Right. I'm building a system for the stage so that I am free to walk around on that stage and do my multiples at will. This was invented years ago, I'm making it smaller now. This box is no bigger than your tape recorder and it runs the whole schmeer. I can record, I can play back, I can add an echo, I can take it out, I can add Vibrola, I can start, stop or rewind the machine, I can put tape part three, part five, part thirteen—I can do anything I want.

I can speak on the mike to the fellow backstage—the mike doesn't go to the audience—and tell him to cut the lighting or get the car ready. Now, this was eleven hundred pounds of equipment when I first built it; now I'm cutting my little black box down to under a hundred pounds traveling weight, and that includes my clothes and my razor.

Are you going to put that on the market?

Now, again, my head being in one place, I want to finish that. When I go out on the stage and get my chops together, I want to find out what has happened, music-wise, in the ten years that I have been in-venting. I know what's happening with music; I want to know what's happening with the audience, what they want.

What about the multiple taping, the sound on sound which is now an essential studio technique that's taken for granted? How did the famous, original eight-track recorder come about?

Mary and I had to move to the East Coast because here's where all the entertainment was happening. Now, working for me, oddly enough, is one of the guys that brought the first tape machine to America confiscated from *Hitler*. This was Colonel Richard Ranger, and he and his privates and sergeants dismantled, piece by piece, the tape machine and brought it to the States, to either Newark or Orange. He put it back together and showed it to me and Bing Crosby and Glen Glenn. A major in the U.S. Army, Jack Mullin, had done more or less the same thing on the West Coast, but it was Colonel Ranger who showed me the advantage of tape over disc, and I immediately turned my head and said, "Ah *ha,* here's where it's at." So, I got *very* close to Colonel Ranger. I hired him to work with me on our TV shows.

So, when I got my first tape recorder, I immediately asked for a fourth head and they asked why and I said I just wanted one. I wasn't *about* to tell anybody what it was for—but it was to make *sound on sound.* And then it entered my mind, if you can do it with *one* machine, why not stack several of them up, stack eight up and do it that way? I took the idea to Westrex, the lab subsidiary of Western Electric, and they didn't think it was possible. I grabbed a plane and went to Ampex, and they built and rebuilt the machine for me. That original machine is in our studio and it's as good as the best machine you can buy today. That's because it was built to last, it wasn't one of those disposable units.

Do you listen to much of what's going on now musically?

I keep up with everything. I had my girlfriend come over here one night and we went through records—thousands of records. She goes through all these records and plays them and I say, "Mark that one, mark down he's good, funky and clean." So she marks it down. After two or three days, I look down that list and there's like a blur—Eric Clapton, Eric Clapton, Eric Clapton. Now, I know when I hear Eric Clapton, he thinks just like this: Thinks just like you press a button, he blocks everything out into a whole story, whether he knows it or not, and that thing starts *here* and ends *there.* I know when he starts how he's gonna end it. I know where his head is at and this guy is predictable. . . . I have kids coming in here to produce a date and a kid said to me, "I got an idea in my head—I want to get a *da-ta-ta-ta* sort of thing," and the kid had never heard of Les Paul and he says he wants to feed this thing back and I'm looking at him like, "Jesus *Christ* almighty, that's a thing I tripped over twenty years ago and now this guy is trying to tell me about it."

But there are a few great—or very fine—guitar players that I listen to. Like Joe Pass and Howard Roberts and Lenny Breaux and, of course, there's George Benson and Big Jim Sullivan over in England. He's a *hell* of a player. And then Alvin Lee comes to see me here, and Charlie

Byrd and George Barnes. I went to see Larry Coryell and he told me how he used to listen to me when he started to play. I'm very interested in how *clean* they play, in what they're saying. There are others that if they turned the fuzz off and turned the level down, they couldn't play at all.

Back to the Log again, do you still use that for anything?

I have two of them now, this one here, this two-by-four Log I built for experimentation—you can slide the pickup around to anywhere you want it. You can use it to find out what your strings are doing and how to make a string that's highly efficient. Say, for example, for experimentation, if Fender comes out with a pickup, I'll run all the checks on it and see what he's done inside. Then I know what he's doing and I know what his level is, what his frequency response is, and then I know what we're doing and we just improve and know why we're better. Which is a very *frightening* thing to realize—that there are so many people in the business that don't know what they're doing. It's just frightening. They just build these guitars and the money is coming in and they don't know what makes it tick. I'm constantly asked questions, dumb questions, questions that, my God almighty, everybody knows. But they don't.

Have you ever stopped to think about the influence you've had on guitar players, the number of them who listened to you? Or of the enormous influence you've had on the course of recording, the echo and the overdubbing?

Well, I don't know. I've been told by a few players—Johnny Smith and Pat Martino and George Benson. I've had some influence on them, but it's never really registered as far as I'm concerned, any more than the multiple recording or any of that. It just seems as though I took so much from the great players—Eddie Lang and Django Reinhardt. Django and I became very good friends. I idolized that guy as a kid and then later, when I went to Paris, Django had quit playing and was fishing with a gypsy camp. To find him, I tore a twenty-dollar bill in half and gave half to a cab driver and told him to go find Django and then he'd get the other half. I did that to two drivers because everybody there said they were Django's cousin or something—out to get your money. Well, Django called the next morning and said, "What are you doing here?" I told him our main reason was to see him, and we had a week off after playing the London Palladium. So, he came over that afternoon and cried and cried. He said he felt like a pig going to slaughter, that on a Saturday night a guy comes along in a pickup truck and tells him to get in and that he would be paid five bucks for playing and one guy would say, "Look, Django, if you don't play that melody then you can just pack up and leave. That's it." And Django says, "Why is it nobody appreciates what I'm doing? I feel as though I'm great." I tried to convince him that he was wrong, that he had many people who really appreciated him and that he *was* great. Then a minute later we were in a cab and he asks if I can read music and I say no. And he cracks up laughing and says, "I can't either."

I say if you got a heart and God gave you all the things to work with, then that's *all* you need. And Django and I became good friends and he of course went back to playing and after he died, his wife gave me his guitar. I still have it in the basement. He could never really understand. He felt as though he really had something to give to the world but they wouldn't accept it. And, unfortunately for many a player, they don't all go down in history as a great and they really should.

On the Road With Cowboy Singer Waylon Jennings

Jack C ———, the federal agent stationed at Gate 56 of the Dallas airport, signaled to his partner when he saw the pair coming. The signal meant "search," and that signal was followed by an announcement to the twenty-three passengers waiting for Texas International Airlines flight 925 to Austin: "TI nine-twenty-five will be delayed momentarily due to transient passengers."

Those transient passengers, the suspicious pair, carried no luggage, had paid cash for their tickets, and were similarly attired in rumpled leather suits, scuffed boots, and hair a little longer than was allowed in the VIP lounge just down the corridor.

Cowboy singer Waylon Jennings and the writer with him slowed down their loping run for the plane as Agent Jack stepped in front of them: "Please step this way . . . *gentlemen*." Jennings carried no identification, and Agent Jack was summoning his superior when a light bulb went on above his head. "Aren't you . . . you're *Waylon Jennings,* ainchoo? I thought you was an entertainer. Hell, glad to meetcha. I *thought* that's who you was. Hell yes, I see you over at Panther Hall. I go over to Panther and get drunk and raise hail ever wunst in a while. Go right on through, gentlemen."

Jennings laughed about it all the way to Austin.

"That reminds me," said the sharp-featured, thirty-seven-year-old country singer. "Last time we was down here, the whole band went over to old Mex and on the way back across the border the customs agent found a roach on the floorboards. I was about to shit—I saw myself doin' ten-to-life in Huntsville—and all of a sudden the sumbitch *recognized* me and he said, 'I'll just take care of this for you, Mr. Jennings.' *Whooo!* And all it cost me was an autograph and two tickets to the next show.''

Clearly, he had arrived as an entertainer when he could cut through officialdom without even trying.

Jennings had just completed a grueling tour of one-night stands in honky-tonks across New Mexico and Colorado, and his return to his native Texas, plus the offhand tribute of Agent Jack, had put him in a good mood and allowed him to relax for the first time in days. "You know how to find Texas?" he asked the writer. "You just go east till you smell it and south till you *step in it!*" The bony angles of his face became smooth in laughter. "And you always know when you cross the Texas line 'cause your wife starts bitchin' and your kids wanta piss and you feel like goin' and stealin' somethin'.''

His laughter died when he checked into the motel in Austin. There was not one but three out-of-town groupies ("snuff queens" in C&W parlance) waiting for him. For most performers, a phalanx of devoted followers is a welcome sign of success, a solid indication of having "made it." Jennings, however, shuns the traditional trappings of the music scene: the expensive drugs and Sunset Strip parties and chattering sycophants. In many ways, he is still the shy musician from Littlefield, Texas, who, as a green West Texas kid, learned about music as a member of Buddy Holly's band. That valuable experience ended abruptly February 3, 1959, when Holly's plane went down outside Mason City, Iowa. Jennings had given up his plane seat to Jape Richardson (a Texas disc jockey known as "the Big Bopper"), and sobered by a brush with death, he returned to West Texas as a deejay.

After years of knocking around, he moved on to Phoenix, where he led a popular local band that was one of the first to successfully mix country music with rock, his days with Holly serving him well. Eventually, he came to RCA's attention, and today, twenty-five albums later, he's becoming known as the acknowledged leader of country music's unorthodox set: a loose-knit group of maverick singers who have successfully defied the Nashville establishment and taken control of their own musical futures. Like Hank Williams two decades earlier, Jennings does pretty much what he wants and, like Williams, his talent enables him to get away with it. He has easily accepted his role as head maverick; what he seems uncomfortable with is public adulation. Earlier, in Albuquerque and Colorado Springs, he had disappeared from the motel when the crush of fans became excessive. Six people hanging around the motel was excessive.

In Austin, he had told no one where he was staying, but there were Francie, Pam, and Estelle camped out in the lobby of the Holiday Inn. Pam and Estelle were a team, as it turned out, and they blitzed every Jennings appearance within a 500-mile radius of their native Denton. They worked in a hospital there and, touchingly, had brought Jennings an offering consisting of massive quantities of cotton balls, baby oil, toothpaste, soap, aspirin, bandages, and first-aid cream. Jennings accepted the gifts graciously. Pam and Estelle were neither self-assured nor beautiful and Jennings knew it, but he invited them to his room to talk.

Francie, however, was more imposing, standing just under six feet, her blond tresses billowing down to her tiny waist. She was dressed in pink hotpants and a straining halter and her eyes were fairly dripping with pink and blue makeup.

"Hi, honey," she breathed. "Ah'll bet yew didn't know I just moved from Atlanta to Hew-ston? Well, ah was just sittin' down theah all *alone* when ah heard on the radio that yew were in Austin, so ah just got my little fanny in geah and *heah ah am!*" She punctuated her speech with flamboyant wriggles of that "little fanny," and Jennings's brow furrowed. Here was a problem. He wanted to rest before the night's show and he owed Pam and Estelle a little attention and he wanted to leave immediately after the show to meet his wife Jessi in Dallas. Francie was going to be a large pain, his expression said. He asked her to wait upstairs in the restaurant.

"Damn," he muttered. "I don't have no idea *what* the hell I'm doin'." He entertained Pam and Estelle briefly, and they were grateful to bask in his glow, if only for a moment.

Francie, however, had a faster race in mind. She was well-known to stage-door guards throughout the South as the smoothest-working circuit rider of them all, and had an uncanny ability to predict a country singer's whereabouts at any time of the day or night. It may well have been, as one jealous rival charged, that she cultivated her own intelligence network of motel clerks, limousine drivers, and backstage guards. Invariably, she had a half-hour head start on the other snuff queens working the circuit, which enabled her to maintain supremacy.

Jennings steeled himself momentarily before entering the motel restaurant, but before he could spot her, she glided up behind him and guided him to a secluded table.

Defeated, he nonetheless upheld the C&W code of ethics, an unspoken rule that country singers cannot be rude to their fans. Unlike rock stars, country performers depend heavily on the income they make playing small clubs, and the patrons in those clubs will tolerate any sort of behavior from their stars—drunkenness, adultery, cruelty to animals—

but they will not stand for a personal rebuke. Word travels quickly of any insult to a fan, and that spells trouble at the box office. So, Jennings picked at his chicken-fried steak and listened for half an hour as she talked—"Waylon, did yew know, ah was the *queen* of the Swingles paper after ah was in Hew-ston just a *week?*"—until he mumbled an apology and half-ran from the room.

"Man," he said, "people like that bug the hell out of me. They just slide right in and take over."

Things became more chaotic after he gained his dressing room at Armadillo World Headquarters, the Austin rock-country hall. Out front, there was already a standing-room-only crowd of 1,800, and the hangers-on in his dressing room were four deep: "Hey, Walen, yew 'member me?" He remembered them and satisfied them with autographs, then retired to the cool darkness of the backstage area. The thin stage partition was beginning to buckle under the crush of Austin's "hip red-neck" audience—three parts young longhairs in Western dress and one part older, moneyed shorthairs. Most of them were already well-fueled on pitchers of Lone Star and Shiner beer, and they were getting im-patient.

Jennings and his band hit the stage and surged into a full-blown version of "Lonesome, On'ry and Mean," and the drunken cheers were loud enough to be heard at the state capitol a mile distant. Jennings seemed almost frightened by the intensity of the crowd response. A fight broke out at stage right between a bantam truck driver and a long-haired youth. They bumped into each other, neither would back down or apologize, and they started throwing beer bottles.

Bystanders joined in—"Who yew pushin', hippie?" "Up yours, red-neck mutha"—until several metal scaffoldings were knocked over and the cataclysmic crash stayed the battle momentarily. Jennings's eyes widened as he dodged a full can of beer that was hurled at his head, but he and the band played on.

Intermission mercifully came and Armadillo manager Eddie Wilson led the band to the dressing room. He was shaking his head. "I've never seen anything like it. Bobby was just out in the parkin' lot tryin' to get some drunks up off the ground and they all swung on him."

Well, said an onlooker patronizingly, that's the way these cowboys get with a beer or two in 'em.

"Cowboys, hell!" said Wilson. "It was hippies *and* cowboys. All of 'em fucked up on wine and reds and all of a sudden they were *brothers,* passin' out together and gettin' up and fightin' together. *Whew!*"

If possible, the backstage scene was even more deranged. Jennings, University of Texas football coach Darrell Royal, songwriter Billy Joe

Shaver, and Armadillo artist Jim Franklin posed for photographs while holding up a giant Texas flag. Royal began expounding on the virtues of a brand of wristwatch that he apparently held a vested interest in. Commander Cody came up on bowlegs to pay his respects to Jennings. "Hi. I'm Cody. Freaky tonight, ain't it?"

Suddenly, a cowboy stiff-armed half the people in the room to get to Jennings. "Hey, Walen!" he whooped. " 'Member when we won district? *Whoo-weee!* Now there was a by-God football team!"

A sedate middle-aged couple from Waco—the male half in red-and-white-striped pants, white loafers, and a red sportcoat; the female in floor-length gown and upswept blue hair—gingerly drew close to Jennings, turning up their noses at the marijuana smokers seated on the floor. The male half thrust his warm paw into Jennings's hand. "Hello, Walen. I'm Richard Wilson of the radio station. We came down here to hear Willie Nelson. Is he gonna be on?"

"No," came the short reply.

Warm Paw persisted. "Well, you know, that drummer boy you had up there tonight, well, we saw him oncet with Willie and he just *passed out* or somethin'."

Jennings took a sip of coffee before answering. "That was Paul English. He's Willie's drummer. His wife just died here recently."

The Warm Paw's wife nodded and beamed at that. She and Warm Paw suddenly found themselves gently shoved toward the door by a statuesque woman in pink hotpants. Francie, having finally caught up with her quarry, wanted him to herself and was clearing the room: "*Please,* Waylon needs to rest just a teeny bit, yew know?"

Jennings rolled his eyes and decided it was time to roll out for the second set. He and the Waylors surpassed themselves. Ralph Mooney, who had spent intermission sipping straight gin in a hallway, unleashed a volley of steel-guitar notes that had even Mr. and Mrs. Warm Paw swaying, if not actually dancing. Jennings reached into his West Texas past for a churning rockabilly set, capped off with the Buddy Holly classic, "Peggy Sue." Partitions at the front of the stage wavered but held, as the crowd surged against them. Those "hip rednecks" would not let Jennings off the stage. Neither would Francie, who found a chair onstage, next to Darrell Royal. There were limpid lovelights in her eyes brighter than the spotlights that followed Jennings.

Waylon finally escaped the stage, leaving a trail of sweat as he made his way to the dressing room. There, he found a chorus of drunks who told him to do an encore, *any* encore. A short drunk, who had suddenly forged an alliance with Francie, was shouting, "Hot damn, Walen, yew gotta do a encore, yew just *gotta!*" Then Francie closed in on him and

Jennings headed for the stage, his only escape. He laid down a blistering version of "Lonely Weekends," ignored the deafening call of the crowd, and sprinted for the exit. The visiting writer, at Jennings's request, had a car waiting there on the sidewalk.

Francie was close behind, but Jennings made it into the car just ahead of her. As the Chevy pulled out, it hit a section of curb and lost a muffler. The resultant din caused a certain concern, inasmuch as the car sounded like a Sherman tank bulldozing through the Ardennes.

Jennings, nonetheless, heaved a sigh of relief. "Francie's a good old girl, she *is*. But it gets down to where it puts me in a bad mental frame of mind, her chasin' me around. But that was one helluva show. That was the *hardest* workin' sumbitch tonight I've ever worked."

A fan, who had crawled into the back seat, simpered that, as far as *she* was concerned, Jennings was better than Mick Jagger.

Jennings laughed a whiskey rumble. "Well, *I* dug it. I got off tonight. Man, I am *soakin'* wet."

The Chevy roared on, its harried driver seeking back streets and looking out for the blue-and-whites.

"Hey," said Jennings, "remember them Smitties? This sounds just like 'em. Back in Littlefield, Mama could hear me plumb down on Main Street and that was twenty blocks away. She'd say, 'Boy, I heard you down there and I heard the siren too, and me up walkin' the floor waitin' on you. I heard you go plumb outta town.' You bet your sweet ass I run out of town."

He found a cigarette and rolled the window down, letting the sweet night air rush in. "Damn, I feel *good* tonight. We took it just right. Hey, let's get something to eat, I'm *hongry*."

Austin not being noted for after-hour eateries, and the possibility of imminent apprehension by police weighing heavily on everyone's minds, Waylon pointed to a row of vending machines at a closed Texaco station. "Pull in there, hoss," he directed. The Chevy rumbled as he loped across the dark concrete. The machines spurned Jennings's quarters and he began kicking them. Anyone passing the station just then would have been treated to the sight of the leading contender for the title "World's Greatest Country Singer" attacking a row of mute machines with hair and shirttails flying. "C'mon, you sumbitch, *give,* damn you!" A few more kicks from his needle-toed black boots and the machines poured out an avalanche of chips and nuts and candy. "*That'll* teach the cocksuckers," Jennings growled triumphantly.

But he was strangely silent as the car pulled into the Holiday Inn and the headlights picked up a solitary figure in pink hotpants waiting in front of the lobby. Francie was tapping her toes impatiently and wanted to know just why the hell she had been kept waiting.

Every Day Oughta Be Christmas and Every Night Oughta Be New Year's Eve: An Excursion With Bobby Bare

Drunk and crazy is exactly what Bobby Bare is not on a misty Tennessee dawn. The creator of some of country music's most rousing concerts and albums (including the classic *Drunk and Crazy*) is droopy-eyed with sleep and moves slowly and carefully as he cranks up his blue-flake bass boat and eases it through the shoals of Old Hickory Lake, near Hendersonville. "I might call my next album *Tired and Sleepy*," he tells me with a wry grin as we clear the mist around the shore and cruise by Johnny Cash's lakeside mansion. Bobby Bare is a good-timer in the grand tradition, but there is one thing he is serious about (besides his family, that is), one thing he will haul his aching body out of a warm bed at dawn for, and that is going fishing. Bare just loves the hell out of going fishing.

Even in Nashville, where everybody is a good catcher of fish (well, there's no nightlife and it doesn't take that long to cut a country album, so what else are you going to do with all that leisure time?), Bare is respected as a man who can catch the hell out of fish. If nobody else is catching fish, Bobby Bare can crank up his blue-flake bass boat and cruise the 400-mile shoreline of Old Hickory until he gets The Feeling. Then, he'll torque down the engine and point to some vague spot. "We'll catch 'em there," he'll say confidently, squinting into the first rays of the morning sun and spitting a glob of Skoal into Old Hickory's blue waters. And, by God, on his third cast or so (or so he says) a monster widemouth bass will strike his lure and fight like a foolish virgin until Bare finally boats it. That's the legend, and it actually has happened.

On this morning, however, Bare is troubled. He doesn't have The Feeling. The fish are apparently suppressing their mental transmissions, or whatever the hell it is that Bare perceives when tracking down the wily widemouth bass, and he is worried that we will have a fishless day. He pops a can of Coca-Cola for breakfast and I fish around in the ice well for an eye-opening can of Budweiser as we cruise on, past Roy Orbison's burned-out mansion, Bare searching for The Feeling and dispatching Skoal spittle into Old Hickory until he decides it's time to get serious and chew on a chaw of Red Man tobacco. The hundred or so minnow in the bait well look up at me and, if fish can look unhappy, those minnow clearly know that they have, at best, eight more hours of the good life in a blue-flake bass boat before a big fish eats them.

"Fish over there," Bare announces around his chaw as he points at a rusted-over boat dock, and he revs up the bass boat to get us there before the fish leave. He makes his first cast and strikes a nice one-pound bream. I make my first cast and take in a lovely one-pound bream. Bare beams at me: he doesn't have to say anything. He has just proved again that he is a world-class fish finder (even though we haven't found the bass yet). We haul them in for a while, tossing back most, until Bare's Feeling passes and he says we should move on. He pushes the Cheater SX blue-flake fiberglas bass boat to its absolute limit and we race by the house where George Jones and Tammy Wynette used to live. Bare mentions a well-known country singer with whom he used to fish until that well-known singer's speed habit made him so perpetually wired that he spent all his time hoping the motor or something equally complicated would break down so he could spend hours fussing with it. "Fishing," Bare tosses over his shoulder at me, "fishing is my only so-called nerve-palliate. We'll go down this way and come back that way. The wind's coming this way, so if we're gonna fish, we oughta fish on the other side of the lake." He spits over his shoulder, and we speed by Faron Young's lakeside mansion.

Bobby Bare is something special in country music, a totally unclassifiable raver who is actually (I think) in complete control at all times of his seemingly out-of-control drunk and crazy show. He has also done some of C&W's best weepers, songs like "The Streets of Baltimore" and "Detroit City." He started out as a rock and roller with "All American Boy" (incorrectly attributed to Bill Parsons), and he still possesses the irreverence and brash innocence that made rock 'n' roll what it once was: Bare himself is the first to tell you that if he gets bored he will do something crazy or at least different just to relieve the tedium. He abandoned his recording career a few years back because he thought it was getting boring and looked around for ways to spice up his tired wax life.

Bare has always been an admirer of a good song and searched for them so diligently that he became known as the best friend an unknown songwriter in Nashville could have. It was Bare who found Paul Craft's "Drop-kick Me Jesus (Through the Goalpost of Life)" and oddities like "Quaaludes Again" and "Rosalie's Good Eats Café," becoming *the* stylist of C&W in the process. He went directly against the Nashville grain of cutting MOR sides, recording the Rolling Stones' "The Last Time"— *treason* in Nashville—as well as other non-trad country songs. His albums *Drunk and Crazy* and *Down and Dirty* are so un-Nashville it's funny. Songs by great writers like George M. Jones (not *the* George Jones), Bob McDill, and Shel Silverstein, and song titles like "I've Never

Gone to Bed With an Ugly Woman (But I Sure Woke Up With a Few)"
made Bare a critic's favorite. Audiences agreed—up to a point. The
"Detroit City" fan tended to frown upon hearing "Quaaludes Again"
(something in there about making love to the coffee table), and vice
versa. Bare tries to pretend that the dichotomy doesn't exist and that
he *has* snared a lot of rock fans. He's got some and his attitude is an
indication why. When Nashville police chief Joe Casey announced not
long ago that sellers of marijuana should get the electric chair, Bare
laughed and said, "Casey should be a concert promoter."

"I dig Italian food," Bare said to me as we walked along Gramercy Park
in New York. "I'd eat shit if you'd put garlic on it."
     He sounded playful. He was wearing his new cowboy hat with its
astounding open-mouthed-diamondback-rattlesnake headband. The
click of our boots was the only sound to be heard as we walked to Pete's
Tavern for a late lunch. Bare related to me the tale of a hooker who
had been found with her throat slit from one side to the other in the
last Manhattan hotel he'd stayed in. His road manager, he said, had
gotten ripped off in the elevator of the same hotel. Bare likes playing
New York but is still uncertain about the side effects of same. A
rattlesnake-hatted cowboy who doesn't know where he's going invites
a certain amount of attention from the legions of predators who prowl
the side streets like hungry wolves tracking dumb lambs. Bare's rattlesnake scared off the wolves. We finally settled down at a table and
ordered plates of chicken livers with beer chasers.
     "I didn't know you could even *get* a chicken liver in New York,"
Bare said. The waitress didn't know whether to serve him or his hatband.
She liked that rattlesnake. They eventually worked out a neat compro-
mise, which enabled us to eat dinner. Waitresses and country singers
have long had a solid rapport, probably because they have a common
interest, which is to make a little money while working very irregular
hours and doing what they want. There could not be a better job than
doing what you want to. There are few openings. Free spirits can wait
at the back of the line: It's a crowded field.
     Well, so what? Bobby Bare deserves to be at the front of the line.
Years and years of standing in line at corporate headquarters hearing a
loud no should have qualified him for a financial yes, which he is finally
realizing. For years, record companies in Nashville pegged him as a
weird guy who tried to record funny songs. Bare got so pissed off that
he formed his own publishing company, and he started getting a lot of
respect for being an honest man—something you don't find every day
in the music business. What's more, he began to be recognized as the
major music talent he is, and that made him work hard at not being a

superstar. He could fade into the woodwork faster than that last Marx Brother could. What a paradox. Bare wanted to be a star, kind of, and he and his record company made sure that he wouldn't become one.

A man who once tried to sell accordions door-to-door for the Antelope Valley Music Company, who had a severe problem when he lived in Alaska because he thought you were supposed to get drunk when it was dark outside, and who shared a Los Angeles apartment with Willie Nelson until their landlady became suspicious after Bare kept buying cheap TVs and stacking them one atop the other as they fizzled out— well, he's not your average country music star.

"Every day oughta be Christmas and every night should be New Year's Eve," Bare told me as we settled down in the bar of the Gramercy Park Hotel to watch the Dallas Cowboys and Philadelphia Eagles slug it out. Bare zapped a good half-ounce of tobacco-colored spittle into an empty glass and the bartender pretended not to notice. A mouse scuttled across the floor and Bare and I decided that a liquid dinner might be our safest course.

At age forty, Bobby Bare resembles a mellow roué, a mature version of the hell-raising rake that he was as a younger man. Back when he was a cocky wise-ass, full of piss and vinegar, a great picture of him with his silver-dollar-studded convertible was widely circulated. That was back when he was starting his second musical career as a young country music star, after his rock 'n' roll days and then a stint in the Army. In 1964, at the age of twenty-three and just hitting with "Detroit City," he was booked with country music legends Chet Atkins and "Gentleman" Jim Reeves on a European tour and created quite a stir. Trouble started in April when the show reached the Capri Enlisted Men's Club in Friedberg, Germany. Here's what *Stars and Stripes* had to say:

> First on stage was Bare, a 23-year-old ex-GI guitar twanger who "stole the show," said club manager Sfc. Grover Noah. Atkins followed but got a cooler reception from the large crowd. Then Reeves came onstage and as he looked around the cheering audience, apparently felt there was too much noise to suit him. "Shut up!" Gentleman Jim shouted at his GI fans. A few voices shouted back, "We want Bobby Bare" in retaliation. In spite of the interruption, Reeves sang a number and had barely started on his second song when the cries began to get louder. GI fans screamed, stomped their feet and thumped glasses on table tops in thunderous unison. Reeves turned abruptly and walked off stage in a huff followed by hoots of derision. Before the next show in the NCO club, the temperamental showman locked himself up in a bus waiting outside and sulked as the rest of the troupe went on with the show. When

his agent asked what the trouble was, Reeves imperiously replied: "I don't play for animals." So when the group got to Munich, both Reeves and Atkins apparently no longer wanted to be upstaged by young Bobby Bare and his "Detroit City" guitar.

Bare smiled at the memory and hoisted a bottle of Budweiser in mock tribute as I handed him the yellowing clipping.

Blair's Jungle Den sits like a scramble of pickup sticks hard against the black waters of the St. Johns River near Astor, Florida, which is sort of near but well removed from Daytona Beach. The Jungle Den is located about halfway between the Atlantic Ocean and Disney World, but its real location is somewhere in the outer reaches of a twisted frontal lobe. Blair's Jungle Den is an old-fashioned stone-redneck fishing camp of the kind James Dickey probably wished he had invented. It's a chaos of dirt roads, minuscule cottages, RVs, and trailers. And crazy fishermen.

Bobby Bare has been coming here every year for the past fifteen years. The Jungle Den has one telephone for incoming calls and it's located in manager Everett B. Blair's office-bait-shop-general-store. If Everett B. Blair likes you, you can totally vanish when you're staying at the Jungle Den. Messages have a way of disappearing. Bobby Bare likes that once in a while; he likes being beyond the reach of agents and bookers and record company PR people and interviewers and everyone else. He also likes to fish for widemouth bass, and the St. Johns River and nearby Lake George are good bass waters. Bare once caught a 9½-pounder downriver in Lake Dexter (downriver is an imprecise term here because, according to Everett B. Blair, the St. Johns is the only river in the world—besides the Nile—that flows north), and he wants badly to break the 10-pound barrier. That's hard to do. Bare is a good fisherman, but widemouth bass are the elite of freshwater fish. They're hard to find and twice as hard to catch. The world record widemouth is 22.4 pounds. The mouth on a bass that size might be a foot across: It will spit out any kind of bait or lure the way you or I would spit out a toothpick. And while the widemouth may not be all that smart, it knows what a hook is and will often play with and then kill your bait fish without coming within a Lotto chance of getting hooked.

Bobby Bare was explaining all this to me at 6:00 A.M. in the Jungle Den's coffee shop while we waited for our eggs and biscuits smothered in brown gravy and hot grits. Just outside the window, a heavy rain was punching needle holes in the surface of the St. Johns River and the wind was bending the palm trees.

"Rain's okay," Bare said as he sucked in a mouthful of the Jungle Den's scalding coffee. "I just don't want no wind. Yesterday the wind was hittin' fifty-one miles an hour and I had a *hell* of a time just stayin' on the lake. If the wind stays down, we'll catch some big ones today."

We were dressed as if for an Arctic expedition: long johns, rain boots, jeans over sweatpants, heavy shirts, and down-filled vests and jackets. We had loose wet suits on over all that. It's cold in the morning out on the lake, but that's the time to go after bass.

"Hell," Bare said as we ate, "I don't really care if we don't catch anything. I just like to get out there. I like bein' out here in the tulies [*tulies* is synonymous with *boondocks* or *sticks*]. Sometimes it bothers me if they start bitin'. It *interrupts* me." He took a big bite of dripping biscuit. "I *would* like to catch the big one, though," he said, laughing.

A knife-like gray Bassfinder X-17 boat rumbled up to the Jungle Den's dock. The driver was wearing a crash helmet with visor and a satin jacket covered with insignia from every imaginable bass-fishing association. It was Len Breehl, our fishing guide. We finished our coffee while Breehl went to get a couple dozen shiners and bullheads from Everett B. Blair for bait. The bigger shiners weigh about a pound and are nine or ten inches long. (Later, when a boatful of redneck fishermen anchored near us and saw us throwing out bait fish *bigger* than what they were catching, one of them hollered, "What'chall fishin' for? *Shark?*" Bare shut them up: "No, *alligator*.")

Once in the boat, we put on crash helmets with visors, Breehl revved up the 200-horsepower Mercury engine, and we blasted upriver. In a minute Bare tapped me on the shoulder and pointed at the speedometer: It read sixty-two mph. That's fairly fast for water travel in a seventeen-foot boat, but then serious bass fishermen like to maximize their fishing time and minimize their travel time.

We pulled up and dropped anchor near a sunken barge on the edge of sunken grass at the mouth of Lake George. When bass are spawning you can fish them two ways: find their beds in the grass in shallow water and throw out small bullheads as bait or try to get them outside the grass using the big shiners as bait. They weren't bedding yet, so we tried the shiners.

The rain was coming down in sheets, it was not yet sunup, and whitecaps were dotting the lake as we threw out our first shiners and kept a careful eye on the cork bobbers that marked their locations. When that bobber starts running away from the boat a mile a minute, you know you've got a bass chasing your shiner.

Bare was happy. "There's not too many things more exciting than seein' a big bass chasin' a damn shiner all around and then takin' it and runnin' with it and then it may come out of the water and dance on its tail and spit out the bait and wave *good-bye* at you and all you see are those huge blood-red gills."

We settled down and stared at our corks. Nothing happened for half an hour or so and no one said anything. It was peaceful: There were no other boats around; the rain let up, and the sun finally poked through the clouds. The only sound was the gentle slap of waves against the boat and Bare's occasional expectoration of tobacco juice into Lake George's waters.

Then my cork bobbed under water, surfaced, and ran to daylight while my reel began to sing with the sound of twenty-five-pound-test line paying out in a hurry. A bass will usually run with the bait, stop, and then swallow it if it feels no pressure (bass are fairly smart). That's when you have to tighten the line, point the tip of your rod at the bass, and then pull the hell back with all your strength to get that hook embedded. When you hook a big one, it feels like tying into a log.

I pulled back as hard as I could, my rod bent in half, and a hundred yards away, in an explosion of black water and foaming whitecaps, a big bass shot out of the water, spit the bait back at me, and danced away.

"Goddam!" Bare was yelling. "That one would go over ten!"

I reeled in my shiner. It was dead: the bass had stripped it clean of scales.

"There's some big ones out there," Bare said determinedly, as he flung out another shiner. He got a run of a hundred yards before his big bass broke water and laughed at him. Bass fever began to get serious about then. I got another hundred-yard run that went for naught and then Bare got a bright idea. Since the bass swallow the shiners tail first and can thus easily spit them out, why didn't we try hooking them through their dorsal fins instead of their mouths, so that by the time a bass decided to spit it might already be hooked?

Sounded good, even to our guide. Bare cast a dorsal-hooked shiner out about fifty feet and in a moment his reel was zinging and he was pulling back so hard he almost fell out of the boat. The water was churning and Bare started to reel in a fighter. It was an eight-pounder, a real beauty. Bare's grin was brighter than the sun. "All *right*," he said, "now let's start *fishing*."

We ran out of big shiners, though, and when we roared back to the Jungle Den we discovered that the Jungle Den was out of them, too.

"The big fish want the big bait," Bare muttered.

Guide Breehl said that he thought he could find some. We headed upriver, past the side canals that were blocked with float-chains and big homemade signs telling you to stay the hell out. Looking up the canals, we caught glimpses of dark houses raised on stilts with boats hoisted up out of the water in riverfront garages.

Breehl turned off into a tributary and cruised up to a fishing camp that will remain nameless. The place was a shambles. An old man sat by the dock in a once-green upholstered sofa that was throwing its springs in every direction. Breehl's boat and the sight of relatively well-dressed strangers brought out a group of silent rednecks who just . . . *observed* us. Bare went into the café/bar to fetch a couple of beers. We got back into the boat and blasted out of there. "You shoulda seen that bar," Bare told me. "It was just full of Whup-ems." ["Whup-ems" is Southern vernacular for barroom denizens who keep an eye out for patrons who are not obvious rednecks. When they spot one entering the bar, they say, "Let's go whup 'em"—which means they want to beat the money out of you for being different. Avoid them at all costs.]

We fished the rest of the day, but the wind was too high to do us any good. Bare did pull in a nice three-pounder with a bullhead, but the wind had chased off the big bass, the twelve- or fifteen-pounders that earlier had been toying with and killing our bait.

Back to camp, as they used to say in *Field & Stream*.

We were staying in a "double-wide," which is real-estate-ese for an extra-wide mobile home, a.k.a. trailer. It had a living room, a carpeted dining alcove, a real kitchen, two bedrooms, and two baths. It also had no running water at first, but that was soon fixed. Bare and I sat down on the imitation Chesterfield in the tiny living room and watched the only channel that would come in on the TV as we sipped at our beers.

"The Canadian equivalent," Bare finally said, "to our surgeon general issued a statement that country music definitely leads to alcoholism. And he was backed up by a doctor in Minnesota who did a study. So UPI called me up to respond to this."

"So, what did you say?" I asked as I fetched two more beers.

"I said," said Bare as he stretched out his feet on the imitation-walnut coffee table, "that if you get involved in country music, that it can not only lead to alcoholism, but to illicit sex, illegal drugs, fame, fortune, and—eventually—insanity."

He laughed and pulled at his beer.

What, I asked, was the whole story behind "The All American Boy," a great early rock 'n' roll single he had done which was attributed to someone else, namely Bill Parsons?

Bare laughed. "I went up to Springfield, Ohio, when I was sixteen. I met Parsons; he was about seventeen. He sang and I sang and we worked together for a while. Then I went out to California and hung out for a while, and he came out and hung out for a while. Till he got drafted. He was gettin' out of the Army about the same time I was gettin' drafted. We ran into each other back in Ohio. He wanted to do a record, so we got this old boy down in Cincinnati who had a studio. We were gonna do 'Rubber Dolly' and 'All American Boy.'

"*Everything* went wrong. We'd got drunk the night before and everybody had hangovers. I tried to play stand-up bass and my bridge broke right in the middle of a take. This was in King Studios, and they were re-doing the studio and we just wanted to get out. It just wasn't a good day at all. We done fucked around for two and a half hours gettin' 'Rubber Dolly' down and I had been workin' on 'All American Boy,' just settin' lyrics to it like an old Ernest Tubb talkin' blues. I was makin' up the lyrics as we went along. We only had about thirty minutes left. We did about six tracks real fast and we split. We went back up to Dayton and sat there drinking beer. This guy Cherokee Lunsford had to pay for our studio time and he wanted to make an acetate of our record for jukeboxes. King's equipment wasn't working, so he went over to Fraternity Records to make one. They heard this record—this was like an hour after we cut it—and they said, '*Jesus!* This is great.' They offered him five hundred bucks for the record."

Bare laughed again at the memory and got a fresh pinch of Skoal. "Cherokee called me and said, 'What do you think—five hundred?' I said, 'Shit, take it, we're sittin' here broke on our ass, man.' So he did. But they asked who was singing and he said, 'Bill Parsons'—who *did* sing 'Rubber Dolly.' He gave me fifty bucks and I forgot about it. Then I went in the Army. I was in basic training in Fort Knox and somebody had a transistor radio and I was listening to the John R. Show on WLAC and he played 'All American Boy' and I said, 'Damn! That's *me!*' I told the guys around me it was me and they all said, '*Shit!*' Then Parsons called me up. He was a nervous wreck. He said, 'Dick Clark wants me on his show, I'm gonna be on the cover of *Hit Parade,* and I didn't do the fucking song. *You* did. What am I gonna do?'

"I said, well, all I know is, there ain't much you can do about it. Take the money and run. So he lip-synched to my voice on Dick Clark."

Wasn't Bare, I asked, outraged that somebody else actually had his first hit?

"Naw. I never was that crazy about the fuckin' record anyway. I got fifty bucks. Parsons got a Pontiac convertible, which they later repossessed. I figured it did work out for the best. If my name had been on that record, people would have expected funny ad-lib songs from me. As it was, as soon as I got out of the Army, I recorded 'Shame on Me,' which sold like a million records, straight up the pop and country charts. Although Chet Atkins signed me to RCA on the strength of 'All American Boy.' He had never really heard me sing."

Bare stood up, stretched, spit a glob of Skoal into a Perrier bottle, and went off to bed to get ready for our 5:30 A.M. wakeup call, but not before he delivered one more curious statement. We'd talked about booking flights back and all of a sudden he said, "You know, I never was afraid of flying until I got married and had children. That's when I decided that I wanted to *live.*"

*   *   *

After her husband went to bed, Jeannie Bare sat and talked a while. She gave up a singing career to be his wife and does not seem to regret it.

"The reason Bare will never be a superstar," she told me, "is that he's too nice. Too professional. Too honest. He is just after the *song*. He's after *quality,* and that's why every songwriter loves him. Other people in Nashville have screwed writers blind and robbed them, but Bare stays on his solitary path. He's stubborn as hell, or perverse, but nobody knows songwriting the way he does. He's obsessed with quality. I listen to the songs first, because he asked me to listen to all the tapes. Then I pick out four songs out of a hundred that I think he should hear. But he'll turn right around after two hundred hours of my listening and then cut just what he was gonna cut anyway. And I *love* it. Because he's *right*."

Bill Haley: The Music Itself Will Never Cause Riots

Bill Haley, who thought of himself as the father of rock 'n' roll and became bitter as recognition eluded him, died as quietly as he lived. He was found, fully clothed, lying in a bedroom of his two-story wood-frame house in Harlingen, Texas, near the Mexican border, at 12:35 P.M., CST, on February 9, 1981. Justice of the Peace Tommy Thompson said that he thought Haley had died of natural causes, maybe a heart attack.

Haley, whose "Rock Around the Clock" in the 1955 film *Blackboard Jungle* heralded the arrival of a new era for young people, apparently was fifty-six years old (press releases gave one birth date; the Texas driver's license found in his wallet said he was born July 6, 1925). The circumstances of his death are still murky. His widow refused to release any information about Haley or his family, including herself. Not even her name. Harlingen police chief Guy Anderson, who was one of Haley's few confidants, said that Haley "had problems. He tried to keep a low profile."

A Harlingen police officer, who asked to remain anonymous, said that Haley—in the six or seven years since he had moved there—had become an immediate cause of concern. He said that Haley had gone out of his way to meet the police force. After that, said the officer, they often had to pick him up while he was wandering along country roads, seemingly lost. The cops would pick him up and take him home, trying to pretend they didn't feel sorry for him.

The same Harlingen police officer said that, on the weekend before he died, Haley had called him at home "six times in ten minutes" and "that he seemed to be hallucinating and just wanted someone to talk to." Haley had just canceled a tour of Germany—where he was still very popular—and seemingly wanted to become invisible again. In Harlingen, few people knew who he was and it'd become obvious that that was what he wanted. He refused to grant interviews and seemed to want to disappear, according to friends.

Self-imposed seclusion in the Rio Grande Valley is a long way from headlining rock 'n' roll shows, but that's what Bill Haley settled upon. He was as unlikely a rock 'n' roll star as you could find anywhere. He was too old and overweight, even at the start, and didn't have the right moves, but he did have the right songs at the right time. Haley was a country-and-western singer and bandleader who accidentally became a rock 'n' roll pioneer.

William John Clifton Haley, Jr., was born in Highland Park, Michigan. His family moved to Chester, Pennsylvania, where he built his first guitar out of cardboard. He left home at fifteen and formed his first band, the Down Homers, which soon became the Saddlemen. For a while, he was a solo act known as the Ramblin' Yodeler.

Throughout the Forties, he played an East Coast version of Western swing with a band lineup similar to that of swing bands (without the fiddle): Haley on rhythm guitar, a stand-up bass, electric guitar, drums, tenor sax, accordion, and pedal steel guitar. Then he started experimenting. "The style we played way back in 1947, 1948, and 1949 was a combination of country and western, Dixieland, and the old-style rhythm and blues. We decided to try for a new style, mostly using stringed instruments, but somehow managing to get the same effect as brass and reeds," he later said.

In the early Fifties, as R&B's dance beat increasingly attracted a young, white audience, Haley began to copy songs like Jackie Brenston's "Rocket 88." He also took on an astute manager, the late Lord Jim Ferguson, who saw Haley's pop potential and was largely responsible for turning the country band known as the Saddlemen into a pop group called Bill Haley and the Comets. The name change came in 1951. Haley later explained the change in musical styles rather glibly: "The musical world was starved for something new . . . the days of the solo vocalist and the big bands had gone. About the only thing, in fact, that was making any noise was progressive jazz, but this was just above the heads of the average listener. . . . I felt then that if I could take, say, a Dixieland tune and drop the first and third beats, accentuate the second and fourth, and add a beat the listeners could clap to as well as dance this would be what they were after. From that the rest was easy. . . . Take everyday sayings like 'Crazy Man Crazy,' 'See You Later, Alligator,' 'Shake, Rattle and Roll,' and apply to them what I have just said."

It was not quite that easy. He worked nonstop, playing house parties (which he called "house-rockin's") and any other jobs he could get in addition to a regular radio show on WPPA in Chester, Pennsylvania. Then, in 1953, Ferguson took him to Essex Records. Dave Miller, the label's head of A&R and promotion listened to some of Haley's songs; when he got to "Crazy Man Crazy" he knew he had a hit. And it was, later that year, but Haley, oddly enough, found himself in the same position as black R&B performers: banned by radio. The vast majority of stations invariably played cover versions of R&B hits, which were more palatable to a white audience when done by an "acceptable" white performer. In Haley's case it was Ralph Marterie, who cut "Crazy Man Crazy" for Mercury. Despite Marterie's exposure, Haley outsold him in the stores: the young white audience wasn't fooled.

In 1954, Haley continued his success with "We're Gonna Rock This Joint Tonight" and "Rock Around the Mulberry Bush." His contract with Essex ran out later that year, and Ferguson took the group to Milt Gabler at Decca.

Ferguson had figured out the business of cover versions and persuaded Haley to cover Joe Turner's "Shake, Rattle and Roll." Haley agreed—but not before he cleaned the song up, dropping lines that were clearly sexual in nature. He later defended the change, saying, "We steer completely clear of anything suggestive! We take a lot of care with lyrics because we don't want to offend anybody. The music is the main thing, and it's just as easy to write acceptable words." If rock 'n' roll was fueled by rebellion, Bill Haley didn't know it.

Even in its sanitized version, "Shake, Rattle and Roll," which stayed in the top ten for three months, was important in that it got rock and roll on major radio stations. That same year, 1954, Haley recorded a song written by Jimmy DeKnight (whose real name was Jimmy Myers) called "Rock Around the Clock." Nothing much happened with it until May 1955, when the movie *Blackboard Jungle* was released. The inclusion of the song on the soundtrack would prove to be a major turning point in the development of rock 'n' roll. There had been other movies about teenage rebellion, including *The Wild One* in 1954 and *Rebel Without a Cause* in 1955, but those films had had conventional big band soundtracks. Not so *Blackboard Jungle*. In addition to the great scene where high school students literally tear up their teacher's collection of "square" records by Bunny Berigan and Harry James, it had Haley and the Comets tearing it up with "Rock Around the Clock" and saxman Rudy Pompilli hanging upside down during his electrifying solos. (Initially, Decca planned to release the flip side, "Thirteen Women," as the single until the movie scored so big.)

The movie's impact was immeasurable, thanks to the raw power of that one song. Comedic actor Howard Hesseman, for example, who was living in Silverton, Oregon, at the time, saw the movie and immediately headed for the nearest big town—Salem—to buy the record, deciding on the spot that he wanted a career in rock 'n' roll. In London's West End, teenagers ripped the seats out of movie houses so they could dance to "Rock Around the Clock." The Comets toured Germany, where they started the first rock 'n' roll riots. The single of the song went on to sell 22.5 million copies.

It was also the peak of Haley's career. With his chubby face and spit curl, he was regarded as cute rather than sexy, and he couldn't compete with the rock 'n' rollers who came after him. His popularity abroad remained steady, however, and he toured off and on for the rest of his life.

Haley always defended rock 'n' roll, but he did so in a left-handed fashion: "The music itself will never cause riots. All the trouble over rock 'n' roll was started by the publicity guys and then a few young hoodlums used it as an excuse to show off. Our real fans know how to behave themselves. Sure, they get excited and stomp and clap, but there's no harm in that. A lot of people blamed juvenile delinquency on us, hot rods, drinking, everything. But rock got the kids off the streets and around the jukeboxes. They said it was a bad influence. Well, we always kept our lyrics clean and we never did any protest songs."

Haley's Comets left him in 1956 after a money dispute and re-formed as the Jodimars, scoring a minor success with "Let's All Rock Together," on Capitol Records.

Haley formed another band and continued touring. Friends say that "something" happened to him when he went to Mexico in 1962 and that he began drinking heavily and never stopped. One of the last times he made headlines was when he was arrested twice in one week in Iowa in 1973 on charges of public drunkenness. Friends say that in later years Haley was obsessed with the fear that his father's insanity was hereditary.

Before he quit giving interviews, Haley talked at length with Roger Ebert of the *Chicago Sun-Times* about his past.

"I wrote 'Rock-a-Beatin' Boogie,' which was the song that gave rock 'n' roll its name. Remember how it started out? 'Rock, rock, rock everybody! Roll, roll, roll everybody!' Well, that started it. And it's never stopped. There's a TV special coming up in a few months about the birth of rock 'n' roll and I'm glad. The story has got pretty crowded as to who was the father of rock. These days, you'd think everybody did it. But we were the first. I haven't done much in life except that. And I'd like to get credit for it."

Chapter 4

Fortitude

Tom Wolfe: Weekend Hipsters

KA-THUNKA-KA-WHOMP! KA-THUNKA-KA-THUNKA-KA-WHOMP-KA-*WHOMP!* KA-THUNKA-KA-THUNKA-KA-THUNKA-KA-WHOMP-KA-WHOMP-KA-*WHOMP!* KA-WHOMP-WHOMP-WHOMPWHOMPKATHUNKAKAWHOMPA KAWHOMPAWHOMPAWHOMPaWHOMpaWHOmpaWHompa Whompawhompa . . . What inna name a Christ we got going on here? This is the famous writer's orderly and even very literary study. I mean, the white bookshelves seem to zoom up about eighteen feet straight and they're just chockablock with, you know, the *heavy* lumber: old Henry Miller and D. H. Lawrence and everybody else up there in gleaming bindings, the expensive first editions, none of those half-price reviewer's copies from the Strand Book Store, where every Saturday afternoon you can see every low-rent book reviewer in Manhattan struggling in with these D'Agostino shopping bags full of review copies—*Scruples!*—staggering down the metal stairs into the basement and weaving through the aisles—tachycardia time!—to finally dump these goddamn shopping bags full of books they've heaved and carried all the way down from West 96th Street, the goddamn bags ripping and *The Complete Scarsdale Medical Diet* falling out on the goddamn sidewalk there at 12th and Broadway, so they scoop it up and finally dump all these goddamn books on the floor there at the back of Strand's basement in front of this rope they have stretched across there, and they avert their eyes and try to look literary—bug-eyed and wheezing and army-navy turtle-necked and Frye-booted, real-Levied literary—while some goddamn pustular NYU lit major behind the rope takes his goddamn sweet time

to sift through the bound detritus and hand them this little chit like it had a bad smell, like it had dogshit all over it or something, and this NYU *twit!* calls out "$27.50!" and they take their dogshit chits and heave their way back upstairs to collect $27.50 and buy a seventy-five-cent paperback of E. M. Forster's that they always meant to read but something always came up and they just never got around to it, but *tonight,* this very night, they *will,* after hitting Zabar's with their remaining $26.75 to get the latest goddamn new cheese and some real coffee, this very night they will read the whole goddamn book and feel very self-righteous and very literary.

No-siree, no goddamn dogshit reviewer's copies of books in *this* here office, this precise, white-on-white office looking out on one of the . . . *better* tree-lined Upper East Side streets, where the author can look right out and see these perfect East Side priapic buds just undulating their way over to Bloomingdale's for more of those crotch-grabbing Jordache jeans that just deliciously creep and slither into every secret fold and fissure.

But—KA-THUNK-KA-WHOMP—the famous writer is not peering out at the undulating buds. He's not even pacing back and forth, stopping to leaf through the fifty-pound *Webster's* dictionary (to see how to spell *hummocky* or some damn thing, for those hummocky shanks, you know) that lies there like the world's supreme authority on its very proper wooden stand. KA-THUNK—the famous writer in his handmade English suede shoes and those transparent socks with the little stripes on them and the handmade suit—*real* buttonholes, nothing off the rack at Barney's for *this* boy—the goddamn writer is standing out there flailing away, just beating the shit—KA-WHOMP—out of this Everlast punching bag—the real thing, just like what they got down at Bobby Gleason's Gym, whamming the bejesus out of this punching bag that he finally decided he needed in his study to combat that goddamn writer's block that just comes sweeping over you like a goddamn migraine and completely poleaxes you. KA-WHOMP! Take that, mutha! Let me meet my quota. That goddamn *quota!* TWO THOUSAND words a day. Count 'em; onetwothreefour . . . it just never stops. 1999 won't get it: twofuckinthousand a *day*. When you're in your agent's office and you're signing that fifty-page contract—you practically get a goddamn hernia just lifting the thing—and you look at that due date for The Work—which is the way they refer to your *creativity,* your life's essence, your goddamn blood and vital juice—you figure mentally, Oh, I can hit about two thousand a day easy.

Well, Tom, boy, nobody ever said a writer's goddamn life was *easy.* Exactly!

(*Sorry,* Tom, boy, but you know how impossible it is to avoid . . . just *kind* of slipping into that Jax-Slax-kind-of-clinging Tom Wolfe-ese just to sample what the air is like at that altitude, and then before you know it you leave oxygen behind and you find that your respiratory system is running on soma or some damn thing. If there is a practicing young American writer alive who denies ever having lifted anything from your style . . . well, we all know that's impossible:::::::am I . . . *right?* Exactly!))))(((((((Perfect!)))))))

Thomas K. Wolfe, Jr., now forty-nine, was an extremely unlikely candidate to be the writer who would happen along in the Sixties and propel American journalism into a new realism that would become known and worshiped and vilified as the New Journalism. Wolfe grew up in Richmond, Virginia—he still retains the careful inflection of aristocratic Southern speech—where his father was editor of the *Southern Planter.* Tom decided to be a Writer and went to Washington and Lee University, where he was surprised to find there was no such thing as a major in writing. He studied English literature instead, was sports editor of the school newspaper, and distinguished himself by wearing a hat and carrying an umbrella, rain or shine. A course in American studies led him to pursue a doctorate in it at Yale. In 1957, as he finished his Ph.D. and still yearned to write, he took a "prole" job as a truck loader to try to get Insights and become a Writer. All he got was drunk after work every day.

He decided that a newspaper job would let him write, and he applied at all the New York City papers. The *Daily News* offered him a post as copy boy for forty-two dollars a week. He was ready to take it, until he heard laughter behind him during his job interview: an editor told him, "We never had a Ph.D. copy boy here before; the *Times* has them all the time." Wolfe foresaw a future of fetching coffee for reporters and decided to rethink things. He bought a job-hunting book, from which he learned how to prepare a résumé, and he wrote to one hundred newspapers around the country. He got three replies. The *Buffalo Courier-Express* and the Worcester, Massachusetts, *Telegram* said no, but the Springfield, Massachusetts, *Union* invited him for an interview and hired him as a reporter. He remembers that his most important assignment was tallying the number of empty stores on Main Street. Wolfe eventually moved to the *Washington Post.* He thinks he got the job because he was totally disinterested in politics: The city editor was amazed that Wolfe preferred cityside to Capitol Hill, the beat every reporter wanted. Wolfe's apartment overlooked the DuPont Theater, which had *Never on Sunday* for an extended run. Every morning he could see the marquee, which read "NEVER ON SUNDAY"—TENTH BIG WEEK, or whatever week it was. When the movie reached its forty-fourth big week, that marquee was a big reminder to Wolfe that *he* was having no big weeks, and he saw that marquee as a big clock ticking his life away. Tom still wanted New York City, so he made the rounds of the newspapers again.

He was lucky. Lewis Lapham (now editor of *Harper's*) had just quit the *Herald Tribune* and Tom got his job. It was there that Wolfe and

Jimmy Breslin and Pete Hamill and others were encouraged by editor Clay Felker to try new avenues in journalism. *New York* magazine, begun by publisher Jock Whitney as the *Trib*'s Sunday magazine, was the birthplace of New Journalism. The *Trib*'s ad campaign was, "Who says a good newspaper has to be dull?" and Felker let his writers take the bit and run. They were encouraged to go beyond the "objective" journalism that ruled daily newspapers, and the result was crisp, alive writing that, more than anything else, made its subjects personal the way fiction did. It was like the difference between Jack Webb, cop (just the facts—but only the facts I like), and Frank Serpico, cop (facts don't tell the whole story). Tom went out to Fort Lee, New Jersey, to interview the widow of slain "rackets boss Tony Bender." Tom couldn't understand, if the dailies called Tony a mob chieftain, why Tony didn't seem to have any money or a big house or a big car. The widow showed Tom the modest house, let him see the "rackets boss' " little woodworking shop, and described the last bag of garbage that the "rackets boss" himself had neatly tied up with string. All of a sudden—all of a goddamn *quick* sudden—newspaper targets became *people*. This irritated most newspaper editors in America. What would later be called New Journalism was ignored or denounced as biased reporting or even fiction. (By now New Journalism has been examined enough so that even William Safire might admit that it's an attempt at honest, personal reporting.)

Tom blazed the national trail by accident. He covered a hot-rod and custom-car show in New York for the *Trib* and treated it as a sideshow, which was what was expected of him—the sort of coverage that any respectable newspaper gives to anything the chamber of commerce wouldn't endorse.

Tom was uncomfortable, though; he sensed these car nuts had bypassed the system and were operating in a stratosphere they had created and knew could exist on its own. *Subcultures*. Tom thought these weird car people were a story.

He talked *Esquire* into an assignment that involved talking to car geniuses in Los Angeles but couldn't make a story out of it. Tom is not a fast writer. He worried and worried over it. *Esquire* already had the piece laid out, was not patient, and directed Tom to type out his notes so a good rewrite man could get on it. Tom sat down at 8:00 P.M. and started a memo to his editor, Byron Dobell ("Dear Byron, The first good look I had at customized cars was at an event called a 'Teen Fair' "); it took all night and ran to forty-eight pages. *Esquire* x-ed out "Dear Byron" and ran the piece as it was: presto, chango, New Journalism! Tom had read history; he knew historical patterns, but he was obsessed by what he sensed to be a new wrinkle. He had stumbled on the fact that the United States of America post-World War II had broken all the rules of history: it no longer took generations for change to take place— after the war, the sudden injection of money into every level of American society had canceled all bets and called off all games. Wolfe was the first to see a major upheaval. The enormous changes allowed subcultures to create themselves despite the fact that the media failed to recognize their existence: Vegas high rollers, rock tycoons, forever-young surfers, Manhattan high-class groupies—America finally was financing a fantasy island for anyone who would lift a little finger. Tom began reporting about a movement that disturbed a great many people, mainly those who controlled the media. The disturbing message from the heartland— from North Carolina, where Junior Johnson's racecar fortunes were more important than Lyndon Johnson's electoral fortunes—was that the aristocracy was finished; that Americans cared about their neighborhoods and their neighbors but not much else. That chauvinism narrowed down quickly to the predictable minimum: me and myself.

Everyone credits Tom for naming the Seventies the Me Decade. What's funny is that he was out of sight for most of the Seventies. He was a late-Sixties hero, especially for *The Electric Kool-Aid Acid Test,* about Ken Kesey and his Merry Pranksters, and also for *The Pump House Gang* and *The Kandy-Kolored Tangerine-Flake Streamline Baby*. But once he pegged the Seventies with the Me flag, he took himself off the college-lecture circuit, where his first question from audiences invariably was "What's Ken Kesey doing?" followed by "How many times did you do acid?" He was not rich, but he was tired of being a Kesey travel guide. Tom was, after all, a journalist, he told himself.

He did take an assignment from *Rolling Stone* magazine to cover the space program, and he wrote a series of four articles that he eventually expanded into *The Right Stuff*. It took him six years to report it, he said, but only six months to write. It takes, he said (and he should know), any writer only six months to actually write any book. The rest of the time is . . . *leisure time,* eh, Tom?

Wolfe does guard his time jealously. He postponed *The Right Stuff* for one year just to polish it after it was written. His magazine assignments are like pulled teeth. He is reluctant to talk about New Journalism, especially after the book he edited, *The New Journalism,* became a magnet for criticism. He caught flak for it from everyone, especially the writers he anthologized.

Tom and Sheila Wolfe seem to live very quietly in their East Side townhouse. Tom's only extravagance seems to be tailor-made clothes. He does not light up the sky at Elaine's. He sits at home in his white-on-white studio and sketches illustrations for *Harper's* and works on outlines of his next book, which will be his first novel and which he hopes will be a sort of New York City version of *Vanity Fair*. He feels New York—*any* major city—should be a central part of a book. Dickens and Zola and Balzac and Thackeray did it, Tom said, so why shouldn't he?

Probably the most striking thing about The Right Stuff *is that it has made you very respectable. You're no longer the hit man who literary people fear and hate. Now you're eminently respectable.*

Most of the things I have done have *not* been sendups or zaps, but those things are remembered somehow. People love a little merciless mockery. So they'll tend to remember something like . . .

"Tiny Mummies," for example.

Yeah. Or *Radical Chic,* particularly, or *The Painted Word,* since, if you even make *gentle* fun of people who inhabit the world that you and I live in or the world of the arts, or anything having to do with expression, they *scream* like *murder*. And of course they have the equipment to bite back, so the fight starts. Everyone kind of enjoys it whether they're paying any attention or not. But *The Electric Kool-Aid Acid Test* was not a sendup, was not mockery or satire.

It was not necessarily a subject the literary world understood or endorsed.

Well, the literary world certainly doesn't endorse the subject of astronauts; it hasn't been a very popular subject. As a matter of fact, one of the things that interested me most was not the space program but military life. I could see that the military, particularly the officer corps, had really been a vacant lot in the literary sense. Serious writers stopped looking at the military around 1919—in any sympathetic way or even empathetic way. It's around then that you start finding the fashion of dealing with the military in a way in which the only acceptable protagonist is the GI, the dog soldier, the grunt, the doughboy, who's presented as a *victim,* not as a *warrior,* a victim of the same forces as civilians.

Did Radical Chic *start with you finding an invitation on a desk at the* Trib?

Yeah. It was an invitation for David Halberstam, and he wasn't even there. I just happened to see it on his desk and there was an R.S.V.P. number. Some people had told me about the thing, but I was not invited, so I called up this number, and I said this is Tom Wolfe, I'm with *New York* magazine, I accept. It turned out to be a defense committee for the Panthers. There was just somebody there writing down the accepts and regrets.

   Incidentally, I came in very openly, with a National Brand stenographic notebook and a Bic ball point pen. I introduced myself to Mr. and Mrs. Bernstein. At the time, they figured anybody who was there was riding the same wave they were. The idea that there might be anything funny about it, or amusing, was unthinkable.

How accurate were your notes?

It turned out I took very good notes. Leonard Bernstein's sister later wrote me a long letter in which she said I did several terrible things, but apparently the worst was that I brought a hidden tape recorder into her brother's home. And I knew then that I was right on course. Kind of a lefthanded compliment. Actually, I knew that if I hadn't been accurate, that would have been the first cry.

I then spent a long time trying to establish the world that they lived in: who they were and why they were interested in this particular cause. It took me an awful long time to work out the *concept.* I had the phrase in my mind already, *radical chic,* 'cause I knew that by then there was a fashionable quality to certain radical causes.

I started writing in the first person, which was a big mistake, telling how I saw this invitation, how I wrangled my way in. I wrote about thirty pages like that, and then it dawned on me that it was useless information and really detracted from the *scene,* which was the important thing. In fact, I find that the use of the first person is one of the trickiest things in journalism, and something that's rarely understood. If you write in the first person, you've turned yourself into a character. And you have to *establish* yourself, you have to make yourself become a character, and you have to have some organic involvement in the action. It's not enough just to be an observer and to use the first-person singular. As the years go by, I've tended to back off from that device more and more.

In his anthology, The Great Shark Hunt, *Hunter Thompson takes a shot at you for always being the observer, never the participant.*

I *must* read that.

I found out that when I wrote this New Journalism book, I managed to waste nine, ten months' writing. I hoped I would antagonize the novelists, 'cause I was touting New Journalism and saying the novel was in disarray. To prove my point, I brought out my aces: Hunter Thompson, Gay Talese, Jimmy Breslin, and a few others. Well, the novelists seemed to be able to contain their emotions, if any, quite successfully [*laughs*]; I haven't seen any of them jumping out of windows. Instead, the only people who got angry were *my stars,* who all ended up despising me for saying they were the shining galaxy of New Journalism.

The next thing I knew, Gay Talese was on the same platform with me at a *More* convention—remember *More* [a now-defunct journalism review]? And there was a panel on the New Journalism. Renata Adler was on it, and she later told somebody that she had had a can of tomato soup or paste that she had intended to empty on my white suit as her comment on the New Journalism, but then somehow she lost the nerve. I had a feeling it was because I was in a pale gray flannel suit that night, maybe it just ruined the picture she had.*

At one point Breslin, I think, said, "There's no such thing as New Journalism, there's only *boutique* journalism and *real* journalism." And Hunter said, "I wouldn't touch New Journalism with a ten-foot pole. I'm a gonzo journalist." As soon as I tried to say, "Here's the great champion of the cause," he says "up yours" with the standard "I'm gonzo."

Actually, I kind of understand their feelings. Each one said, who the hell does Wolfe think he is, lumping me into his raggedy battalion?

The battalion that is wrecking the novel?

Well, they didn't care one way or another about the claims I was making for the form or the way I was putting down the novel. It was just the idea that I could put them in a category. I suppose if one of them had written the thing, I would have had the same reaction.

I would think the astronauts weren't eager to talk to you, some weirdo saying, I'm from Rolling Stone *and I want to investigate your private life. Obviously you didn't say that; how did you go about it?*

They weren't all that tough. By that time, some had left the astronaut corps. They were a lot looser about the whole thing, they were no longer under the *Life* magazine contract. I think many had become rather bored with the way astronauts had been described. They tended to be pretty open if they agreed to talk at all. A few wouldn't be interviewed. Alan Shepard told me that he only cooperated in documentary ventures that had a scientific purpose . . . later on he indicated that he had read the *Rolling Stone* pieces and didn't particularly like what was there; I don't know why. Neil Armstrong said he had a policy of not giving interviews and didn't see any reason why he should change it. I think he had hopes, and perhaps still does, of writing his own book. All the Mercury astronauts who were still alive—[Gus] Grissom was dead— were willing to talk and were cooperative.

---

*Renata Adler recalls, "My memory is a bit hazy, but as I remember it, it would have been soup, probably vegetable, poured over his head, not his suit."

Was John Glenn open?

Very open. I spent a day with him when he was campaigning for the Senate in 1974, the year he finally won the primary against Howard Metzenbaum, who had beaten him just a few years before. Then I spent an afternoon with Glenn after he won; he was actually pretty generous with his time, as senators go, and he was very helpful.

I've been surprised by the number of reviews that found my picture of John Glenn negative. I wasn't trying to send him valentines, but in my mind he came off as an exceptional and rather courageous figure. He did a lot of unpopular things. He told off a lot of people, and he almost lost his flight by telling the administrator of NASA and everybody else that Lyndon Johnson couldn't go into his house, that he and his wife didn't want him in there. That took a lot of courage.

When did the notion first strike you—of course it should have been obvious to everyone—that the original astronauts were not the Boy Scouts who were presented to America?

I guess from the first conversation that I ever had with any of them. It's not that they bragged about their exploits or talked about things like driving these wild races on the highway. At the same time I was starting this thing, in late 1972, there had been reports in the press indicating trouble in paradise among the astronauts. Buzz Aldrin's nervous breakdown had been revealed. That was the same year there was a stamp scandal, which wasn't really much of a scandal, but nevertheless it made people stop and ask, "What, astronauts took a cut of some stamp sales?" One of the astronauts had just become an evangelist. Two or three had been photographed with long hair, and this was immediately interpreted by newspapers and magazines as a sign that there were astronauts who were turned into hippies, which never happened as far as I can tell.

Perhaps because the general whitewash of the astronauts' flaws had gone to such an extreme at the beginning, the least little crack was overinterpreted. To this day, so many people think that most of the astronauts who went to the moon have suffered breakdowns or become alcoholics. It just isn't true.

For a while there was the assumption that this voyage was traumatic because it removed them from all familiar environments, and that this just had devastating effects on these simple men who weren't prepared for it. The truth was, they had had such sophisticated simulations that there was very little new to see when they reached the moon. By the time Armstrong got there, he had had probably five hundred simulated missions in replicas of the Apollo command module, with moving pictures of the moon, based on films that had been brought back by manned and unmanned vehicles. I think it was false for Armstrong to have delivered some apostrophe to the gods or some statement of poetic awe about what he had seen, 'cause he had already seen it all simulated in such high fidelity, how the hell could he pretend there was something startling about it? So he said it's "a small step for man, a giant leap for mankind." When I asked him about it, he said, "Sure, I worked on it for a couple of weeks."

How did you get the notion to cut this book off where you did? The idea of the end of innocence—I believe you make the point that the astronauts' parade was, in a sense, the peak of American innocence.

I think that was the last great national outpouring of patriotism. There was some of that with Gordon Cooper's flight, but it was much bigger in the case of Glenn. By the time Cooper flew in 1963, there were many signs that the United States and the Soviet Union were reaching some sort of rapprochement, so that there wasn't the tension about the flight. The cold war was still a big thing at the time of Glenn's flight.

I liked your characterization of the press as the proper Victorian gent, that the press was reverent through all this. Did you really review all the clips, or was that a generalization about the way Americans perceived those astronauts?

I noticed things like James Reston's piece on the astronauts. If for any obscure reason anyone wanted to finish off James Reston, all you would have to do is reprint that piece.

Where he wrote, "This is a pretty cynical town, but we were misty-eyed" and so forth, after the astronauts' parade?

Yeah. And reading that stuff also pulled together some thoughts I had had along these lines. I'll never forget working on the *Herald Tribune* the afternoon of John Kennedy's death. I was sent out along with a lot of other people to do man-on-the-street reactions. I started talking to some men who were just hanging out, who turned out to be Italian, and they already had it figured out that Kennedy had been killed by the Tongs, and then I realized that they were feeling hostile to the Chinese because the Chinese had begun to bust out of Chinatown and move into Little Italy. And the Chinese thought the mafia had done it, and the Ukrainians thought the Puerto Ricans had done it. And the Puerto Ricans thought the Jews had done it. Everybody had picked out a scapegoat. I came back to the *Herald Tribune* and I typed up my stuff and turned it in to the rewrite desk. Late in the day they assigned me to do the rewrite of the man-on-the-street story. So I looked through this pile of material, and mine was missing. I figured there was some kind of mistake. I had my notes, so I typed it back into the story. The next day I picked up the *Herald Tribune* and it was *gone,* all my material was gone. In fact, there's nothing in there except little old ladies collapsing in front of St. Patrick's. Then I realized that, without anybody establishing a policy, one and all had decided that this was the proper moral tone for the president's assassination. It was to be grief, horror, confusion, shock, and sadness, but it was not supposed to be the occasion for any petty bickering. The press assumed the moral tone of a Victorian gentleman.

I say Victorian gentleman, because it's he who was the constant hypocrite, who insisted on public manifestations of morality that he would never insist upon privately in his own life. And I think that one tends to do that on a newspaper. Less so in a magazine. A newspaper seems to have such an immediate tie to the public. Television doesn't have it. Newspapers do. I'm not entirely sure why, but it makes newspapers fun to work for.

It also leads to these funny sorts of reactions. People *never* read editorials. All newspapers know this. And yet if you would publish a newspaper without editorials, it would be as if you had sold your soul to somebody. Everyone would ask, in effect, "Well, where are the editorials? They must have sold them. They're taking something on the side." And so newspapers are quite right to run editorials. It all has to do with this moral assumption.

Hell, to this day you can't get anything in newspapers. I think of this as the period of incredible shrinking news. I'm really convinced that there's less news covered in America now than at any time in this century. Television creates the impression that there's all this news because the press has become very incestuous and writes stories about the press, with all these marvelous phony wars about television and what it does or doesn't do. But television as a news medium has no reporting at all, really, except for some cosmetic reporting done by so-called Washington correspondents, who usually stand in front of some government building with a microphone covered in black sponge rubber, reading AP or UPI copy. In effect, every shred of news on television comes from either the wire services or from *non-events,* to use Daniel Boorstin's phrase—the press conference, the basketball game, and so on. So you then have to ask, "What are the wire services giving us?" Well, the wire services are totally creatures of local newspapers. Those big wire services just cannibalize local newspapers. Suddenly you're up against the fact that there's no competition in most parts of the country *at all.* I doubt if there are five cities where there is still newspaper competition. There's a little bit left in Los Angeles, a little bit left in Boston, and some in New York, but not much. Maybe one or two other places. When this happens, the monopoly newspaper cuts back on its staff—always happens. They just stop covering local events—too expensive. And they'll hire children from journalism schools at the lowest possible scale. They'll let them work for a couple of years, send them to the Statehouse, 'cause at the Statehouse they can pick up four or five stories a day handed out by public relations people. That's your local coverage—canned items from the Statehouse. When these people have had enough experience to begin getting good, getting a feel for reporting, they manage to get rid of them or ease them out of the job because they will be wanting more money. They will also be wanting to create heat; it's very hard for a managing editor—an older man—to resist if a young reporter says, "Look, I dug up a hot story." There's still enough pride in the business, so it's hard to say, "Well, forget it, kid, we're not interested in hot stories here. We just want the wire-service stuff and a few handouts from the Statehouse and that's it."

So really, what you're seeing on television via the wire services is just getting smaller and smaller. It's really very sad. I don't know how much corruption there is at the local level, but there's never been a better time in the century for there to be corruption in local government, because the press is not gonna spot it.

Is this kind of head-in-the-sand policy deliberate on the part of the publishers?

I don't think it even gets to that exalted level; it's just that since there's no competition, why knock yourself out and send a larger number of reporters to cover, say, the federal courthouse or city court, why beat your brains out by doing it better? And it's only the occasional newspaper that has pride, a kind of lingering, vestigial pride in the business, and tries to do a job right.

Television, which has the money to do the reporting, has gotten away so beautifully *without* doing it that it's not about to start. Within the television news operations there's such a premium put on *not* being a reporter, everyone aspires to be the man who *never* has to leave the building: the anchor man, who is a *performer.* The reporters are called researchers and are usually young women, and the correspondent on television is a substar, a supporting actor who prides himself on the fact that he doesn't have to prepare the story. You talk to these guys and they'll say, "Well, they sent me from Beirut to Teheran, and I had forty-five minutes to get briefed on the situation." What they should say is, "I read the AP copy." The idea is that as a performer, you can pull together this news operation anywhere you go, and the whole status structure is set up in such a way that you're *not* going to get good reporters. Just try to think of the last major scoop, to use that old term, that was broken on television. I'm sure there have been some. But what story during Watergate? During Watergate there were new stories com-

ing out every day. None were on television, except when television
simply broadcast the hearings. They can do a set event. And that's what
television is actually best at. In fact, it'd be a service to the country if
television news operations were shut down *totally* and they only broadcast hearings, press conferences, and hockey games. *That* would be
television news. At least the public would not have the false impression
that it's getting news coverage.

Truman Capote talks about the nonfiction short story. What is that about?

It's interesting that it's important to people like Norman Mailer and
Capote to call what they do in nonfiction—if they think it has literary
value—a novel or short story. It reminds me so much of the impulse
that made Fielding call his novels "comic epic poems in prose." In the
eighteenth century, when he was writing, the novel was a very low-
rent form. The reigning form was epic verse, particularly the epic drama.
Actually, Shakespeare wrote in the form of the epic drama, classical
verse, classical drama, and many times he chose classical subjects. As I
said in *The New Journalism,* Fielding made this claim for both *Joseph
Andrews* and *Tom Jones,* which is another way of saying, "You've gotta
take me seriously." And the fear is that you won't be taken seriously if
you're considered part of a low-rent form. Mailer called *Armies of the
Night* the novel as history; history as a novel.

Throughout the world of letters, a curious thing is going on in which
all sorts of fiction writers have been struck by the power of nonfiction,
good nonfiction, in this era. And they also are instinctively aware of the
power of realism. They try various ways of tapping into this current.
It was so interesting to see E. L. Doctorow start backing away from
the fable in *Ragtime.* It's a typical modern fable in many ways, but
Doctorow also started using real names, usually of dead people—of
course avoiding problems of libel. And the book would not have
been . . . it would hardly have been noticed if he hadn't done that.

Gore Vidal, you may remember, wrote a curious novel called *Two
Sisters,* in which he used real people like Jacqueline Kennedy and fictional
people. And it was also about that time that William Styron did *Confes-
sions of Nat Turner.* In the old days, such a novel would have been based
on Nat Turner, but would have changed the name of Nat Turner to
something else. Well, this one again tried to draw on the current of
realism, and the reader is led to believe that this *is* the story of Nat
Turner, when of course the novelist had to fill in a few gaps. All of this
was during the period in which the fable was sort of fashion. But the
fable wasn't working. Not only were the writers of fables losing readers,
but they were losing publishers. There was a depression in the stock
market about 1973, and it had a terrible effect on the publishing industry.

A lot of publishers just began lopping the deadwood, as they saw it, off their lists. This meant experimental novels had to go. And that, I think, indirectly began to have a lot to do with this backing into realism. It's sort of like somebody leaving the presence of the king: bowing backward, bowing and walking backward, but getting the hell out of there very rapidly. So I have a feeling that by 1984, well, in a few years, there'll be a whole new vogue with realistic novels. It's so obvious now that that is the direction for the novel to resume.

I believe it was in the New Republic *that Mitch Tuchman wrote that the reason you turned against liberals is that you were rejected by the white-shoe crowd at Yale.*

Wait a minute! Is that one by Tuchman? Yeah, oh, that was great.

He talked about your doctoral dissertation.

Yeah, he wrote that after *The Painted Word*. It went further than that. It was called "The Manchurian Candidate," and it said in all seriousness that I had somehow been prepared by the establishment, which he obviously thought existed at Yale, to be this kind of kamikaze like Laurence Harvey—I think that's who was in *The Manchurian Candidate,* wasn't it?—to go out and assassinate liberal culture. I loved that. And he's talking about Yale. When I was at Yale, William Buckley was writing *God and Man at Yale,* saying that it had been taken over by the Left and that the Left was pouring all this poison into the innocent vessels of the young. Tuchman's saying I turned on liberalism is amusing in itself, because it would indicate that I had either been or pretended to be a liberal and then had turned on my comrades for some devious reason. All I ever did was write about the world we inhabit, the world of culture, with a capital *C,* and journalism and the arts and so on, with exactly the same tone that I wrote about everything else. With exactly the same reverence that the people who screamed the most would have written about life in a small American town or in the business world or in professional sports, which is to say with no reverence at all, which is as it should be. And these days, if you mock the prevailing fashion in the world of the arts or journalism, you're called a *conservative.* Which is just another term for a heretic. I would much rather be called a conservative in that case than its opposite, I assure you. Of course, the word *liberal* in itself doesn't exist anymore. Nobody talks about liberals or liberalism.

The Left no longer exists in America. There *are* leftists, but they have no terrain. There is a swing away from the political fashion of the Sixties. It doesn't mean anything more than that. The disappearance of the Left is something that deserves book treatment, and I don't pretend to know exactly how it happened, but it happened in one year, in 1970. In May 1970, the Left reached a peak of power with the shootings at Kent State.

You've never really written about politics or wanted to. In fact, I heard that you advised Hunter Thompson not to, that if he did, he would lose it.

Oh, I think writing about politics was probably one of the biggest mistakes Hunter ever made. I believe he is interested in it, which astounds me. I think his gifts, which are tremendous, are wasted on American politics, except possibly in an event like Watergate—which he didn't write about, I don't think. Because this country is *so* stable politically. It really is an extremely stable country.

It doesn't matter who's president.

Oh, I don't think so either. That's why I'm not too concerned about who gets elected in 1980. The real lesson of Watergate was, what a stable country! Here you've got the president forced out of office, and yet the tanks don't roll, the junta is never formed. I don't think there was even a drunk Republican who went out and threw a brick through a saloon window! Everyone *enjoyed* it. That was the greatest show on earth. Everyone sat back and watched it on television and enjoyed it when Jerry Ford, who had been handpicked by the man they just threw out, stumbled from one side of the country to the other. And then they elected the guy who for three years wore picnic clothes [*laughs*]. Carter's *too much*. I think if they ever do the presidential portrait of him, they should take him to the bow of the *Delta Queen* in his cutoff Levi's and Adidas shoes and have him lean against the railing with Rosalynn in her khaki harem pants! And there you have it!

Have you always been a real clothes horse, really careful about clothes?

The first time I remember being interested at all in clothes was after I saw *The Kiss of Death* [1947] with Richard Widmark as Tommy Udo. That was his first big role, he was the villain; Victor Mature was the hero. It was a gangster movie. I was at Washington and Lee, and there was a custom, I guess you'd call it, of conventional dress. It was an all-male school, and everyone had to wear a conventional jacket and tie. I guess I just wanted to put a *spin* on the custom without transgressing the rules, so I decided on these dark shirts.

Now when I think back on it, I have done the same thing ever since, which is to wear rather conventional clothes and put a little spin on it, such as to wear white where you'd ordinarily wear navy, black, or things of that nature. Style, men's clothing, has very rigid presumptions about it, and if you really experiment, suddenly you're out of the ball game. You could certainly cut a striking figure by wearing a royal blue caftan everywhere you go, but you would remove yourself from most transactions of life. So if you want to have any fun with it, it really has to be rather marginal. But the interesting thing is that marginal things seem outrageous at first.

I also think I was the only person on campus who wore a hat. And I know I was the only person who carried an umbrella every day. When I got to my next stop, Yale graduate school, I fell into great confusion, because the grad school was full of genuinely eccentric people, and to try to be eccentric in the midst of a zoo full of eccentrics was a lost cause. The currency was debased. At the same time, it was no use trying to dress very conventionally because there was a whole campus full of undergraduates who were dressed very conventionally.

It was a very confusing time for me in terms of dress. My last couple of years there I discovered long hair, and that was very unusual. When I say long hair, I'm not talking about hair down to the shoulder blades. That was still the period back in the Fifties, when everyone's ears stuck out and the sun shone through them.

Finally, when I got to Washington, I started having clothes made because I discovered a traveling British tailor. There were actually several who advertised in the back pages of the *Manchester Guardian* air-mail edition. They would set up shop in a hotel room. The samples used to always be on top of the bureau. You'd go look at all these samples books and pick some material. They'd make you whatever you wanted.

Is that when you discovered real buttonholes?

Yes. Then, once I got into it, this tailor told me the names of his customers, rather indiscreet of him, and some turned out to be very famous people. That was the basis of a piece I would later write for *New York* magazine, called "Secret Vice," about the buttonholes and so on.

When I came to New York I decided I should start getting clothes made in this country so I could get fittings, because there were some rather bad mistakes, though not as bad as you would get with a Hong Kong tailor. So I went to a tailor here in New York and picked out a white material to have a suit made for the sumertime. Silk tweed is actually a very warm material, so I started wearing the thing in the wintertime. This was the winter of 1962 or 1963, and the reaction of people was just astonishing.

Long hair at that time outraged people. It was a real transgression. I did a story on Phil Spector in 1964, and he had hair about as long as the Beatles'. The things that were yelled to him on the street—I mean the *hostility*—were just amazing.

The hostility for minor changes in style was just marvelous. I had a great time. I was really getting into the swing of things. I remember my friend Bill Rollins, who was one of the great figures on the *Herald Tribune* at the time. Every time I came into Bleek's or one of those places where newspaper people met, he'd say, "Here comes the man with the double-breasted underwear." I rather *liked* that. In fact I loved the idea. I've always been waiting for someone in an interview to ask me what I sleep in.

Okay, I'll bite. What do you sleep in?

I think I would say double-breasted pajamas with frogging. In fact, it's not true. I actually wear nightshirts.

Brooks Brothers nightshirts?

No, my mother's made me a few that are really nice. I've also got these chain-store-look ones with the alligator; I don't know who makes those—they're like a long polo shirt. But I much prefer the idea of the double-breasted pajamas. I mean I *bought* some; they really aren't comfortable. They have a big lapel, you know, and piping around the lapel and collar.

Strangle you while you sleep.

The cinch drawstring on the trousers was always uncomfortable, and the big collar tends to make you perspire. But those things are so *beautiful,* with all the buttons and the frogging; that's the way people *should* sleep. Which brings me to one final note on style. It's still possible to have fun with clothes if you're willing to be pretentious. That still annoys people: pretension in dress. In fact, this summer I was in East Hampton visiting some people who took me to a party. I was wearing a four-button seersucker jacket that buttons up really high—I think it is actually Edwardian—with a little tiny collar and a white tie with small, far-apart black stripes, and I had on a collar pin and cuff links, white serge pants, and white cap-toed shoes, which are real English banker shoes, only I had them made in white doeskin. I had on some sheer white socks with black stripes to pick up the stripes in the necktie—I'm the *only* person who would confess all this to somebody. Pretty soon I noticed that I was the only man in the room—and this was a party of maybe sixty people—who had on both a jacket and a necktie. I think everyone had an income far in excess of mine. Finally this man came over to me; he was a little drunk, but he was also angry. He asked, "What's the idea of the *rig?*" I asked, "What do you mean?" He said, "The *tie,* the *pin,* all this stuff." So I looked at him, and he had on a polo shirt and some kind of go-to-hell pants, and he had this big *stain* down the front of his polo shirt, right down the middle, right down to his belt line. I said,

"Well, gee, I guess I can't keep up with the styles in these parts. How do you do that bright stripe down your polo shirt?" He looked down sort of in surprise and said, "That's sweat, goddamn it, that's *sweat!*" He suddenly was very proud of it. I could see that I had landed in the midst of the era of funky chic.

You know when I write certain things and it turns out that I'm correct, it amazes me, I must confess. When I wrote that thing, funky chic, I never dreamed how correct that was.

On several occasions, most recently in the Polo Lounge in Beverly Hills, I'd just be standing around and people would come up and ask me if there's a table available, because I'd have on a suit and necktie. It's really odd, but you can have fun if you're willing to be a bit pretentious. Wear some trick outfits. If it's worth it to you.

Does it ever get in the way of your role as the observer?

No, most often the opposite has gotten in the way. In the beginning of my magazine-writing career, I used to feel it was very important to try to fit in.

To be the chameleon?

Yes, and it almost always backfired, most notably when I went to do a story on Junior Johnson, the stock-car racer, one of the first stories I did for *Esquire.* I was quite aware that he was from the hills of North Carolina. A lot of moonshine and ex-moonshine runners were involved with stock-car racing at that time, Junior being one of them. I thought I'd better try to fit in, so I very carefully picked out the clothes I'd wear. I had a knit tie, some brown suede shoes, and a brown Borsalino hat with a half-inch of beaver fur on it. Somehow I thought this was very casual and suitable for the races; I guess I'd been reading too many P. G. Wodehouse novels. I really thought I'd fit in until about five days after I was down there. Junior Johnson came up to me and said, "I don't like to say anything, but all these people in Ingle Hollow here are pestering me to death saying, 'Junior, do you realize there's some strange little green man following you around?' "

I realized that not only did I not fit in, but because I thought I *was* fitting in in some way, I was afraid to ask such very basic questions as, what's the difference between an eight-gauge and seven-gauge tire, or, what's a gum ball, because if you're supposed to be hip, you can't ask those questions. I also found that people really don't want you to try to fit in. They'd much rather fill you in. People like to have someone to tell their stories to. So if you're willing to be the village information gatherer, they'll often just pile material on you. My one contribution to the discipline of psychology is my theory of information compulsion.

Part of the nature of the human beast is a feeling of scoring a few status points by telling other people things they don't know. So this does work in your favor.

After that, when I did *The Pump House Gang,* I scarcely could have been in a more alien world. I did the whole story in my seersucker rig. I think they enjoyed that hugely. They thought of me as very old. I was thirty-odd years old, and they thought of me as very stuffy. They kind of liked all that—this guy in a straw boater coming around asking them questions. Then it even became more extreme when I was working on *Electric Kool-Aid Acid Test.* I began to understand that it would really be a major mistake to try to fit into that world. There was a kind of creature that Kesey and the Pranksters, practically everybody in the psychedelic world, detested more than anything else, and that was the so-called weekend hipster, who was the journalist or teacher or lawyer, or somebody who was hip on the weekends but went back to his straight job during the week. Kesey had a habit of doing what he called testing people's cool. If he detected the weekend hipster, he would dream up some test of hipness, like saying, "Okay, let's everybody jump on our bikes and ride naked up Route 1." They *would* do that, and usually at that point the lawyer, who didn't want an indecent exposure charge on his life's score sheet, would drop out. Kesey explained this theory of testing people's cool, his notion that there're lots of people who want to be amoral, but very few who are up to it. And he was *right.*

How did you come to write Acid Test?

This goes back to 1966, the year after *The Kandy-Kolored Streamline Baby* came out, and I had written a whole bunch of articles that eventually became *The Pump House Gang,* but I didn't want to bring out another collection. It just wouldn't seem like a step forward. I was really casting about for another book to write. About that time, Henry Robbins, who was my editor at Farrar, Straus & Giroux, had gotten Xerox copies of some letters that Larry McMurtry had gotten from Kesey, who was then in hiding in Mexico. These letters were marvelous, paranoid chronicles of his adventures and lamentations about the strange fate that had befallen him now that he was a fugitive. And I got the idea of going to Mexico, finding him, and doing a story on the life of a fugitive.

I bought the ticket for Mexico City, and somehow, before I went there, Kesey sneaked back into the U.S. and was arrested by the FBI just south of San Francisco. I went out to the jail in Redwood City where they'd put him, and I met all these crazy-looking people hanging around. There were people trying to get me to take books to Kesey with I Ching coins slipped into the binding. They turned out to be Pranksters. I didn't know anything about these people and what they were up to. I knew that Kesey had been involved with dope, because that's what he'd been arrested twice for. I assumed that dope must be what accounted for their strange appearance. Stewart Brand was one of the first ones I met. He wore a piet in his forehead. A piet is a disc, a silver industrial disc; I don't know what they were used for. They reflected the light in some strange way. They had a very geometric sunburst design.

They had these white coveralls on with pieces of American flag sewed on. Only a few of them had really long hair; it was more just *strange* rigs and gear. They were very open and invited me to this place, this abandoned pie factory where they were staying while they waited for Kesey to get out. It was down in the skid-row section of San Francisco, worst place I ever saw. Very *hard* on a boy like me, that life. It got more and more interesting. I'd learned that some of them had been down in Mexico with Kesey, so I started pumping them for information—about the fugitive life. They kept saying, "We'll tell you about that, but that isn't what it's all about." I said, "Well, what is *it* all about?" And they said, "It's the unspoken thing." It gradually began to dawn on me that this was a *religious* group, a religion in its primary phase. It began to seem even important to me. The sociology of religion is one of the things I'd picked up at Yale graduate school.

One learns that every modern religion, from Hinduism to Buddhism and Christianity on to the present, started with a primary group, a small circle of disciples, as they're called in Christianity, who have an overwhelming experience that is psychological, not neurological—a feeling, an overwhelming *ecstasy* that they have interpreted in a religious way and that they want to enable the rest of the world to have so it can understand the *truth* and the *mystery* that has been discovered.

The Pranksters were no exception. Their neurological experience had come through LSD, but that wasn't so unusual either. The Zoroastrians were always high on something called *haoma;* to this day no one knows what it was, but it was obviously a drug. By the time I met Kesey, he was already starting to promulgate the concept *beyond acid;* the idea that LSD could only take you to a certain level of understanding and awareness, but that you couldn't become dependent on it. Having reached the plateau, you must move on without it. He announced this new truth to the movement and was much criticized for it, because by this time, 1966, the rest of the movement was having a helluva good time still getting high. They didn't want to hear this. But this is exactly what Zoroaster ended up doing. He said, now boys, we've got to start doing it without this *haoma* stuff. A little astral projection if you please, maestro!

How did you come across the third great awakening and the Me Decade? Was that originally a lecture that you were doing?

I think I did it for *The Critic;* I used "the third great awakening" in that.

One of the few things I learned on the lecture circuit, which I have abandoned for the most part, was the existence of these new religious movements and some insight into what they were like. I would begin to meet members of religious communes who had come to my talks in hopes of hearing about Ken Kesey and the Merry Pranksters, whom I was not talking about any longer. I would talk about art, and the first question would be, "What's Ken Kesey doing now?" And I can't tell you how many times that happened. I began to see that I was perceived as a medium who could put them in touch with the other world. And all these people were patiently listening *just* to get to the question period, or to get me alone to ask, "What's Ken Kesey doing now? What's he really like? Where can I find a commune? Are we running our commune correctly?" *God,* I used to get all these letters—I could have started a column like "Dr. Hip Pocrates, Advice for Heads."

Well, the other question that everyone asks, I recall, is how many times you'd taken acid in order to do Kool-Aid Acid Test, *and you said you hadn't, which disappointed everyone greatly.*

Yeah, I think they really wanted me to be on the bus. In fact, I never was.

You went off in private and took acid, just to see what it was like?

Well, I actually did it once during the writing of the book; I'd started writing the book, and then I thought, Well, this is one little piece of reporting I haven't done. So I did do it; it scared the hell out of me. It was like tying yourself to a railroad track to see how big the train is. It was pretty big. I would never do it again. Although at several places I went to lecture in the years that followed, people would put things in the pie that was cooked for dinner—not LSD, but a lot of hashish, marijuana baked into things, or methedrine. People would pop poppers under my nose, things of this sort. They thought they were doing me a favor. But one of the reasons I wrote *The Electric Kool-Aid Acid Test,* one of the reasons I thought it was important enough to write about, was that it was a religion; Kesey's group was a primary religious group.

And you could see how just such a group developed, as if you'd been able to have been a reporter when the early Christians were forming and then again, running into students who would tell me they had formed communes, and who were very frankly religious and would call themselves Jesus people. They said they didn't use dope, but they all *had*. In the beginning the whole Jesus movement was made up of former acidheads, and when they said they didn't use dope, in most cases they really meant they didn't use chemical dope. Anything you could grow was quite all right. That meant that marijuana was okay, peyote was okay . . .

. . . mescaline was all right, mushrooms, et cetera.

Yeah, if you would go to the trouble of making it. Those things were all okay. The people in the psychedelic world had been religious but had always covered it up. There was such a bad odor about being frankly religious. I mean Kesey would refer to Cosmo, meaning God; someone in the group used the word *manager*. Hugh Romney [a.k.a. Wavy Gravy] used to say, "I'm in the pudding and I've met the manager." Or they'd say, if they were getting into a very religious frame of mind and began to notice a lot of—what's the word when two people pick up the same thought at the same time? Probably *coincidence* is the right word, but they had another name for it—they would begin to say, "Well, there's some real weird shit going down" or "Brothers, this is the holy moment," or anything like that.

In the early Seventies, the mood of all this began to get more and more frankly religious, and the idea that this was the third great awakening popped into my head. Because I had remembered from graduate-school days the first awakening and second great awakening, out of which came Mormonism. Then I began to read about it. I saw that the Mormons, for example, had been just like hippies and had been *seen* as such. Just *wild* kids. They were *young* when they started. You think of Mormons as being old and having big beards. They were *children*. They were in their early twenties. Joseph Smith was twenty-four years old— he was the leader of the band. And they were just *hated, more* than the hippies were hated. And Smith was lynched. He wasn't hanged, but he was in jail in Carthage, Illinois, and it was invaded by vigilantes and they shot him to death. That's why Brigham Young took the group out to the woods of Utah.

And I think that movement is growing bigger and bigger. There's such a . . . yearning in everybody—there always has been—for blind faith. There's no such thing, I think, as rational faith. It isn't faith. And people always want it, one way or another, me included, although I hide it from myself, as do most people who think they are really sophisticated and learned. But this is something people really *want,* because blind faith is a way of assuring yourself that the kind of life that you're either leading or *intend* to lead is inherently and absolutely the *best*. That's really what it's all about.

Now is a great time for new religions to pop up. There are people who get religious about jogging, they get religious about sex, and you talk to some of these people who are avowed swingers—they'll *bore your head off.* God, it's just *painful* to listen to them. Fifteen minutes in a roomful of these people is like turning your head into a husk. Health foods have become the basis of a religion. Let's see, ESP, of course, flying saucers, *anything* is fertile ground now. There's a new messiah born every day. That's why Jimmy Carter made such a colossal mistake in not preaching. He'd gotten away with murder as it was, getting elected as a born-again Christian. *That's* what people wanted. If he had just ranted and raved for the last three years about the depravity of the people, they would have *loved it.*

You've collected an impressive list of critics and enemies.

That's not hard to do, as we mentioned earlier, if you're willing to treat the world of critics and artists and journalists the way *they* normally treat other people. If you really want to accumulate a list of enemies, you can get it soon enough. There were finally so many extraordinary insults in print about *The Painted Word* that I began having fun by putting them in categories. Tuchman's *Manchurian Candidate* critique was under a huge list of political insults, most of them saying I was a fascist, but some also saying I was a communist. There was another category of what I thought of as X-rated insults, which came about as follows: Right after *The Painted Word* came out, a well-known abstract-expressionist painter was at a dinner at which he said, "You know, this man Wolfe reminds me of a six-year-old at a pornographic movie; he can follow the action of the bodies but he can't comprehend the *nuances.*" Which incidentally is rather a reckless metaphor or conceit to set up for yourself, if you're defending contemporary art, because that's pornography, and I become the innocent child. Quite aside from that, I loved the notion that there was someone in this day and age who professes to find *nuances* in a *pornographic movie.* The next thing I knew, in *Time* magazine there is a review by Robert Hughes—the art critic, I think he's called—and he says, "Wolfe is like an eleven-year-old at a pornographic movie." [*Laughs.*]

Regarding John Russell's review in the New York Times . . .

This is the man who, at the age of, well, I guess he was in his late fifties, had risen to the eminence of first assistant to Hilton Kramer of the *New York Times.* I only mention his age because he mentioned *my* age. He rather flattered me by saying I was a little too young to understand all these things. He changed the image somewhat. He said I reminded him of the eunuch at the orgy who can follow the action of the bodies but cannot comprehend the nuances. I suppose he was afraid that some of the readers might find the image of the child in the pornographic movie somewhat sexy, so he changed it to the eunuch; nobody would find that very sexy.

It became indirect proof of a point that I was making in *The Painted Word*—just how small a world the art world is. As far as I know, neither of those men was at the dinner party. But this conceit, this metaphor, quickly passed around to the three thousand souls who make up the entire New York art world.

It became doubly funny when I really began to realize that in contemporary art, there is almost no sexual content *whatsoever*. It's one of the few major movements in art history where there is no sexual content. Even in pop art, what few sexual images there are, such as Wesselmann's nudes, are so highly stylized that there is no sensuality. In effect there's a very determined effort made to remove the sensuality, from nudes, for example. Let's see, there were a lot of psychoanalytic references.

Some [critics] were rather simpleminded, along the lines of how sick or neurotic I was. There was one woman who was much offended by *The Painted Word,* and she wrote to Bob Shnayerson, who was then the editor of *Harper's,* where the piece first appeared, and she berated him for letting *me* exacerbate my well-known mental affliction—psychosis or neurosis, I forget what she called it—by publishing this piece. And it was really more *his* fault than *mine,* because after all, I was *sick.* It was a shame, a terrible chapter in what had been the rather great history of *Harper's* magazine. I happened to see a copy of the letter and I ran into her at a party. So I said, "I must tell you, I happened to see a copy of what you wrote, and you could do me a great favor if you would explain my affliction to me, because I believe that prophylaxis is a good thing to aim for in mental health as well as in such areas as tetanus and diseases of that sort. At the very least, I expected a little dissertation on obsessional neurosis or something of that sort. Instead she suggested that I perform a crude anatomical impossibility on myself and then left the party. [*Laughter.*]

But that was the *passion* of the response to that piece. I found that there are people who take art more seriously than politics. Everyone seems to understand that underneath it all, politics is a game. But art *really* is religion to some people. Creativity is the new godhead and the artist is a receptor of emanations from the gods. It is the fulfillment of a prophecy made by Max Weber, who said that in the twentieth century, *aesthetics* would replace *ethics* as the standard for moral conduct. I think we see a lot of that now.

Tell me, where are you going to turn your eye next? Are you at loose ends, or casting around?

I'm doing something that I've had on my mind for a long time, which is a *Vanity Fair* book about New York, à la Thackeray. When I went to Leonard Bernstein's party, it was with the idea of gathering material for what was going to be a nonfiction book, which *could* be done, incidentally, if you could find enough events or scenes like that to move into. My impulse now, though, is to try to do it as a novel, since I've never done one, and to just see what happens. I'm also very much aware of the fact that novelists themselves hardly *touch* the city. How they can pass up the city I don't know. The city was a central—character is not a very good way to put it—but it was certainly a dominant theme in the works of Dickens, Zola, Thackeray, Balzac. So many talented writers now duck the city as a subject. And this is one of the most remarkable periods of the cities. Who has been the great novelist of New York since the Second World War? Nobody. Or Chicago or Cleveland or Los Angeles or Newark, for that matter. My God, the story of Newark must be absolutely amazing.

So you're going to be out prowling the streets?

Well, I don't know if I'll be charging into people's houses, but I will have to do a lot of reporting. There's more good material out there than in any writer's brain. A writer always likes to think that a good piece of work he has done is the result of his genius. And that the material is just the clay, and it's ninety-eight percent genius and two percent material. I think that it's probably seventy percent–thirty percent in favor of the material. This ends up putting a great burden on the reporting, and I don't think many fiction writers understand this.

Wasn't that part of the first big attack on the New Journalism? They said, well, the material is just there; it's the inspiration, the genius of the novelist that does something with it. If it's a reporter digging something up it's just journalism, raw material lying around; anyone can pick it up.

Yeah. I'm sure I went into this in the introduction of *The New Journalism,* but novelists in the nineteenth century understood that no one writer had enough material, and they would go out and do reporting as a matter of course. And Zola especially—he wrote a lot of his novels serially—would spend two weeks of the month doing reporting with a notebook, and the second two weeks he'd spend writing the episode. There's a scene toward the end of *Nana,* a very important scene at the races at Longchamps; he just went out there and soaked up all this material. It's not just a matter of your saying, "Here's the episode I want to write, so now I'm going to hang some accurate details on the story." The *material* leads you to the story. I don't know exactly what Zola did in that case, but I have a feeling that he came up with an entirely new and more exciting story because of the material he ran into.

I know that in one part of the book, there's the image of a golden bed, which is one of the great symbols in French literature, and he found it through reporting. He wanted to do a novel about a courtesan, Nana, so he arranged an introduction to meet a real courtesan, and he went to her house, and he was greatly disappointed to find out that she was far too urbane and cultivated to serve as a model for the kind of woman he wanted to present. He wanted really just an animal, a sexpot who had a tremendous power over men of all sorts. While he was there she showed him her bedroom, which featured a bed with golden posts done by goldsmiths at enormous cost, with all sorts of priapic cherubs and nymphs with shanks akimbo springing out of it. That stuck in his mind and he used it, he gave it to Nana in the novel. It became a symbol of the decadence of the Second Empire. You know, you wouldn't *dare* dream up such a bed, even if you had the power to dream it up in the first place. But the fact that he actually saw it gave him the idea in the first place, and then the confidence to use it.

TINY, or Texans in New York

The following is excerpted from a speech that Chet Flippo was scheduled to deliver to the 1984 convention of New York Friends of Texans in New York, which was, unfortunately, canceled at the last minute due to certain attendance problems.

I have been asked to speak to you on this occasion on "Being a Texan in New York" and all that such a heavy responsibility entails. So be it. I had wondered if perhaps we Texans in New York had disappeared, had tossed our ostrich-skin Lucchese boots and our anteater-skin belts and pheasant-feathered ten-gallon skimmers into the great Gotham melting pot, and that no longer did a peculiar odor follow us around, a loathsome stench that identified us one and all to passersby as yahoos in wonderland.

I went on a fact-finding mission down in Dallas, the center of the universe, and discovered that folks in Dallas don't dress that way and perhaps never would, at least if they could help it. Dallas, I found, adores New York, thoroughly approves of everything about it (except

Harlem and Queens and Brooklyn and the Bronx. And Staten Island. And maybe the Lower East Side), and envies it so. Restaurants, shops, shoppes, clubs, klubs throughout the Big D all set their watches—Rolex or Piaget—to Manhattan time. And they all think—hell, I used to think it—that there is some kind of weird Texas Underground in New York, some kind of damn underground railroad taking on fresh shipments of human flesh from SMU and Rice and UT and Baylor and moving 'em on up north and then dispatching them into key work posts in the marble castles of Madison Avenue, important broadcasting positions in the networks on Sixth Avenue, pin-striped bunkers on Wall Street, and influential galleries on trendy West Broadway. But it's mostly a chimera. (Mostly.) Real Texans in New York are invisible. You already know who some of the identifiable TINYs are: Walter Cronkite, Dan Rather, Liz Smith, Tommy Tune, Phyllis George, Bill Broyles, Dan Jenkins. A real TINY might appear to you as just another guy huffing and shoving down Madison Avenue in the standard-issue Brooks Brothers pin-striped-up-to-the-ass rig with the meaningless rep tie. But you have to look for the swagger, the swagger that says "I may be wearing this clown suit with a ridiculous pork-pie hat and carrying a hideously expensive leather lunch box but in reality Ah'm a stud from Texas with six-shooters on both hips and Ah'm gone to kick some ass. Some Yankee ass."

The powerful Texans who are fleecing the minions here do not want to be identified. That's wise. They do not wear Texas Asshole gear. They wear Burberry and Paul Stuart and F.R. Tripler and Brooks Bros. gear. The last True Professional New York Texan was the esteemed author and social observer Larry L. King, and he himself broke camp and lit out for Washington, D.C., where he settled down with the winnings he got from scribbling *The Best Little Whorehouse in Texas*, a magnificently Wagnerian overmyth of what was in actuality a grubby little Texas henhouse. But that was what the Texas myth used to be about: a febrile romanticism that sailed off to New York in a zig-zag course, trailing its bedraggled feathers all over the East Coast and back again to the Third Coast—which is, of course, what Texas is now calling itself in its head-swelled bid to become a major movie-making center.

But allow me to backtrack a bit. As far as I can tell, and I posit this modestly and reluctantly, nothing much seemed to happen till I moved from Austin, Texas, to New York in 1974. Oh, there was Tex Guinnan, the Runyonesque saloon queen pouring bootleg hooch back there in the thirties, but there weren't many Texas footprints here after that. As far as written history is concerned, Larry L. King was the only TINY with enough backbone to actually stand up and be counted as a TINY in 1974. When I landed here that year from Austin, King immediately took charge of me. "Bah Gahd," he rasped on the phone my first night here, "Ah'm gone ta take you ta Elaine's, bah Gahd. Takin' you ta Elaine's." And he did. And that was when I first realized why TINYs exist. They love to talk. In the Sixties, most expatriate Texans went to California because all they wanted to do was drugs and psychedelic music. Texans are gregarious and cannot talk in California because no one in California can talk. So Texans stated to move to New York. The best thing about New Yorkers is that they love to sit around in delis or coffee shops or bars and just schmooze and talk the hours away. Same as Texans, who like to talk as big as the sky and would never entertain the idea of living elsewhere.

Larry picked me up at the Drake Hotel and hauled me up to Elaine's where Elaine herself sat us down at a Power Table. What a revelation for an old country boy! Elaine's was just like a Texas bar where everybody sits around and bullshits and says hidy to the other people. Real homey. Larry was a true star there. He had on one of those old cracked-leather vests you can buy at the army-navy store in Austin for $7.98 that barely contained his belly. He was marvelous company. He could even out-bullshit the late Slim Pickens, the man who inspired the word *bullshit*. Larry could good-ol-boy it better than any man, dead or alive. His voice, tempered by decades of "whuskey" and tobacco intake, was a rumble that could shake glass. And he was the real thing. He had actually worked for LBJ and told him where to get his ashes hauled. Yankees, my first night in New York, actually crouched at his feet and marveled aloud as he sipped from his bottomless tumbler of whuskey and told marvelous lies with such gravelly charm that even me and Elaine believed him. But he could bullshit anybody and come out ahead. So he was the number-one TINY.

Then a dangerous idea emanated from one person, who shall remain unidentified. This person decided that there actually were TINYs and that they should meet each other and have parties and such like. And that there should actually be such a thing as Texans in New York. So the first Texans in New York party was held on Texas Independence Day in 1976 at O'Lunney's on Second Avenue, an average Irish bar in a neighborhood of superlative Irish bars. It turned out to be such a big deal that *The New York Times* actually sent a "cultural news" reporter to cover what was essentially an amiable beer bust. The *Times* story made the wire services, and I was pleasantly surprised to hear from yahoos back in Texas who had been convinced I was a total zero only to read in their daily Texas newspaper (q.v.: *The New York Times* Syndicate) that I was quoted as a big-deal TINY who said profound things like, "Well, we're just folks here trying to have fun."

Texans soon became yesterday's version of today's Eurotrash crowd.

We used to gather at Dan Rather's posh swankienda, where Liz Smith would serve "Texas Tea" (Lone Star beer) and Lynn Wyatt would cook up sizzling nachos and Stanley Marcus would describe the next new Texas shopping mall that would be built in midtown Manhattan and Van Cliburn would come and play his new Texas concerto which was sure to knock the next Soviet/Russo/Commie competition dead on its head. That used to happen. Things are a bit slower now.

Rosemary Kent had her Texas tailgate party at a car and truck dealership on West 57th Street in Manhattan and served bottles of Texas beer from pickup trucks. That was bearable, but then Bloomingdale's (which is really only a wing of the Smithsonian) actually built a life-size replica of the Lone Star Café inside its flagship store. A New York copy of a New York copy of a Texas honky-tonk? I stayed home behind a securely locked door that day. The gears were starting to come off the wheel.

A low profile (especially after such Texas un-pluses as the portrayal of an extremely uncouth LBJ in *The Right Stuff*) is now highly desirable in cool New York. No room for yahoos in this world capital city. TINYs therefore became just like flu germs: invisible and unwanted.

(I must here confess that in my stylish Manhattan apartment I do have two ice trays in my icebox that make Texas-shaped ice cubes. I also have a barbed-wire Texas Christmas wreath. And two sets of longhorns. Oh, and that Lone Star electric beer sign in the kitchen. And there's the old Armadillo World Headquarters poster in the bathroom. And the horseshoe over the bedroom door. But none of that really means anything.)

After that first TINY party at O'Lunney's, everything went pretty much downhill at a pell-mell pace. By the next party, you practically had to stay home and bolt the door in order to escape the crush of drunken hatted-and-booted Texans and pretenders. We had become, sadly, the New Irish. Instead of Paddy and Mick, we were Bubba and Hoss. The Lone Star Café, where the alleged party now took place, was a dead ringer for a Blarney Stone at the end of the St. Pat's parade: yokels upchucking to the right of you, rubes pissing on their own $79.95 Tony Lama look-alike boots to the left of you. And nowhere to run or hide. Real TINYs started pulling in their reins right then and there. How wonderful, after all, is it to be a quaint character with all the charm of a puking high school senior from Tenafly? I mean, I know real TINYs who have actually undergone speech therapy to try to shed their so-called accents. (That some of them came out sounding like refugees from Cape Cod, the Main Line, or Belgravia is unfortunate but true.)

What do you think Wall Street TINYs did after mulling all this over?

Ran right to the closet, of course. They trampled each other in their rush to Brooks Bros. and Barney's and Paul Stuart and F. R. Tripler and J. Press for camouflage layers of protective clothing.

The reason TINYs do not have a real club (read: physical plant) in Manhattan—and don't ever let anybody bullshit you on this—is because no grown person really wants the genuine, stinging stigma of being seen walking willingly into something called the Texas Club. The images that come immediately to mind involve white patent leather shoes and red polyester Sansabelts and loud drunken men named Bubba and louder drunken women named Ethel (who actually answer to "Skeeter"). It wouldn't quite be the same as going to the Yale Club, now would it?

New York's honky-tonks were abandoned long ago (two years, give or take a few months) to the true pretenders: tourists from anywhere, teeners from Jersey and Long Island, and dyed-in-the-wool-cap knownothings from everywhere. We were treated to the spectacle of the original Oakland cowboy, one Billy Martin, opening the first Western wear store in Manhattan. Billy Martin is too short to wear a ten-gallon hat. Halloween night, October 31, 1983, at the Lone Star Café was a case in point. Perennial Texan in New York Kinky Friedman (of Kinky Friedman and the Texas Jewboys fame) was the headliner. His band included some stellar side musicians: Sweet Mary from the legendary Austin band Greezy Wheels, twice-legendary keyboardist Augie Meyers from the thrice-legendary Sir Douglas Quintet from San Antonio, and honorary-Texan-by-dint-of-excess drummer Corky Laing from the notorious heavy metal group Mountain. Musically, it was a great night: a splendid mix of Texas-Jewish humor, Tex-Mex rock 'n' roll, and Eastern-rock energy. In the audience were Abbie Hoffman, several Manhattan magazine editors and writers who like to drink at loud bars, and a clutch of roaring Australians—who seem to act like real TINYs. Two editors got up and demonstrated why they are not entertainers, Augie Meyers said he was tired of being a TINY and was exiting for California or Texas, at the very least; Kinky said he didn't know what to do anymore, although he was continuing his collaboration with New York deejay Don Imus on a so-called Broadway play about a Texas evangelist who was God's other son; and most bystanders considered themselves lucky to be honorary Texans (the Lone Star is the State of Texas's embassy in New York, even though its owners can't get DPL—diplomatic—license plates, which may have been the reason behind the Texas movement).

Then we had the sad, slow decline of some of the hottest TINYs. Texas Joe Armstrong, former boy-wonder publisher of *Rolling Stone* and *New York* and *California* cashed it in as founder and publisher of a big-bucks magazine called *The Movies* that went belly-up. The reason? Apparently, Joe's only backer was a Texas money man who got magazine-shy after a few issues and backed off. New York money was not forthcoming—read, not confident—about the venture.

Likewise, my tri-coastal friend Bill Broyles had been brilliant at running *Texas Monthly* in Austin and then picked up *California* magazine, becoming a certified media golden boy at age thirty-seven, when he was tapped on the shoulder by Katharine Graham to head up *Newsweek* as its fifth editor in ten years. He could not lose. He had all the right credentials. After he moved in, I started hearing disquieting reports that the *Newsweek* staff was . . . sort of . . . ignoring Bill. I got a quiet phone call in the middle of the night to the effect that Bill was all of a sudden spending a lot of time playing touch football out there in the Hamptons. His, uh, resignation finally came in January. *Newsweek* publisher Kay Graham, who runs through editors the way I run through used cars, was "greatly saddened" by Bill's, uh, resignation.

And remember Houston whiz François deMenil, he of the Schlumberger Oil de Menils, who moved hisself on up here from Houston or wherever to set himself up as A Presence? He put his boots up on a desk in a penthouse office at 745 Fifth Avenue. A more expensive or desirable New York address you'll be hard-pressed to find. Looks right out over the Plaza Hotel and Central Park. Movie location type of place. And François was going to make movies. His penthouse office had suede couches and shiny blond shelves crammed with actual bound scripts and high-tech Japanese equipment. Took a lot of meetings, François did. I took a wonderful meeting with him at "21" and he told me he planned to make a lot of movies. Apparently, he still plans to make a lot of movies. Who doesn't?

And there was the curious case of Molly Ivins, one of the best political reporters and writers ever to come out of Texas. A mainstay at the liberal Austin outpost known as the *Texas Observer*, she long ignored the flattery of *The New York Times* before finally succumbing and becoming a TINY and a *Times*er. But once she climbed on board, trouble started. Maybe she was too big for the *Times*. At least one *Times* editor questioned her loyalty to the American Way of Life, given her previous affiliation with the maybe-radical *Texas Observer*. The *Times* shipped her off to Albany, and then to Denver, and then into cold storage. Molly got her back up and quit and hauled it on back to the Big D to write a column for the *Dallas Times-Herald*.

Nevertheless, there are TINYs who are in hog heaven. Be assured of this: Anyone in New York who is powerful and from Texas does not ever talk about either being powerful or being from Texas. He just goes about his business quietly and before you know it his wallet is $10 million thicker and yours is just sucking wind.

Some Texas–New York priorities are never quite sorted out. *Texas Monthly* hired New York writer James Wolcott to be its movie critic. Apparently, no writer in Texas had ever laid eyes on the silver screen. Conversely, the New York Public Library has installed former University of Texas scholar Vartan Gregorian to ride herd over its miles of stacks. Maybe it all evens out in the end.

Dallasite Shannon Wynne, who runs what seem to be the hippest clubs in the country (clubs such as Nostromo and Tango in Dallas), slips into Manhattan quite often to see what the new downtown clubs are up to. He takes notes. Then he sneaks back to Dallas to go them one better. The Lone Star Café in New York got national publicity because of the iguana sculpture by Texas artist Robert Wade on its roof. Shannon left the Lone Star in the shade when he put Wade's musical frog sculptures on Tango's roof: The Dallas city council went crazy and Tango got international press.

Not long ago, a young Texas executive quietly told me about a deal he had just closed with a Fortune 500 company. The deal will likely never be made public: no glowing press releases or shimmering parties or even a mention in Phil Dougherty's advertising column in the *Times*. The deal? Multi-million dollars' worth of art objects and cultural projects designed to upgrade the company's image. Five years ago, the deal would have been hosannaed with the loudest PR trumpets the company could muster. No longer. Why? Pinstripes ultimately win out over polyester. You don't hustle your balls in public anymore. A lot of this started with LBJ. LBJ hustled his balls in public ("I never trust a man until I've got his pecker in my pocket" and "You're asking the leader of the Western world a chickenshit question like that?" are two fondly remembered LBJ quotes). You just don't do that anymore, unless you want to sound like some peckerwood high school football coach from North West Low Rent, Texas (White Trash Branch), decked out in white patent leathers and red polyesters.

Texans, bless their polyester souls, are slowly grasping the concept that they are living in the twentieth century. They are funny creatures indeed. They're sometimes like a raucous convention of buzzed British, Australian, Irish, and Japanese businessmen visiting a transvestite whorehouse. They try to Texan it out and come out looking just a little bit foolish. It is hard, after all, to wear a vomit-speckled tuxedo with élan. After Six, indeed. But Texans do have a different kind of hitch in their get-along, as Don Meredith likes to say. And when they get outside the

Lone Star State, and especially when they get to New York City, they get real different. Like Sam Houston, who was the ornery president of the Republic of Texas. Whenever he got tired of being a full-time Texan, he used to light out and go live with the Indians in East Texas. Loincloth and all. Squaw and all. He had figured out a simple lesson that not many people have ciphered to this day: Being a full-time Texan is not an easy gig.

It's a lot to live up to. Perhaps the spirit of Sam Houston and Lyndon Johnson, of Sam Rayburn and Billie Sol Estes and John Connally perseveres and endures like Johnson grass growing up through the concrete of Manhattan. I mean, if Tommy Tune can be a certified Texan in New York superstar, then there's hope for us all.

Larry L. King was the last white man to be a professional Texan and to this day he won't reveal how he did it. That was when he was still a "drankin' " kind of man and before he wrote that Texas version of *The Sound of Music* about that petty little cathouse and before he went off to a special camp where Texans learn how to not drink whuskey. He was, though, the prototype for the TINY. The last time I went to a TINY function, Roy Blount, Jr.—by default—ended up acting as most Texan of the TINYs. And he's from Out-of-State. A pitiful state of affairs. It's a hell of a job to fill. Big shoes to step into. Some job description:

WANTED: Male, middle-aged, beer gut, whuskey voice, with endless repertoire of tasteless jokes about women and sex and blacks and Jews and bodily functions and football and Texas A&M; intimate knowledge of LBJ's tasteless jokes about the above; familiarity with the Willie Nelson–Dolly Parton joke. Must claim to have once had a beer with Don Meredith and have a twenty-year-old girlfriend from SMU named Muffin (or Skeeter) whose daddy would kill on sight any beer-gutted professional Texan hosing his daughter. Should owe books to at least three New York publishing houses that are threatening to sue him. If New York law allowed it, he would be one enormous walking bar tab.

He or she is also pretty big in the heart department. If I told you that right now, at 1:30 in the morning, I could call up people whom I have never met and who have never heard of me and drag them out of a warm bed by telling them that I'm a fellow Texan and invoking the name of a fellow Texan and get these people I don't know from Adam to: a) loan me money; b) bring over some chicken soup; c) bring over some bourbon; d) bring themselves over for a party; e) help me out of a sticky job situation; f) get a job (or at least an internship) for my worthless cousin; g) help me with a bad tax problem; h) loan me a Willie Nelson album; and if I told you that all of that is possible and in fact has been done by this writer, well, then, God help me, I am telling you the truth about Texans. About TINYs, anyway.

So what does it all mean? What's the cosmic overview from a TINY perspective? All I can say is that I spent last week back in Austin on the set of a movie that Willie Nelson is doing. It was wonderful. The air was so sweet you could drink it. I had not seen a 360-degree technicolor blue sky in a year. The Tex-Mex and bar-b-q places were incredible. Dinner on a terrace overlooking Lake Travis at sunset was, after years in gray Manhattan, like rediscovering color. I seriously thought about moving back to Austin. Except that condos in Austin cost the same as condos in New York; I could not find a twenty-four-hour newsstand or a twenty-four-hour coffee shop or a twenty-four-hour deli; I got tired of the local newspaper, which is basically nothing but a conduit for the wire services and local advertising; and I got tired of the view of Town Lake, which is dominated by hideous $500,000 concrete-block condos that my Austin friends derisively call the "Beirut Towers" and that in fact do resemble the bombed-out structures in Lebanon. The freeways are as bad as in L.A. I got tired of driving into endless grid-lock on a stupid loop around Austin that was not even there until the damn Yankees started moving into town. Austin was once a walker's paradise, an intellectual settlement set down in the midst of the Phil-istines. It was the only civilized Texas city. Now, New York City is, at least for me.

An Interview With Chet Atkins

Chet Atkins is a hard man to fathom until he struggles through an aimless hour of polite conversation that is meant as a prelude to an interview and suddenly jumps to his feet and leads the way out of his very formal office in the RCA building in Nashville. "C'mon," he says as we're already on the back steps, "let's get out of here. I feel like a damn prisoner."

As is befitting a man who is both guitar legend and country music's praised and cursed prime mover over the past two decades, Atkins is private and introspective to a degree that is almost intimidating. It's not intentional; that's obvious as he stretches out in his Mercedes 450 SEL and cruises through the afternoon streets and talks of this and that: what is Springsteen going to do, he wonders, and what about these Bay City Rollers and what do I think about Monty Python?

It's very apparent that Chet Atkins didn't get where he is by being some kind of know-nothing shitkicker, which was the usual picture of anybody out of Nashville. He came out of the deepest poverty in rural Tennessee; as a child he was so shy as to be almost autistic and as a young adult was fired from job after job, but he still went on to become the best-known guitarist ever and, as RCA's Nashville chief of A&R, one of the most important record executives.

He played rock guitar on the Everly Brothers' hits, signed Roy Orbison, and played on Elvis Presley's sessions as well as Hank Williams's. He has produced or signed or accompanied on records people from Ann-Margret to Al Hirt to Floyd Cramer to Jim Reeves to Eddy Arnold to Red Foley to Dolly Parton to Porter Wagoner to Don Gibson to the Browns to Hank Snow to Jessi Colter to Willie Nelson. His protégé, Jerry Reed, is one of music's hotter guitarists. He signed Waylon Jennings and then dared to try to tell him to get a haircut. It didn't work. He signed Charlie Pride despite dire predictions that a black country singer would mean the end of RCA Records in the C&W market. He broke the country production mold by banning steel and fiddle from sessions and introducing horns and strings. Whether you like it or not, his Nashville Sound made it possible for country music to enter the future. He also, along the way, played with Homer and Jethro, Bill Carlisle, Archie Campbell, Mother Maybelle Carter, and Kitty Wells, and in the past year has cut albums with fellow guitar pioneers Les Paul and Merle Travis.

He's played the Newport Jazz Festival and these days listens mostly to Art Tatum. He's played with Arthur Fiedler and the Boston Pops but still recalls touring with a freak caravan that included the "Human Lodestone" ("a man who could increase his weight so he couldn't be lifted"), a one-armed banjo player, and a man with such short legs that "he could urinate just by lifting one pant leg."

He played the White House, and the autographed picture from JFK is still up in his dining room, near the autographed picture from Paul McCartney and the gold records he produced for Perry Como. George Harrison wrote liner notes for one of his albums, *Chet Atkins Picks on the Beatles*. Merle Travis, one of the greats in guitar history, autographed a picture to him thusly: "My claim to fame is bragging that we're friends. People just don't pick any better."

Now a vice-president of RCA, Atkins divides his time between the office and playing concerts. He was born June 20, 1924, near Luttrell, Tennessee.

Did you always have the aim in life to be what you became: the best-known guitar player in the world, a prolific producer, a major force in the development of country as well as pop music over the past twenty-five years?

I always wanted to be known and respected for the guitar and I wanted to be a superstar. Instead I wound up being a semi-star. But I think in this life you've gotta be careful where you aim because you go right where you aim. I wanted to be known as a good guitarist and that happened. I wanted to be a record producer and that happened. I wanted to be on albums when they first started and that happened. I wanted to sell and that happened. You've just got to use your intelligence and work at it. Man, I came from the worst poverty you can imagine, in Appalachia. I remember malnutrition, I remember being hungry. I said to myself when I was a kid, I'll never be that way again. I guess for me the guitar is the symbol of that.

I hear you never travel without one.

That's right. If I'm somewhere and I don't have one with me, I'll go out and buy one. I might not play it but I want to know it's there. I guess it's like my security blanket. I came from a fifty-acre farm between Luttrell and Corryton. These were whistle stops on the Southern Railway, which went to Middlesboro, Kentucky, which was a health spa. So I was raised between these two little whistle stops back in the holler. My father was a teacher and evangelist-type singer; he would travel around with preachers and sing. I think I got most of my talent from my mother. She could sing and play piano and she was very emotional and my dad wasn't—he was kind of tough and, musically, he was a little mechanical. . . . I had asthma really bad when I was a kid and worked on the farm when I could. My dad and mother separated when I was five or six and she married a guy who could play two or three chords on a guitar. Back along about that time there was a tourist camp over on Highway 11 and me and my brother and stepdad would play over there and put a hat in the corner for people to put loose change in. That was about the first money I ever made—a few cents.

Did you get any music training at all?

I picked up most everything I know—somebody would pass through that knew a chord that I didn't and I would steal it. I remember when I first discovered G in the second position—boy, I *marveled* at that. I didn't know that was possible. I played it for a week.

What was your first electric guitar?

I had an old acoustic Silvertone that's now in the Country Music Hall of Fame. I had an old radio I had sent away to Chicago for and made an amp—really a PA system—and for a pickup I used a contact mike with a clamp where you could attach it to the bridge, and that was my first electric. You know, the stupid thing was we didn't have electricity where I was living.

I used to take it to town, to Columbus—I was living in Georgia with my dad—and take it to the church and play it there. I kept it until I became a professional. It would oscillate and sound like a motorcycle going by.

What were the first songs you heard that impressed you?

Our national anthem was "Wildwood Flower." Everybody played that. But the first country music I was exposed to was Jimmie Rodgers, on records, and my brother played guitar and sang some of the mountain songs, things that were country back then. Jimmie Rodgers was all right but he was a little simple, for my taste. I remember my stepdad used to come in drunk a lot and we had some Blind Lemon Jefferson records, "Matchbox Blues," and he bet me I couldn't play the runs. And I'd play all the runs and he'd get mad 'cause he didn't play them that well. But the first music that ever really excited me was when I got to listening to the radio and I'd hear pop tunes with different chord progressions that I never heard before and harmonies I had never heard before. I worshiped Benny Goodman's sextet and I liked to hear each guy improvise—I didn't like regimentation.

I heard you were fired a lot in the early days.

I never wanted to be a sideman and I always had problems with bands I worked. Back in those days when you worked at a radio station, your value was determined by how much mail you'd pull. I didn't pull a lot of mail because I was experimenting around and playing a lot of what I wanted to hear. I was trying to play a little jazz and I didn't draw mail, so I got fired a lot.

Where did you hear jazz? I wouldn't have thought there'd be much around in the South.

Well, I started in the early Forties on a radio station in Knoxville with a group called the Dixieland Swingsters, and they played a little Charlie Christian kind of jazz. At that time all radio stations had transcription services, so I could lift George Barnes and Les Paul transcriptions out and listen on weekends and at night. That's when I first heard Segovia—that's when I first heard Django Reinhardt.

Did you ever meet Django?

Yeah, I did. I met Django in Chicago in 1946. He played the Civic Center up there with Duke Ellington and I saw the show. He played great—I remember he knocked out all the musicians in the band. And so I went backstage—which took a hell of a lot of courage. I got the only autograph I've ever got in my life. I didn't know until I read his biography that he was illiterate. That's all he ever learned to write. And I've still got it. The only one.

Did you talk to him after that about picking?

He couldn't speak English and I couldn't speak French. Just stood and grinned at him and he grinned back and he knew I was a real fan because he patted me on the back. But that tour was a fiasco for Django. *Time* magazine just chopped him up, made fun of him. They said, here he's gonna come to America and show how to play guitar. They made fun of him and he was just brokenhearted because he really did teach this country how to play guitar. He got on a boat and went back to France. He had an awful lot of drive, Django did in his playing. Hell of a beat. I heard most everything he ever did and I never heard him slow down.

How do you trace over the years the development of your style and how did you become "the world's greatest guitar player and fingerpicker"?

Yeah, and that damn "world's greatest guitar player" is a misnomer. I think I'm one of the best-*known* guitar players in the world, I'll admit to that. But there are so damned many people now who play the style I play and can play their own, and there are so many people who can play better jazz. But I kind of was the evangelist for that style. For fingerpicking, me and Merle. I think me more than him because he wasn't making albums. But . . . my stepdad played with a thumbpick and three fingers—just played rhythm that way, and he would play a bass string and an arpeggio with his fingers. The guy that used to cut my hair played "Spanish Fandango" with his fingers and I learned to do that. I just always loved the effects I could get with my fingers. I never wanted to be a Django, never wanted to be a Les Paul or George Barnes. Back in those days, *everybody* played with a straight pick except a few hillbillies like my stepdaddy who didn't know any better. And I don't know why I loved to do it but I never wanted to play with a straight pick. So when I was about fourteen, I heard Merle on the radio and I didn't know what in the hell he was doing but I knew he was fingerpickin'. I started trying to play like I thought Merle would play and I was playing with a thumb and three fingers. I didn't know he was doing it with a thumb and one finger. And that was luck, see, because if I'd been in Cincinnati and seen him I'da wound up playing *exactly* like him. Later on I met him and he said, how'd you learn to play with three fingers, and I said, hell, I thought that's what *you* were doing.

Back in those days I was kind of ashamed of my picking. But for some reason or other I held on to it because I could always walk in a radio station and get a job.

At what stage in your career did you really kind of settle in your style? Knew you had it under control and that's the way you should play?

Well, the minute I heard Merle I knew that was what I was gonna do. But there was still a lot of limitations to the style. I had to search and search to find a key to play certain songs and some songs I couldn't play at all because I didn't know a lot of chords. I figured out ways to play the melody and the rhythm at the same time, and I learned also if there's a difficult spot where I couldn't play melody and rhythm at the same time, I'd break and make a solo out of that part. But I was very limited. When I first got a job playing solos, I could only play "Maggie," "Bicycle Built for Two," "Bye, Bye Blues," "Seein' Nellie Home." So the boss at the radio station would come down and say, you gotta learn more tunes. And so, to keep my job, I searched to find tunes that I could play and I'd use different tunings—tune the E string down to D and play tunes in D sometimes instead of C to get the range I wanted. But it was trial and error. I just had a damn guitar in my hands sixteen hours a day and I experimented all the time. That's the way I learned to do harmonics—I saw steel players doing a similar thing.

One day I thought, I wonder what would happen if I played a harmonic and then a pure note, so I had my arpeggios worked out like that and I just strummed along. But I always played most every tune I played in sharps 'cause I had to have those open strings. I learned to play "Yankee Doodle" and "Dixie" at the same time—I don't know why. That almost run me crazy.

Who on radio and records were the biggest influences before you heard Travis?

George Barnes and Les Paul. See, Les and my brother were working together and I'd hear Les do all that fancy finger work and I'd think, what the hell is he doing? And my brother would write me to explain how Les did some of that.

Didn't Les give you a guitar?

No, my brother gave me a Gibson L-10 guitar that Les had had designed, and that was one of the happiest days of my life. I never met Les until I was working in Springfield, Missouri. This guy was watching the show through the glass—a dressed-up, nice-looking fellow—and I thought, well, I will knock him out, you know, I'll impress him. So I played a Les Paul chorus and played a lot of fast runs and he came in and introduced himself and said, I opened up this goddamn station in 1931, or something—you know, I was so embarrassed because I played one of his choruses. So he thought I was a thief, I guess, and I was to a certain extent—but he was too because he couldn't play a damn note without Django.

Before you went full time with RCA and you were still playing sessions, didn't you work several with Hank Williams?

Yeah, those were easy. Hank had an awfully big ego. Tried to write a song every time he picked up a guitar. When I started recording with him, his style had already been set. They used that dead-string guitar and that's what I did for him. He wasn't in shape a lot. Sam McGee used to say he was so skinny his ass rattled like a sack of carpenter nails when he walked. The last session I did with him was "I'll Never Get Out of This World Alive." And I thought, how ironic. He did it and then went over and sat down and was so weak that I thought that song was prophetic. And it was. When I first came down here I was anxious to meet him because of "Lovesick Blues," which is the best damn country record ever made. I wrote a little back then and Hank said let's go out to the house and try to write one. I was awe-struck being around him. But we finally knocked out a couple—I've forgotten 'em. But he'd come up real close to you and say, "Listen to this, hoss," and he'd sing "Jambalaya" or "Hey, Good Lookin'," and that bourbon breath would knock you down and he'd say, "How you like that?" "Great, Hank." He'd say, "You damn right it is."

Didn't you play on Elvis's first RCA sessions? How did that come about? Were you then head of RCA Nashville?

Well, I moved here in 1950—I came in as third guitarist with the Carter Sisters and Mother Maybelle—and I was featured on the Grand Ole Opry for fifty dollars a week. Steve Sholes—remember there was no Music Row here then, it hadn't started—but Steve Sholes would come in with portable equipment and record acts here. We'd rent a garage somewhere or something and set up this portable equipment and he would call me a few days beforehand and tell me he wanted to record Pee Wee King or Don Gibson or this one or that one. So I would hire the musicians and we'd get in the studio—I've always been kind of domineering around musicians, so I'd tell everybody what to play.

So Steve Sholes more or less picked you as his man in the field?

I guess he saw that I had a little talent and he kept saying how he'd love to build a studio in Nashville and have me run it. This was around 1952–53 and I didn't pay any attention; I thought it was too good to be true. Then about 1955–56, RCA built a little old block building down here. And what happened was that Mr. Sholes discovered Elvis Presley and talked RCA into spending $40,000 for Elvis. Well, all of a sudden Mr. Sholes was a big man in the company and he didn't have time to come to Nashville to record. Back then we would cover a lot of pop hits. We would do "Sincerely" with Johnny and Jack and "Oh Baby Mine," and we'd cover a pop hit and have a country hit on it. Mr. Sholes kept getting busier, so by and by I had everybody and was working sixteen hours a day and making hit records left and right and getting a few thousand a year for it. But I loved what I was doing.

Back to Elvis—what was that like, cutting with him?

Well, I hired the musicians. I got Floyd Cramer on piano and Hank Garland and Scotty Moore and myself on guitar and Buddy Harman on drums and the Jordanaires to sing backup. First I tried to hire the Speer Family, a religious group, but I couldn't get them. This was for "Heartbreak Hotel" and "I Want You, I Need You, I Love You." I set the session for the afternoon and he came in with pink trousers with blue stripes and he was real nice. He'd yessir and no-sir you to death. He was very respectful, a little too much. He was singing and split his pants. One of his boys went to get him another pair and he threw the split pair in the corner. A girl who was working for the Methodist Publishing Company in the same building asked me what to do with the pants and I told her you better hang onto them, that boy's gonna be famous. She said naw and six months later there she was on "I've Got a Secret" with Elvis's pants.

What was the session itself like?

I would offer suggestions on how to do a song and he would welcome them. I played rhythm. He had Lamar with him, a big, fat boy, and Lamar would say, "That's fantastic, Elvis. That'll sell three million. Play that sumbitch again." Lamar finally got up to saying, "That'll sell seven million," and I thought, yeah, he's probably right.

What other sessions did you play with Elvis?

I really don't remember. I played on "Are You Lonesome Tonight?" after he got out of the Army. But I finally quit working sessions with Elvis because he started doing night sessions and I wanted to be home at night with my family.

When you were producing someone like Jim Reeves, were you consciously trying for a pop sound?

We were consciously trying for pop sales and we used violins and intentionally left out the steel guitar and fiddle, because at that time you couldn't get a record played pop if it had steel on it. That only happened a few years ago when Dylan came in with steel—people started accepting it. And fiddles, scratchy fiddle . . . couldn't even get pop play with a fiddle till, I guess, the Rolling Stones did "Honky Tonk Women" ["Country Honk"]. So then the kids would buy those records. They're like sheep, just follow whatever they think is the in thing. But I always tried, like with Reeves, I tried to make good records that had a pretty sound. The only playing I have to go by is what I like, and luckily I'm kind of square—and if I like a song it's pretty sure that the public will, because I'm square.

So we had a lot of success and the Nashville Sound evolved—it just evolved like the Grand Ole Opry—there was no planning to try to get a different sound. I've always felt that any records you make you gotta get a hook in it somewhere and get something different. We weren't sitting down and saying, okay, let's start a Nashville sound or anything like that.

Do you think it would have happened or would have happened as fast if you hadn't been the one in the position? You really changed the course of it.

I hear that all the time but I can't see it. If I were sitting off looking at it maybe I could see it. But I've always been involved in all kinds of music. I've been playing—tried to play—a little classical guitar for twenty years. And I was a country musician. And I was into jazz a little—fifties jazz, what I consider to be a great era of jazz—so you know I could use little chord progressions and those things that I've heard and do it in a country way to where it wasn't offensive. I think that is the great advantage I had.

How did the Floyd Cramer piano sound come about? That was a big change for Nashville and even for pop with his "Last Date."

Well, I love things that are different. Floyd Cramer—there was something so damned different from what anybody'd done and we did it and it changed the whole damned music business. It really headed it in a new direction, and it *was* country, too, and I'm proud of that. And I didn't do it. It was Don Robinson who came up with that style, but I beat Floyd over the head till he learned how to do it.

What happened to Robinson?

He's still around. He just never tried to do anything with that style. He would send me demos all the time of that stuff and, oh, they just tore me up because it was such a fresh, new sound. He sent a demo on "Please Help Me, I'm Falling" and I cut it with Hank Locklin and it was a smash hit. Don should hate me but I don't think he does. I think he understands. I just loved the style so much and Floyd was my piano player. . . .

When I first started running the operation here, I was scared. I was scared to hire musicians, scared to spend money—scared to hire voices 'cause it cost too much and I didn't know anything about economics. Finally, I'd been in there a few months and hadn't done much and I thought, the hell with it, I'll spend the money and make great records and either get fired or sell some records. So I became my own man when we made "Can't Stop Loving You" with Don Gibson and "Oh, Lonesome Me." He sent me a demo and had a bass drum on it going boom, boom. So we put a mike on that drum and an equalizer and we turned it up so we could hear it—hell, nobody ever heard a bass drum on country records and I think that was part of the charm of "Oh, Lonesome Me." So after that we made a lot of them.

Haven't you since apologized for the Nashville Sound?

I've said that I hope country music doesn't completely lose its identity—and I apologized for anything I did in taking it too far uptown, which I sometimes did because we were just trying to sell records. To sell records you gotta surprise the public, give them something different all the time, because there's only so many directions you can go—strings, horns, or go backwards and do it the way we used to do it twenty years ago. The point I was making was that if it was *my* fault that country music had moved farther uptown, well, I was sorry. But I want to sell records, too.

Why did you cut back on producing so much—just tired?

It's such hard work now because of the sixteen track—I keep telling Les Paul I'm gonna slip up behind him and kick his ass, because it's all his fault. You know, he's the one that talked Ampex into building that three-track, then eight-track. Back when I was having so much success, it was easy because you did it all in the studio, put it on two tracks, shipped it to New York and that was it. Maybe it had a few mistakes—maybe the sound could have been better—but it had all that spontaneity in it. And when I'm making records I never worry about a bad note in the band or anything. It doesn't matter a damn to the public. If a guy's singing sour or something or out of tune all through the record, it will turn people off. But you're selling *emotion*, and that's all that matters. You gotta be careful in a studio because you got certain musicians who will work thirty minutes on finding the right chord, and that's not important, it really isn't.

What's your method of being a producer, handling both the technical and musical aspects of it? In other words, can you write a chapter about how to be a producer?

I think the one thing that you gotta have to be a producer is the ability to spot a good song. And then there are a lot of other qualities, such as programming the right song for the right artist. But the main damn ingredient is knowing the song. And then if you have any other talent— if you're a musician, good at arranging and all that—that's a help. But I think one of the most important things is enthusiasm. Some of the greatest producers I know are guys that don't know a damn thing about music, can't hum you a tune, but they're so enthusiastic. That's a quality I've never had because I'm a bit of a pessimist. I know that you can make a great record but that doesn't mean it's gonna be a hit. You've gotta have the sales, the emotion, and the exposure. And so you got a lot of strikes against you and the odds are that it *won't* be a hit.

Did you ever count up how many gold records you played on or produced?

No, I haven't. I don't think about the past that way too much—'cause hell, there's always another one. I've done well, not as well as some people, but I think I did exceptionally well, considering I was handling about thirty-eight to forty artists. Just run 'em in and do four songs a session, not really spend a lot of time on each record.

How did you know that electronics would have so much to do with music when you were just starting?

I didn't really. When I first started playing seriously, electric guitar was just starting. So it was a case of wanting to sound like somebody you heard on the radio, and the persons I heard of course were Les Paul and George Barnes. They played electric guitar and, you know, it was a bigger, nicer sound. I just wanted to play an instrument that could be heard, that would project much better than acoustic. I've always known that there was a lot that could be done with guitar and always had ambitions to play the guitar like Boots Randolph plays sax—the kids do it now but I can't stand all the volume. And that's the direction it's gone in the past few years. You can get more emotion that way, can sustain and change the decay of a note, and do it with pedals, fuzz, and sustaining gadgets.

You seem to shy away from adding gadgets—the simpler the guitar the better?

Well, I do because I think people appreciate purity. I think gadgets come and go but purity is what will be remembered—like a Bill Monroe or Doc Watson, to me that's real good and pure, and that'll be good years from now. I think a guitar is meant to sound like a guitar and I can't understand why people try to make it sound like another instrument. Gadgets are fine behind a singer, which I do once in a while. I use a phaser for a chorus or two. You need to, because, in an hour, electric guitar gets a little old—I like to change, use an Echoplex onstage, which enhances the sound a little bit. But I've always wished, if I could go back and do things over, I think I would probably be more of a purist. I would just study guitar and play tunes more related to *me*—like tunes from the South, country songs—and I would try to be more a folk artist than country artist because I think you have more longevity.

What would be your advice to young players?

I think a person playing guitar needs to read some books or get lessons from a good instructor at first. They just need someone to explain to them the proper use of the fingers of the left hand, whether they play with fingers or picks. I've known a lot of guitar players down through the years that were really restricted when they played with three fingers. It's really a four-fingered instrument—and five when you use your thumb—and some guys figure it out without lessons; they figure out the proper fingering. I didn't discover that for quite a few years. I didn't use my little finger a lot and it really held me back. But that's very important. Tuning is important. A lot of players get lazy and play a little out of tune. That's not necessary. If you're gonna play, I think you should have respect for your instrument and play in tune. It's so much easier to learn now. See, when I was a kid, there was nobody to listen to except some neighbor that played three chords. Now you can buy *Guitar Player* magazine and all kinds of instruction books, see somebody do it on TV, hear it on a record and slow it down. So it's a lot easier. When I was playing I was kind of in a wilderness; I was just groping in the dark.

What's your favorite guitar?

Past month I've been playing a prototype of a solid body that Gretsch is going to put out. I've been wanting to get into a solid body for years but Gretsch couldn't make one that I liked. They finally made this one. They call it the High Roller and I like it a lot.

What do you want in a guitar?

First I like good action. Because I pull strings a lot and I play harmonics a lot, which means you have to bar and pull notes with the other fingers. And I like a guitar that sustains very well because I play in the high register a lot and I like simplicity as far as controls go. I soup 'em up a little—maybe file the nut down if the strings are too high for the nut. And if they have bad frets I'll refret them. I'll also change the capacitor so that when you throw the switch it doesn't knock the highs off too much. Mainly I like a guitar that will tune up well. But I have several great classic guitars and I have one that Mr. Hascal Haile of Tompkinsville, Kentucky, built for me. It's kind of a flamenco guitar.

You practice every day?

I try to but I don't. I'll practice for three or four days all day and then go maybe a month without practicing. But I try to at least strum—if I don't strum a guitar every day it bothers me.

Basically, how do you describe your technique?

Well, the technique I play is pseudoclassical, which came about from just experimentation, 'cause I never had heard a classical guitar player. I just—to get a percussive effect on the rhythm—I mute the strings with the left hand sometimes. Most classic guitar players do that too, for effect. The only difference is that I use a thumb-pick, which has advantages and disadvantages. The main disadvantage is that you can't change the tone like you can with the flesh on your finger. With your thumb you can play with your nail and get a harsh sound or with the flesh of your thumb you get a pretty, soft sound. The disadvantage to that is that I can play a lot of fast runs with a thumb-pick and nails, which is a lot harder to do without a thumb-pick—impossible almost, because you have to get your hand extended out from the strings when you play with your nail. It's just not easy to play fast three-finger runs.

What about tunings?

I believe in playing most everything in a standard tune. I think that's the reason that Spanish guitar is as popular as it is and accepted as a legitimate musical instrument. Because it has a standard tuning. I tune an E string down to D a lot, like a lot of people. I also tune the A string down to G and the E string down to D, which is similar to playing an A where you have two open bass strings—you get a wider tonal range. I play a few tunes in a D major tuning mainly because the fella who wrote 'em, wrote 'em in that tuning—John D. Loudermilk; he's a fine composer. When I was a kid all you could buy was a set of guitar strings.

People didn't know anything about gauge then. You didn't buy a string by gauge. What I would do was I would use a first string for a second, second string for a third and so forth—I did that for years because I found that the guitar had a much prettier sound if the strings weren't too tight and it would sustain a lot better, and for a first string I would go buy a banjo thumb string, which must have been about a nine or ten gauge. I had to make up all my sets that way by buying banjo strings.

Do you still wear gloves to protect your hands every time you go out?

I do a lot and always in winter. I haven't had a broken nail in a year. My nails aren't strong anyway, and you get out in the cold weather you can just bump 'em against anything and they break.

Have you tried taking gelatin to strengthen them or using coating?

I'm too lazy to take gelatin and I thought there might be side effects from that. But I put polish on before a performance and then take it off. But the glove really saves my nails. I file my nails a lot, too. You get a little rough place on a nail, you need to smooth it off right away or it'll break. Sidewalks and the sides of buildings are really good to file your nails on. People on the street always say, "What in the hell are you doing?"

Have you thought about insurance for your hands?

[*Laughs.*] That's a little vain. But if you lead a normal life, you don't have to worry. I use 'em when I need 'em. But I stay away from saws. They're dangerous.

What about hand-crusher shakes? How do you avoid those?

I get those a lot. But I get mad at myself because if you watch it they can't hurt you. You grab their hand first and jam it up with their thumb so they can't hurt you. Some people really have very strong grips and don't think but are going around mutilating people.

You're one of the few guitarists whose fingers you can't hear squeak.

I don't know why that is. Unless it's that I always rub my fingers around my nose and get a little oil on them. Also, I don't have real thick calluses, which will make you squeak. But you know I'd love to be like Segovia and play with all that power and squeak, but he's the strongest player there's ever been. As far as technique, I never really practice scales or anything. I never tried to be real smooth or clean.

When you're cutting a song yourself, do you ordinarily improvise as you go along or will you go by a stock chart?

When I'm recording a tune? Sometimes I will have learned the tune off the music but most of the time I will just learn it off the tape. If it's a new tune I'll learn it off the tape by ear and check the music to see that I've got it right. And then I try to change the chords or phrasing to a better way. I try to always get some surprises in, even if it's a standard. I try to play some substitution chords here and there. When you're a soloist like I am, it's hard to play a damned thirty-two bar tune for two and a half minutes and make it interesting. You've got to modulate, do something, give it a little different treatment. It's easier when you have a band—let somebody have a chorus. But you know I get out onstage— I play three or four concerts a month with symphonies and by myself and get out there and I haven't been practicing the tunes—and think, *what in the hell* am I doing here? In front of all these people I'm gonna embarrass myself!

Are there any rock guitarists that you kind of liked their work, paid attention to?

Yeah, I like some of them. Duane Allman knocked me out before he got famous. He used to hang around with my daughter a little. And I went with her one night to hear him play—I think he was playing better then than when he got on records. He was playing with great coordination—slow blues, then he'd put in a lot of fast notes and they'd all come out on the beat, and I admire that in a guitarist, that quality. I liked Jimi Hendrix—he played interesting sounds, all the gadgets and everything. And Albert King is one of the greatest I think. Lonnie Mack is a fine blues picker. Roy Buchanan is my favorite of all those guys. I think he plays *so* tasty and with such a great beat. He's my favorite really. And jazz, I like Lenny Breau. But you know, you hear some great choruses on record and you hear some bad stuff, too. It's like our country records—there's a lot of trash out there but a lot of good stuff, too. I like the guitar on Linda Ronstadt's record, "When Will I Be Loved"—Andrew Gold, that guy is terrific. It's an Allman Brothers type of thing, of course. I think the greatest chorus last year on record was in "Midnight at the Oasis"—Amos Garrett.

When was it that McCartney was here?

He was nice—when he first came to town he said he wanted to meet me. He's the nicest kid. He was telling us how they wrote "Yesterday"— that was "Scrambled Eggs" first, that was the title. Well anyway, he's telling about the first time he ever tried to write. His dad had written a tune—he remembered his dad and uncle trying to write words to it—

and Paul played it for me—and it's a pretty good little tune, kind of a "Darktown Strutter's Ball" tune—and I said, "You know, why don't you record that sometime for your dad, it would be a great present." I told him I did that for my dad and he sure appreciated it. So Paul called me one night and I got some musicians together—it was kind of a Dixieland sound—and they recorded it and released it in England. It was called "Strolling in the Park With Eloise," and me and Floyd Cramer played on it.

But he knew a lot of the stuff. He'd ask me, did you play on this with the Everly Brothers? I played guitar on all their records, most of their hits.

The Everlys—how did you and they determine what kind of sound they needed?

Oh, we just experimented around. Floyd would suggest that I play a lick or something or they would or I would come up with something. But Don [Everly] and I were both big on Bo Diddley and what a great sound that was. I'd shown the Everlys to Mr. Sholes at RCA and he wasn't impressed with them. And they tried all over town really—they were hitchhiking around town. I felt sorry for them. So the minute Don got a recording contract, I remember I saw him in the alley down behind the Opry and he said we're gonna record for Cadence and will you play some Bo Diddley, and I said *right!* So we did "Bye Bye Love," I guess it was. First time we did the Bo Diddley thing. We played different chords where Bo just played the same two or three chords, and you know that's something that hadn't been done on a pop record or kid record until that time. But it kind of disintegrated after a while; there was fighting between the publisher and Archie Bleyer [their producer], and the kids couldn't get along with Archie or the publisher, and it kind of fell apart—it was sad. It got so the sessions weren't any fun to work because of all the bickering between all these people. It got so I didn't even want them to call me when they were gonna record because they couldn't agree on anything. I made an album with them though, a couple of years ago, called *Pass the Chicken and Listen*—good album, didn't sell any, but one of the best they've done in recent years. I think Don and Phil would still be big if they would just switch over to country like so many of the old rock stars are doing—Crash Craddock, Twitty, and those guys. But they won't do it. And of course they're not together now and I talked to them about it but they want to stay in the groove they're in. I played on most of the hits. But they didn't record an awful lot.

Roy Orbison—did you sign him to RCA?

Yeah, I signed him up. He made some records—he'd been on Sun—had a couple of records did pretty good—"Ooby Dooby"—and we made a few records; nothing happened. And he left and of course he had a lot of success after he left us for Monument. He's one of the ones that didn't make it with me. He says he thinks it's because he kind of stood in awe of me and all the people over here and when he went out on a little label he could express himself a lot better. I suppose that is true. When he got away from us he had a lot more confidence in his ability.

In the Sixties, did the rise of the Beatles and Rolling Stones cause you any concern or change the thinking of record company executives?

Yeah, it did. But Elvis had already had the greatest effect, of course. When he came on, some people had the idea that the trick was to have a heavier drumbeat and then you would sell like Elvis. That wasn't true. We went through a period there when country music was at its weakest, because we were floundering, wondering what to do. We finally found out the thing to do was just to stay country because the fans were still out there and would still buy the music. But for a few years we did fumble around trying to grab some of the rock sales. All that had really settled out by the time the Beatles came along, and I think they just influenced us to make better records, find better songs and better arrangements and so forth.

Do you think it was inevitable that what's being called progressive country is coming from outside Nashville by people not considered country?

I guess it was because of mass communication, but I didn't expect it so soon. Mr. Sholes always told me that music would get closer and closer together, all the different forms, until it finally amalgamated and became one music. And it sure is moving in that direction. I hate to see it happen, but hell, it's almost that way now. You know, you listen to the Eagles— "Lyin' Eyes," that's a great country record. They could be from Nashville. The only thing that separates them is geography, and I think it's more of them borrowing from us than us borrowing from them.

Does it ever bother you that you don't have a young audience?

I've always been a semi-star. My audience gets older and older. But once in a while I'll read *Guitar Player* magazine and some kid will say he listens to my records and it makes me feel good. Yeah, it bothers me. 'Cause I *wanna* appeal to the young people too.

What would you consider now to be your greatest failures, successes?

I don't know—my greatest—hell, you know I just feel so lucky to be able to make a living picking a guitar. I never dreamed it would happen because we were so far back in the sticks. I used to daydream, I could hear people introducing me, saying, "Here he is, the world's greatest guitar player," but never really thought it would happen. I don't know why I didn't just take a straight pick and play like George Barnes or Les Paul. But you know, I *never* had any desire to do that—I wanted to be me. Somebody'd come up and say, "Les Paul, Merle Travis, George Barnes"—oh, it would make me sick and furious. I just never wanted to sound like them. I wanted to sound like *me*, 'cause I guess my intelligence told me that's the only way I'd ever get anywhere. So I would copy licks from pianos and I didn't know the limitations of the guitar, but I knew I could fool around and figure out how to do most any lick with my fingers where I couldn't with a straight pick. I just had that burning desire to play pretty tunes on a guitar and I worked my ass off to do it. But I've—I'm proud of what I've done. I've spread the gospel of fingerpicking, and when I was playing guitar nobody did it and I first started—and now the *whole fucking world* is playing finger style. Even if they play with a pick, they reach down with their fingers and break a few arpeggios and stuff, and I'm proud of that and I think some day, some writer will remember. Kids forget—they say, Chet Atkins, who in the hell is that, you know. I think when history is written in the music business, somebody will remember and realize I did that and I'm proud of it.

Phil Ochs, Troubadour, Dead

The last sad chapter in singer/songwriter Phil Ochs's up-and-down life story ended April 9, 1976, when he hanged himself in his sister's house in Far Rockaway, Queens. Ochs was thirty-five years old.

Although Ochs's clever, biting lyrics earned him fame during the Sixties as the troubadour of the New Left, his musical career had been ailing for years and he had, according to family and friends, grown increasingly despondent. "It blew everyone away," said Doug Weston, owner of the Troubadour folk club in L.A. and a longtime friend of Ochs. "He had a great many friends, but he felt estranged from them. Phil was a very romantic person and romantic people are easily disillusioned, and when that happens it can be very deep."

Last December, Ochs moved from Manhattan to his sister Sonny Tanzman's house in Queens. In Manhattan he had virtually lived in the streets, moving from one hotel to another or staying with friends, who were concerned about his drinking. When he moved out to Queens, he stopped drinking and spent much of his time playing cards with his sister's three children. According to friends, Ochs had been trying, off

and on, to write again, but had lost his confidence. He talked of myriad projects, mostly unrealized: producing a recording session with a young Dylan soundalike named Sammy Walker; organizing a Save New York City benefit; opening a nightclub in SoHo and going into movie production.

Ochs's last real public performance was October 23, 1975, at a birthday party for Mike Porco, owner of Gerde's Folk City, the scene of Phil's early triumphs. During an evening of all-star sets by the likes of Dylan, Joan Baez, and Jack Elliott, Ochs (wearing Dylan's hat) sang a poignant—if hoarse—set of "Jimmy Brown the Newsboy," "There You Go," "Too Many Parties," "The Blue and the Gray," and a moving version of Dylan's "Lay Down Your Weary Tune" that drew praise from its composer.

That party amounted to a dress rehearsal for Dylan's Rolling Thunder Revue, but when the Revue pulled out of town four days later, Ochs was not on the bus. Close friends said that Phil had "understood" that there would be a place for him on the tour but that the invitation was never tendered because of his "unpredictable behavior" and drinking, and that he understood that, too. The whole Rolling Thunder business stirred controversy even in death: "Phil Ochs was drowned in the Thunder" was how New York's WBAI summed up its feelings during its radio tribute.

Ochs and Dylan had had a stormy relationship over the years. They met in the early Sixties when they were the center of a tight circle— including Dave Van Ronk, David Cohen/Blue, Tom Paxton, and Eric Andersen—that hung around the offices of *Broadside*, the mimeographed topical song publication. Dylan was clearly the star, while Ochs was clearly number two; but Ochs believed he could go just as far as Dylan. Dylan could be cruel about this competition: When Dylan first played "Can You Please Crawl Out Your Window" for Ochs, Phil said he didn't think it would be a hit. Dylan turned on him, ordering Ochs out of the limousine they were riding in with the parting shot, "You're not a folksinger; you're just a journalist." Ochs later laughed about the incident to Dylan biographer Tony Scaduto: "He wasn't used to being criticized." Still, it marked the end of their friendship. Ochs saw Dylan at a house in Los Angeles and Dylan started screaming abuses at him. Ochs left and broke out in hives. "I think he's clinically insane," he told writer Jules Siegel. "If I didn't admire him so much, I'd have to hate him. In fact, maybe I do hate him."

During the past two years, after Ochs moved back to New York from Los Angeles, he and Dylan came to something of a truce. Ochs helped organize the 1974 Madison Square Garden tribute to Salvador Allende at which Dylan appeared. Then, not long after *Blood on the Tracks* came out, they ran into each other on MacDougal Street and Ochs chided Dylan for getting away from topical writing with a gentle "*Blood*'s not good enough, Bob." At the time of Ochs's death, Dylan was in Florida rehearsing for the Southern swing of his Rolling Thunder tour. A friend who talked briefly with him said Dylan was "shaken" by the suicide, but would have no statement to make.

Phil Ochs was born in El Paso, Texas, on December 19; grew up in New York; was graduated from Staunton Military Academy in Virginia; then entered Ohio State University in the late Fifties. He spent his first two years there as a non-major. Then Ochs was jailed for fifteen days in Florida on a vagrancy rap, and it was there that he decided to become a writer. Back at Ohio State, he declared himself a journalism major and began publishing a little radical sheet called *The Word*, in which he wrote that Fidel Castro (together with John F. Kennedy, Ochs's major political influences) was the greatest figure in the western hemisphere in the twentieth century. The hostile reaction to this remark brought Ochs his first disillusionment with journalism.

At the same time, his roommate, Jim Glover, gave him a guitar and Ochs started writing songs. They formed a folk duo called the Sun-downers and dropped out of school, working bars in Cleveland for a while before Ochs split for New York City. He landed right in the middle of the *Broadside* crowd, writing topical songs (he didn't call them protest songs) with the best of them.

Mike Porco, whose Folk City was a buzzing center of activity, remembered Ochs dropping in for hootenanny nights. Porco booked him for his first professional gig, August 6, 1962, at Folk City. "He wasn't an excellent singer," Porco said, "but you could listen to the words. Next to Dylan, he was the biggest draw."

"He was fantastic back then," David Blue recalled. "He was drawing on all that political energy. He had it all plotted out, how both careers would go—his politics and his music. He showed me graphs for the next six months, how the rallies would go, how the records would sell."

The peak of the political music movement came at Newport in the summer of 1963 when Ochs, Dylan, Pete Seeger, Paxton, and Baez held "broadsides"—workshops on civil rights and banning the bomb. Kennedy's assassination changed things: Dylan drifted toward rock and told Ochs his writing was "bullshit, because politics is bullshit." Ochs was unconvinced. His first album, *All the News That's Fit to Sing*, came in early 1964 and featured "Talking Vietnam" and "Talking Cuban Crisis." Less than a year later *I Ain't Marching Anymore* was released and the title song, "Draft Dodger Rag," and "Here's to the State of Mississippi" (revised after Watergate days to "Here's to the State of Nixon"), firmly established Ochs as the leading protest singer/songwriter. Dylan was denounced by rad-libs for abandoning protest, and *Sing Out!* proclaimed Ochs his successor.

Jerry Rubin said Ochs's music "expressed the political feeling of our generation. His guitar was always there at the service of the people. His death robs the Sixties' political people of their voice.

"I saw Phil four days before he died and he seemed in real psychic pain, he seemed to no longer have a cause—there was no reason for him to live anymore. He had often talked about suicide—he once asked me if how you died connected with what happened to you after death. I tried to get him into therapy or yoga, but he just wouldn't help himself. What more can I say? He was so tied to political changes that when that spirit went down, he went down with it."

Donovan, a protest contemporary of Ochs, agreed with Rubin's assessment. "Phil was an intense boy who seemed to be trapped in a pre-'64 radical stance and didn't transpose his work into what you might call the flower-power movement. He remained a hard-nosed radical." He remembered the last night he saw Ochs, at a party in Donovan's honor at Tommy Smothers's. He was "completely out of proportion—with the press, agents, and the whole Hollywood schmaltz." Donovan said that "Phil didn't necessarily love me that night; he thought all folks who made money off folk songs and didn't feed the world were crazy. He didn't realize that we'd begun to love the world to death instead of bombing it to death, that the children were the future and the radical stance had to go. . . . "

His third album, *Phil Ochs in Concert*, got as high as 149 on the *Billboard* chart in 1966, and "There but for Fortune," which appeared on the album, became a hit for Joan Baez in 1965. The next year he produced his finest album, *Pleasures of the Harbor*, proving he still had the deadly sting of satire in his pen with "Outside of a Small Circle of Friends," though the title song was a study in lyric gentleness.

Tape from California (1968) and *Rehearsals for Retirement* (1969) received less notice than their predecessors. The latter album's cover was a picture of Ochs superimposed on his tombstone.

"After Chicago in 1968," said his brother Michael, "things began to fall apart for him." David Blue agreed: "Phil was totally a child of the Sixties. He was a political animal and that political energy was his only source. When that started to go, he started to wither."

As his popularity waned, Ochs had one last inspiration: he put on a gold lamé suit and played rock 'n' roll at Carnegie Hall in 1970. There was a bomb scare during the show, he had to win over a very hostile audience, he badly cut his right hand when he angrily broke into the box office, but he thought the whole affair was fantastic. A&M recorded the concert but released it only in Canada as *Gunfight at Carnegie Hall*. "That was the big turning point in his life," David Blue said. "He believed in that record so much and A&M wouldn't put it out. I heard it; it was good. He really felt let down." Mike Ochs disagreed: "Jerry Moss [A&M's president] kept him on the roster to the end. No matter how crazy he was, whenever he had an idea Moss would listen and just ask how much money he needed."

Throughout the Sixties, said former manager Arthur Gorson, Ochs seriously thought he would be assassinated, he was so politically volatile. "He thought he was risking his life by singing. When he finally realized he *wasn't* in danger, he got depressed because he felt he wasn't politically relevant anymore."

He began to run dry. In a tasteless move, A&M once sent out buttons that read, "Inspire Phil Ochs." Ochs wrote a half-dozen pieces for the *Los Angeles Free Press*, including one on the death of Bruce Lee. He traveled extensively, going to Chile with Jerry Rubin, to Australia, and to Africa, where his vocal chords were permanently damaged when he was mugged in Kenya.

His last big public appearance was at the War Is Over rally in Central Park on May 11, 1975. He sang "The War Is Over" before 50,000 people and it was a touching moment—reality had finally caught up with his ten-year-old song and it was pathetically clear that antiwar songs and singers were relics from the past.

Ochs went downhill fast after that. He played four shows for Porco at Folk City July 30 and 31, but some customers at the last show complained of Ochs's drunkenness and a few asked Porco for their money back. He drifted, drinking, staying in cheap hotels or with friends in SoHo.

He turned up in September at the Chelsea Hotel, registered under the name "John Butler Train," perhaps a play on John Wayne, one of his favorite media heroes. As Train, Ochs was charged with assaulting a woman friend in New York and was arrested for drunkenness in L.A.

"He got a raw deal," said Barbara London, one of his SoHo friends. "I saw him sleeping in the street. He *was* savable and the people who could've helped him didn't seem to want to. Now they're going to have a big benefit."

A tribute concert has been planned for May 28 at Felt Forum, with half the proceeds going to Phil's daughter Meegan, twelve (who has been living in California with Phil's estranged wife, Alice), and half to charity. No performers had been definitely named at press time, though Dylan, Baez, Seeger, and Lennon were mentioned.

The Sunday before he died, Ochs stopped by Folk City for a tequila sunrise. "He looked pretty heavy," said Porco, "and I said, 'Phil, you're not losing weight.' He said, 'I'm not doin' nothin', I can't lose weight.' When Phil was on a bender, he would do all the talking, but when he was sober, he was very shy, wouldn't use a curse word. I said, 'Phil, have you been writing anything?' He said, 'No, Mike, I haven't been doin' nothin', just takin' a rest. I haven't got the head right now to write. Maybe one of these days.' I said, 'How's the stomach, you gettin' better?' He said, 'I went to the doctor, but I'm not perfect yet.' I said, 'Well, Phil, you care for another one?' He said, 'No, I have to meet somebody, but maybe I'll come back.' He smiled—he had one of the nicest smiles. He walked out and that was the last I ever saw of him."

Phil Ochs was cremated the day after he died, in accordance with his wishes. There was no service, in accordance with his family's wishes.

Part Two

THE NOTORIOUS

Chapter 5

Pride

Jerry Lee Lewis and the Elvis Demon

The Elvis demon came over him after he lost count of the number of drinks he had knocked back in the dim recesses of Bad Bob's Vapors, the cavernous supper club and watering hole out on East Brooks Road that is his favorite Memphis haunt. He was hunkered down at the ninety-foot-long bar, under the Vapors' dusky red overhead lights, which barely pierced the vast smoky reaches of the place. The sound of Elvis came at him again and again. Was it the phone or the jukebox or the demon murmuring to him? Elvis's voice, silky and insistent, was calling to him, calling to Jerry Lee, calling to the only legitimate pretender to the throne. The demon whispered, "Come to me, I need you, I need Jerry Lee. Come to Graceland. Elvis is in trouble. Elvis needs Jerry Lee. For nobody else understands the demands of the kingdom and the power of rock 'n' roll."

Jerry Lee had been swilling V.O. straight up—Coke on the side, please, Killer—since mid-afternoon with a series of Vapors regulars. "Buy you a drank, Killer?" "Three dranks, Killer?" He had never had a shortage of friends to drink with in Memphis. And plenty of them were quick to offer the pills and powders that fueled Memphis rock 'n' roll. Plenty of drinking and doping buddies to empathize with Jerry Lee's rotten luck over his long, ill-starred career in Elvis's shadow: "Killer, you was screwed! You shoulda been the King! They jacked you over!"

That November night in 1976, Jerry Lee knew he was making a mistake but just couldn't stop himself. After all that V.O. and Coke and God only knew what else, he switched over to Champagne. The dull red glow from the lights in the Vapors was throbbing and throbbing. There was a red shift in his brain: Goin' to Graceland! Goin' to get Elvis! I'm comin', El, I'm comin'!

His house in Mississippi is protected by a black-and-white picket fence, with the pickets painted to look like piano keys. The archway above the driveway gate reads "The Killer." But for the vagaries of fate, God, and the archangel known as Satan, this would be the shrine of rock music and Elvis would have been summoned to these gates. Instead, Graceland, a few short miles to the north, will always be the home church of rock 'n' roll.

   This sprawling red-brick suburban ranch house is more understated than Graceland. One reason for that—apart from Jerry Lee's wildly fluctuating fortunes over the years—has been his long struggle with the IRS. On more than one occasion, IRS agents have swooped down on Chez Killer with caravans of tow trucks and hauled off his earthly treasures: gilt-trimmed Cadillac Eldorados, big Lincolns, Jeeps, Rolls-

Royces, antique Fords, motorcycles, tractors, jet skis, a mechanical bull from Gilley's, jewelry, guns, and musical instruments. "They treated me like a dog," he said of the first IRS raid. Such seizures have become almost routine.

Now, at the beginning of 1989, he's down to his last Cadillac and has filed for bankruptcy again. At age fifty-three, he's mounting what may well be his last stand. To say he does not understand money is to woefully understate the case. He will never know how many millions he has made and how many were stolen from him and how many he spent and gave away. In his salad days, he operated only in cash—shoeboxes full, glove compartments full—and that's when the IRS started sniffing around. As the son of a moonshiner, Jerry Lee is suspicious of banks and revenuers alike. These days, he says, he doesn't have a dime in his pocket and relies on wife Kerrie to take care of business.

When he appeared before bankruptcy court in December of 1988, he said that he had signed a contract with the producers of the movie *Great Balls of Fire* "about eight" years ago entitling him to between $200,000 and $250,000 as a flat fee for his authorized life story. "They want me to do several things that I may or may not do," he said. He avowed that he had not received any record royalties in years and was not signed to any recording company. He said he had no assets beyond his listed exemptions in his bankruptcy petition: $30,000 for his Nesbit, Mississippi home; $500 in cash; $1,500 in household goods; $250 worth of books; $3,500 in clothes; and $10 equity in two leased cars—a 1983 Cadillac and a 1986 Corvette. He said his monthly income was $4,000 and his monthly expenses were $7,800. He said his debts totaled $3 million, and two-thirds of that was owed to the IRS. The remainder was owed to twenty-one creditors, including nightclubs and hospitals (and $119 to the Waldorf-Astoria).

At the door of Chez Killer on this Sunday afternoon, which happens to be Elvis's birthday, I am greeted by two white stone lions flanking the door, three very-alive large guard dogs, and an even larger live-in bodyguard. "Jerry Lee's expecting you," he says, ushering me in. "Get you a drink?" The inside of the house, with the exception of music industry trappings and a proliferation of pianos both large and small, is remarkably similar to that of many middle-class Southern houses I have been in—furnished in Sears' best with the ubiquitous satellite dish out back. There's a sort of sunny, knotty-pine, overstuffed cheeriness to the place that I would not have expected of Satan's favorite rock 'n' roller, nor of a man who has managed to live with hellhounds on his trail.

*   *   *

He staggered out, through the electrically locked double set of front doors, out into the vast asphalt reaches of the eight hundred–car parking lot, and finally found his custom Lincoln. One hand had a death grip on a bottle of Korbel; the other grasped a .38 pistol. He tossed the gun onto the dashboard, ground the ignition, and burned rubber all the way out of the Vapors parking lot onto Brooks Road, where he hung a swerving, squealing left onto Elvis Presley Boulevard and set sail due south for Graceland. Elvis was the once and future king, but he was pissing away the kingdom and the glory. Only Jerry Lee, truly the sole living man capable of being the King of Rock 'n' Roll, knew how El felt. Only Jerry Lee could save him from himself and from the wasteful retinue of parasitic courtiers and handlers whom Jerry Lee knew to be sucking the very lifeblood out of Elvis. "I'm comin', Elvis! Hold on, brutha!"

Then Jerry Lee and his wife Kerrie appear. It's very apparent she's the main reason he's a changed man—as changed as Jerry Lee Lewis will ever tolerate. In the Eighties, his life and career hit absolute rock bottom. He was near death from drugs and alcohol several times—although some said it was from the Devil coming to collect his due. Cousin Jimmy Lee Swaggart, before his own personal devils ruined his career, had even come around trying to save Jerry Lee.

But it has been sixth wife Kerrie McCarver Lewis who has brought Jerry Lee around. She's a handsome, exuberant woman of twenty-six (to Jerry's fifty-three) who rushes to show me around the place as Jerry Lee trails along ("Get you a drank?" he asks solicitously). They've been married since 1984, and she is the mother of Jerry Lee's only surviving son, Jerry Lee III, who is now two years old and the Killer's delight. As the last male of the Lewis line, Jerry Lee attaches a great deal of importance to his heir. He has lost two sons—one drowning in his swimming pool and the other in a one-car wreck. Along the way, he also lost wives number four and five—one drowning in the swimming pool, the other of an apparent drug overdose.

Kerrie, number six, says she has known Jerry since she was a kid and her singing group, the McCarver Sisters, recorded "Whole Lotta Shakin' Goin' On." That was in 1973, and in the years that followed she would run into him at the Vapors or Hernando's or some other roadhouse. (She also got him into the Betty Ford Clinic in 1986. It wasn't her fault he checked himself out as soon as they rolled him out at six in the damn morning and told the Killer he had to clean his own room.) "We just got to be friends over the years. We kinda just like dated around. Then he came in to Hernando's [Hernando's Hideaway, another favorite Jerry

Lee haunt] and picked me up off the stage in the middle of a song in front of everybody and said he wanted to get married and I thought he was joking. It upset him badly that I just flaked it off, and he left. The next time I saw him, he was announcing his marriage to Shawn and I was like heartbroken. I didn't know what I had done. So then, after the tragedy [Shawn's death] and all, that was a bad thing. After it was over, he started comin' back in [to Hernando's] and we started datin' again and never quit. I guess we still are. Five years now in April we'll be married. That's five years *solid*. Most of his marriages, like to Myra— that was thirteen years but they lived together maybe two years out of that. And I think Jaren's was ten or twelve years and they lived together six months. So we've been together five years out of five years. It's been *great*. Since Lee was born and God gave Jerry a second chance to be a father again, all he wants to do is stay home and play with Lee and watch TV and do his shows. We're pretty boring now."

"Now, this is the original piano," Jerry Lee says, stopping in the hallway to rest a hand affectionately on a weather-beaten, stove-up old Starck upright piano. "This is the one my daddy bought for me when I was a kid and he mortgaged the house for it. It's goin' to the Smithsonian. Get y'all a drank?" We walk on down the hall past childhood pictures of Jerry Lee and his two closest childhood friends, his cousins Mickey Gilley and Jimmy Lee Swaggart. They are no longer close: Jerry Lee has dismissed Gilley's country-music style as pseudo–Jerry Lee, and he and Swaggart have been at loggerheads over the years about which one is or is not serving the Lord or Satan. Both grew up in the fiercely primitive Assembly of God church, and Jerry Lee himself was consecrated and used to preach until he gave himself over to the Devil to play rock 'n' roll.

We walk on down the hall. Without comment he passes his bedroom door, which has two objects on it. One is a name plate, of the kind an executive would have on his desk. It reads JERRY LEE LEWIS. The other is a small iron cross with the inscription "As for me and my house, we will serve the Lord."

Sacrilege! The iron gates to Graceland do not swing wide to admit Jerry Lee, the only true friend of Elvis. Even after Jerry Lee's Lincoln sort of nudges the gates, they bend not. The gatekeeper, instead of recognizing and admitting the guest, betrays him by calling the police. In the flashing red lights Jerry Lee flings the devilish bottle of alcohol aside: He forgets to roll the window down first and it shatters. His pistol is observed. A number of police officers approach with guns drawn. "Jerry Lee, was you fixin' to go up there and shoot Elvis?" "Hail yes, Killer!"

                          *   *   *

"Kerrie, where's the limo?" Jerry suddenly asks.

"What do you mean, sweetheart?"

"I thought there'd be a limo. There always is."

He looks quizzically at Kerrie. It turns out he's due in half an hour at Graceland as the superstar guest of a national live radio show commemorating Elvis's birthday. A great honor and one that Jerry Lee did not exactly expect, given his relationship over the years with the King and the fact that his fans don't exactly overlap with the Elvis fanatics who will be weeping and wailing and holding candles up all over the place at Graceland. Still, what better choice than the man who could have stepped into Elvis's shoes. Obviously, Jerry Lee is pleased to be going. He's dressed to the nines in a three-piece suit, gold stickpin, the works. Even a little pancake makeup for the photographers who will surely be there. But where the hell is the limo? There ought to be a limo.

"Well, Jerry, I'm sorry," Kerrie finally says. "I guess they forgot. I'll drive you over, honey. C'mon."

He can't wait to get going and picks up a bottle of V.O. from the kitchen counter and starts out the door, bottle in one hand, white porcelain pipe in the other. "I'll see you over at Graceland," he calls to me over his shoulder. "Fix yourself a drank to carry along."

In addition to Kerrie and Jerry Lee III, another major factor in the reemergence or rehabilitation of Jerry Lee is that for the first time in his career he seems serious about allowing someone to manage him. His new manager, an old Elvis hand named Jerry Schilling, is one reason why Jerry Lee was invited to Graceland on Elvis's birthday.

"I was reluctant to take Jerry Lee on," Schilling had told me the night before in the lobby of the Peabody Hotel, scene of many past Jerry Lee and Elvis episodes. "You can guess why. He had a history of being unmanageable. He called me a little over a year ago. At that time he had only a few little club dates and the IRS wasn't going to let him play those, because they would attach all his monies. I had no idea at first the extent of the IRS problems. But Jerry told me he felt he had never really been managed and that it was his fault. He said he felt he had one big shot left and felt he was ready. He said he would consider only two people: either me or Colonel Parker. I was rather shocked. My deal with Jerry is this: he has a road manager traveling with him, he pays his taxes, he does his shows, and he stays straight. And that's what he's doing. It's scary to look back: Not much over a year ago he had basically no career. Now I think we're about halfway there. Last year, Vegas laughed at me when I tried to get him in there. Six months later I got him into Bally's. Now there's three hotels bidding for him. I had him open for X at the Universal Amphitheater and he twice tried to back out. But they loved him. My plan was to regain his credibility. Then I wanted him to do this movie soundtrack [for *Great Balls of Fire*]. They wanted to go other ways—use the Sun masters or have Dennis Quaid sing it; they didn't want to deal with Jerry Lee. But he wants this bad. He wants a hit record more than anything in the world. This movie is just a means to that."

People familiar with the music business in general and Jerry Lee in particular find it amazing that a movie is being made about him while he's still alive. The production has not had an easy history. Producer Adam Fields says he first started pursuing Jerry Lee eight years ago and finally succeeded in locking up rights to a Jerry Lee story by a deceptively simple ploy: He got exclusive movie performance rights on the two songs without which it would clearly be impossible to make any kind of a Jerry Lee movie, namely, "Whole Lotta Shakin' Goin' On" and "Great Balls of Fire."

He then secured movie rights to the book *Great Balls of Fire,* written by Jerry Lee's third wife (and second cousin) Myra with a co-writer. It was Myra, you will recall, whose marriage to Jerry Lee when she was but thirteen effectively ended his rock 'n' roll career. As the book points out, that career spanned only 569 days, from "Whole Lotta Shakin' " to the fall. Although based on her book, the movie, scriptwriters Jim McBride (director) and Jack Baran (first assistant director) point out, of necessity covers only that portion of his life up to the end of his rock 'n' roll career. Baran says, "If you were a kid in 1958 and loved rock 'n' roll, all you knew or heard was that Jerry Lee married his cousin and stopped making rock 'n' roll records. But what actually happened was great drama. He was effectively drummed out of the business for that marriage. He was made a scapegoat for all of rock 'n' roll, but that was what happened. We also wanted to show what made him what he was, and much of that was the religious conflict, especially with his cousin, Jimmy Lee Swaggart, the battle between God and Satan."

He gets up from his canvas director's chair to ready the morning's first shot. "You know," he says, laughing, "I grew up in the Bronx and there rock 'n' roll was make-out music. It wasn't of the Devil, like it is here in the South. So, what we've tried to do with Jerry Lee is deal with it on a mythological as well as a realistic level. We really wanted to make a musical, not a rock video. We really tried to show his roots: you know, if you take a black left hand and a white right hand and put them together, you've got rock 'n' roll. And that's Jerry Lee." He strides toward the camera: "Fuck rehearsal! Let's shoot this!"

*   *   *

Saturday night the lobby of the Radisson is all a-twitter. Time for the wrap party. The word is that Jerry Lee himself will drop in. The three Elvis look-alikes who are staying in the hotel are in and out. I check for messages to see if Jerry Lee will ever see me or if in fact he's even gotten my messages. Earlier, I went by Bad Bob's Vapors for a drink and the owner, Dr. Ed Franklin, told me, "Oh, yeah, Jerry would come around and talk about Elvis like he was fixated with him." Oh, yeah, I thought, smiling, like isn't that charming. How long ago was this—thinking it was like three years ago. "Oh, it was last night," Franklin said. "He sat right over there and just went on and on about Elvis."

Last night I met Dennis Quaid. Quaid, who is portraying Jerry Lee, is very much in character, everyone says. He was very friendly, though, introducing himself after a spell at playing the white grand piano in the hotel lobby. He's a good musician and it's obvious that an actor who is not also a gifted musician could not have carried the role. Quaid said that he and Jerry Lee had come to a "real understanding." At the bar, Dennis had proudly shown me the gold ID bracelet Jerry Lee had given him. "I had asked Jerry Lee if I could borrow something, to help while I studied him. He gave me this. He bought it right after 'Whole Lotta Shakin' ' came out for like thirty bucks. And he gave it to me. He said he could never ask for it back."

Whereas Quaid had eagerly sought out Jerry Lee, the movie's director, Jim McBride, had no such desire. "I tried to keep Jerry Lee at arm's length because I thought it would get us into a lot of trouble, but we really needed his help for the music. He was very difficult, but we got some great music on him. The plan was to make it a musical, not a rock movie, to have the music advance the story. Reading the book opened my eyes in a lot of ways to what he is, which is a true independent spirit who said fuck you to the whole world, this is what I will be. He has the attention span of a child—he was very suspicious of the whole thing. It was Dennis who really forged a trust with him. I tried to discourage Dennis from hanging out with him too much. But he and Jerry Lee had to kind of lock horns and they came out of it pretty much liking each other. It took Jerry Lee forever to read the script but when he finally did he was livid. He demanded meetings, to change every-thing. So we have this meeting in the lobby of the Peabody. He's got his copy of the script, it has stuff scrawled across every page: *LIES, LIES, lies*. He singled out the scene where he and Sam Phillips argue about hell—that came from a Sun tape. But he said everything that comes out of that whore Myra's mouth is a lie. Finally, after the ranting and raving, I said, look, you know and I know we're not gonna change everything. But if there is one thing that is really wrong that you want

changed, what is it? He said, speaking in tongues, because it is blasphemy. I said, that's it? He said, that's it. So we took it out. He was
happy. I suspect he doesn't know anymore what the truth really is. He
changes from day to day."

"A funny thing about Jerry Lee," scriptwriter Jack Baran was telling
me, "is that when we started researching this movie, the first thing that
struck me is that there are very few instances of Jerry Lee ever saying
anything. He's so elusive. He gives interviews but he never gives himself
away. Even the one thing we had on tape from Sun Records—the
hellfire-and-damnation talk he had with Sam Phillips when he was cutting 'Great Balls of Fire'—Jerry Lee denied ever saying any of it. When
we sent him the script, he wrote 'LIES' across every page. He's revised
his history so much that I don't think he even knows the truth of it
anymore. I'll be curious to see how your interview goes, if he says
anything to you at all."

Jerry Lee sends word that he has decided to see me and—adding an
element of surprise—is en route to my hotel at that very moment. By
limo. I elevator down to the lobby just in time to see him sweep in.
The doormen and hotel staff are bowing and scraping—"So happy to
see you, Mr. Lewis." It is too bad the three Elvis look-alikes are out
doing their Elvises—A Musical Celebration show over at the Orpheum
Theatre (where Jerry Lee once defied U.S. marshals who tried to serve
him with a writ)—rather than here to add a little gloss to Jerry Lee's
entrance.

We retire upstairs. Jerry Lee settles in by the window, puts his feet
up, and unwraps and slowly lights a cigar the likes of which I have
never seen before. It is only about twelve inches long, but it is a very
Killeresque gesture. He regards me with the blackest eyes I have ever
seen, eyes that are at once challenging and assessing. Much has been
made of people being afraid of Jerry Lee up close—no doubt for good
reason. It's pretty apparent that he susses out whatever attitudes and
fears you bring to the encounter and then works on those.

"Now, just what is it you want to know, son?" he asks very brusquely
and matter-of-factly. Not unfriendly. Just a man who knows there are
no surprises left for him in this life. I open my mouth to reply but he
interrupts: "Now, where are my manners? Let's get you a drank, son.
What're you drankin'? Now, Jerry Lee will have a . . . triple V.O.
straight up, Coke on the side. You?" He studies me.

"Uh. Make mine a double Black Jack straight up, water back." No
use trying to outdo the Killer. He nods appreciatively, puffs away at
his giant stogie, and regards the ceiling, waiting for me to say something.

I study him before replying. He is wearing a crisply pressed three-
piece double-breasted pin-striped blue suit and flashy white web-weave

shoes. Physically, he looks every bit his fifty-three years and more: this man has lived hard.

"Well," I venture. "Was Jimmy Swaggart preaching to you as a kid, as the movie suggests?"

"Naww. *Nooo.* I preached before Jimmy did. He was mean as hell. He didn't preach till he was seventeen, eighteen years old. Oh, yeah, I preached for three years before Jimmy did. Jimmy used to come and hear me preach. You can't get Jimmy to say amen to that but it's true. But when he did bust loose, he got *with* it."

Yeah, I say, I've heard him preach about you many a time.

Jerry cackles with laughter. "Oh, *yeah,* he had to have *somebody* to blame things on. And he always goes back to me. You know somethin', I knew this was comin' up someday—his thing with the whores. See, any time Jimmy ever made a little bit of a wrong move I would be blamed for it. So I did. And I probably well could be blamed for it."

Well, I say, were you surprised at all by his getting caught?

"Not at all," he says after taking a reflective puff on his cigar. "No, sir. I wasn't surprised. I was *dumbfounded* a little bit. But not surprised. He made a bad mistake there. I think where Jimmy went wrong, I think a servant of God like that, if you're gonna go that big time on it, the television, the radio, and the whole works, and be the businessman he is and have the millions and millions and millions of people following him like he did, and like he probably still does to a certain extent, then he should have lived up to that. Yes, sir. This cigar bother you?"

I avow that it does not. I say that I feel the ministry is a heavy calling.

Jerry Lee stabs the air for emphasis with his torpedo of a cigar. "Yes, you're right. It *is* a heavy calling, and it is strictly a calling. It has to be from God, it has to be sent from God—now whether or not he can handle it, that's something else, you have to work that out through God, and through his son Jesus Christ. But Jimmy—see, where people are really jeopardizing themselves is leaving out the third party of the Trinity, which is the Holy Ghost. The Father, the Son, and the Holy Ghost. They waver away from that and that's one of the main factors that we have that people just don't want to get into."

And why is that, I ask.

"They don't want to believe in the Holy Ghost," he says flatly. "They don't want to accept the Holy Ghost, they don't want to have to believe in the evidence of the Holy Ghost, which is speakin' in tongues. They don't want to accept this. See, the Holy Ghost will not dwell in an unclean temple, that's for sure. And that's somethin' me and Jimmy twenty-somethin' years ago had a big knockdown drag-out out on Coro Lake here in Memphis. He came out to my house and we got in a big argument about the Holy Ghost. I didn't have no idea what was goin' on with him. And he said, 'I think if you're saved, you can go to heaven.' I said, 'Well, if you're saved you can go to heaven, I hope.' He said, 'You know what I mean.' I said, 'No, I really don't.' But I knew what he was leadin' up to."

Jerry Lee takes a long sip of his V.O. and a shorter sip of his Coke and continues. "He said, 'Well, I think Baptist people go to heaven too.' I said, 'Well, *God*, Jimmy, what are you talkin' about?' He said, 'Well, do you gotta have the Holy Ghost to go to heaven?' I said, 'Just a minute, Jimmy. I'm very surprised at you, you know. You're talkin' about somethin' here, the way you were raised, the way you have been preachin', and now all of a sudden you say you don't gotta have the Holy Ghost to go to heaven. I mean, you're a full-fledged Pentecostal preacher and now you're sayin' you don't have to have the Holy Ghost to go to heaven. You ain't preachin' the full gospel, son. You're headed for a fall because of that.' And he *did* fall. That's the reason he fell. *Absolutely*. I've never said that to anyone [pointing at my recorder]. He run from the Holy Ghost, from the Truth. He was sayin' people can be saved without havin' the Holy Ghost. He left my house mad; he said, 'C'mon, Frances, let's get out of this den of iniquity.' You *must* have the Holy Ghost, in this day and age we're livin' in. *Anybody* can get saved, sure, that's no problem. But gettin' the third party of the Trinity, which is the greatest gift God has sent down here to us, is the *Holy* Ghost, man. You can conquer *hell* with the Holy Ghost, you can conquer *Satan* with it."

Does Jerry Lee Lewis have the Holy Ghost then? If anybody's music was ever inhabited by the spirit, it's yours, Jerry.

He speaks, slowly and solemnly. "Yes, sir, I *do*. It's a very *unusual* situation with me and the Holy Ghost. I, I've had the Holy Ghost all my life. I've always been such a believer in the Holy Ghost and such a fighter for the Holy Ghost, uhm, even in things I've did—and I don't claim to be right by a long shot—I knew I had strayed completely away from God. But for a matter of fact I know that the Holy Ghost never left Jerry Lee Lewis. Now that's strange, but that's a *fact*."

A knock at the door. Is there anything we require?

"Yeah," Jerry Lee says, eyes lighting up. "Could you find me a nice young blonde about seventeen years old and that'd probably finish me off in about thirty seconds. Do you believe this old man said that. I'm deficient in a lot of things but I won't screw up that bad." Cackle, cackle.

I say I think the Mann Act is still on the books.

"What's that?"

"That's where you go to prison for taking underage girls across state lines for immoral purposes."

"Well, I'm not familiar with that, Killer. I always married mine." He gives me the Jerry Lee glance, a sort of quick, sharp sideways look from under his eyebrows. Stephen Toblowsky, who plays Sun Records' Jud Phillips in the movie, calls it a "cross-eyed penguin look," which is the perfect description.

Are you happy, Jerry Lee, happy with the movie?

"Yes, sir, I'm pretty well satisfied with it. You know, the script and everything, they're making a movie and it took me a long time to consider even doing it. I wanted a movie like Jerry Lee Lewis was, *really*. I mean don't leave out anything but tell it like it was. But they've rewritten these scripts and everything usin' Myra's script, that little ole book she come out with, and it's nothin' but a bunch of damn *lies*. Lies. Excuse my French. *Durned* lies. And, uh, she was hostile at the time she came out with that and they took it and they're using it in this movie and that's got me worried a little bit. But like I said, these people are very smart folks, they know what they're doin'. And I just hope that they don't . . . [he looks at me fiercely] make me *mad*. Now, the music in it is fantastic and that's the only thing I cared anything about and they didn't seem too big-time interested in that at first. Dennis wanted to sing at first, and that was *ridiculous*. That would be like crammin' a wet noodle up a wildcat's ass." He laughs enormously.

"So I went in and re-recorded it all. And I did it in a handicapped situation. They really weren't into it. I had to do it myself. I went in and did it and they couldn't believe what I was doing. They said, Jerry, there's no way you could ever beat the original 'Whole Lotta Shakin' Goin' On,' and I said, you believe that? And T-Bone Burnett said, yeah. And I said, well, then I don't need you for a producer. I said, yeah, I can beat it. If I didn't I wudn't be in this studio. But I beat it in one cut. T-Bone said, you have made a believer out of me."

Can you tell how much of the movie is you and how much is the myth?

He answers seriously, rolling his whiskey glass between his palms. "I don't know. I haven't seen all of it, to tell you the truth. There's nobody really knows what happened around then, you know. And they have me dividing up my money with J. W. Brown [Myra's father and Jerry Lee's bass player] and that's not true. J. W. Brown didn't get no money of mine."

In the movie he gets fifty percent.

Jerry Lee is scornful. "Hail, no. He wadn't gettin' *five* percent. Only time he ever got fifty percent was when we were makin' twenty-five or thirty dollars a night. When it got up to fifty or a hundred dollars a night I cut him back. I said, Jerry Lee can't pay you this much. I put him on a salary of two hundred and fifty a week. And all this in the movie is distorting, distorting, *distorting,* and is not true.

On the other hand, I remind him, this movie can help.

He answers me by singing. " 'On the other hand there's a golden band.' Yeah, but now you're gettin' into a different situation. And that makes me wonder, too. I never wanted to do anything—if it will help me, if it will better me in the eyes of the people, to distribute my thoughts, to spread my thoughts of the Holy Ghost and things like that, if it will clarify a lot of things in people's minds, then I don't care what they say in this movie or what they do. But I want it very well understood that when this comes out on screen that there's gonna have to be a second movie shot. This one covers really, like you say, eighteen months of my life, and I think these people think these eighteen months of my life are a big deal, and I don't think it was quite as big a deal as they think it is. What's gonna make this movie is the music. All this bullcrap they're shootin' about Myra and Jerry Lee Lewis in a Cadillac and eatin' popcorn and bull*shit* like that, they don't even know what they're *doin',* man. It could've been a movie if they'd done it right: it's music, it's rock 'n' *roll.* My life—eighteen months, man, that ain't *nothin'* to do with my life. That wadn't even a steppin'-stone."

But, I point out, that's where you hit so big and then the revelation in London of your marriage to your thirteen-year-old cousin ended your rock career and—

He angrily cuts me off, sitting up to point an index finger at me. "The marriage wadn't *nothin'* to do with that. Sam Phillips and Sun Records is what screwed everything up. He dropped his distributors and dropped ever'thang, I come back from England and I had no distributors. Columbia Records offered me ten—[pause] million [pause] *dollars* for a five-year contract. I can prove what I'm sayin'. See, nobody knows anything about this. And I had to linger around on Sun Records. I cudn't get off of Sun Records. Sam Phillips—he made me stick around for five and a half years, near to six years. Sam had all my money, never paid me no more money. Sumbitch owed me about [pause] *thirty* million dollars. He ain't paid me a penny. Sam Phillips. Shit. He's worth over a hundred million dollars at least. He owns half of the Holiday Inns. *Rillly* [mocking my "really"]."

So, I say, the business of your marriage and the public backlash—

He interrupts: "You don't think, over a period of all these years, he didn't owe me thirty million dollars? Shoot. I used that for a figure of speech. I'd be glad to settle with him for a million. I'd be glad to settle with him for, uh, uh, twenty dollars if the man would sit down and talk to me."

Will he do that?

"Naw. Ain't no sense to it. Anyway, he fucked me up bigtime. For years and years and years. See, I had a three-year contract with Sam and I had one year left with Sun and that's when I hit—big! time! Well, he brought me another contract, two-year with a three-year option. And, uh, I asked Jud, his brutha! I said, what do you think? Do you think I oughta sign this contract? He said, well, Jerry, I think Sam has been good to you, I think you should stick with him. Pull the regular percentage again. No guarantee, no nothing. Sheeit. Give me a break. I had to go through this crap, man. I had to suffer for five and a half years on Sun Records, when I could've been on Columbia Records, a major label—I never would have had no downfall at all."

It wasn't the public reaction to your marriage that stopped your career?

"*Sheeit* no. I never stopped drawing crowds. I had bigger crowds always. Hell, I was drawing bigger crowds than Elvis Presley was for two or three years after that and didn't even have a hit record."

But, I say, didn't Sam and Jud make you sign the letter of apology to the industry about the marriage and it ran in the trades?

By now steam is coming off his forehead and he's gulping V.O. "I don't even know what you're talkin' about! [I start to relate the scene in the film where he—weeping—signs the apology.] That's a goddamn lie! I just heard about that scene yesterday. I tell you, that's the damndest lie I ever heard in my life! I didn't never apologize to a *motherfucka* in my life! *Never!* Sheeit! You think I'm apologizin', baby, you wrong! I don't wanta hear that shit! They might oughta take that outta the movie." He takes a quick drink and several prodigious puffs on his cigar. "Preach it, Lewis!" He falls silent.

"I coulda went with Columbia Records, I coulda sold more records, been bigger than ever. But you know, it was like Elvis Presley and Tom Parker and Sam Phillips and all of 'em conjured all this shit up and kept it on my head. But I've had to let the years go by, and I've had a lot of hit records on Mercury, a lot of big, big hits. And you know my biggest hits are yet to come."

We drink in silence for a bit. I feel the Jerry Lee glance alight on me. "Uh, Jerry Lee, when did you meet Elvis? Was it at the Million-Dollar Quartet session at Sun?"

"That's right. Yeah, I knew he was a real fuck-up right there because he wouldn't get up off the piano bench and let me play. He just kept on playin' and playin'. He said, 'Jerry Lee, I've come to the conclusion that everybody should be able to play the piano.' I said, 'Hell, I've been tryin' to tell you that for two hours.' He didn't mean nothin' by it. He said to me, 'I'd rather be dead if I can't be king of rock 'n' roll.' I said, 'Well, El, I'd rather, too.' "

He gets up and opens the window to let some of the smoke out. Still standing, he addresses the nighttime Memphis sky out the window. "Elvis was scared to death of Mr. Parker, like a monkey on a string. I went out to see him open in Vegas. Elvis sent a Lear jet for me. He said, 'Jerry Lee, I don't trust these people. I want you to tell me the truth.' He was a monkey in a cage. I tried to tell him what I saw, but he was too far gone. And they kept him like a monkey in a cage. And when the monkey in the cage started acting up and getting out of control of the carnival barker, instead of throwing him peanuts the way they always had done, they started shooting little balls of Demerol to him. The monkey eventually thought he was King Kong and finally they buried the monkey. But the carnival barker kept right on going. The end."

He is silent for a moment, studying his glass. Then he shoots me the glance and an impish grin and says, "It's true!"

What's the truth about the gate episode?

"Elvis had been calling me for several days—he had Linda Thompson, his girlfriend, calling me. I get on the phone with Elvis and he's saying, you got to come out here. I am so *depressed* I don't know what to do. He just sounded pitiful. He had called many times before but I just hadn't felt that the blind could lead the blind, you know. I didn't feel that I was in that good a shape to go out to Elvis's house. I got to be honest with you, I was pretty loaded that night at the Vapors. I'd been drinking whiskey pretty heavy and then I got over onto Champagne, hell of a note. Then Elvis called and I said, awright, I'll go out there and straighten him out."

He laughs heartily and drains his glass. "Mistake number bigtime one! So I got into this long ole Lincoln of mine, this Mark I had. I had a bottle of Champagne between my legs. I arrived at Elvis's house. And at the Vapors Charlie Foreman had given me this .38 derringer pistol; it's at Swaggart's house now. It was brand new, and never been fired, beautiful gun. I took it and put it in my glove compartment. He said, no, you can't have a concealed weapon. Put it on your dashboard. So I throwed it up on my dashboard and forgot about it. I whipped into the drive—the front end of that Lincoln looked like it was thirty miles long—and I hit the gate. That gate shook and it looked like Elvis doin' a show. Two tons just a shakin'. The guy he had working the gate wasn't his Uncle Vester. It was a new boy and he come over there and he knocked on my window and he looked at me. I was tryin' to roll my window down, but instead I was puttin' my seat back. I said, what is this, boah? He said, well whatya want? I said, well, I wanta see Elvis Presley. Elvis called me to come see him. This boy didn't know who I was. Now, I thought I had put down the window on the right side and I threw this Champagne bottle out and the window was up so I knocked the whole window out. Well, that scared him to death. Then he saw that pistol and his eyes got this big around and he cut and run! He called the damn cops. And I sat there and the next thing I knew I was surrounded by five or six po-lice squad cars. This cop was talkin' to me and I knew him and he said, 'Jerry Lee, this looks *bad*. What're you doin' with that pistol? Were you gonna go up there and shoot Elvis with that pistol?' I said, 'Hell, yes, if I can get up there!' I figured if they were that damned stupid to ask a question like that, then I'm gonna answer 'em stupid! He said, 'Well, I just think the best thing to do with you is just take you downtown.' I said, 'Whatever you think.' We got in the squad car and we was ridin' downtown and I said, 'You know somethin'? You gonna lose your job, boy, you know Elvis did call me. El's waitin' on me up there.' And this boy like to got fired. A couple of 'em *did*. He was about to make lieutenant so they let him slide. But he never pulled a stunt like that on me again. I was *right*. Elvis waited on me five or six hours up there. He never knew what was goin' on.

"Now, I *did* hear a different story where somebody called him and said Jerry Lee is sittin' down there with a gun and Elvis said, 'Lock him up.' But I find that hard to believe. But I never pushed it after that. I never tried to go back anymore. But the whole thing was just so stupid. They were wrong. I was right, son. Now am I, Jerry Lee Lewis, gonna shoot Elvis Presley? *Shooot. Damn.* I mean I had to sit down and explain this to Lisa Marie, you know. She asked me about this and she worships me and she really respects me. Good kid. She was really serious about this. And I told her the truth and everything. She understood. Good-lookin' little gal, too! As a matter of fact, Lisa Marie cud ve-er-ry well be my next wife!"

I am surprised. "Jerry Lee? In this life?"

"In this damn century! Would you believe, this year?"

Well—what would Kerrie say?

"That's her problem. I ain't never promised nooobody no rose garden."

Do you, I wonder, fault Elvis?

"Elvis was—he was an asshole."

"What do you mean, Elvis was an asshole?"

"I said it!" He's defiant. "He backed it up! That's all I know. He was a *dummy*. He proved it. Now, don't get me wrong. I loved the man. But he was one of the most greatest talents there has ever been in the world. And he wasted it. He had no backbone to go with it. His backbone was made of jelly."

People always say, I say, that if you had had someone like Colonel Parker you would have been Elvis.

He snorts. "If I woulda had Tom Parker, I would have murdered that sumbitch the first week. He wouldn't have lasted till the water got hot. Matter of fact, he better walk lightly around me *now*."

Another knock at the door: our drink order being taken again.

Jerry Lee calls out, sotto voce, obviously joking: "You got any good strong dope? I'm not choosy, brother, I am what I am. Thank you, Killer.

"Now, son, you wanted to know what made me? What made me. When I was in the school in the first grade, the teacher told me, she said one and one was two. I said, now wait a minute, how do you know? And right then we had a big problem. She said it was. I said now I don't believe that shit. How do you know it ain't three? Now, you know what I was tryin' to say. She got upset and called my mother up there, and it's been that way ever since. Now, she was right, one-hundred percent right. But at six years old I didn't feel that anybody could teach me anything. Don't tell me that one and one is two. And don't tell me that Jerry Lee Lewis isn't the right kind of person. Because Jerry Lee Lewis is the right kind of person. If he wadn't the right kind of person he'd be *dead*. Or in jail. Now, that's Jerry Lee Lewis's success. The way it is. I am what I am."

The Perfect Pitch

The deal, that's all this business is about. . . . Listen, if Paul Newman comes in and says he wants to play Gertie Lawrence in Star!, *you do it, that's the nature of the business.*

—John Gregory Dunne, *The Studio*

In the beginning was the pitch, and while it was not necessarily good, it was certainly effective. Satan was the first pitchman and, when he made his presentation to Adam and Eve, he set the standards for all time: "Have I got a deal for you!" Similarly, Moses had to do a convincing pitch with the Ten Commandments; Martin Luther was great with his Indulgences; David Stockman had his Rosy Scenario. Not much has changed.

Before the deal comes the pitch, and this cycle of pitch and deal pretty much dominates and determines business and enterprise in this country. If you can't sell it, it isn't real. Likewise, there can be little doubt that there is no place that lives and dies by the pitch and deal as much as Hollywood. Empires and fortunes spun from dreams and fantasies are of necessity based on wishes and hopes: there are no concrete foundations for the dream machine.

Pitching is usually discussed in salesmen's terms, but when you think about it, baseball is perhaps a more apt analogy. Just as in baseball, the Hollywood pitch may be wild, controlled, over the backstop, out of the park, or a down-the-pike strike. And the pitcher, to be truly effective, must have terrific control, enormous self-confidence, and a hell of a delivery. A very early example of the fastball pitch involved tycoon Howard Hughes, who was just starting to flex his oil-money muscles in Hollywood. In 1926, an actor named Ralph Graves pitched Hughes—to the tune of $40,000—a project called "Swell Hogan." Even though the movie was never released, Graves's pitch to Hughes—"It'll make a hell of a movie"—remains a Hollywood classic.

That's the kind of chutzpah you need to deliver a pitch in Hollywood. Of course, you should try to say a little more than that when pitching studio executives, but then rules are made to be broken. French director Jean-Claude Tramont sold the idea for *All Night Long* to Twentieth Century-Fox executives just by saying he wanted to do a movie about night workers. The history of *Texas Chainsaw Massacre II* sheds light on the pitch process. Director L. M. "Kit" Carson tells how it came about: "I went in with [producer] Tobe Hooper to see Menahem Golan [head of Cannon Pictures]. We had the first two acts down on paper. I started explaining how this was Leatherface killing people in Dallas on O.U. Weekend [when the University of Texas plays its annual football game against Oklahoma University], with drunks falling out of windows and throwing toilets out of windows. Menahem stopped me and said, 'Ooh, I'm scared already.' Then he asked, 'Are both you guys from Texas?' We said yes. Then he said, 'Okay, go make the movie.' Not your usual uncomfortable pitch meeting. I didn't have to act the movie out."

A usual pitch meeting is one or more writers and maybe a producer who likes their idea meeting with one or more studio executives. The latter call the shots, which is why pitch meetings are usually held at a studio (although power-breakfast meetings are increasingly the vogue). The writer's job: to sell the executive on an idea. The executive's job: to resist the pitch unless it's a can't-miss project. It's not unlike a sales pitch in any other line of business. The writer has anywhere from three to thirty minutes to pitch a line of goods to a presumably shrewd buyer. "It's a real Willy Loman kind of thing," says screenwriter Mitch Glazer. "It can be terrifying. You have no control over the time and place of the meeting. You have to be able to sell something immediately. Used to be you would have a script to show them. Now, it's a real high-concept kind of delivery. You have to describe the thing in one sentence."

High-concept is both bane and blessing. Selling an idea with a few words is great, in theory—until, that is, you try it. Try describing *Gandhi,* for example, in a few words. ("Pacifist frees a nation"?) Or *Gone With the Wind.* ("War love story"?) Or *Chariots of Fire.* ("Guys in their underwear run races"?) You can see that pitching is indeed an art. I've heard of only one one-word pitch that was really effective (and I don't mean "Stallone" or "Streisand." Words like that mean star-vehicle and that's not what we're talking about here. Vehicles don't need to be pitched; they drive themselves). The word? Gold. The concept? Ancient Egypt and mummies and pyramids and so on. (*Gold* is still not a motion picture, not even in turn-around.)

Glazer is fortunate in that he usually has partner Michael O'Donoghue with him at pitch meetings. This allows them to do, as O'Donoghue says, "a kind of good cop–bad cop type of presentation. That's one way of doing it. You have to realize that there are no guidelines for this sort of groveling. They have leash laws for writers in Hollywood, you know."

Most pitchers agree that there are certain plans they can make and certain precautions they can take to try to grease the skids: try for a morning pitch, preferably early in the week; plan your strategy beforehand, even to the point of practicing your spiel before disinterested friends; never pitch alone; never pitch stoned, drunk, or half-asleep; never make a formal pitch in an informal setting (that's why there are meetings). Television writer David Felton says that "the art of pitching is something that takes years to learn. You have to know the terminology. Like, 'franchise' is very big this year, as in 'This is the Cosby franchise.' My best concept was 'Police Woman Centerfold.' And that's all it was; a concept. I pitched it to an exec at Universal and he looked at me for two seconds and said, 'My job is that Universal is a man dying of thirst and my job is to bring it water. A period-piece comedy is not water.' All I can tell you is that something makes sense when you sell it and it doesn't when you don't." Felton also recommends against arriving with a lot of words down on paper and strongly advises against "leave-behinds"—that is, hard information down on paper that you leave behind for executives to read later on. They might change their minds, Felton says, when they take a hard look at something they just invested in. "Don't give 'em too much information."

The late Orson Welles was good at that. He once tried to borrow $50,000 from Harry Cohn for *Around the World in Eighty Days.* Cohn wanted collateral. Welles offered to direct a future movie for Cohn.

"You got a story?" Cohn asked over the phone. Welles looked around the room and spied a wardrobe woman reading a paperback book titled *The Lady from Shanghai.* "Yes," said Welles. (It actually became a movie, although the book it was based on was *If I Die Before I Wake.*)

Then there are the pitches that were better off never made. *Heaven's Gate,* described as the biggest disaster in Hollywood history, was originally optioned by Twentieth Century-Fox and then put into turnaround once Fox's production head decided it was too "bloody and nihilistic." United Artists then turned it down because of its "mayhem/ murder." Unfortunately, UA eventually made the film, only to have it sink the studio.

There probably hasn't been a better summation of the pitch than that delivered by ace screenwriter William Goldman, of *Butch Cassidy and the Sundance Kid* fame: "You walk into the executive's office with your producer leading the way. Introductions follow. Then the standard circling chitchat: 'Been here long?' 'Actually, I was born in Westwood.' 'A native? Are they legal?' Chuckle chuckle chuckle. During this sizing-up time, the executive is trying to answer one question: 'Who is this a------?' He knows you're not Mario Puzo because Puzo wouldn't be there talking about taking twenty-five thou for an iffy project like this. The executive undoubtedly has read something of yours—a treatment, a story maybe, an earlier unmade screenplay. And he's talked with the producer who has probably glanced at the same material. But are you the one?"

That's the hard question. Are you the one? The one with the hot idea, the one who can bring that idea to life, the one who can produce magic? Are you the one who can make the magic pitch while sitting in the hot seat? Kit Carson says he finally got over his dread of pitch meetings a couple of years ago, when "I finally decided that I shouldn't be intimidated by the offices and the formalities of the meetings. I said to myself, 'Well, I could just get up and walk over and p--- on this guy's desk. He doesn't scare me. That's when I got my confidence at pitching.' "

Michael O'Donoghue, a writer who became infamous on "Saturday Night Live" (remember his macabre "Mr. Mike" segments?) makes it a point to wear sunglasses and chain-smoke cigarettes in pitch meetings. Even so, he has had his shaky moments. "I met with Frank Price to pitch a movie about giant insects taking over the world. Now, Frank Price is the man who turned down *E.T.* So this dark science-fiction vision that I had, he hated. Five minutes into the pitch, I could see that he was thinking, 'Who let this . . . person into my office.' But I had to keep going like nothing had happened. Pitch etiquette requires that you continue. Once, a producer pitched me on a movie about a serious type lawyer and I stood up and said, 'I don't feel this is my cup of tea.' Well, he was horrified. It's like you have to finish the dance once it's started. So, Frank Price, he didn't call the studio guards, but I think he would have liked to."

Any producer or studio executive will tell you that the perfect pitch doesn't exist. But, if it did, it would contain the following elements: it would be totally original even though it was just like the last really big movie; it would be a perfect vehicle for whichever star is hottest at the moment and therefore is considered a lock at the box office; it wouldn't cost much to make; and it would carry the right demographics (which, at the moment, as any moviegoer knows, involves the teenage audience). Of course, any writer will tell you that the perfect pitch is totally original, is unlike any other movie that came before, will win not only an Oscar but a Pulitzer Prize, is not just a star vehicle, and will earn the writer the respect of "real" (i.e., book authors) writers.

One man who has seriously studied the matter of pitching is Jim Sarnoff, who just happens to be an agent. He has developed the following principles of the perfect pitch:

1. Meet only with executives who have the power to give you a deal on the spot.
2. Your client must be someone the executive or buyer has expressed interest in before the pitch meeting.
3. Your client, in making the pitch, should be passionate enough about the idea to convince the buyer it is a fresh idea, no matter how unoriginal it really is.
4. Most importantly, you have to leave the meeting with a deal. If a deal doesn't result, it's not a good pitch meeting.

Pitch meetings come in many different forms. Walter Shenson, who produced the Beatles' *A Hard Day's Night* in 1963, almost fell into that project. United Artists London director Bud Orenstein called Shenson and asked him to make a low-budget film with the Beatles, mainly because United Artists' record affiliate, UA Records, would get the soundtrack. The forty-five-year-old Shenson balked at first, protesting that his own children were driving him to distraction with their Beatles records. However, he finally agreed to go to London and see what was up.

Once there, he met with director Richard Lester, who almost begged to be allowed to direct a Beatles movie—which, of course, existed only as an idea: Beatles + Movie = Success. Next, Shenson met Beatles manager Brian Epstein, who told him, "The boys want to make the film; can we come to your office?" The pivotal meeting with the Beatles eventually took place in a London taxi. The script was the last part, and least element, of the whole negotiation.

Two decades later, another movie by a Beatle was done far differently. Paul McCartney decided to write the script for what later turned into *Give My Regards to Broad Street* on a whim. Stuck in a London traffic jam one afternoon, he began to toy with a thought: "What if the master tapes to my next album got lost in a traffic jam?" Eventually, he set about writing a screenplay, which even he admitted was more a set of ideas than a screenplay. And then he pitched it around. To find that nobody bit. He finally went to producer David Puttnam (*Chariots of Fire*), who found Paul a director and producer and suggested that Paul finance the production himself. So he did: "I was funding it. It wasn't too high a risk and I hadn't even thought too much about the cost. I was just approaching it artistically. I thought, 'I'm going to be in it, and I'll just have to believe in myself.'"

Once he had completed ten minutes of cut film, McCartney put the ball in the hands of his father-in-law and financial advisor, New York attorney Lee Eastman. Eastman shopped those ten minutes around and Twentieth Century-Fox made a deal. *Broad Street* ended up costing only $9 million to make, but it was such a total and complete box-office disaster that rental fees can't even be guessed at.

Other pitches can be just as nebulous, if not as obviously successful. Director George Stevens once went before UA head Arthur Krim and hyped him on the idea of making *The Greatest Story Ever Told*. Krim gave him the "go" sign on the basis of little more than that. When Stevens was finished, Krim had an expensive, boring flop of a movie on his hands.

Producers Don Simpson and Jerry Bruckheimer had no trouble pitching *Top Gun* to Paramount but, oddly, the key to the movie's success was a pitch made in Washington, D.C. As Bruckheimer explains: "We decided it was wise to meet with the Pentagon and enlist their aid and support at the outset—make them our partners as it were. We couldn't have done the film without Pentagon approval. So we pitched them the genesis of the idea, the story. They were very excited and they said they would love to do it with us, with two stipulations. First was that the film be totally authentic and accurate. And second was that it show some semblance of commitment to Navy life. We had no problems with that. So the Navy helped us. And charged us a whole lot of money for it."

There are pitches and then there are pitches. *Echo Park,* a surprise hit with the critics in 1986, represents the growing trend away from the standard-pitch movie: Hollywood was barely involved, and there was no formal pitch meeting per se. The original idea for the movie began with director Robert Dornhelm and scriptwriter Michael Ventura talking about collaborating on a movie about the Los Angeles they knew, rather than the "glitzy L.A." they usually saw on the silver screen.

Once Ventura finished a script, Dornhelm—who is Austrian—pitched the idea to the unlikeliest of benefactors, the government of Austria, and came away with a grant to start pre-production. He got another grant from Weinfilm, an independent production company in Austria. Then he took the script to Bill Wyman of the Rolling Stones. Wyman, who is interested in doing film music, kicked in with another grant. Finally, Dornhelm contacted producer Walter Shenson (*A Hard Day's Night*), who also put in some money.

"We shot the whole thing for about nine hundred thousand," Ventura said. "We got real good people cheaply. Tom Hulce had shot *Amadeus,* but it hadn't been released yet and the industry word was 'Who wants to see a two-hour opera picture?' So Tom was not real hot yet. It was a total shoestring deal. We had no permits to shoot, so all our outdoor shots were 'stolen.' For example, we had Susan Dey running around in her underwear in downtown L.A. No cops around to provide security. Our security was a few of us standing around holding lead pipes.

"Any independent film has a history something like this. In studio work, it's usually a development deal. I've done those and I would never do one again unless I was walking in with a director who was ready to do the picture. A writer alone gives up his authority to the producer and the executive. You're just an employee, once the deal is signed.

"My first development deal was for *Roadie,* several years ago, for UA. Unfortunately for me, UA started *Heaven's Gate* right then and all of UA's time and energy went into that."

What a studio head looks for in a pitch is highly individualistic, of course, but Don Simpson is a good case in point. Simpson, who with his partner Jerry Bruckheimer has produced *Flashdance, Beverly Hills Cop,* and the current hit *Top Gun,* was for ten years head of production at Paramount. As such, he was on the receiving end of twenty-five to thirty pitches a day. This is what he looked for in a pitch:

1. "On a gut, an instinct level, I would look for a notion or idea that grabs me immediately—not high-concept, because I don't believe in that.
2. "Then I would say, 'Does this lend itself to a terrific venue, a terrific arena, a terrific environment within which to set a movie?'
3. "Then, 'Is there room to tell a terrific, taut, emotional story within these confines?'
4. "If the answer is yes, I ask, 'Is there room to populate this landscape

with a character or a group of characters that are absolutely dramatic and riveting?'

5. "If the answer is yes, then I ask, 'Well, is there the opportunity for the thing to be about something in even the most subtle way?'

6. "If the answer's yes to that, I ask, 'Can I put all these elements together in two hours of screentime and will it be a movie that I want to see?' If the answer's yes, then we do it.

"As a studio head, that happy combination would happen before me only about twenty-five percent of the time. But seventy-five percent of the time I had to move ahead anyway because it was my job to service the distribution pipeline of the studio. I had to make fifteen to twenty movies a year, and you can't like fifteen to twenty movies a year."

Simpson, like most Hollywood veterans, doesn't believe in the perfect pitch. "I don't think it exists. The only perfect pitch is the one that gets the job done. If a pitch sells the idea succinctly, economically, and dramatically, I think it's perfect."

He also dismisses the theory that many current movies were filmed only because they were tailored to a certain star. "As a studio head," Simpson says, "I think a vehicle doesn't make anything better or worse. As far as I'm concerned, if something is conceived as a vehicle, it's better off as a car."

He would probably agree with legendary movie tycoon Sam Goldwyn, who once listened impatiently as a writer pitched him about an important "message" film he wanted to make. Said Goldwyn finally, "If you want to send a message, call Western Union."

The Love You Take Is Equal to the Love You Make: A Profile of David Geffen

I knew that I couldn't live in an apartment in Brooklyn like my parents. I had to find a way out.

—David Geffen

He was a genius—that is to say, a man who does superlatively and without obvious effort something that most people cannot do by the uttermost exertion of their abilities. He was a genius at making money, and that is as un-

common as great achievement in the arts. The simplicity of his concepts and the masterly way in which they were carried through made jealous people say he was lucky. . . . but he made his own luck. . . .

—Robertson Davies, describing a character who is not David Geffen in his novel *Fifth Business*

Thirty-nine-year-old David Geffen, *wunderkind* no more (starting to silver around the temples in fact) but again a power in show business, delivers his silver Porsche to the slightly sullen but properly obsequious parking attendant at Le Dome on Sunset Boulevard on a properly sun-silvered day. No tinsel-city-metaphor crap for him today, though.

"As far as movies go, this is a ghost town," he tells me as the maître d' hustles to seat us. Geffen is unshaven, wearing a *relaxed* striped Oxford-cloth shirt, faded Levis, white socks, and tennis shoes. More than a third of the tanned and well-tailored movie and record executives in Le Dome do a curious half-bow out of their chairs as he passes: "Hel-lo, David!" "David!" "Call you later, David!"

He nods and waves to people he knows, sits, and orders a bottle of Evian water. ("Half a glass of wine and I'm *gone*. *Half* a glass.") He knows and says that half a dozen years ago those same moguls would have regarded him as the invisible man. Even though he, David Geffen, had once been the most powerful young lion in show business.

When you list his early accomplishments, you almost need a series of those Lions Club brass plaques: Brooklyn College flunk-out; University of Texas flunk-out; CBS-TV usher; mailroom boy at the William Morris Agency in New York; major booking agent; biggest manager of rock acts in the Sixties; founder of Asylum Records, the most prestigious rock label of the early Seventies. Then, before he turned thirty-five, Geffen was named vice-chairman of Warner Bros. He quit for a spell of what might rudely be called navel-gazing, taught at Yale for a while, and then decided to come out of retirement. Geffen Records' first signings were Donna Summer, John Lennon and Yoko Ono, and Elton John. He helped put together the Paul Simon/Art Garfunkel Central Park concert, and for his troubles Geffen Records got worldwide rights to that record outside North America. No mean feat.

Soon after, Geffen Films, which no one had heard about before, produced *Personal Best* and signed up a number of other projects. Geffen also decided to check out Broadway. *Dreamgirls* was the first project he got involved with and, typically, he had signed Jennifer Holliday to a recording contract before she 1) got into the show; 2) got thrown out of the show; 3) got reinstated after he interceded with director Michael Bennett; and 4) became the show's singing star. Guess which record label will have the first Jennifer Holliday album. Guess what label has the *Dreamgirls* cast album.

Our Geffen is also one of the co-producers responsible for bringing *Cats* over from London to Broadway and he has invested in Athol Fugard's *Master Harold and the Boys*. In other words, David Geffen is the master of making the Deal. And the Deal, after all, is what day-to-day business in any business is all about. (By the way, Geffen is also a member of the Board of Regents of the University of California.)

Back at Le Dome, David Geffen ignores the deal-makers while he studies the menu.

"Chicken," he announces. And so it is chicken we will have. He closes his menu authoritatively and looks around the room with sharp, quick glances—the glances of a street kid always on the lookout. Brooklyn glances. David Geffen lives half the time in Beverly Hills and the other half on Fifth Avenue in splendid surroundings; but he will never forget his Brooklyn uprising.

He does not, for example, believe in power lunches. "Ma Maison is the power restaurant here," he says, sipping his inevitable glass of Evian water, "but I don't go there. I don't like to measure such things and see how important I am. I don't go to Elaine's anymore." He may well be the single most influential figure in pop music today, but the trappings are few, the attitude very low-key. Back in his first career (Geffen retired at age thirty-five as the result of a false cancer diagnosis) he was a bit more flamboyant: Rolls-Royces, living with Cher, being seen in the right spots. The new Geffen is less hyper and invests in art and theater with people like the Shuberts. On this afternoon, he has a quiet lunch and then heads back to work in his silver Porsche.

The Geffen Los Angeles offices are extremely unprepossessing: the second and third floors of a three-story building with a faux-chalet appearance on Sunset Boulevard. There is no sign outside, no marked parking places, none of the visual flash one finds at most record companies. Overhead, to say the least, is very low.

Just as David Geffen somehow always seems to be sporting a day-old stubble, so does his office exhibit a vaguely disquieting air of impermanence. There's a thick maroon carpet and a luxurious tan corduroy couch for visitors. Unlike most record executives' dens, which are chockablock with gold and platinum albums and pictures of the exec backstage with the stars, there is absolutely nothing mounted on the walls. There are two small framed posters leaning against an off-white wall. One has the engraved words: "And in the end, the love you take is equal to the love you make." The other is an autographed poster announcing the Calvin Klein–sponsored benefit concert by Elton John for New York City's parks. There are also two low end tables. The one by the couch has a large crystal bowl full of Bit-o-Honey candy bars on it. The other is, in effect, David Geffen's real office. It's situated right by his Eames chair, where he sits all day, looking out over Sunset Boulevard and making phone call after phone call into the entertainment world. His ten-button phone on that low table is where he does business. He has never had a desk, he writes nothing down, he seems to file nothing, and during the course of the day his bamboo wastebasket fills with papers he discards once he's committed their content to memory. A fund-raising letter from Alan Cranston lands alongside an invitation to visit Menachem Begin in Israel.

Geffen hooks a leg over the edge of his Eames chair and starts working the phone. "Linda," he calls to his assistant, "get me David Horowitz on the phone." Linda is Linda Loddengaard, Geffen's longtime right arm. They met one night years ago on the sidewalk outside the Troubador, the Los Angeles nightclub. (This was just before Geffen and two partners started the Roxy, a rival night spot, because they were irritated by the Troubador's booking policies.) The only job-related question Geffen asked Loddengaard before hiring her was: "Have you ever filled out AFM [American Federation of Musicians] reports?" She said, "No," and in the past dozen years or so she has filled out maybe four of them. When Geffen retired in 1975 after selling Asylum Records, he had Loddengaard retire with him, just to make sure no one else hired her. When he decided to plunge back into the business, she was reactivated. She likes working for Geffen. "He's a fascinating man. Obviously I wouldn't be here if he weren't."

She gets David Horowitz, who is an executive with Warner Communications, on the phone for Geffen. Geffen is meanwhile sorting through his mail—art catalogs, wine catalogs, the trade magazines, a pitch from Easter Seals. "Linda, send a hundred dollars to Easter Seals," he says, and then Easter Seals lands in the wastebasket beside Alan Cranston and Menachem Begin.

"David! How are you! . . . Asia [a new rock supergroup on Geffen Records] will be a multi-platinum album! It's a dream come true. David, do you realize Geffen Records will gross between forty and fifty million in domestic [U.S. only] sales this year?"

Geffen's phone calls are usually short and to the point, albeit cordial. He likes to get to the heart of the matter at hand. As one of his employees says, "David is a very quick read. He's always ahead of you and he's never afraid to make a decision."

"Linda! Did we RSVP yet for Diana Ross's birthday party Friday?"

Geffen flips through *Women's Wear Daily* and then *Architectural Digest*.

Above Linda's desk is a beautiful old poster from the Depression, one of a series of Mather inspirational lithos. This one shows a diver above the following message: "Diving for Success—those who plunge head-long into their work come out with its prizes. Mean it and you'll make it." More of the huge framed posters start arriving by messenger. Geffen has bought all the Mathers he could find. He puts the phone down long enough to come out and inspect them and reads one aloud: "Repeating our mistakes ruins our records. Let's make each miss improve our aim. Only hits win." He chortles with delight. "Linda, I want one of these hung in every office."

Is that, I ask, to motivate his employees?

Geffen looks surprised. "No, it's to motivate *me*."

Back to the Eames. "Linda, get me Paul Simon." Paul Simon is out. "Get me David Lieberman [a prominent rack jobber whose company places records in shops]."

"David! This is going to be a number-one album. If you rack it early enough there won't be any returns. Also, I wanta tell you the Elton John LP is a *hit*. The single is across-the-board AOR [album-oriented-radio], AC [Adult Contemporary radio], and pop. It's a hit before the album ships. You're not gonna get hurt with this record. It's a good record and I wouldn't tell you that if it weren't. And *Dreamgirls*. This is the finest cast album ever recorded. It cost me four hundred thousand to make it. It's the first pop album to come out of Broadway." He laughs. "I'm gonna sound like *everything's* a hit."

Geffen winks broadly between phone calls when I remind him he was once called the "Billy Martin of the record business" but that his attack has mellowed. "I'm not sure what they meant by that Billy Martin stuff," he says, laughing.

"Bernard! I want you to know that I have the album to *Cats*! *Cats*. No! I have the *right* to make the cast album. I just thought you'd like to know that."

A quick afternoon break for a cool Evian water. Geffen jumps up and tells me about the first time he saw L.A. He paces the room, his graying black frizzy hair haloed by the sun bouncing in off Sunset Boulevard. "I graduated New Utrecht High School [in Brooklyn] and the next day I delivered a car, from the newspaper, it says 'Drive a car to California.' So I delivered a car to California and I got to—my brother was going to law school at UCLA and his girlfriend's brother drove me around Beverly Hills.

"I remember as I was driving through Beverly Hills and all I could think was how angry I was at my parents that they chose *Brooklyn* instead of Beverly Hills. I thought, 'Why the fuck would anybody *not* want to live here? *Look* at this. This is fabulous!' I thought, fuck! I'm gonna live *here*. As though the choice were between Brooklyn and Beverly Hills. Fortunately, now my life is structured so I can spend six months in L.A. and six months in New York. So I'm connected to both places. It must be what I want 'cause this *is* what I've done with my life."

A quick phone call to Mo Ostin and Warner Records. "Mo, have you heard the news on the record? At Lieberman it's number nine, at Sound Unlimited, number one. It's a breakout. I tell you, it hasn't even begun yet. And I want everybody who has a musical to come to me. *Dreamgirls* is a classy package and I'll do that with *Cats*."

A call to Frank Barsalona of Premier Talent, the largest booking firm in the country. "Frank! It's already Top Ten in every major chain in the country. It's A-rotation with Lieberman. I think we have an album here that can do five million copies. People are excited to play the record. When's the last time you heard that?"

David Geffen has not become known as a supreme deal-maker for nothing. He cut his first deal in 1964 when he was working in the mailroom of the William Morris Agency in New York. The guy he replaced had been fired for lying about his educational background. The agency had written to the college he'd claimed to have graduated from and found out otherwise. Geffen put down that he'd graduated from UCLA and then, since he was in the mailroom, after all, sat back and waited for the letter to come back from the UCLA registrar. When it did, he steamed it open, slipped in a forgery attesting to one D. Geffen's B.A., sealed the letter back up, and sent it on its way.

Geffen kept his job, and was soon booking and then managing acts, among them Laura Nyro, Joni Mitchell, Crosby, Stills & Nash—every singer/songwriter from the sixties practically. His own record company came next. But let Geffen tell the story. It is a sun-splashed L.A. afternoon and we are riding down Rodeo Drive in his Porsche en route to lunch. Asylum Records was started because of Jackson Browne, says Geffen, as we weave in and out of traffic.

"Jackson sent me a letter with a picture, this very attractive young guy, and I thought, 'Bob Dylan sent me an eight-by-ten glossy once and I threw it out,' and my secretary, thinking he was so attractive, listened to Jackson's tape and told me, 'You really have to listen to this.' So I started Asylum because I couldn't make a deal for Jackson. I tried to sell him to Columbia, Atlantic, and they all passed. I went to Ahmet Ertegun at Atlantic and I said I got this guy, the greatest, I'm very enthusiastic. Ahmet listened to the tape and says, 'Lousy guitar player and lousy singer.' I loved singers of their own songs so to me he sounded great. I went to Clive Davis and he passed. I got nowhere. I went to Ahmet and said, 'Listen, honestly, I'm doing you a favor with Jackson Browne, he's gonna be a big star.'

"Ahmet said, 'Listen don't do me no favors.' I said, 'You're gonna make a fortune, I *promise* you!' He said, 'I tell you what, I already got a fortune. Why don't *you* put up the money, you make the record, you make the fortune.' Which is how Asylum Records got started. I started the company with Ahmet and it was a very good deal for me because they weren't that interested in it. They were just accommodating me because I was this important manager.

"Within two years they bought it from me for seven million and I don't know what to make of it; I was this kid from Brooklyn. Seven million was more than I could imagine. They more than made their money back on it in six months. I said, 'Oh, shit! I gave the company away. Seven million is *nothing*. But Steve Ross, the head of WCI, made a new deal with me because it was clear to him that they had made such an incredible deal that it wasn't right for me and that it would not inspire me to keep working if they didn't compensate me correctly. So he made a sensational deal and it kept me with them and working."

Geffen expertly guides his Porsche into a parking garage and shortly we're at the head table at La Scala, another Geffen favorite. After ordering Evian water and pasta appetizers and making sure the restaurant has fresh shrimp, Geffen continues with his career saga. "So I left them with a fantastic record company, *jewel* record company. At that point I thought, 'Well, I've done this, I don't want it. Fuck the record business. On to the movie business!' Well, the movie business back then became a nightmare [*Oh God!* was one of his signings], because I'd gone from running my own company to having a big title but not really running the company and I was in a state of constant frustration. . . . I have no sense of politics, since I've never worked in big companies, and Warner Pix was a highly politicized situation and I was just fucking up constantly because I didn't realize you had to check with this person and send a carbon to this one and all the stuff people learn growing through the ranks of a big company. I had *no* idea. I was like a schmuck, completely naïve. By the end of the year I had stepped on so many toes without intending to do so that I had to get out. And did.

"Then I was confused. I didn't know what the hell to do. So I started teaching [at Yale]. Thought, I'll figure this out. I tried for three and a half years to figure it out. I hadn't figured it out and I started to panic and said, 'Oh, shit! *What* am I gonna do?' Then I went to Barbados with Paul Simon and I kept on asking him, 'What am I gonna do?' 'Look,' he said, 'the first thing you have to do is *begin*. You don't know where it will take you but *unless* you begin, you're always waiting to begin. *Start!* Just decide to go!' So I knew I had to do that. And so I did. Started a record company and it's grown into Broadway and the movies and it's not even two years old."

Geffen stopped his monologue to enjoy his shrimp, which were not inexpensive. He was the picture of a happy man.

Various Hollywood movers and shakers stopped by our table, all of whom offered the services of various directors, writers, stars or starlets should Geffen Films need them. At one point, Geffen felt sufficiently moved to try to answer my question of what exactly goes into a Deal.

"*Well*. Let me put it this way. I'm very good at understanding what numbers are about. I think I forgot trigonometry a very long time ago. But I know . . . I *can certainly negotiate* a deal. I know where the numbers are, what all the effects are on interest rates, and so on. Deals are all different. See, I don't think the cleverness comes from being able to negotiate a good deal, that is to say, the best terms or whatever. I think the *smart* in making a deal is picking the correct *material,* the correct *artist,* making as good a deal as you can with that artist or that material. There are *no* bargains, first of all, in life. I've never seen any. And I'm *not* looking to make a bargain. Because a deal in which somebody else is unhappy or I'm unhappy is a bad deal. It's gonna break somewhere. If I see that a deal can't be made comfortably for everybody, I just pass. Because I know that my life will be *shit* from this deal. In the area of deal-making in show business, I am capable of functioning in any area of it and making a good enough deal. I'm always afraid of the guys who are so *tough,* you know. I always think, Uh-oh, it's gonna be a tug of war here. There are attorneys who intend to make a fair deal. There are other attorneys who want it *all*. If by some stroke of good luck you happen to do well, they're back in five minutes to renegotiate. Generally speaking, I think the record business is filled for the most part with very decent people. I can't exactly say that I think the movie business is filled with decent people. I think it's filled with a high level of mean-spiritedness, and more people are vested in other people's failures than maybe *any* business in the world. . . . For *me,* I find it pretty easy to sail through the community. Particularly because I have one thing which is unique in this community. I have the support of Warner Communications and Steve Ross [reportedly to the tune of a $100 million blank check]. It's not a question of *clout;* it's a question of *backing.*"

After a respectful silence and a cup of coffee, I venture to say that that doesn't happen to everyone.

"*Name another one,*" Geffen replied quickly. "I can't. Can you?"

Holmby Hills is my idea of Southern California. Or at least Geffen's corner of it. He has just bought Marlo Thomas's hillside home and turned it into a realtor's sales pitch: solid Tudor manse on five acres with L.A. and ocean views, orange trees, big pool, et cetera. At 10:30 in the A.M., as I arrive at the Tudor and head for the bathhouse to change for a swim before lunch, I can hear iron being pumped. Geffen, who had never been in shape in his life, has done so. He had a gym built into the house and hired an instructor five mornings a week, no rain checks. Michael Bennett, who directed *Dreamgirls,* strolls out to the pool with me. He has stopped over in L.A. to discuss theater with Geffen. Bennett is pleased with Geffen's association with *Dreamgirls,* and feels that Geffen can fuel the next generation of cast albums.

Geffen, still huffing and puffing from his hour-and-a-half workout, joins us at poolside.

Everything is perfect, which I now expect from Geffen. The refrigerator in the bathhouse is stocked with Henry Weinhard's Private Reserve. There are Braun electric lighters at every table around the pool, even though Geffen seldom entertains. Lunch is exquisite and served at the right intervals by a staff that manages to remain unobtrusive.

"You know," Geffen says, as he supervises a very properly served luncheon, "one changes. Five or six years ago I went to the Russian Tea Room with Tony Perkins and his wife. Tony said, 'Caviar appetizer for everyone.' I said, 'Oh, no, not for me.' Because I'd *never* tasted it. Perkins said to me, 'You're just crazy, caviar's fabulous, how do you know you don't like it?' I say I know I don't like it and order chopped chicken liver. Perkins tells me he insists I eat one little piece. I said, 'I'm going to vomit if you make me eat this.' Everybody at the table drove me so crazy I took the tiniest little bite off the corner, thinking, I'm gonna throw up, literally. And I say, 'Gee, this tastes *great.*' And my world expanded so much because of that particular incident."

Geffen in New York City is only a trifle more hyper than Geffen in Los Angeles. In his Fifth Avenue apartment, high above Central Park, he sits at a small glass-topped table beside the window and works his phones. Behind him is a David Hockney painting. Over by the stereo wall is a Magritte. Tiffany lamps cast a soft glow over a wall of Tiffany vases. On the stereo is Donna Summer's next album, which Geffen assures me will be *the* big album of the year. He could be right. It sounds better than anything she's done before. And there's an expensive reason for that. She *had* recorded a double album produced by Georgio Moroder, but Geffen didn't like it and, in a move unusual in the record business, refused to issue it. Instead, he finally persuaded Quincy Jones to produce her and he's justifiably proud of the result.

The dining room table is covered with fresh roses and orchids, each in its own little crystal vase. Over lunch, as Summer sings "The Lush Life" in the background, Geffen tells me of the only irritant in his otherwise very enjoyable life. Robert Towne, who wrote and directed *Personal Best,* seems to be suing Geffen, Steve Ross, and Warner Bros.

Pictures, to the tune of $155 million, for breach of contract, fraud, defamation, and coercion. Towne wants $50 million in punitive damages from Geffen alone, and claims Geffen coerced him into signing an agreement whereby he gave up *Greystoke,* his Tarzan script.

"I will tell you about Robert Towne," Geffen says flatly, and it's one of the few times I can sense his temper rising. "Robert called me after Warner Brothers had pulled the plug on his film and he had been turned down by everyone else. The movie was simply gonna disappear. He begged me to pick it up. He's an old friend of mine and I read the script, which I thought was wonderful. Without taking the precautions that are necessary in a venture like this, I said yes. It never occurred to me that it would turn into this nightmare. Later, I realized what a disaster it was. He lied about the budget.

"I mean in this lawsuit, he charges that I annoyed him with long phone calls." Geffen laughs heartily. "The fact of the matter is, the great thing about the phone is that you can always *hang it up.* Or you don't *have* to pick it up.

"But I visited the set one day and found Robert in a condition that was not inspiring to confidence. But still I hung in there with him. I never fired him, which in retrospect I should have. He went way over budget. I called the production manager and asked how much money it would take to finish the film and what the shooting schedule was. He said he'd been instructed to not give me that information. I said, 'What do you mean? I can close down this film tomorrow.' He said, 'No you can't.' I asked why not. He said, 'Well, Robert saved all the shots between the two girls for the end, so if you close it down, there is no film.'

"I thought about it and about how sick and demented this kind of behavior was. I closed down the film and took possession of the negative." Geffen is clearly warming to his subject now, and talks faster and more animatedly.

"I did not let it go back to shoot until there was a signed contract and an agreement that beyond an agreed-upon budget Robert would be responsible for the overage. So, finally, a movie that was supposed to cost seven and a half million cost sixteen million. The reason for the lawsuit is that half a million of Robert's own money was put up for completion by selling *Greystoke* to Warner Brothers. That's something *he* initiated. So, he went over budget and spent his own money and now he wants it back.

"Oh." Geffen laughs. "Incidentally, he served *The New York Times* before I was served with the lawsuit. So that was the first I heard about it. Finally, Robert Towne has done some very good work as a writer, and as a director he has a lot to learn. Films are a *business* and most directors have a sense of responsibility to the costs of the film. Robert has no such sense. He's doing himself a disservice by suing Warner Brothers, Steve, and me for $155 million, which is larger than the gross for *Star Wars*. That's typical of his excess."

He fell silent. It's unusual to hear Geffen vent his spleen in such a way. But he was not finished yet.

"You know," he says, a bright gleam in his eye, "the episode with Robert Towne reminds me of the song by Oscar Brown, Jr., about the snake. A woman finds an injured snake and it begs her to take it in and help it. She's afraid to, but it charms her into it. When the snake is completely healed, it *bites* her. She says, '*Why* did you do that?' And the snake says, 'You knew I was a snake when you took me in.' "

And David Geffen laughs uproariously.

Chapter 6

Covetousness

Rock 'n' Roll Tragedy: Why Eleven Died in Cincinnati

We didn't call it festival seating. We called it animal seating, because when they came in, they came in like a herd of cattle.

—A Riverfront Coliseum employee

At about 7:15 on the evening of December 3, 1979, Larry Magid sat down to dinner with Frank Wood in the luxurious Beehive Club, a private club in the upper reaches of Cincinnati's Riverfront Coliseum. Wood, who is general manager of the city's premier rock station, WEBN-FM, remarked to Magid, who is head of Electric Factory of Philadelphia (one of the country's leading rock promoters), that the crowd streaming onto the coliseum floor far below them for that evening's Electric Factory–promoted Who concert seemed to be quite orderly. A "happy crowd," he said, not at all like the rabble that had disrupted previous "chain-saw concerts" there, like the Outlaws' fighting crowd and Led Zeppelin's mob. The crowd below them was sprinting to get as close as possible to the stage, in the grand tradition of "festival" or unreserved seating. By agreement of the coliseum management (the coliseum is privately owned), Electric Factory, and the Who, mostly general-admission tickets had been sold: supposedly 3,578 reserved seats in the loges at eleven dollars each and 14,770 general-admission tickets at ten dollars each.

A few of those thousands of young people—the youngest was four years old—had blood on their shoes as they ran happily down the concrete steps into the "pit," the seatless area in front of the stage where the true fanatics stand throughout the show. But no one noticed. Some of the people who paused—dazed—beside the green-and-white pizza stand just past the nine turnstiles at the main entrance had no shoes on at all, and some had lost other bits of clothing. But other than that, inside the hall, it just seemed to be business as usual: the familiar ragtag rock 'n' roll army staggering into the hall after five or six hours of waiting outside in the cold for the doors to open and keeping warm and happy with herbs and beer and wine and each other.

Magid and Wood continued their leisurely dinner. They still had plenty of time before the Who would come on, which would actually be about twenty minutes after the scheduled starting time of 8:00 P.M., because the band would be preceded by clips from the film *Quadrophenia*. Cal Levy, who runs Electric Factory's Cincinnati office, cruised the aisles. Things looked okay to him. He had noticed at about 1:30 that afternoon that a large crowd was congregating around the main entrance—two banks of eight glass doors each, situated in a large V. Levy had found coliseum operations director Richard Morgan and asked him to put into effect a special security procedure they sometimes used, which was to station guards at ramp entrances and allow only ticket holders onto the plaza at the main entrance, thus eliminating the gate-crashing element. The coliseum's entry level—the concourse and plaza—is reachable only by a bridge from adjacent Riverfront Stadium, where most people park, and by ramps from street level. There were no police on the spacious plaza at 1:30. Levy suggested to Morgan that some should be there. Sixteen arrived at 3:00 P.M. and by four there were twenty-five. The coliseum hires off-duty police to patrol the outside, and for security within the coliseum employs guards from the Cincinnati Private Police Association.

At about 6:30, Lieutenant Dale Menkhaus, who headed the twenty-five-man detail outside, decided that the eight thousand or so people who were now packed around the banks of doors were beginning to present a problem. The doors weren't scheduled to open until 7:00, but the crowd could hear the Who conducting its sound check and wanted in. It was thirty-six degrees and the wind coming off the Ohio River made it feel much colder. Menkhaus later said he told Levy and Morgan to open some doors; Levy told him the doors couldn't be opened till the sound check was over. Menkhaus was also told there weren't enough ticket takers. Morgan, as is the case with all coliseum employees, has no comment.

At 7:00 P.M. the Who left the stage. No one inside the coliseum knew that while they ate dinner and conducted business as usual, waiting until the appointed time to admit the "animals," just outside those front doors the horror had already begun, a horror under a full moon, a horror of chilling magnitude that will probably never be fully explained.

On June 28, 1976, a young man named Richard Klopp sat down to his typewriter in his apartment on Auburn Avenue in Cincinnati. He was slow to anger but he was angry. That morning he had gone out bright and early to buy tickets to see Neil Young and Stephen Stills at the coliseum. He got to Ticketron an hour ahead of time because he wanted good seats, only to find that tickets were sold out because they had gone on sale three days before the date advertised by Electric Factory. Klopp was already unhappy about the last two Electric Factory shows he'd been to, so he said, "By God, I'll send them a concerned citizen letter"— and just to be sure they didn't blow him off as some rock druggie, he decided to send carbon copies to the city council, WEBN, Ticketron, and the Cincinnati public-safety director.

Klopp wrote: "The two concerts that I have attended (the Who and Paul McCartney) were both sold out on a 'festival seating' or general-admission basis. What this means for the promoter is more money; for the concertgoer . . . this means that he'll probably have to sit in the aisles or on the floor . . . jeopardizing his safety and the safety of others. If a fire or general panic were to break out, many, many people would be trampled to death. . . . Because civil people like to avoid these kinds of conflagrations, many concertgoers make a point of arriving at the coliseum two, three, and even four hours before the doors are 'scheduled' to open. At the Paul McCartney concert, for example, I arrived at 5:30, two hours before the doors were to open. After a span of two hours, several thousand people had congregated on the plaza in front of the doors. When they were finally opened (a half-hour late) the mass of people pressed forward, literally crushing those by the doors. . . . This is what happens when tickets are sold on a 'festival seating' basis, and it is no festival."

On the night of December 3, 1979, as Richard Klopp was caught up in the horror on the plaza and saw his wife swept away from him in the crush, it didn't immediately occur to him that what he had forecast was suddenly happening to *him*. He was just trying to survive. Klopp is six feet two and weighs over 200 pounds, but he went down; the pressure from those behind him toppled him. He was flat on his face on the concrete, and those marching, charging feet were all around him. It was no great comfort that city councilman Jerry Springer had actually replied sympathetically to his letter—no one else did, and Springer never *actually* was able to get anything done. What Klopp felt, oddly, as he wondered whether he would live or die, was *anger* at Cincinnati's establishment, at the forces that made him get a general-admission ticket when he wanted a reserved seat, at whoever it was that wouldn't open those doors to relieve the crowd pressure. He seldom went to rock concerts anymore, but he had really wanted to see the Who and had gone to Ticketron an hour early. All tickets had been sold by the time he got to the window; he saw scalpers buying a hundred tickets each. Klopp ended up paying sixty dollars for tickets for himself and his wife.

He had gotten to the plaza at 2:40 the afternoon of December 3 because he wanted to be sure they got good seats; he had brought a book with him to read. That book, *Structuralist Poetics* by Jonathan Culler, was still in his right hand as he lay on the concrete. Someone, miraculously, helped him to his feet and he was back in the crush, his arms pinned to his sides. At one point he was within five feet of a closed door, but he had no control over his movement. At times his feet were off the ground. Despite the cold, he was drenched in sweat. He couldn't breathe. He and everyone around him had their heads tilted straight back, their noses up to try to get some air. He noticed that an actual steam, a *vapor,* was rising off the crowd in the moonlight. He would later be angered to read that it was a "stampede," because to him it was a concentration of too many people in too small a space with nowhere to go but forward— people in the back were yelling, "One, two, three, push!" but they didn't know people in the front were falling. There was little noise. Some people tried to calm those who were panicking. Some shouted, "Stay up! Stay up or you're gone!" Some chanted, "Open the fucking doors!"

The forward crush continued and pressed up against those closed doors; the crush had started around 6:15 and ground on for an hour and a half or so. Klopp noticed that there were actual human waves swaying like palm trees in a hurricane. He saved his life by seeking out the eye of the hurricane, and he was swept out of the crush.

He couldn't find his wife. He ran to the first policeman he saw and shouted, "What are you *doing*? People are getting *trampled* up there." The policeman looked him over and asked, "What do you do for a living?" Klopp replied, almost in shock, "Working on a Ph.D. in language." The policeman said, "Well, you just used a dangling participle." Klopp, caught up in the absurdity, said, "I think I know more about language than you do." The policeman smiled. "Well, don't tell me how to do my job, then." Klopp lost his temper. "People are getting *hurt*." The policeman said, "Well, we can't do anything." Klopp finally got inside and found his wife.

A few feet away, Mark Helmkamp was pleading with a policeman to do something. He said to the cop, "Here, take my ID and bust me for false information if you don't believe me." He said the policeman told him to move along.

A day later, Helmkamp was still furious. "I was greatly disturbed by WCPO-TV's depiction of us as a drug-crazed mob. There were too many people and just two doors open. It was an incredible bottleneck; it was a slow squeeze, not a stampede. I was stuck in it for forty-five minutes. I went down twice and wasn't sure that I would make it. I saw guys with blue lips—they couldn't get oxygen. I saw, I think, four ticket takers after I walked over all the shoes to get in. I couldn't keep my feet on the ground the whole time. I kept my arms in front of my chest to keep from getting crushed. People were climbing up on other people's shoulders. Some people went berserk and started swinging their elbows. That was the only blood. There was no group panic. After I saw the dead people, it sunk in. Dead. Just dead. It pissed me off to see Uncle Walter Cronkite blaming *us* for this."

The doors were officially opened at 7:05; according to eyewitnesses, four doors out of the sixteen were open, and two of those were closed and blocked at times by guards with billy clubs. From where he was in the crowd, Phil Sheridan saw only one door open. "It looked like they attempted to open more, but the crowd was so tightly packed it was useless. I was maybe fifteen rows of people back, staring at this door, and it hung like about six inches open and they finally sprung it open and that's all I remember till I got inside. I could see people smashed up against the doors that weren't open. I had ahold of my girlfriend and my buddy grabbed me by the shoulders and I took him by the hand and we started to make our way through the turnstiles. Well, in that ten or fifteen seconds it took us to get our act together, we were now inside between the doors and the turnstiles and the door was a frenzy and they're still trying to take tickets! God, it was insane! I was three abreast in this goddamn turnstile, which was only eighteen inches wide! People were getting hurled in and shoved through the turnstiles and the ticket takers were still saying, 'Hey, where's your ticket?' The initial rush came about six-thirty because that's when people smelled blood, you know, the magic hour, they're finally gonna open the doors for us. There was continuous pushing till seven and then the doors opened shortly after that. God, this one girl, it must have been twenty minutes before the doors opened and all of a sudden I feel a tug on my arm; it's this girl, and her head was at my waist and she said, 'Excuse me, my feet are back there somewhere.' She was *horizontal.*

"I went back out to look for my friends; I saw—and this is after the show started, which was about eight-twenty—I saw the same scene. It was still crazy. It was crazier between the outside doors and the turnstiles than it was outside, 'cause by then people were really going for broke. I found my friend Bill and he said he saw people going over the tops of the doors, he saw bodies piled in front of the door, and people were going over them and around them any way they could. At about nine, I saw more waves of people. I looked outside and saw what must have been thousands of dollars' worth of personal articles strewn everywhere, these terrible piles of shoes, shoes trapped in that chain-link fencing behind the turnstiles. I wonder about the kinds of injuries that weren't reported."

The twenty-five-man police force outside finally found the first body at 7:54 P.M. After the ambulances and the fire department and the fire chief and the mayor and the city safety director and the Flying Squad from the Academy of Medicine and additional police and the TV crews and everybody else got there, they finally understood that this was serious. Cincinnati proper put on its serious face. TV crews were asking onlookers if drugs and alcohol hadn't caused this "stampede."

Mayor Ken Blackwell—this was his first day on the job—was summoned from his dinner with House Speaker Tip O'Neill and said it looked to him like this awful tragedy had been caused by "festive seating." It was his decision to continue the concert, lest the many thousands inside riot if the show were stopped.

Promoter Larry Magid said he first learned of the trouble at 8:45 from a coliseum employee and went backstage to tell the Who's manager, Bill Curbishly, that there were four dead, "two ODs and two crushed." According to Curbishly, the fire marshal arrived and said he thought there was a mass overdosage. He wanted to stop the concert; then he learned that the deaths were due to asphyxiation and that people were still being treated on the plaza level.

Curbishly told him it would be senseless to stop the concert, that there could be a riot and people might stampede back across the plaza. The fire marshal said, "I agree with you totally."

By the time the show was over, Curbishly knew of eleven deaths. He told the Who that something serious had happened and they should hurry their encore. After the brief encore, he took them into the tuning room and told them of the deaths. They were devastated.

"Initially, we felt stunned and empty," said Roger Daltrey, three days after the concert. "We felt we couldn't go on. But you gotta. There's no point in stopping."

Lieutenant Menkhaus said sixteen doors were open and Cal Levy echoed that; Electric Factory attorney Tom Gould said nine to eleven doors were open and Roger Daltrey said three were open. Dozens of eyewitnesses told *Rolling Stone* that never during the trouble were more than four doors open and that only two were open most of the time. The coliseum management still refuses to say how many tickets were sold, how many guards were on duty, how many ticket takers or ushers there were or anything else. Curbishly said Electric Factory paid $7,800 to the coliseum for ushers, ticket takers, interior security, and cleanup.

Including emergency exits, there are 106 doors at the coliseum (although John Tafaro, spokesman for the coliseum, would not confirm or deny this number); why at times only two at the main entrance were open will be a point of speculation for some time.

When Riverfront Coliseum first opened on September 9, 1975, with a concert by the Allman Brothers, an usher on duty named Donald Fox said that the coliseum had too many outside doors and that gates rather than glass doors should be installed at the main entrance on the plaza. His was the first of many warnings that were ignored. Riverfront Coliseum was trouble waiting to happen.

Riverfront Coliseum exists because a man named Brian Heekin wanted a hockey team in Cincinnati and therefore needed an arena. Heekin, his brother Trey, and their friend William DeWitt, Jr., all great sports fans, were the guiding forces behind the coliseum. In the early seventies, Brian—whose great-grandfather formed the Heekin Can Company, which was the family's fortune and its entree into Cincinnati's relatively small business and social elite—had tried to buy the Kentucky Colonels of the American Basketball Association and bring them to Cincinnati; he lost out to now-Kentucky Governor John Y. Brown. But Heekin really wanted and sought a National Hockey League team. When Cincinnati began talking about a renewal project for the riverfront area, Heekin popped up with the idea of a big indoor sports arena there. He initially wanted the city to build it and lease it to his Cincinnati Hockey Club (later changed to Cincinnati Sports Inc.). The city came close to financing and building such an arena. Heekin tried and failed to get local banks to finance an $18-million arena. Heekin was offering the city an NHL team, the ABA Colonels, and a World Team Tennis franchise. When it seemed to him that the city was not going to help, Heekin decided to build his arena in the suburbs. All of a sudden he got what he called "unbelievable" pressure from local businessmen to build at the waterfront. And all of a sudden he began getting local support. The chamber of commerce got behind the idea, the governor offered to help with state revenue bonds, and then, before anyone knew what was happening, the chamber of commerce called a press conference on August 8, 1973, to announce that a sports arena would be built at the riverfront; that local banks and savings and loan associations would put up $10 million in state industrial revenue bonds; that $4 million would come from Heekin's Cincinnati Sports Inc.; that another $4 million was forthcoming from city, state, and federal funds; and that a final $1 million would come from leasing the arena's posh sky boxes to wealthy patrons. Heekin's newly formed Cincinnati Coliseum Corporation bought three acres of land next to Riverfront Stadium from the city for $200,000. The McNulty Company of Minneapolis drew up the plans, and the Universal Contracting Corporation of Norwood, Ohio, was contracted to build it. The city ended up using state highway funds and federal funds to build the elaborate sky bridges that connect the coliseum concourse to street level. Thus, all the concrete right outside the coliseum doors is city property. That's where the eleven died.

Heekin never did get the NHL franchise he said he had, nor did he get a World Team Tennis franchise. The Kentucky Colonels did play a few games there before pulling out. Gradually, as with so many such arenas around the country, rock shows supported the place. Instead of an NHL team, Heekin got the World Hockey Association Stingers, hardly a major draw. When the WHA folded and the Stingers were absorbed into the Central Hockey League, Heekin's corporation got what was said to be a settlement close to $3 million and the Stingers continued to play in the coliseum, paying rent of $4,000 a game. The Stingers played there two nights after the Who and drew 869 paying fans. The University of Cincinnati basketball team still plays games at the coliseum but has reportedly considered pulling out in the past because of heating problems, among other things. At the start of one game between two other teams, the players sat huddled in blankets because the temperature inside was in the forties. After the Who show, the NCAA decided to reject the coliseum's bid for basketball finals there, although the NCAA claims the decision had nothing to do with the tragedy. Promoters canceled the two remaining rock shows of 1979 after the Who show. Local journalists said the coliseum's future was not bright. Big events there the past year have been a tractor-pulling contest and a Jehovah's Witnesses convention.

The coliseum's first fatality came on October 4, 1975, when seventeen-year-old Thomas Lambert, pursued by police who said he had cursed them, jumped or fell to his death from the plaza level to the street below.

Security problems have been noticeable at the coliseum. In March 1976, police officer Walter Scott told the *Cincinnati Enquirer* that there had been many incidents in which coliseum personnel refused to co-operate in emergency situations. He said he was worried that a life-or-death situation might arise. On August 3, 1976, when Elton John played the arena, there was big trouble. A crowd of about two thousand rushed the doors. No one was hurt badly, but police and fire officials found numerous fire-code violations, including locked exit doors. An editorial in the *Enquirer* the next day said that things weren't right at the coliseum during rock shows but concluded: "We'd be surprised, though, if the Elton John fracas is repeated anytime soon." On August 5, 1976, fire captain Ed Schneuer told local media that problems were getting worse at the coliseum because of festival seating, and that kids were gathering there earlier and earlier because of it. Fire captain James Gamm said that festival seating was a problem because, in a case of serious trouble inside the coliseum, bodies could "pile up in a major catastrophe."

City councilman Springer said publicly that festival seating caused a "climate of disorder." Brian Heekin disagreed, saying that Springer was not qualified to comment on people's behavior at concerts and that kids liked festival seating. Heekin also said he wouldn't mind talking with city officials about the problem of people urinating outside the coliseum.

Also on August 5, Brian Heekin, coliseum operations director Richard Morgan, and security director James Madgett were each charged with one count of failure to comply with ten lawful orders of the fire chief regarding building-code violations at the Elton John show. "The city is just trying to cover its tracks," Heekin told the *Enquirer*. "It's city property outside the doors."

According to the *Cincinnati Post,* Heekin pleaded no contest to the charge and was fined a hundred dollars. The charges against Morgan and Madgett were dismissed.

On August 8, 1976, an unnamed security guard at the coliseum told the *Enquirer* that festival-seating concerts were always oversold—he thought they were crowding 20,000 into the place.

On August 11, 1976, an editorial in the *Enquirer* said, "There is no reason to justify a ticket-selling procedure that encourages early congregation on the . . . plaza. Experience has shown repeatedly that gatherings of this kind are open invitations to trouble. . . . Management would be prudent in installing staggered rails so that ticket lines could more easily be kept orderly."

That same day, city manager William Donaldson organized a task force to draw up a plan for security at rock shows at the coliseum. "We want," said Donaldson, "to make sure their operation never again is an occasion for risk to the citizens of Cincinnati."

Three of the seven members of this Public Safety Study Team were from the coliseum: Heekin, Morgan, and Madgett. The other four were from city government. Their report, issued August 24, 1976, said in so many words that in the future everything would be fine and dandy at the coliseum. Section Three of the report, regarding festival seating, said: "The matter of 'Festival Seating' (nonreserved seating) was briefly discussed; however, no recommendation is being made at this time. The team felt that we should first evaluate the results of improved fire safety and security methods before taking a firm position on seating arrangements. It would seem that if Fire Prevention Code requirements and security needs are fully met, that the method of seating may become a secondary concern."

A week earlier, on August 13, 1976, Mayor Bobbie Sterne had asked for a study of seat sales at rock shows and recommended that all seats be reserved.

And before that, on August 6, 1976, fire chief Bert Lugannani sent a memo to a city council member in which he said there were numerous fire-code violations at the coliseum and that the number of guards and open exits was not sufficient. The chief also addressed himself to the matter of festival seating: "Selling a concert on a general-admission basis (festival seating) allows for sale of a ticket for each fixed seat and each specified standing area (i.e., 15,800 seats; 1,800 people permitted on the arena floor). Placement of the stage prohibits viewing the concert from approximately 4,000 of the seats sold. Those persons have no recourse other than to congregate in the exit way if they desire to watch the performers. It has been recommended that the concerts be sold on a reserved-seat basis. It was felt by the responsible coliseum officials that this would create an economic hardship." Nothing was done. A second city safety report produced a similar nonreaction.

"Cincinnati as a city," said one member of the local "rock 'n' roll establishment" who preferred not to be identified, "expects rock fans to be like Reds fans—who are actually worse. It's like you're supposed to be going to church. It was only a year ago that the Bengals allowed banners at the stadium. Maybe this happened because rock fans were regarded as lower than sports fans, who can do anything they want. Maybe this is a city that wants to be cosmopolitan without regarding rock fans as anything but a nuisance. But a nuisance that provided a lot of money. The coliseum was built as a sports arena. But rock 'n' roll kept it afloat." The coliseum refused to comment about this.

There were other red flags that were ignored. Fleetwood Mac played the coliseum a month before the Who, and even though seating for the Mac show was completely reserved, there was a bottleneck at the entrance because, according to an eyewitness, not enough doors were open.

The night of the Who concert, business continued as usual until eleven people died. Some blamed the victims for their own deaths, even though it has been proved that some of them—like David Heck, who got out of the crush and went back in to try to help others—died while trying to stop the madness even as police ignored them.

*   *   *

Cincinnati moved quickly to blame "festival seating" for the tragedy, although no one explained why festival seating had been permitted for so long at the coliseum when previous concerts had proved it dangerous. No one explained why even though Ticketron claims ticket sales were limited to eight per person, scalpers were spotted leaving outlets with stacks of tickets. In the week after the concert only city councilman Jerry Springer said there should have been someone at the show with the authority to open the doors when there was obviously a disaster in the offing. No one said who could have had the authority. It had been business as usual for everyone. Dozens of concertgoers told *Rolling Stone* that they had been treated like so many sheep to be herded through so many doors. The *Cincinnati Enquirer*'s banner headline of December 5 read: ALL DENY BLAME FOR TRAGEDY. And that's probably where it will stand. After the show, Pete Townshend said he felt partly responsible because, "It's a rock 'n' roll event that has created this, and we feel deeply a part of rock 'n' roll." Local commentators tried to pitch drugs and alcohol as the reason for the alleged "stampede."

This writer visited the coliseum and got as many "no comments" as he could use for ten years.

Electric Factory's Cal Levy did agree to talk, however. Levy, who actually was the show's promoter—Magid had come in just to see the Who—was visibly shaken. He contended that he had no control over the opening of doors or the number of guards.

He paced his attorney's office in the twenty-sixth floor of Carew Tower in downtown Cincinnati, stroked his beard, and said, "Hey, I'm no Bill Graham, okay? I just think that when all the facts are known, all the reports are completed, that it will show that there was a combination of things that brought about an uncontrollable situation on that plaza.

"All the procedures used Monday night were the procedures that were implemented on all the previous shows where nothing ever went wrong."

Could he have had the authority to order those front doors opened when it became apparent they should be opened?

"No. Our only responsibility is to get the group onstage, to pay for staffing at the coliseum [although he said he had no responsibility for the size of the staff]." He said Electric Factory had provided "peer security" (i.e., young people who are not in uniform) for the floor-level general-admission area and had arranged to have paramedics and ambulances ready.

Electric Factory's attorney, Tom Gould, said he thought that everybody concerned had a zone of responsibility and that everybody discharged "what they thought was in the best interest and was the right thing to do." Levy and Gould both said that maybe no one was at fault; perhaps it was a natural disaster.

Levy was quick to point out that Electric Factory had promoted Cincinnati's first outdoor rock show, the Eagles, at Riverfront Stadium. "We had fifty-two thousand kids, general admission, and the same parties involved in the planning. Dale Menkhaus and I worked extensively on the security. And nothing happened. But what I think we're faced with here is unusual circumstances that all merged at one time and in one place. Maybe there were enough doors; were they open early enough? Was there a high level of drugs or intoxication? The music from the inside?"

But, he was reminded, things had gone wrong before. Some earlier shows had been violent.

"I can't deny that there are problems at shows; it happens everywhere in the country, right? Nobody could predict it, and I don't feel anybody could have controlled it."

Soon thereafter came the first of what will undoubtedly be an unending series of lawsuits. Todd Volkman, who was allegedly injured, filed a $1.2-million class-action suit (which can be expanded to recover tens of millions) against the promoter, the coliseum, and the Who, but not the city of Cincinnati, on whose property he was allegedly injured. A second, filed by Betty Snyder, mother of the late Phillip Snyder, does name the city as one of the defendants. In that $10.25-million suit, the city is accused of negligence in its failure to follow the advice from its own Human Relations Commission to ban festival seating. It also alleges the city police were negligent in failing to enforce drug and liquor laws. (The police reported twenty-eight arrests for drugs and disorderly conduct on the plaza the night of the concert.)

One local lawyer said gleefully that there isn't enough liability insurance in the world to cover the potential lawsuits that could come out of the Who show. Under Ohio law, parties who feel injured physically or emotionally (a hot line was immediately set up for the emotionally warped) have two years to file suit.

The city of Cincinnati registered immediate civic outrage. No more festival seating, *probably,* said the city government. A task force was set up to find out what was wrong. Frank Wood of WEBN-FM was named to it. He said that he was not sure what the task force could do, all he knew was that he had read in the morning paper that "I'm not allowed to point a finger at anyone, and I think that's a shame." The task force has no subpoena power, and it was widely viewed in Cincinnati as window dressing.

The coroner's office said the dead apparently died from "suffocation by asphyxiation due to compression" and "suffocation due to accidental mob stampede." Toxicology tests for drug or alcohol residues in the victims are forthcoming.

An editorial in the *Cincinnati Post* said the coliseum had been the city's "citadel of lawlessness." Mark Helmkamp called home to tell his folks he was okay and he got a pot lecture. The victims were blamed.

Promoters across the country blamed festival seating. Larry Magid said that he felt terrible and that he personally didn't like festival seating, but that's what the kids wanted. A kid in Cincinnati printed up a few T-shirts that read I SURVIVED THE WHO CONCERT.

Roger Daltrey, weary and shaken, said, "It was really a freak; it's not a nightly occurrence, you know."

The mayor of Providence, Rhode Island, canceled the Who show there, saying that after two performances the Who was averaging 5.5 fatalities per show. Angry kids marched in Cincinnati and in Providence to say that rock 'n' roll should not be automatically blamed. They got little support.

Misadventures in Paradise: Keeping Up With Jimmy Buffett in the Land of Sunshine, Greenies, Fins, and Bikinis

He is dedicated as ever to certain indecencies and shall we say reversible brain damage . . . he was among the first of the Sucking Chest Wound Singers to sleep on the yellow line . . . this throwback altarboy of Mobile, Alabama, brings spacey up-country tunes strewn with forgotten crabtraps, Confederate memories, chemical daydreams, Ipana vulgarity, ukulele madness and, yes Larry, a certain sweetness. But there is a good deal to admire in Buffett's inspired evocations from this queerly amalgamated past most Americans now share. What Jimmy Buffett knows is that our personal musical history lies at the curious hinterland where Hank Williams and Xavier Cugat meet with somewhat less animosity than the theoreticians would have us believe.

—Tom McGuane, from the liner notes to *A White Sport Coat and a Pink Crustacean,* 1973

Six years after *White Sport Coat* put Jimmy Buffett on the musical map, he still resides in his curious hinterland, but he's moved it farther south. On this radiant summer afternoon, Buffett's bar-hopping in the Caribbean and taking on a glow that rivals the tropical sun. But his reverie is abruptly shattered by a chance remark:

"You know, Jimmy, you really oughta drink a lotta pineapple juice. It'll make your come taste *sweet!*"

The blond, bronzed, pigtailed woman who says that to famed Caribbean rake Jimmy Buffett almost falls off her barstool laughing as he blushes a pulsating scarlet through his tan. Joining in the merriment are assorted loungers, loafers, aging hippies, and members of Buffett's band—the Coral Reefers—who are scattered around the veranda of L'Entrepont, a harborside bar on the island of St. Barthélémy. Buffett, fighting to regain composure, declines the pineapple-juice advice and signals for another "greenie" (Caribbean for Heineken).

In the interest of various individuals' marital harmony, it should be noted that Buffett, thirty-two, does not know the woman in question, although she, like most members of this expatriate community of young Americans, takes a proprietary interest in Jimmy. He is *theirs*—he used to run a little marijuana through the islands himself, and he lives the life he portrays in his sun-drenched, saltwater-dappled songs of Caribbean romance and adventure.

And the local drug smugglers—Lord, they swear by the music and would no more make a run in their boats without Buffett cassettes on board than set sail without a few cases of greenies. And now, through a curious coincidence, Buffett has dropped anchor at St. Bart's, a smugglers' haven. From L'Entrepont, I can see about two dozen seaworthy vessels besides Buffett's own fifty-foot ketch, *Euphoria II.*

St. Bart's is a tiny, splendid island. Its populace is packed with sun-baked American and European hippies with lots of money and no visible means of support. They sit around all day at places like the topless and sometimes bottomless beach over by the Hotel Jean Bart, drinking pineapple juice and greenies. At night they slip their boats out into the opalescent waters to take care of business. No wonder Buffett is taking a break from recording his new album, *Volcano,* at George Martin's AIR Studios in Montserrat to rest and relax on St. Bart's. Ever since Jimmy tired of Key West's growing commercialism and left there in 1977 for Aspen (subletting his house to Hunter Thompson), he's been looking for a foothold in the Caribbean, and St. Bart's seems to be the ideal spot.

When I'd called him from New York about our meeting in Montserrat, he'd suggested this stopover. His directions sounded simple enough: "Fly to St. Maarten and charter a boat or plane to St. Bart's.

Wait for me at Le Select Bar." Still, I've been a little gun-shy of Buffett's sense of time and space since the first time I didn't interview him. It was in 1972 in Austin, Texas. Buffett was playing solo at a little folkie joint called Castle Creek and in those pre-platinum days he and I were on the same pay scale and social stratum. He put on a brilliant show and I decided to give the boy a break and splash him across the pages of *Rolling Stone*. He peered at me through a haze of Lone Star beer and agreed to meet me the following afternoon. Five years later, we finally got around to the interview.

Times have *not* changed. During his recent summer tour, we made an abortive attempt to meet in Charlotte, North Carolina. I got there all right, only to discover that Buffett had mistaken Charlotte for Charleston, West Virginia. What I mean is, his songwriting is a little sharper than his grasp of geography. Still, I took him at his word this go-around and, after landing safely at St. Bart's grass airstrip, set off for Le Select Bar.

Le Select is a legendary bar in the Caribbean, a real crossroads for smugglers and other exotic charlatans. It's a tawdry, open-air, white-washed-stone joint with outhouses that would make a sewer rat gag, but the clientele makes the place, I suppose. Naked hippie children crawl across the floor, hard-eyed hippies whisper conspiratorially in English, French, and Spanish at the bar, dogs wander in and out. I settled in for a series of beers and, after the regulars huddled and decided I wasn't from Interpol, one of them volunteered the information that Buffett *might* well be on the island.

"Big party last night," one of them whispered to me. "Everybody on the island was fucked up. Lots of acid. Buy you a greenie?"

Four hours later, I began to wonder whether Buffett had perhaps . . . *forgotten* he'd promised to meet me. I mean, a guy who claims that his two major influences are the pirate Jean Lafitte and Mitch Miller might have something else on his mind other than meeting a reporter.

"I enjoy this life as a jester/Seems to keep me moving around," Buffett sings in "Stranded on a Sandbar," one of his new songs, and that's a pretty fair self-assessment. Much like Jerry Jeff Walker (who first introduced Buffett to Key West and the Caribbean way of thought), he's a rambling, good-timey troubadour who can also rock out when the spirit seizes him. His recent success seems both accidental and incidental: a journalism major in college, a failed Nashville songwriter, a former reporter for *Billboard* who writes witty and unconventional songs. Any guy who's penned such minor classics as "Why Don't We Get Drunk (and Screw)" and "My Head Hurts, My Feet Stink and I Don't Love Jesus" is maybe operating with his own particular vision of the universe.

Two more greenies, I decided, and then I'm leaving. Head for the beach by the Hotel Jean Bart for a couple of days, then fly back to New York and tell the boss, "Sorry, no story there. Didn't work out."

Unfortunately, my route to the beach takes me by L'Entrepont and Buffett, spying me, flaps off the veranda in his ragged cutoffs and T-shirt. "Hey, *where* you been?" he asks solicitously as he hugs me. "We saw your plane come in. Siddown. Have a drink. Man, have you ever seen anything like this? The Coral Reefers are getting a tan for the first time in their lives!"

How can you get mad at a rogue like that? All you can do is slip into his Caribbean mind-set and wait to see what happens.

"Listen," says Buffett, "the album's going great. We'll go out to the boat after a while and listen to some tapes. Russ Kunkel is drumming on it and he's *perfect* for the group. On Monday James Taylor's coming down to do some vocals with me and he's bringing a couple of his brothers. How you been?"

Beaming almost paternally, he looks around the table at his Coral Reefers, scatters a sheaf of greenbacks across the table, and says, "Let's go out to the boat."

Buffett pads barefoot down to the quayside, where his rubber dinghy is tied up. He cranks up the outboard engine and we thread our way past anchored yachts in the lowering light and board *Euphoria II,* a lovely, spotless craft. In the cabin, Buffett pops open fresh brews, puts on a cassette of rough cuts from *Volcano,* and sits down beneath a framed picture of himself in the Oval Office with Carter and Mondale. "That photo does wonders for customs inspectors," he says wryly, as "Survive" comes over the speakers. "Eat your heart out, Billy Joel!" he shouts. "Aw, I'm just kidding," he adds, although it *is* a Joel-like piano song.

"Survive," I say to him, is really a departure from previous Buffett songs, which tend to gather themselves in two distinct camps: sensitive ballads or clever wordplays. That pattern was set with his first ABC album, *A White Sport Coat and a Pink Crustacean,* which was one of the unheralded sensations of 1973, alternating ballads like "He Went To Paris" with funny, goofball songs such as "Why Don't We Get Drunk."

"I know what you mean," Buffett agrees. "Hell, I sat down one day and listened to Billy Joel's *52nd Street.* I like Billy Joel, I think he's a good writer. But I just sat down and said to myself, 'Well, *goddamn.* I can do one of those if I want to.' That really made me get off my ass and look seriously at this whole project. So that's the way I made *Volcano.* I went back and listened to *A White Sport Coat . . .* and *A1A,* which was probably my most popular album, and I just said, '*Shit,* I can write a Billy Joel song.' "

Volcano is a long way from Buffett's first album—the 324-copy-selling *Down to Earth,* released in 1970 by Barnaby Records (he didn't care; Barnaby gave him $500 to buy a new guitar). Another Barnaby album and a series of records on ABC solidified his position in the early and mid-Seventies as the perfect composite of a rocking folkie: wittier than John Prine or Steve Goodman, sunnier than Jerry Jeff Walker, and harder edged than the wimps (who know who they are). He left a failed marriage in Nashville for the good life in Key West with Jerry Jeff (with whom he wrote "Railroad Lady" on 1973's *White Sport Coat,* a song that became a country classic after Lefty Frizzell recorded it). His commercial success was moderate, although his cult following was fanatical and he soon drew exalted admirers like James Taylor and the Eagles. The breakthrough year was 1977: *Changes in Latitudes, Changes in Attitudes* sold platinum, "Margaritaville" went gold, Irving Azoff signed him to Front Line Management, and he toured with the Eagles; 1978's albums, *Son of a Son of a Sailor* and the live *You Had to Be There* sold well. But Azoff himself has guaranteed that *Volcano* will be Buffett's biggest album ever. I'll be greatly surprised if it's "not Top Five."

"Volcano," the title song, comes on the boat's cassette deck and Buffett smiles at its Caribbean cross-rhythms. "I'm really proud of this," he says, fetching more greenies from his tiny refrigerator. "Actually, Keith [Sykes, a Coral Reefer] and I sort of wrote this together. The Reefers went to a little bar on Montserrat one night and heard this great 'woop-wop' band and told me about it. So I went to the bar, the Cafe La Capitain—there are bars and then there are *bars* and this one's a classic."

Was the woop-wop band sound similar to reggae?

"Oh no," he replies seriously. "Down in Montserrat they don't particularly like Rastafarians. It's a misconception that all Caribbean music is reggae. Most of the down-island stuff is more calypso, happy, good-time music. This band was more like a calypso kind of maranga. It had a guy who played a long blow pipe and a banjo-uke player. The next day, I had laid out four working titles for the album, but none of them really grabbed me, and I was wondering, 'What the fuck can I call this record?' Then I looked out the window at the volcano [Montserrat has an active volcano] and I went *ding!* I'm gonna call the album *Volcano.* So I said, 'Now we got to write a song called "Volcano." ' I went to the studio and Keith was fooling around, playing a little Caribbean shuffle, that little *da da da.* He said, 'You know, they play everything in F down here.' I said, 'Well, hell, why not? I've never written a song in F.' So we wrote it and I said. 'Well, hell, let's go get the guys from the bar, we need the woop-wop sound to make it authentic.' I had already written the chorus. 'I don't know where I'm a gonna go when the volcano blows.' So we got the woop-wop band to come in and play and it was perfect. It just felt so goddamned natural."

Buffett rewinds the tape and plays "Volcano" again to make sure I catch the references to Three Mile Island and the Ayatollah. "You're serious, for once," I observe.

"Hell, it wasn't planned," he assures me. "I had this nice melody and I wanted some clever lyrics. What I do best is write catchy lyrics, and with Three Mile Island and everything else that's happening it just worked out perfect.

"When I played it back for the locals, they got off on it. Even the cooks at AIR came out of the kitchen to listen, so I knew that I had hooked a little bit of authenticity. It was fun for once to take some shots at real things like Three Mile Island."

He turns the volume up and we go out on deck to watch the moonrise, which apparently is a big deal with St. Bartians. The pungent odor of marijuana wafts over the harbor and we can hear a Buffett tape blaring from a nearby yacht. We stretch out on the teak deck and Jimmy takes a long toke on a joint. "Ahh," he says, "when the moon comes up you're gonna hear this bay *howl.*" Amazingly, when the china white moon rises, there *are* wolflike howls emanating from various boats. You can see distant hands cupped around glowing joints and hear glasses clinking.

"Is this paradise for you, Jimmy?" I ask lazily from my prone position on deck. He replies, laughing softly: "It's *close,* eh?

"I may buy land here," he says. "There're two acres for sale next to David Rockefeller's house. Shit, I may buy them. Why not?" Hard to argue with that.

"Let's get some pizza," he says. "There's a great place here that just serves champagne and pizza. Ahh, I can't *stand* it. What a tough life."

We cruise back, tie up the dinghy at the dock, and start hiking up the hill from the harbor, past Le Select, from which issues Buffett's song "The Captain and the Kid." The Select regulars, who are beyond cool, look out and holler "Hey, Jim, howzit?" It seems they will do *anything* to prove how hip they are and how it's not a big deal that Jimmy Buffett hangs out on their island. They passed their ultimate test a few months before, when the Rolling Stones discovered St. Bart's and moved in for a spell. Cool prevailed.

Buffett gives the regulars a perfunctory wave, plucks a jasmine flower, and sniffs it. "Oh," he says, "just think. I could be recording in New York City. Match *this,* Fifty-fifth Street." "Fifty-*second* Street," I correct him. Buffett laughs.

I decide that I like him: "Yer all right, Buffett. I understand you're accidentally rich." He laughs again. As we enter the Momo–Pi–Polo tavern, all the locals gather around us, except for two swarthy guys in the corner, who seem to be closing a major dope deal. And the waitresses cannot give Jimmy enough attention.

"Last night," Buffett says with a sigh as the first bottle of champagne arrives, "we drank twenty-five bottles of champagne in here and never got around to eating. And that was just the beginning. *Lord*. I got to settle down. I got a record to finish."

"Horseshit," I say. We toast each other. Blond American hippie women pop out of the woodwork. Good Christ, St. Bart's should be declared illegal. "A long night tonight, eh Jimmy?" I ask. He just rolls his eyes.

About $200 later, we leave Momo-Pi-Polo. "Tell you what," Buffett says, "while you're here, I really oughta show you Le President. It's a wild disco out in the hills, a great place." We locate Buffett's rented Mini-Moke, a bastardized open-air Jeep. He revs it up to about seventy-five mph and off we roar down a dirt canyon road. The owner of Le President welcomes him with open arms and starts playing calypso disco; local versions of "Stayin' Alive" and such. Within a half-hour, the place fills up with Anglos. Jimmy tires of the excessive attention before I do and we retire to the bar to talk some more about *Volcano*.

"I booked studio time as soon as I heard George was building a studio in the islands," he says. "I've always wanted to record down here. The energy's incredible. We've done eight tracks in ten days—we freaked out those British cats at AIR 'cause we worked so fast and drank so much. I'd wake up Fingers [Greg "Fingers" Taylor, the Reefers' harmonica player], he'd knock off a hot solo and go back to sleep."

Tales of Buffett's past drunken adventures abound, usually about his days as a down-and-out singer/songwriter in Nashville and Key West. Parties just seem to spring up around him. Tom Corcoran, a Key West photographer and writer who's been with Buffett since the beginning, shakes his head in amazement when I later ask him to tell me the most outrageous thing Buffett had ever done.

"It'd take *days* to think of it. Back when he literally didn't have a buck for dinner, my wife and I'd have him over for spaghetti and we'd start out with a few beers and things would just *build* from there. We wrote a few songs together before things got out of control. You know about the Buford Pusser [*Walking Tall*] incident? I think that was in Nashville. Jimmy came out of a bar and had no idea where he was, so he climbed up on top of a Cadillac to look around and try to get his bearings. Only problem was, the Cadillac belonged to Pusser, who happened along and damn near killed Buffett.

"There is one thing," Corcoran continues, "that he's never told the press. He became a hero in the Caribbean a couple of years ago when he saved two shipwrecked sailors. We were sailing from St. Maarten to Anguilla, where we spotted a bar. We decided to drop in for some Heinekens. But before we reached the island a freak storm hit us, the temperature dropped thirty degrees, and the winds hit gale force. We had run out of fuel and had to just ride it out. Finally the storm passed, and the wind just died, which never happens in the Caribbean. We were dead in the water.

"Then we spotted these two old fishermen—the Vanderpool brothers—who'd been wrecked by the storm and were hysterical. Buffett got 'em on board and we calmed 'em down. Still, no wind. Finally, Buffett said, '*Goddamnit,* we'll go ashore and trade these two guys for some beers and some fuel!' So he and Groovy [Buffett's captain] put on their bright yellow foul-weather gear, grabbed a hand-held VHF radio, rowed the dinghy ashore, and went into town. Buffett announced he had the Vanderpools.

"The locals just freaked. They gave him some fuel and a lot of beers, we took the Vanderpools home, and the whole island turned out for a celebration. They paraded Buffett through town in the back of a pickup truck, with everybody cheering. He's *amazing.* He turns a shipwreck into a party."

Now, however, Jimmy Buffett may be slowing down a bit. There have been major changes in his life. His marriage to the smart and lovely Miss Jane (whom he doesn't deserve) and the birth of their first child this year seem to be stabilizing him. He's selling *Euphoria II* for a smaller sloop, and he's gotten a bit more businesslike in the wake of hits like "Come Monday," "Margaritaville," and the platinum success that followed his switch from a Nashville management firm to Azoff's sleek Front Line organization.

Even so, it's sometimes hard to tell just who's doing the managing. I was sitting around one afternoon with Buffett, shooting the shit over coffee, when he slowly started getting steamed up. He picked up a phone and called Azoff—collect—in Los Angeles.

"*Goddamnit,* Irving!" he yelled. "I told you not to wire money down here. It never arrives! Now this is what I want. Call somebody at Bayshore [Studios] in Florida—the Eagles are there—and have him fly down here *today,* with two thousand dollars in cash. And twelve Ping-pong balls." There was a short silence. "*Yes, twelve Ping-pong balls.* There's not a goddamn Ping-pong ball on this island." He hung up, laughing. "Hell, let's go get some beers and go water-skiing. Tonight we'll be able to play a little Ping-pong."

I buy us another round in Le President and ask him, "Buffett, do you think you're growing up? This new album, from what I can tell, shows a lot more depth in your writing—no more 'Cheeseburger in Paradise' kind of stuff. Are you really maturing, or is your vision of the Caribbean just changing?''

He laughs nervously. Serious questions make him tense. "Well," he finally replies, "I think it's a bit of both. Probably more of me changing. I've *always* written in the Caribbean; I can still tap it for a lot of material. I won't get tired of it as long as there are those goddamn five-block lines for gasoline in Santa Monica and the Ayatollah is declaring everybody on his shit list. It's an escapist situation here, but I think I can take it to the point where I'm maturing, and apply that to where I would like to be as a writer.

"I am pleased with this album. I wrote just about all of it on the boat. I came in totally prepared for once. I caught a lot of flak over the last LP, the live one in 1978. People either loved it or hated it. I figured, 'Goddamnit, it was cut live and that's the way we *are* live.' It didn't get much airplay. But I don't care. It sold well.

"After that, I wanted to lay back and maybe return to a *Changes in Latitudes* . . . or *A1A* kind of thing, to settle back into that kind of writing. I had six months to work, so I came down here to just sit on the boat and get into a schedule and write every day. I think this is the *best* fuckin' record we've done. It's like bringing that feeling of the past to what's happening today. There's something for everybody, from 'Fins' to 'Sending the Old Man Home.' It's clever stuff.''

Buffett drains his greenie and seems embarrassed at talking so much. I suddenly feel the unmistakable nudge of a large, firm, and braless female breast on my right arm. The nudging becomes insistent. I look to my right. The breast is attached to a rather attractive, although hopelessly drunk, young woman. *"Please* introduce me to Jimmy," she whispers.

Buffett, whose radar is pretty good, calls for the check. We shower the bar with money and depart. He is silent as he races the Mini-Moke up the road, scattering gravel and dirt. "Let's check out the club at the Jean Bart," he says.

"Buffett," I ask, "what's this business where you once said Mitch Miller and Jean Lafitte shaped you?"

He roars with laughter. "Well, *well,* well. Did I say that? Mitch Miller, for *sure.* In the old days. *Sing Along With Mitch.* Who didn't. I remember that very well, because I was ten or eleven at the time. But Jean Lafitte was my hero as a romantic character. I'm not sure he was a *musical* influence. His lifestyle influenced me, most definitely, 'cause I'm the very *opposite* of Mitch Miller.''

And what of Tom McGuane's Buffett-related line about the hinterland where Hank Williams and Xavier Cugat meet?

"That's a great sentence McGuane [Buffett's brother-in-law] wrote. I think it's still true, even more true now. I never thought of myself in those terms till he wrote that. But it *was* pretty much descriptive of what I've wanted to do. That is what my progression has been through all the albums. *Volcano* is about as representative of that statement as anything I've ever done. A good mix."

"But what about the song 'Fins'?" I press. "That's totally off the wall and can be interpreted as being either sexist or feminist—about lounge lizards hitting on young girls."

"I *know*," Buffett says. "I cover all the bases on that one. It's just one of those things that come about on the road. 'Fins' was an in thing with the band, just a term for checking out chicks. A 1979 version of 'Girl-watchers.' But I think it's got a little more class. It's really about land sharks who live in bars and feed right after dark. My audiences picked up on it and starting 'finning'."

Buffett demonstrates finning by taking his hands off the wheel and wagging them above his head: *"Fins up! Or,"* he says as he lets one hand wilt like a limp penis, "Fins *down*. Finettes. Fin soup. Fin pie. Fins everywhere."

He skids the jeep into the parking lot of the Hotel Jean Bart. The hotel's club, the Frigate, is supposed to be closed but Buffett raps on the door anyway. A bouncer inspects us through the peephole and we enter yet another disco. This one is totally out of hand. The crowd is composed of drunken tourists who remove bits of clothing while they dance, and sharp-eyed local guys who lean coolly against the bar, evaluating the night's prospects and biding their time.

"Fins. Land sharks," Buffett murmurs as he goes off to find the men's room. I dance with an American who, after about thirty seconds, asks me if she can meet Buffett and then tries to perpetrate some kind of sexual act *right there* on the lighted dance floor. I can sense the locals at the bar toting her up.

"See you around, darlin'," I say as I rezip my pants and head toward the bar.

"As a fellow journalism-school graduate, Buffett," I say, "I advise you that this place is getting weird and they're gonna be after you pretty soon."

"I know." He nods soberly. "About time to head for the boat."

"But lemme ask you something," I interject. "When did you first take on the Caribbean as your personal friend?"

"I think it's always been there," he says. "I once read a great passage in *The Commodore's Story* to the effect that 'if you ever grow up on a body of water, you know it's connected to another one.' My grandfather [a sailing master] told me sea stories, tales about the Caribbean and how exotic it was. That was a lure. I grew up on Mobile Bay and I knew it would connect to white, sandy beaches and palm trees—which don't exist around Mobile Bay. You *know* that you can gain the access if you have the courage and the spirit of adventure within you to get out on the water. It *does* link you to any other place."

His eyes take on a faraway look. "Time to go back to the boat."

The next time I talk to Buffett, he says he is en route to Hawaii to open an Eagles show there. I can't help recalling Miss Pigtails in St. Bart's and her pineapple-juice instructions. But Buffett is with his wife, and I don't have the heart to remind him that Hawaii is one big pineapple field. I mean, fresh squeezed probably does the job better than the canned variety. . . .

Chapter 7

Lust

Rocking Havana: Yanquis Find Rebellion, Repression, and Bad Cigars

Their radio, the young Cuban couple's battered but precious portable Panasonic, is the most important thing in their lives. It's their only link to the world of rock 'n' roll, blue jeans, and what amounts to a fairyland of freedom compared to the Marxist military state of Cuba. Fidel Castro Ruz may have outlawed rock & roll, but he can't outlaw the radios that suck in the sounds of the music from the States.

I first saw Preston and Maruja, with their radio-cassette player, literally hiding behind a tree near the beach by the Hotel Marazul, where I was staying some thirty miles from Havana. I'd just had a strenuous encounter with a loyal young communist, an encounter that ended with him saying to me, in loose translation, "Live free or die, imperialist motherfucker whore!" He and I obviously had different ideas about what "living free" meant, and his riposte culminated a small debate about the respective roles of the U.S. and Cuba in the Vietnam–China conflict. Cuba's position is amply demonstrated by the dozens of VIETNAM VINCERA ("Vietnam Will Win") billboards dotting the lush, green countryside and by Fidel's oft-quoted "We Must Be Ready for Anything" speech (his manifesto denouncing China and declaring Cuba's solidarity with Vietnam).

I was in Cuba to attend the Havana Jam, a historic (and nonpolitical) three-night music festival of U.S. and Cuban musicians on March 2, 3, and 4, 1979. It was the first such event since before the Cuban Revolution, but my communist opponent was more interested in the global success of Marxism than in musical hands across the ocean. The Havana Jam was in fact an unofficial affair: CBS Records President Bruce Lundvall set up the concerts with the Cuban cultural ministry without the official sanction of either the Carter or Castro administration. The festival was of no great importance to the majority of Cubans, who did not even know about it. The young communist knew about the Jam since his family was well connected politically and thus entitled to tickets. The presence of such musicians as Weather Report, Kris Kristofferson and Rita Coolidge, Billy Joel, the CBS Jazz All Stars, Stephen Stills, and a like amount of leading Cuban groups meant little to him. Solidarity with the people of Vietnam was more important.

I had started walking back to the hotel, and halfway through the stand of tall pines that separated the beach from the hotel, I heard a *"psst!"* coming from behind a tree. *"Psst! Señor,* mister, *monsieur?* You are being *avec* with *con los Americanos?"*

We finally settled on French as the common language, and I established that I was *un CBS Americain*. Preston, Maruja, and their Panasonic emerged from behind the tree. Initially, I wasn't sure about them, especially after suddenly being immersed in a country that is part late-Fifties nightclub flash and flesh show, part banana republic inefficiency and poverty, and part military stockade that seems permanently mobilized.

Cuba's brand of communism is unique: I saw floor shows in Havana that far outstrip anything in Las Vegas or Paris, yet media censorship is total. I had to register with the foreign-affairs ministry, which stationed agents in the hotel to supervise American journalists. I was most curious about the state of things for young people in Cuba. Unfortunately, said Luis Llerandi, my foreign-affairs overseer at the hotel, such interviews would not be possible since I was in Cuba purely to see three concerts. Luis had just left the beach when Preston and Maruja approached, and I had no way of knowing if they were government agents or what.

It soon developed that they were regular kids, rock & roll fans. Preston's words spilled out excitedly. Who was I, was I a famous rock star that perhaps he had heard on one of the radio stations from Miami? I am being journalist from *Rolling Stone? Fantástico! Rolling Stone* is being hottest item on Cuban black market, next to Levi's, rock 'n' roll records, and American cigarettes.

Preston and Maruja, it turns out, are both students at the University of Havana, but they'd rather be at, say, Ohio State or Miami U. They are not great fans of communism or Castro.

Preston looked nervously over his shoulder. "The police are watching the beach," he said. I scoffed. He jumped nervously: "Oh, *no*. Remember what country you are in. We should not be seen talking to you. We could be arrested. We must go. You are getting for us maybe invitations [tickets] to see Billy Yo-el and Krisanrita?"

Can't do, I said. The Cuban cultural ministry is handling the whole thing. Since the invitations were free, why hadn't Preston and Maruja gotten a pair? Maruja spoke up: "The invitations went to the communists and the Russians. Young people could not get them. Tell Billy Yo-el and Krisanrita that the people that are being seeing them are not being the people who love them. Remember, this is being communist state." I suddenly recalled that the charter flight that had brought the musicians and journalists down from New York City had been insured by CBS for $120 million.

Maruja looked at me pleadingly: "You are getting for us maybe copies of *Rolling Stone?*" Sure, I said, come on back to the hotel with me. They both recoiled. "No," said Preston, "the police are there." It turned out he was right.

While Preston and Maruja lurked in the woods, I went back to the Marazul, enjoyed a refreshing saltwater shower (the room was going for ninety dollars a day), dressed, and went back to the pine trees with an armload of copies of *Rolling Stone,* two cartons of Winstons, and cassette tapes of the Stones, Billy Joel, Kristofferson, the Bay Hays (I mean the Bee Gees), Beatles, et cetera. Preston and Maruja almost wept with delight. I'd just given them what amounted to goods worth hundreds of dollars on the black market, but it wasn't the monetary value that overwhelmed them. It was just that this was stuff they would never otherwise have had the chance to get. The only other thing they wanted was my Levi's, which Preston told me would go for about 150 pesos (almost $200) on the black market. I kept them on.

Preston insisted on taking me to Havana to visit his house "even though it is only poor apartment." I'd love to, I said, but my man Luis at the hotel isn't real keen on journalists jumping the tour and seeing people not on the approved list. I can't hop in a taxi, because the *Yanquí* journalists have to clear everything with Luis, and besides, there aren't any taxis at the Marazul. Preston said to forget the cab; I should get on the same Havana-bound bus he and Maruja would take. I should board it at a bus stop two blocks from the Marazul and pretend not to recognize him and Maruja. Again, I scoffed. Preston became serious: "I have friends who are in jail for 'crimes against the revolution.'" He seemed genuinely frightened, but at the same time he couldn't pass up the chance to get next to *Yanquí* rock 'n' roll, at least get as close as he could. I went back to the hotel and told Luis I had contracted a sudden headache and would pass up the afternoon bus tour of selected museums. He clucked solicitously.

I got on the number 162, an aging British Leyland bus, paid my twenty centavos (about twenty-five cents), and found standing room next to Preston and Maruja. I drew a few curious stares from the other passengers, but nothing serious.

Everyone in Cuba, it seems, rides buses. Few people own cars, and the ones who do have pre-revolution (pre-1959) American cars. This is 1955 Chevy heaven. Cuban mechanics are wizards (they're still repairing 1949 Studebakers and 1948 Hudsons). We rode past the José Martí youth pioneer camp, where thousands of kids were waiting on the highway for rides after finishing their mandatory two weeks of indoctrination. Soldiers were hitchhiking all along the road; olive drab as far as the eye could see. The bus turned onto the *malecon*—the spectacular seawall road that separates Havana from the Gulf of Mexico—and passed Morro Castle, built in 1642 to protect Havana's harbor.

We disembarked in Old Havana and walked down Monserrate past the Museum of the Revolution, which was Batista's palace before Castro took over. I wanted to linger and look at the *Gramma,* the luxury yacht Castro had used to invade Cuba from Mexico (the boat, about sixty feet long, is encased in glass with armed soldiers guarding it), but Preston and Maruja hurried me on. Old Havana was in many ways depressing. The streets were filthy—even by New York City standards—and the once-beautiful eighteenth- and nineteenth-century Spanish houses were deteriorating. Laundry on once-lovely balconies was billowing in the breeze. At almost every corner were anti-Chinese pro-Vietnam posters put up by the CDRs (Committees for the Defense of the Revolution— block associations and de facto communist watchdogs on a local level).

We turned left on Brasil Street. From outside, Preston's house was impressive, a Dresden-china blue structure with an imposing wood door marked by a large oval peephole. The interior was another story. The stairs were grimy. Preston's apartment amounted to a peeling stucco closet, taller than it was wide. The building, once a single-family home, had been subdivided into a dozen cubicles. His kitchenette had a hot plate, on which he brewed me a cup of coffee, a real luxury in Cuba (many of the finest restaurants do not have coffee at all). Preston proudly served it in a chipped cup. He put the *Some Girls* cassette I had given him onto his Panasonic and turned it up. *"Fantástico!"* he said. He had heard only "Miss You," on Miami's WGBS, from which he had also learned the only English he knew.

While I sipped coffee, Preston and Maruja scanned the copies of *Rolling Stone.* Then they started hitting me with questions. Who won the Grammys? Who is bigger in the U.S., Andy Gibb or Barry Manilow? What is Paul McCartney doing now? What has happened to John Lennon? I said Lennon was now a dairy farmer. Preston was incredulous. "The leader of *los* Beatles is now being *campesino? Fantástico!*"

Three of Preston's friends (two students and a dentist) came in bearing bottles of Hatuey beer. They pressed me with more questions: The males wanted to know if I'd met Raquel Welch or Dolly Parton. The females wanted to know about Warren Beatty and Kris Kristofferson.

Preston and his friends poured out their souls. They want to leave Cuba right now. They want rock 'n' roll and Western movies and Levi's. They love Kristofferson because they saw him in *A Star Is Born.* Preston does not give "two shits" about Marxism and he begged me to print what he said, because "I am not speaking with just one voice. I am speaking with many voices, of many of my friends, who are feeling the same way as I am. We are all not being communists here." His friends nodded. "We not all are being Marxists. That is not freedom."

"Perhaps you are getting us invitations to the show tonight?" Preston asked.

I'll talk to Krisanrita, I said.

"What was the show last night being like?"

Well, I said, Weather Report, one of the best American jazz groups, had opened the show, and it was terrific by any standards, especially the solos by Jaco Pastorius and Joe Zawinul, and the fog-machine effects. Two Cuban groups had followed, Conjunto Yaguarimu and Orquesta Aragon, and I was partial to Orquesta Aragon's melodic charango music. Preston curled his lip: "That is *old* people's music. There is nothing in Cuba now that is *our* music. We listen to WGBS in Miami and WLAC in Nashville and WLS in Chicago and sometimes when the weather is right we see 'Soul Train.'"

"So then what else happened?"

Well, I said, the Fania All Stars ("Latins from Manhattan," as Dexter Gordon called them) played and the Cubans walked out in droves. *"Fania* is a girl's name," Preston explained, "so why should we see such a group?" Beats me, I said.

Maruja, who had disappeared earlier, returned, shyly holding up a slender joint. *Cristo,* I said, that is *dope.* That surely means jail here? They smiled. "We are trusting you," Maruja said. "Please to smoke with us." I did. It was Cuban home-grown marijuana and not all that good, but the sentiment outdid the product. We all smiled at each other as Maruja put on a Stones tape. Fidel may be exporting his soldiers, but he has a potential opposition at home.

I asked them about Cuban music. They shook their heads in disgust. "All Cuban music is old people's music," Preston said. "The nightclubs are very bad. They are for the tourists. The music is very bad, it is the music of the 1950s. It is as if there is no *now*. Musically in this country, it is always yesterday. Havana is a capital of two million people, but there are being only three clubs where young people go where there is being tapes of American music. Is very bad."

Is there, I asked, being very careful with the question, an underground in Havana? They didn't understand the concept of "underground." I tried the term "opposition."

"It's impossible," Preston blurted out. *"La póliza* is everywhere. They are everyone. Life was better before the revolution, I am thinking, except now life is better for free education and free health. But the intellectual life is gone; everything is conducted for the Communist party. The Communist party is a giant octopus. Fear is everywhere." What can you do? I asked. "Why, nothing!" Preston said. "Nothing is possible."

It was time for me to head for that night's performance. Everyone gave me a formal handshake, except for Maruja, who gave me a lingering kiss. Hands across the ocean, so to speak.

I arrived early that night at the Karl Marx Theater, a.k.a. Teatro Carlos Marx. The theater looks uncomfortably like an American department store, with Marx's signature spilled across the facade of the building in ten-foot-high neon letters. The police were arresting kids trying to sneak in. The Russians were lined up, already looking bored. I took my seat in row seven; a Cuban "guide" sat near the aisle to "protect" *los Americanos*.

The Karl Marx Theater is Cuba's version of Carnegie Hall; a very plush, 4,800-seat venue. The big problem, as even Bruce Lundvall admitted, was that all the "free" tickets were indeed handed out to loyal communists. Lundvall said he could never get a straight answer from the bureaucrats about ticket distribution. I got one answer when I spotted Preston and Maruja in the crowd: They'd bought invitations for ten pesos each (about $12.50) on the black market. So much for Marxism.

The CBS Jazz All Stars opened, and were not at their best, mainly because that afternoon they'd been permitted a sound check of about two and a half seconds, while the Cuban groups got two hours. Still, seeing a trio of John McLaughlin, Tony Williams, and Jaco Pastorius was electrifying, as were performances by such greats as Stan Getz, Dexter Gordon, Woody Shaw, Eric Gale, Jimmy Heath, and Percy Heath. Trying to crowd all that into forty-five minutes was not fair, and they knew they'd gotten short shrift. The musicians had not *needed* to come to Cuba, several told me later. They came because they thought they'd be welcome, but I couldn't find a one who said he'd like to return. Getz, who'd been the inspiration for this Havana Jam (about two years ago, he, Dizzy Gillespie, and Earl Hines got off a cruise ship in Havana and jammed spontaneously with Cuban groups), was very unhappy. "This is too institutionalized," he said. "The government took it over."

But it was not a bad night for music: Stephen Stills played better than I'd ever seen him, and he even jumped into the crowd with his transmitter guitar. Preston and Maruja were delighted. "We have never seen anything like that," Preston told me. Stills drew a tremendous response when he performed "Cuba Al Fin," a Spanish song of solidarity with the Cuban people he'd written especially for the occasion. Unfortunately, when Stills got backstage, he was attacked by Cuban officials for playing longer than his allotted time.

The Cuban group Irakere, which CBS now has touring America as an opening act for Stills, closed the night with a lovely set of classical Afro-Cuban-Mozartian jazz. But many of the American musicians, disgusted at the treatment they'd been receiving and the isolation they felt, didn't see Irakere. Instead, they gathered at the backstage bar and got drunk on rum and listened to a Richard Pryor tape. On the bus back to the hotel, two well-known jazz musicians—one white, one black—got into a bitter racial argument.

Havana Jam's third night opened with a Cuban group so bad that an American engineer fetched me to listen to the sound as it came over the mixing board. "This is Ricky Ricardo forever," he said, and he was right. Dexter Gordon walked by, heading determinedly for the bar. "This is too much," he said. "I've seen nothing but the hotel and this concert hall. I thought they'd at least let us jam with the Cubans. But we got nothing."

Krisanrita did well, especially after Kris dedicated "The Living Legend" to "your commander in chief, Fidel," and got a standing ovation. When Kris came offstage, he admitted being "scared shitless," but he got the only backstage ovation the American musicians accorded *anybody*. Percussionist Willie Bobo slapped Kris on the back and told him, "I always knew there were white niggers but I never saw any till tonight!"

Kristofferson said he didn't intend to make a political statement: "I told the audience that this song could have been sung for great revolutionaries like Zapata, Che Guevara, and Jesus Christ. I was just rapping about building bridges between people."

Following Krisanrita were Sara Gonzalez and Pablo Milanes, two prominent members of the Cuban *nueva trova* (the new song movement), rather like folk singers. I asked Preston what he thought. "Old music," he said. "I am waiting to see Billy Yo-el."

Billy Yo-el closed out the festival with a bang. When he jumped on his piano, the kids in the crowd surged past the guards and really tried to get down. If the Cuban government thought they were keeping rock & roll out of their country, Joel proved them wrong, prompting the American press to dutifully record that he had proved rock & roll can still be subversive.

I was standing in the wings with some of the CBS Jazz All Stars, though, and their comments suggested that *they* thought *anybody* with three chords could get *any* kids up out of their seats and dancing. They were also, they said, "highly pissed off" that Joel was the only musician who refused to allow CBS to record and videotape his performance. That made for some ugly words between Lundvall and Elizabeth Joel, Billy's wife and manager. After all, CBS had laid out about $235,000 for this affair and hoped to release a series of albums as well as a TV network special. Losing the closing act would leave a big hole in the records and film. Elizabeth Joel told me that "we just don't want another album out when we've done so much already." One CBS Jazz All Star said Joel's decision was "a slap in the face to the rest of us. We agreed to come down and so did he. Now he becomes a prima donna."

Lundvall said he couldn't explain Joel's decision. It did not make for great relations between Americans. Stephen Stills told a sound engineer: "Never have so few worked so hard for so little."

And whatever goodwill the Americans retained toward Cuba disappeared at José Martí Airport when they were forced to wait more than seven hours before clearing customs, while Russian tour groups were breezed through. The sight of dozens of the best musicians in the world standing there and spontaneously singing "I Love New York" while shaking their fists at the Russians is not something I will soon forget.

I have never heard as much complaining as I did on that flight back to New York. Just after takeoff, the pilot came on the PA system and drew cheers when he announced, "Those of you on the left side of the aircraft can lean out and spit on Havana."

I was sitting with Tony Williams and asked him what his feelings were. "It was not what I thought it would be," he said, lighting up an American cigar. "Even the cigars weren't any good. There were a lot of unfriendly people. I had hoped there'd be some interchange with the Cuban musicians, that I'd get to jam with some of their drummers, but they *deliberately* kept us isolated. They wanted to flaunt their power."

Still, I couldn't forget the expressions on Preston and Maruja's faces after Billy Joel's set. They came up and hugged me, as if the whole damned thing had been my doing. And Maruja said, "Thank you, United States of America, for giving us rock 'n' roll. Otherwise, we would never have seen it."

Uma Karuna Thurman

She is being talked about as a New Age teen goddess; as a golden thoroughbred sired by Kosmic Karma out of the Age of Aquarius; as some kind of shimmering new breed of creature so exotic that she does not even breathe oxygen. And it fairly well pisses her off.

Her exquisitely shaped nostrils flare beautifully, she tosses her magnificent blond mane, and fixes her piercing blue eyes on me and tells me flatly that she thinks it's all a load of crap. "When you're starting out and really haven't done anything yet, people just want to make some kind of phony hype about you," Uma Karuna Thurman says, pausing to take a puff off one of my cigars and a sip from her glass of Southern Comfort. She is making some kind of spectacular impression on the other late-afternoon denizens of New York's fabled Rainbow Room. Sixty-five sun-splashed floors above Manhattan, happy hour takes on

an added dimension with seventeen-year-old model-actress Uma sharing a table and her views on the world with this writer and the room at large.

To start with, she is over six feet tall and a marvel of genetic design in ragged denims and baggy sweater. She is physically perfect, right down to her one charming imperfection: a crescent-shaped scar positioned perfectly on her left cheekbone. The one piece of jewelry she is sporting is a button that reads "To Hell With Rambo and All He Represents. Vietnam Veterans United to Prevent World War III." And she is outspoken as only a seventeen-year-old free spirit can be. Although the fact is not remarkable to her, Uma is somewhat representative of the New Age label she's been branded with.

She was born in Woodstock on April 29, 1970. Her father, Dr. Robert Thurman, is a Buddhist scholar and professor with close ties to the Dalai Lama. His first wife was Christophe de Menil. In Millbrook he met and married former Ford model Nena von Schlebrugge, who had been married to Timothy Leary. The counterculture bloodlines were impeccable. Enter the perfect child. "Uma" means number one. "Karuna" stands for compassion. Uma was precocious, even for such an enlightened household as the Thurmans', where the Dalai Lama was a sometime houseguest. Uma spent her first and thirteenth years living in India. And along the way she became a very independent, strong-willed young lady. She left home for Manhattan two years ago to pursue an acting career. She is still in high school and is about to start shooting on her fourth movie, *Dangerous Liaisons,* with the likes of Glenn Close and John Malkovich. (The previous three were the low-budget *Kiss Daddy Goodnight,* with Matt Dillon's brother; *Johnny Be Goode,* with Anthony Michael Hall; and *The Adventures of Baron Munchausen,* with Robin Williams and many others.)

But we get ahead of our story. Back in the Rainbow Room, Uma and your correspondent are smoking cigars and drinking and having a big-time shoot-the-breeze. The Manhattan business people streaming in stare openly at Uma, wondering just which starlet she is. Uma knocks back another slug of Southern Comfort and is startled when I tell her that that was the drink of choice of my late friend Janis Joplin. Even though the sixties are to Uma "just like ancient history," she is fascinated by Joplin. We talk about the Sixties for a while, which Uma says intrigue her but no more so than any other decade she hasn't known. "I was born in 1970 and, if anything, the bulk of my independent life has been in the Eighties."

She pauses to take in the spectacle around her. "You know," she says, "this is only my second interview. In the first one, the first thing the woman said was, 'We understand you are fucking Warren Beatty. We understand you are fucking Richard Gere.' " Well, welcome to the wide world of journalism, I tell her. She laughs heartily.

"Why didn't you ask me about Richard Gere? That was the big thing in the *Star,* the pictures," she says. I tell her that I knew that Gere was a family friend and nothing more because of his interest in Buddhism. She purses her lips and nods, leans back, and pulls on her cigar. I have to remember that, despite everything else, Uma is still only seventeen, has no media coach or major agent whispering in her ear, and is still not versed in all the ways that a fairly public person can be skewered. Fair play requires me to silence the tape recorder for a moment and deliver some fatherly advice on the many media traps awaiting her. (And to maybe order another drink. Maybe not.) She is delighted to hear some of them, dismayed by others, but fascinated nonetheless.

She also wears her career on her ragged sleeve. I ask her why she is pursuing acting so single-mindedly. Her reply is as sunny as the room. "I just want to be good at what I do—and be happy. Acting is a special way of communication. It's like music—you can sneak up on people and get to them and they won't even know it." She takes another sip of Southern Comfort and says that what really got her into acting was *Breakfast at Tiffany's.* And not because of Audrey Hepburn. "It was because of Holly Golightly," Uma says, ever so breathlessly. "Holly Golightly was a major character in my fantasy mind. I actually liked the book better than the movie. But Holly was it."

There are, uhm, certain similarities, perhaps, somewhere, if someone really searched for them, one guesses. I ask her if she feels she missed any part of her childhood because of the way she was raised. Uma says she feels it's "an amazing concept" that things could be missed that were never experienced, and furthermore, she says, gathering steam, it's a real waste of energy for people to agonize over fantasized perceptions of what their lives should have been and, for example, just look at her, which I do. She is just seventeen, she says, and she's very happy with herself and wouldn't undo a minute of her life, even if "it would have meant an easier and sillier and lighter dream life of being in the Brady Bunch."

We have a good laugh, as do the people at the next table. Perhaps the word "seventeen" hangs a little too long in the air. At any rate, the Rainbow Room's vice squad appears at our table in due order to inspect the "young lady's ID." By the time they do so, she is drinking ice water. And talking seriously again, presumably about her career. "Playing it safe is really a bore," she says. "If you can't risk it all, you can't win it all." Then she winks at me as we get up to leave.

Chapter 8

Anger

Christopher Durang Explains It All for You

Christopher Durang looks like a choirboy. He was, in fact, a devout Catholic as a boy. But he was named after Christopher Robin, not St. Christopher, and the only thing devout about what's being called his "anti-Catholic" play is the righteous opposition rallying against it. The theater's "bad boy" is worse than a combination of Lenny Bruce and Paul Krassner, say Catholic priests who have taken to their pulpits to condemn Durang's play, *Sister Mary Ignatius Explains It All For You*.

The fact that *Sister Mary* is the hottest thing on off Broadway really does come as a complete revelation to Durang, who wrote it as self-therapy after a string of critically acclaimed plays that were every bit as dark-humored and socially vulgar as *Sister* flopped, both on and off Broadway. What's a sick humorist to do these days?

Chris Durang doesn't know. He is thirty-two years old, worries about his weight and his air conditioner, eats only Nabisco Spoon-Size Shredded Wheat for breakfast, enjoys being a semi-recluse on the Upper East Side, and writes some of the most vicious and funny black humor around. *The New Yorker* called Durang "one of the funniest playwrights alive," the *Times* has virtually adopted him, and the *Post* went so far as to christen him the "jolliest maverick of the younger American playwrights."

All that praise despite the fact he has yet to have a play run longer than three months in New York, has never been seen having lunch with Joseph Papp, and, according to most critics, has yet to even write an *ending* to one of his plays. His Author's Notes are often agonized appraisals and re-appraisals of what the ending should have been.

Small matter. Durang, after a handful of plays, has early on earned a reputation—some would say notoriety—that many an established playwright would envy. He claims to be indifferent to all the hoopla, although he *can* quote accurately from reviews. It was Durang who told me that Richard Gilman, who sponsored his application to the Yale School of Drama, had savaged *Sister* in a review in *The Nation.* Who reads theater reviews in *The Nation?* Lapsed Catholic playwrights, apparently—when they're not *not* reading reviews. Likewise, a writer who will do any of the following (in his plays), as Durang has, is obviously not afraid of offending people: write that there's nothing premature about premature ejaculation because our society is so fast-paced that everything must be done quickly; kill the Pope after calling his doctrine "Papal wee-wee"; dwell on the problem of nasal intercourse; dare pray "Give Us this Doris Day"; name a war baby "Missing in Action"; write a song called "Don't Sit Under the Atom Bomb With Anyone Else but Me"; or call homosexuality "that thing that makes Jesus puke."

But when one sifts through the evidence and the Broadway and off Broadway gold dust that seems to get spread around everywhere, there seems to be an unavoidable conclusion that Christopher Durang may yet become the bridge between Broadway and off Broadway. He doesn't know anything about that and rejects the notion out of hand when I posit it. As any self-respecting playwright would. After all, who would want to shoulder the legacy of a Sondheim or Simon?

In fact, Durang still feels the sting of his only Broadway venture, a perhaps overly ambitious musical called *A History of the American Film* that had a brief run at the Anta Theatre in 1978. Although it was a very clever parody of American history as seen through the movies, its unwieldy title ensured its premature demise.

The Nature and Purpose of the Universe, his first New York–staged play, included such risqué lines as "Your family is the bane of Maplewood, Mrs. Mann. My husband has been attacked in the garage by your pansy son twice now, and just last week we found your little son's penis in our driveway." Durang may have even been irreverent to the theater itself in *Das Lusitania Songspeil,* the cabaret act that he co-authored and performed with longtime friend Sigourney Weaver. In the revue, Durang and Weaver suggest that Brecht was heavily influenced by Sondheim when he wrote "Everybody Ought to Have a Maid" and say that Brecht and Sondheim collaborated on *Private Lives of the Master Race.* The same revue included a skit called "Welfare Mothers on Parade (We Piss on You)." As far as I could tell, no theater bus tour from Long

Island or Jersey put it on their itinerary. No, but Broadway is dependent on the farm system, on such young, irreverent off-Broadway writers.

Durang's *Beyond Therapy,* a quirky urban comedy that starred Weaver, is set for a Manhattan revival this spring. Lily Tomlin saw *Sister* and asked Durang to write a script for her. If ever the world is ready for—or at least receptive to—Christopher Durang's distinctive sense of humor, it seems that time is now.

I decide I have the perfect joke for the Durang sense of humor one Sunday afternoon as I shoot up to his Upper East Side place. We walk across East 86th Street and settle down in a Greek coffee shop so comfortable that ageless women in minks sit in booths for hours reading Agatha Christie. Durang himself attracts such women and reads such books ("I like books that are soothing").

We order coffee and I tell Durang my joke: "Jesus Christ, right? He checks into a motel, right? And he hands the manager a hammer and some nails, right? And he says, 'Can you put me up for the night?' *Can you put me up for the night?*"

Durang ponders that while he takes a couple of swallows of hot coffee and, finally, does not laugh. He does force a polite smile, however. For Christopher Durang, humor is no laughing matter.

Back at his sublet on 86th and Park, which is as dark and gloomy as his peculiar vision of life, Durang turns out to be surprisingly modest and soft-spoken. "I own nothing but a typewriter and maybe a fork," he says seriously. The only personal touches are a few framed photographs propped up on the mantel—Durang and Sigourney Weaver performing together in *Das Lusitania Songspeil,* pictures of the casts of *Beyond Therapy* and *A History of the American Film,* the Obie he received for *Sister Mary,* a picture of Elizabeth Franz as Sister Mary. "I just have those up there to remind me that I live here," Durang says, almost apologetically.

After lunch we sink into the overstuffed couches of what he calls his "TV room." The whole room is painted an incredibly depressing dark brown color that seems to actually *defeat* light. The sun doesn't shine in here. I dimly make out a giant blond-wood Zenith TV console, undoubtedly one of the first ones made.

"This is where I lose the world," Durang says. He is a very private person and does not run loose on the town when he's not writing. You probably will not run into him at Elaine's or the Odeon. He *was* once on TV. He and Sigourney Weaver chanced to be on the "Joe Franklin Show" the very day the nail-in-the-coffin reviews came out for his play *Titanic.* Franklin, mercifully for Durang, had not heard of the play. Another guest on the show was a nutritionist. Franklin turned to Durang and Weaver and intoned: "Acting and nutrition." Weaver carried the ball on that one.

No, Durang prefers the background. He has sung and acted on stage—well, according to eyewitnesses—but he likes anonymity, as befits someone whose favorite author is James Thurber. "My favorite cartoon," Durang tells me over glasses of ice water in his dark TV den, "is Thurber's 'With you, Lydia, I have known happiness and now you say you're going crazy.' Do you know that one? My mother and I loved it." He falls silent in the thickening gloom.

Besides his upbringing as a Catholic, Durang's loss of his mother seems to have most affected him. Both obviously inform *Sister Mary*, his most powerful play yet. It's a bittersweet mix of jibes aimed at the Church's infallibility and inflexibility as well as an exploration of how those doctrines can wreak havoc on one's private life. The play's turning point, an emotional speech by one character about the long, slow, torturous death by cancer of a mother, is blatantly autobiographical: Durang's mother died such a death, long after he had lost his faith, and it embittered him.

"I actually had no idea that *Sister Mary* would play that funny," he tells me slowly. "Because, I was really just—it came right after a period of when I wasn't writing. *A History of the American Film* had just closed on Broadway and I'd spent a long time working on it and I was depressed about that. And my mother was dying of cancer, a very long death. Four years already, and after *Film,* she was dying slowly for another two years.

"And," he continues, "I hadn't written anything in a very long time. I stopped trying to write with a specific idea, with a production in mind. After having been on Broadway and thinking, 'Well, where will the next dollar come from?', I decided to try to let go and just write something that interested me and so I started with this nun talking. When my mother was dying—it's very hard to offer comfort to someone who's dying. One of the comforts was religion. My mother did believe, but she didn't feel all that comfortable with a strong belief. One of the sisters had that belief. Anyway, that started me remembering all the things that I had been taught.

"And how they were supposed to apply. But I, unfortunately, didn't believe. So, I guess I got thinking how I felt like I had no answers for anything and was wondering how the Church had an answer for everything. I decided to have a nun explaining everything, starting with the solar system, which she goes through *very* quickly. I started to make it two acts, because one-act plays are just not commercial. It couldn't go to two acts. Then I decided to finish it, just so I *could*. Because for a year and a half, I hadn't written anything new. So, in retrospect, it feels very pure, because I wrote it for *myself*."

He looks as satisfied as I have ever seen him.

Durang's route to Yale Drama was a circuitous one. A truly Catholic boyhood in Morristown, New Jersey. Parents (father, architect; mother, homemaker) who regularly took him to Broadway shows. He began writing little playlets as early as the second grade, when he discovered that dialogue "got to the meat of things so quickly." Young Durang also acquainted himself with Catholic guilt early on. Even before the age of seven—what the Church considers the "age of reason"—he understood that he needed to start going to confession because, as Sister Mary Ignatius explains, "Once we turn seven, He feels we are capable of knowing." His first Catholic problem came a bit later. "I remember when I read *Portrait of the Artist as a Young Man,* I had such an identification with Stephen Dedalus. I guess the sin of masturbation was too embarrassing to confess. And when you don't confess mortal sins, then you don't go to communion. Your parents are suspicious why you don't go to communion, so you stop going, and that's a mortal sin, and they add up and add up and then you go to one sermon where they do a *hell-fire* number on you." He pauses to mop his brow.

"*So,* from the seventh grade to the ninth, I was basically in a state of mortal sin because I made the mistake of confessing masturbation to a monsignor, who was furious with me, who just intimidated me. It's simply one of the things you learn: you learn to take gut classes in college and you learn that monsignors are very hard-line. I was so traumatized from this one confession that I decided I'd never do this awful thing again. I lasted three weeks. So then I quit going to confession for two years. That *meant* for those two years, that if I died, I would have gone to hell. It was very upsetting."

Durang got even with the Church when he was thirteen by staging a play in which a girl scandalously let slip a shoulder strap. At the same time, he was entertaining the idea of entering the monastery. Instead, he entered Harvard.

"I was very distressed by how depressed I got. I pretty much stopped writing. I just sort of didn't do anything. Just went to the movies obsessively. When I went to Harvard, I assumed that I would find all these radical Catholics all over the place, like the Berrigans. I just presumed that's who'd be at Harvard. The Catholic society I found there was very traditional and very kind of clubby. I really hated it. And found it stultifying.

"The only thing I found was a Jesuit house connected to the divinity school, so I was more comfortable there. I went there for probably six months to Sunday Mass. But I just stopped believing for all the various reasons one does stop believing. Late in my freshman year, which *is* fairly late at that sort of thing."

(This is clearly not the same Durang who would later write in an appendix to one of his plays: "Actors who take too many pauses should be shot.")

So here we have a fairly moony but sharp writer who was known around Dunster House for his quick wit and for exclaiming, "I'm Marie from Romania" (they say you had to be there). He was not part of the real theater crowd, like Tommy Lee Jones was. Instead, he popped up with a revue called *The Greatest Musical Ever Sung*.

"When I came out of this two-year slump, I came out of it with a very—I don't know what word to use, but a bitter sense of humor, dark sense of humor, that suddenly informed my writing. I wrote *The Nature and Purpose of the Universe,* which got me into Yale.

"There *was* a lot of Catholicism in that play, actually. I think I just suddenly changed my sense of humor or my outlook or something. This was also a sort of psychological rush of expression that was coming out of a lot of confusion and anger that would then come out in this weird comedy, 'cause I remember I really cackled away as I wrote. I really did, laughed *out loud*."

Durang blossomed at Yale. The introvert from Dunster House became the hale fellow in the communal dining room of the Hall of Graduate Studies, with a Sigourney Weaver at one elbow and any number of talented writers and actors and actresses at the other. Wit and wisecracks flew like wisecracks and wit, they say.

Robert Brustein, Yale Drama Director, encouraged the young playwright and the results were quick in coming. Durang began to turn out any number of admirable pieces for the Yale Cabaret, which changed shows weekly. (Meryl Streep appeared in a play that Durang wrote with Albert Innaurato, although no one paid much attention to the fact until she became famous.)

It was during his stay at Yale that Sigourney Weaver became one of his biggest fans: "His plays were practically all I did at Yale. There was so much glee in him. His plays reflect that. He's taking on bigger bites of things now. Chris looks like *such* a choirboy and he writes these *malicious* plays. His plays *are* becoming more powerful and perhaps less playful.

"He has an amazing sense of truth about his characters. You can trust him. His sense of truth is wonderful. He's only interested in the human element. Chris writes straight from his heart."

After Yale, Durang developed a comfortable (for him) indecision, starting with the usual lingering-in-a-college-town job. Although he was hired as a typist at the Yale Medical School, he was soon given a job writing to potential organ donors and explaining that Yale was booked up forever, so they should make other plans for the disposal of their remains. (Perhaps not surprisingly, Durang *liked* that job and kept many of the letters.)

After Brustein kept finding him fellowships, Durang finally moved to New York City—against his own better judgment. However, even while his bank account hovered in the double digits, Brustein had regional theaters doing his plays. So don't shed any tears over the shoe leather that Chris Durang went through, slogging up and down Broadway every day, mile after mile. He didn't have to walk that far. While he may not have been making any money, he did have the most fearless satire in town and was quicker to offend in his plays than anybody Joe Papp was producing.

When I last met Durang for lunch, I asked him the question that invariably occurs to anyone who has read his plays: "Why don't you write endings to your plays?" "I do." Okay.

"Come to think of it," I pressed, "just what is your vision of the world?"

Durang trotted out one horror story after another about *Catholics* who had been shafted by the universe. I mean real horror stories. Maimings, rapes, unspeakable acts. What about endings?

He said, seriously, that he *has* written endings to most everything he's written. Which made *me* recall that Durang had told me that one of the first times *Nature and Purpose of the Universe* was performed was at Smith College; Durang's mother brought one of her friends to savor the triumph, not realizing the content. Said Durang, "Their faces were so funny to see, they really looked as if they had both just been slapped or as if someone had come and defecated right in front of them. It just made me sort of giddy."

What about endings? Again he answered seriously. "I don't think that there are any solutions in life, so I don't see any in my plays."

Well. With that in mind, why don't we just kind of stop this thing right here.

When There's No More Room in Hell, the Dead Will Walk the Earth

Monsters do exist—in us and among us. They walk in our shadow. They can prey on us more as we fear them less. We should know. We created them. Now we try to tell them to go away. Our new and knowledgeable ways provide a certain freedom for the dark creatures.

—George A. Romero, director of *Night of the Living Dead*

Night of the Living Dead has been described as "the most horrifying, stomach-churning charnel in the history of horror." That description makes its creator, George Romero, chuckle. He's a large, bearlike, affable man who looks more like he should be directing *Benji* than what

he's doing right now. What he's doing right now is hanging out in the Monroeville Shopping Mall, near Pittsburgh, up to his armpits in blood and gore. He's directing a sequel to 1968's *Night of the Living Dead,* which *is* a terrifying chronicle of the dead coming back to life and eating the living. The day before, I had watched the uncut version (it's heavily edited for TV) in his New York office—right after eating a hearty lunch. I kept it all down but there were moments when I thought I wouldn't, for it is one strong movie—the banality of evil personified; slow, deliberate zombies coming after you and catching you and eating you alive. Run them over with a truck and they get right back up and keep lurching after you; blast hell out of them with an elephant gun and they reel for a moment but keep on coming. Glassy-eyed stares and lunging arms that can smash through a wall to grab you and rip your arm off and beat you to death with it. And then eat you. I mean there is no way to *reason* with these creatures.

That's why, when Romero asked me if I wanted to be a zombie in the sequel, *Dawn of the Dead,* I almost knocked him over getting to the makeup table in the "Community Room" of the Monroeville Mall.

"Regular or special zombie?" asked Tom Savini, the makeup and cosmetic special-effects whiz.

"What's the difference?"

"Regular is just dead and decaying. Special means you're *really* deformed."

"Gimme the works. Ugly as possible."

"You picked a good night," said Savini, as he started putting gray pancake makeup on my face. "Tonight I'm gonna behead one of the zombies. I play one of the bikers who break into the mall and I ride by with my machete and *whoosh!* off goes the head and the blood spurts up—that's the fun of it. I've never chopped off anyone's head before and this is creative."

Next he started working a latex mold onto my cheek, along with gray lipstick and brown eye makeup. "You didn't get to see the zombie that walked into the helicopter blade, did you? We made a foam latex head full of gore, with two fire-extinguisher pumps full of blood off camera. When that blade shaved that head, it was like slicing an egg, it was *beautiful.*" A little bit of yellow hair spray and he was done. "Okay, you're dead."

I looked in a mirror and almost fell over: there was a living corpse staring back at me, with a terrible gaping wound across its cheek. Clayton Hill, one of the "lead zombies," came over and slapped me on the back. He looked deader than I did. "I could see," he said, "that you *really* wanted to be a zombie and I appreciated that, I can see you're into it. Some of these zombies around here don't care that much."

We walked through the mall's upper level, toward Penney's, where the night's first scene was being shot. Since it's hard to film gun battles with the mall full of customers, the crew was shooting every night from midnight till dawn. With the mall brightly lit, almost glowing, and the stores all closed and the hallways deserted save for a few wandering zombies, I began to mentally slide into the fantasy Romero had working here.

Hill was carrying a Thompson submachine gun as we walked. A retired air force officer, he's the film's weapons coordinator, but he really likes being a zombie.

"This is supposed to be a horror movie," he said, "but it's also an action thriller. It's a whiz-bang. We've fired thousands of rounds of blanks; every type of weapon available.

"Now, let me tell you about being a zombie. When you go into your zomb, you're in a fantasy. I go into the role feeling I *am* the living dead, I can't focus on things, I can't get it together. I researched it in books—the wide-open eyes, the clutching hands, the slow movements. Then I made my own zombie. I asked George and he said, 'Be your own zombie.' I intend to be the *best* zombie there ever was. I want people to come away from this movie saying, 'Wow, he was a *good* zombie.' Sharon, the nurse zombie, got into her zomb so heavily the other night, she made herself sick. We've got some good zombies. When we were shooting the exteriors and it was zero degrees, there was this three-hundred-pound guy showed up every night in a bathing suit. He said, 'I'm not cold. I *love* it.' "

"The zombies lost in *Night*," I said, "but don't they win here, don't they start getting smarter?"

"Maybe the bad guys win here," he said, "and I like the switch—but I'm *not* sure the zombies are the bad guys because we *can't help* being zombies. I love zombies."

We reached Penney's, where Romero was shooting and reshooting a dialogue scene with the four human heroes, and I took the opportunity to study the script. At the moment, it had no beginning and two endings. "Some directors work from day to day," Romero told me. "I work from moment to moment."

The plot, loosely told, is this: The dead are returning to life and eating the living. Four human heroes flee the city in a helicopter and land on the roof of a suburban mall. They kill off all the zombies inside (kill the brain and you kill the zombie), secure the outside doors and set up housekeeping in the mall. They live the good life for some months until a scavenging gang of (human) bikers breaks in to get their share of Baskin-Robbins and Sony Trinitrons. In an extraordinary scene, twenty-one bikers on their hogs crash the doors and, with machine guns blazing, try to rape the mall. The zombies follow them in and there are fierce battles between heroes and bikers, bikers and zombies, and heroes and zombies. The surviving bikers flee and the zombies get two of the heroes. The remaining man and woman—in one ending—get away in the helicopter, which is dangerously low on gas. In the other ending, the woman kills herself by leaping into the helicopter blade. The ending is still unresolved, as is the problem of explaining at the beginning what is happening and why.

As I listened to the dialogue in the scene in front of Penney's, I caught one line that began to offer an explanation. The four heroes are trying to figure out what's going on and one of them says, "It's something my granddaddy, who used to practice *macumba* in Trinidad, told me: 'When there's no more room in hell, the dead will walk the earth.' "

"George," I asked, "where did you get that line?"

He laughed. "I just made that up. *Truly.* On a drunken night when I was really crashing to finish the script and I thought that was kind of nice. It was from something Dario Argento [the Italian director of *Suspina,* who's doing the sound effects and score for *Dawn*] told me. My family is Cuban and Dario said, 'Well, you have a Caribbean background and that's why you're into the zombie thing; zombies originated in Haiti.' I said, well, all right, and I just figured that's something a voodoo priest might say. Whee! I'm just having fun, man."

George Romero, at age thirty-eight, is understandably a bit apprehensive about the reception that *Dawn of the Dead,* as his first "big" production (with a budget approaching a million dollars), will receive. His film reputation remains rooted in *Night of the Living Dead,* which, done for about $114,000, was a critical masterpiece and has grossed almost $11 million.

After studying drama at Carnegie-Mellon in Pittsburgh, Romero did TV commercials for years until the *Night* idea came to him. After its success, he was deluged with offers to do a *Night II.* He became "paranoid" about it and turned completely away from the horror genre. His next movies did not do well: *Jack's Wife* was briefly released as *Hungry Wives,* and *There's Always Vanilla* was briefly released as *The Affair. The Crazies,* which Romero feels was a prototype for *Dawn,* was not successful but may be rereleased.

In the meantime, he mined the Pittsburgh area for commercials and began doing network sports documentaries (such as *Juice on the Loose*) and political spots for Lenore Romney, among others.

In 1973, he wrote the sketch for *Dawn* and at the same time formed a partnership with New York stockbroker Richard Rubinstein. "Up until that time," said Romero, "I really didn't have any kind of pipeline into the operative industry at all. I was operating out of Pittsburgh very naïvely. Then I started to get back into it."

He foresaw a film called *Martin* as his "reentry" to directing films. *Martin,* which was shown at Cannes and has not yet been released in the U.S., is a "quiet" Romero horror film. Already acclaimed in Europe, *Martin* is more or less a modern-day vampire story set in a small town near Pittsburgh. It is, of course, sympathetic toward (or at least understanding about) the vampire.

We moved down to the ice rink for Tom Savini's beheading scene. Stardom finally called me: I was cast as one of the zombies who try to snatch Savini out of a motorcycle sidecar while he chops off the head of the zombie behind me. Romero offered only one bit of direction: "Okay, zombies, remember this: That's *your food* on that motorcycle and you *want* it. Get as close to it as you want but that cycle is *not* going to swerve out of your way."

Before the scene, Clayton Hill caught me over by a potted palm, where I was putting dirt under my fingernails. "Really into your zomb. I like that."

I stationed myself in the Pup-A-Go-Go stand and the minute Romero yelled "action" something remarkable happened: My eyes went out of focus, my hands clenched grotesquely, and I developed a lurching gait as I went after that motorcycle. I *wanted* that food and I almost got it. By the time the scene was shot twice—once with a mannequin that is beheaded—I was out of breath and my pulse was pounding.

"Maybe there's a little zombie in all of us, eh?" George said only half facetiously.

Sharon Ceccatti, the nurse zombie, came up to congratulate me as I caught my breath. "Is it always like this?" I asked. "You bet," she said. "Most mornings I go home and I *shake*. I can't sleep."

"This is beginning to feel like Dachau," a man beside me was saying later as we watched a zombie get his hand—very bloodily—cut off in a door. "This is far beyond Sam Peckinpah." The man speaking was Gary Zeller, who supplied the weapons for the film and handled explosives and breakaway special effects. Among many other projects, he worked on both *Godfather* films. He is one of the few crew members not acting in the film. "I didn't want to," he said, "this is getting depressing. Twenty gallons of blood used, animal intestines for the zombies to eat—this morning I was eating a corned beef sandwich and somebody said, 'Hey, that's a prop.' We use corned beef in some of the artificial arms. Real amputees volunteered, makes it look real. I've rigged over five hundred bullet squibs. We kill 'em every possible way, burn 'em, shoot 'em, blow their heads off. It's good there's some comic relief now and then because this movie runs like a machine gun.

"It's funny how this gets to you. This morning I was cleaning one of the Tommy guns in my motel room. I had just showered and was nude and I hear a key in the lock and the door opens and this businessman is standing there with his suitcases. I automatically train the gun on him and his mouth hits the floor. I say, 'Get outta here and don't say nuttin' about this.' He just ran. But really, man, I want to get back to New York. I feel like I'm out on the edge here, on the edge of civilization."

At seven every morning, the *Dawn* crew starts shutting down. At 7:05 every morning the mall's computer turns on the Muzak. Also at 7:05 a group of cardiac patients arrives, with a doctor, to stroll through the mall for "exercise under stable weather conditions." The zombies start filing out and the cardiac patients start filing in. Life in the mall. A clerk arrives early for work and she isn't wearing any makeup and one of the film crew says to her, in all seriousness, "Hey, zombie, are you through for the night?"

After a long night of killing zombies, George Romero sat down to a big breakfast at the Sheraton Inn-On the Mall. One of the motel's features is a "Mall Shopping Weekend Plan, $49.95 per couple." That amused Romero a great deal.

I mentioned to him that I liked the mall better at night, that the zombies seemed to have more purpose than the shoppers.

"That's how I got the idea!" he said. "I know the people who own it, and I went through the mall, empty, one time and I said, "Holy shit! That's the *perfect* place for the fulcral episode where we can show the false security of the whole consumer America trip. That's why this is in color—*Night* was black and white—because of the mall. So I wrote a little sketch about it and then put it in a drawer while I did some other things. I'm really surprised no one else picked up on the idea, because now there are these shopping developments where you can live on top and work and shop down below and never have to leave the building. That's a *trip*. In this film, the mall becomes the *cause*. The four heroes get in there to get some Civil Defense water and food and then they rack out and this consumerism, it's too tempting for them to resist. They arm themselves heavily, they become banditos fighting for all that stuff."

Are the bikers then supposed to be an antidote for them or are they actually an exaggeration of that: racing through the mall at a hundred miles an hour and scooping up color TVs?

"I think they're the ultimate of what the heroes are becoming, fighting for control of the Mothership. In fact, when they first see the raiders, the bikers coming over the hill, Peter takes off his new watch and all his other shit and that's a flash toward realization. The raiders are consumerism at its extreme and they just storm in there and go bananas and then of course that causes the downfall. But the heroes, even though Roger is dying at that point, he still has his candies and radios and shit . . . and that's why they're so extreme in their garb during the attack scenes, all the crossed gun belts, fighting over microwave ovens. I mean . . ."

He doubled over with laughter. Romero has a weird slant on the world, to say the least. With *Night* and *Dawn* he has filmed some of the most explicit violence imaginable and yet he can argue, convincingly, that it's detached violence because it's directed at *things* rather than people; that the zombies become merely so many insects to be swatted aside. At the same time, he's starting to make the zombies smarter and more sympathetic because he genuinely likes them. On a set, he resembles a giant, bearded shepherd with his poor dead flock shuffling after him. Sometimes he refers to his zombies as "sharks," which is a startling but dead-on comparison.

Zombies have been staples in horror films for decades, I said to him after his laughing fit, but until *Night of the Living Dead,* they were harmless and ineffectual. *Night* made them deadly dangerous enemies. Where did he get his zombie notion and where will he take it?

He answered seriously. "I originally wrote *Night* as a short story, following a character through three stages. It was from Richard Matheson's book *I Am Legend,* which became a lot of movies: *The Last Man on Earth, The Omega Man,* it was done three or four times. My story was in three parts: the beginning of the phenomenon, which was *Night.* The cusp, as I call it, is *Dawn of the Dead,* a cusp or balance where we feel the zombies will take over because they have the mall at the end. By the end, the mall looks just the way it does during the day. And in the third part, the zombies *will* take over and become the operatives. Zombies in the White House.

"The zombie was just an intriguing character, it *is* a sympathetic character. It always has been, really. Lugosi always had a bunch of them working for him. But they never got a piece of the action before. There's a sequence in *Dawn* that really shows the change. When the raiders first invade the mall, they're really dealing cavalierly with the zombies, to the point of throwing pies, and then there's a sudden turnaround that puts the zombies where I'd like them to be. The raiders get their comeuppance."

Despite Romero's avowal that he's just making "comic books," I reminded him, he gets very close to a message when he talks about "human sellouts" and "operatives" versus the "alternate society."

"Well, *Night* is obviously part one of that. The revolutionaries appear but the operatives are still on top. *Dawn* is the midpoint in the seesaw and then the dead take over and the operative society collapses. But human sellout . . ."

Another attack of laughter toppled him for a moment.

"The sellouts," he finally continued, "the scientific community is saying, 'Let's *feed* 'em. They're *wasteful.*' They eat only five percent of a body and then the body's intact enough to revive and it comes back as a zombie. The government says we should feed them and control that pattern—which seems *probably* what those cats would do. So if someone has died in your family, cut them into meal-size bits."

He was roaring with laughter and the businessmen at breakfast around us began throwing odd looks toward our table. George wiped tears of laughter from his eyes and went on: "That's probably the way it would go. My idea to take it further is to actually have human operatives that are trying to preserve their own kind of operative situation and in fact *using* the zombies initially, training them to serve their own needs. There are beginnings of that in *Dawn*. I show a few flashes of intelligence or at least a learning capability in the zombies. If there are human sellouts that first start teaching them to do things so that they become *really* operative, then it's *over*. But that is also what's happening to *us,* those kinds of monsters, our corporate monsters that prey on us more as we fear them less. I mean, that's this whole false security concept of the mall, being funneled into it, the temple to consumerism, the mall. And being perfectly happy, you know, absolutely lulled by it and yet eaten by it like that."

But isn't that temple, the mall, also fragile in the film?

"Fragile? If you attack it in a direct manner, yeah. I mean, it's fragile only to the extent that it doesn't need to attract you. I mean, you can just walk away from it. Which is another reason I like the character of the zombies because you can . . . if you don't get involved with them, you're okay. I mean, you can just push it away."

Romero paused, obviously feeling he had gotten carried away with philosophy. He laughed. "I do think of my films as morality plays, even though my reputation is, you know, splatter films and like that. But I think of them as very moral. The splatter and everything else is the format. . . . I mean, I'd be willing to put the POW! BANG! SUPER! on it. It's comic books, man, it's paperbacks, you know, that's what they are. I want *Dawn* to play like a cowboys and Indians movie. I'm trying to see if I can get past all that violence and just hoot and holler and cheer and throw pies and shit."

★   ★   ★

A few weeks later, George finally decided which ending to use (we're keeping it a secret) and he had worked up a beginning, which had worried him greatly. He was criticized in *Night* for having a *deus ex machina*—in that case a radioactive satellite—activate the zombies. *Dawn* will begin with a TV newscast—with the film's credits over—just announcing that the zombies are out and about. I called him up to suggest that recombinant DNA would be a good cause, but he wouldn't hear of it. "I want it to be unexplained because the zombies really just come out of *us* rather than a third party. It just happens."

A Star Is Borning

Lola from Budapest is a bit of a psychic, among other things, and one afternoon not long ago, when she settled into her customary front-row seat in NBC's Studio 3A in Rockefeller Center for the taping of the

"Tomorrow" show, she just naturally started divining things and reading life lines and such. Lola from Budapest—that's the way she's billed on her business cards and fliers—offered to hypnotize Tom Snyder when he strolled out to warm up his audience, and he good-naturedly declined. Lola from Budapest adjusted all her parcels and bags and turned to me to check out the old life lines and to ask who would be on the show. Lilli Palmer she knew. Maureen Reagan she knew. Jim Carroll she didn't know.

"Well," I said, "he's sort of a singing poet, a street kid alive with the rhythms of the city. He was even nominated for a Pulitzer Prize for a poetry book and . . ."

(Oddly enough, a phone call a few days later to the Pulitzer Prize committee revealed the fact that Carroll as well as his fans only *thought* he had been nominated for a Pulitzer for his book, *Living at the Movies.* When I told Carroll that I was stripping him of his so-called nomination, he said that "some lady" at Viking Press had written him a letter telling him that Viking intended to enter his book for Pulitzer competition and that he had since lost the letter. So, apparently, has Viking.)

Lola from Budapest cut me off. She was dubious. "I wait till I hear him," she said. As a skeptic, she was a definite minority member of the studio audience, about half of which was young and black-leathered-up-with-silver-chains. I recognized many of the Carroll chain gang from his show the night before at the Ritz. It was only his second New York rock 'n' roll performance—as opposed to his poetry readings at St. Mark's and such places—but there was no doubt he was the hottest ticket in town in a season when rock's big events, like the Plasmatics' Cadillac explosions, were causing giant yawns all over town, from Hudson all the way up to 86th Street. Jim Carroll, former teenage junkie, whiz-kid poet, basketball legend who went from Lower East Side asphalt courts to hardwood-floored gyms and prep-school uniforms at Trinity, seemed to be about two minutes away from full-fledged rock-and-roll stardom.

Everybody was talking about the republication of his teenage-junkie book, *The Basketball Diaries,* and about his new album, *Catholic Boy,* and that great teenage flame-out song, "People Who Died," from that album, which had become an underground-radio sensation even before the album came out, and that had people in radio tip sheets, like the influential *FMQB Album Report,* saying radio things like " 'People Who Died' is phono-matic sales stirring rock" and "best new candidate for hot phones."

A young poet whom Ted Berrigan called "the first truly new American poet," who was signed to Rolling Stones Records, and whose New York rock debut, last July at Trax, featured no less a guest guitarist than senior Rolling Stone Keith Richards (who has a nodding acquaintance himself with the ins and outs of junk) was one hot number indeed.

There can be little doubt that Carroll the poet is a far subtler and sharper persona than Carroll the rock 'n' roll lyricist. Carroll the poet could write (in *Living at the Movies*), "I sleep on a tar roof/scream my songs into lazy floods of stars . . . a white powder paddles through blood and heart/and/the sounds return/pure and easy . . . this city is on my side," in the poem "Fragment: Little N.Y. Ode." With "Sure . . ." he wrote a devastatingly funny junkie's apologia: "I got/a syringe/I use it/to baste/my tiny turkey." Carroll the rock lyricist doesn't come close to such economy of wit.

But Lola from Budapest knew none of this. Tom Snyder, who is big on bringing up his Catholic upbringing at any opportunity, picked up on *Catholic Boy* right away and decided that Carroll might pep up an otherwise moribund moment or two.

At the rehearsal before the show's taping, Carroll had been noticeably nervous and had broken out in cold sores. The four Secret Service agents who accompanied Maureen Reagan kept giving him the cold eye, and they pounced on him the first time he went into the makeup room.

Carroll, a rangy, gaunt-faced, six-foot-two character with pale-red hair, nervously paced the sound stage, lighting one cigarette after another. "I'll have a hard time," he said to me, "trying to pretend that it's Snyder and not Danny Aykroyd I'm talking to. I'll just try to steer him away from drug questions and just quote from *The Basketball Diaries:* 'Junk is just another nine-to-five gig in the end, only the hours are a bit more inclined toward shadows.' "

It turned out Snyder was easy on Carroll and went light on the drug subject and didn't even mention the *Diaries* passages where Carroll spoke of hustling gay men. Snyder talked about Catholicism and patent-leather shoes that reflect up girls' dresses. Carroll was still nervous and kept digging one too-white leather jazz shoe's toe into the red carpet of Snyder's little round turntable of a set, just a couple of feet from where Snyder's brown teddy bear sits beside his chair, always just out of range of the camera.

Lola from Budapest liked Carroll at first. "He is beautiful," she leaned over and whispered to me. "He will do well in future. He has sense of humor and is ambitious. Good-looking boy."

Her smile faded a bit as Carroll talked about how he was a product of Catholicism, "redeemed through pain, not through joy," and how Christ's forced march with the Cross and subsequent crucifixion were "just like punk rock."

Snyder assumed his deep-think mantle and asked if Carroll perhaps mightn't think that some people—but certainly not Snyder—mightn't think that such a statement bordered on blasphemy.

Carroll ground his toe into the carpet: "No." He said that since he was six years old he had been looking for a vision, a sign from Christ, but had never gotten close, even that time he invited Christ home to watch the World Series with him and Christ was a no-show, and that he figured that the reason Christ put him on permanent hold was that Christ spent twenty-four hours a day giving a buzz to all these born-againers who seem to have a direct celestial hookup. That got a studio laugh, and it also generated several hundred unhappy letters from members of the Moral Majority around the country.

Carroll talked about how basketball had been his great equalizer when he was a disadvantaged kid and how he could go one-on-one against any rich suburban kid and whip him and how he had gotten onto heroin when he was deathly afraid of marijuana because at that time, in the early Sixties, everybody said that marijuana was addictive. He squeezed in his nine-to-five quote and then got up and sang "Wicked Gravity," a song "about transcending."

Snyder had been refraining from smoking on camera because it was a national anti-smoking holiday or something, and he raced over to the corner of the studio and lit up a cigarette. Lola from Budapest did not respond to "Wicked Gravity" as enthusiastically as did the chains-and-leather gang, although, it must be said, many normally dressed people who wore cloth seemed to like hearing Carroll's rather emotionless delivery of lyrics about doing it all night without touching, and seemed to like the Jim Carroll Band's cheerful full-speed-ahead attack, very reminiscent of the Stones or Faces on a sloppy good-time night when the sound of rock 'n' roll is a slightly menacing, don't-tread-on-me metallic anthem of the young and free. The music, loose and raucous, had a commitment to the rock 'n' roll tradition of exuberance and rebellion; the words were biting and cold and totally impersonal, as detached as a commuter who is late for the 6:23 and finds his path blocked by a blathering Moonie. Maybe Carroll planned it that way and maybe he didn't, but the combination of fire and ice—hardly new, anyway, in any kind of performance and especially so in the arena of rock poetry—provides a conveniently articulated urban sensibility for the urban inarticulate who went into cold storage after Jim Morrison died and who thought Patti Smith was a pale substitute and hid out downtown during disco and Barry Manilow. The no-morals majority of hard-core New York rock fanatics doesn't mind at all if Jim Carroll sounds a little bit like Lou Reed or David Bowie, just so it's still the cold-steel-and-concrete sound of the city, a sound that provides a personal, alien soundtrack for those who don't fit in—or who like to think they don't fit in.

When Jim Carroll finished "Wicked Gravity," Lola from Budapest's facial expressions seemed to indicate that she was working up a re-evaluation of Jim Carroll. "What is your opinion?" she asked me. I said I thought that the jury was still out and that I liked some of what he did. Lola from Budapest grasped my hand and shook her head: "He has no emotions. He is schizophrenic. Maybe drug addict. Maybe homo-sexual." I couldn't bring myself to tell her that those were precisely the qualities required to become a rock 'n' roll star circa 1981 in this town. The requirements are stricter than the college boards.

"I was vulnerable, but they said I was mesmerizing," Jim Carroll was telling me as we walked east on 54th and crossed Broadway after his band rehearsed one afternoon. "*Mesmerizing*. That was the word. That's what got me into rock 'n' roll."

I remembered a chilling moment from his Ritz show. I was sitting at a balcony table, thirty feet above the true-grit fans packed in front of the stage, where Carroll was half-chanting and half-singing "Nothing is true" ("everything is permitted"), which strikes me as half-baked Nietzsche, but you never know how many people actually chart their lives according to pop-music lyrics. I felt a sudden pressure on my shoulder and turned to see a pale young man climbing up on my table. "Excuse me," he said, "I need to jump off your table here." "Well, why?" I asked, trying to stall him before he or someone he might land on got hurt badly. "That's what he wants me to do," the young man said, gesturing toward the stage. "Well," I said, grabbing his ankle, "he told *me* he doesn't want you to kill yourself." The young man smiled vacantly and climbed down off the table and patted me on the head: "You're a good man." He wandered off, singing "Everything is per-mitted."

I didn't even mention that to Carroll as we walked along 54th, the main reason being that he was already nervous enough about even existing as a semi-public person without taking on the burden of the psychos who turn up in the wake of any known face. He'd been visibly shaken by the press of autograph hounds who had trapped him in the NBC lobby after the Snyder show. He's still getting his street-smarts back, he said, laughing. One of the first things that happened to him when he moved back to New York from California, where he'd gone to kick smack and methadone, was that he got mugged right outside Radio City and the mugger wasn't satisfied with Carroll's $300 and came back and broke his nose for him.

He's not quite the same cocky young poet who was published as a teenager in *The Paris Review* and had people like Jack Kerouac and William Burroughs cheering from his corner and had Allen Ginsberg and Anne Waldman as friends. And he had been one of the best basketball players in the city and had been a poor Irish kid who got a scholarship to Trinity and had been a pioneer long-hair-doper-cool-guy-athlete who excited some people because he could dunk a ball backward and excited other people because he could dunk a ball backward while stoned and then write about it. Even though he was a "scholarship guy," a poor kid thrown in with New York's rich, he fit in well at Trinity. He was a certified star basketball player and he was quick-witted enough to bluff his way through classes and he had a street swagger and he took out glamor girls who went to the Professional Children's School, little foxes who were already in show business. Some of his classmates remember that he was as swift a bullshit artist as there was. They still recall that he once wore a fake arm cast to school to get out of baseball or football practice—especially football, because everybody could tell right off that he detested physical contact. And while it says in *The Basketball Diaries* that the book was written between his twelfth and fifteenth years, some of his classmates say it was more or less rewritten and polished between Carroll's fourteenth and eighteenth birthdays, and closer to the eighteenth than the fourteenth.

Jim Carroll and I turned up Sixth Avenue and stopped in O'Neal's for a Coke for him and a beer for me. He is off drugs and drinks only an occasional shot of tequila. He still has a rancid memory of the time he had his stomach pumped out after chugging most of a fifth of Scotch and then passing out in the snow up in Inwood Park and almost losing parts of his fingers from the frostbite. What a drag for a young romantic. To this day, the smell of Scotch turns his stomach, he said as we slid into a booth at O'Neal's. He lit a cigarette with jerky movements and talked in nervous spurts, looking around the room at nothing in particular.

Why, I asked, has he not identified Trinity in the *Diaries,* calling it instead a "posh private school."

"I thought I'd get sued." He laughed, and he loosened up a little. "As it is, they're all thrilled by it at Trinity. I still go up and see Frank Smith, my Latin teacher."

After Trinity—Carroll didn't bother to attend his graduation ceremonies—he did a month of college before dropping out to be a star teenage poet and druggie. Artist Larry Rivers hired him as an assistant, and Carroll stretched canvases and sharpened pencils at Rivers's 14th Street studio and lived in Rivers's 91st Street apartment. "I was only getting off three or four times a day [on heroin]," Carroll said, "just to stay high. I wasn't into doing it for a lifestyle, just to write and to nod.

At night, I'd go out and hustle, make some money. I wound up just staying up there and baby-sitting Larry's kids. Which was great. I'd walk them down to the zoo and meet my connection at the fountain on 72nd near the boathouse. On a rainy day, I'd meet him at the Museum of Natural History, because he loved those big panoramas. I think heroin makes you like things like that, miniature little landscapes. Junkies tidy up always. So, if you kept a system like I did—I didn't have a partner or old lady to hassle with—I kept everything very neat.

"I loved Larry," he said after a sip of his Coke and a fresh cigarette. "If there was anybody from around that art scene who had an influence on me, it was Larry. This was a real cool dude. I even started to imitate his walk. He's the only guy who ever had that effect on me in the art world. Frank O'Hara might have—if I'd known him. I *followed* Frank O'Hara one day when I was first into poetry, followed him home from the Museum of Modern Art, because I knew he worked there. This was like two months before he died. I followed him in a taxi and he got off at Astor Place and I followed him up to Tenth Street and Broadway, right across from Grace Church—you know Poe's poem 'The Bells' was written when he was living near there, about the bells in that steeple. But, to me, it's the place where Frank O'Hara's last apartment was. I followed him to his house. I'm sure he didn't notice me. But of course I always got told by poets that 'Frank would have loved you.' He seduced every guy on the scene—all the straight guys too. I made it a point never to sleep with any guys in the poetry scene, except, you know, the gay guys, which were plentiful, you know, in the older-generation school of New York poets. But I'm sure with Frank I would have wound up in bed. He was an idol."

Carroll cupped his cigarette in his hand and sipped at his Coke and looked off at nothing. "I was the young protégé," he finally continued. "They really took me in the way they didn't take in younger poets who came along later. I came along at the right time."

What happened, I wondered, that made him flee New York for northern California in 1974 when he thought he was nominated for a Pulitzer?

Carroll looked me straight in the eye. "I knew I was gonna kill myself if I stayed in New York. I was fucking around too much. See, I was on methadone then and I was starting to buy extra bottles because when you're on a certain dose you can shoot as much heroin as you want and not feel it. The theory of methadone in New York is to keep them on as high a dose as allowed, 'cause then you can't feel junk even when you shoot it and you can work; it just gets you straight. You feel it when you're first on the program, but after a month you don't even feel it. But the methadone program in Marin County was like a college dormitory; they really helped you get off junk. It was still real tough. Methadone's an insidious drug, infinitely harder to get off than junk. I kicked junk cold fifteen times; the withdrawal symptoms peak after about three days and last about eight days.

"But methadone is a month of physical torment at the very least. You can't get any sleep to escape it. I hate even thinking about it. But at any rate, I came out of it. And then I just became a recluse. I'd take my twelve-mile hike with my dogs up along the coast."

Carroll jumped up to get a fresh pack of smokes. I suddenly noticed that the happy-hour crowd around us was leaning in very close to listen.

When Carroll got back, I asked why he thought he should go into rock 'n' roll.

He smiled. "When I'd do readings, people would say, 'Mick Jagger reading poetry—you should do rock 'n' roll.' I said, 'No way, man.' I respected people's singing voices then. Forget it. Even when Patti [Smith] did it. Her lyrics were better than her poems, to me. But Patti wasn't as accepted and didn't have a reputation in the poetry scene like I did. I was supposed to read with her the first night she did it with music, with Lenny [Kaye] playing guitar behind her, but I got busted in Rye, New York, because I was visiting a friend who had some hash. So I was in jail.

"But my connection with New York in my recluse period was reading about CBGB and punk rock and Television and Blondie and Talking Heads, and one by one they all got signed up by record companies and came out to San Francisco to play the Old Waldorf. I checked them all out. Then Patti came out, and I did that show down in San Diego with her. I got this band together. Rosemary [his next-door neighbor, whom he married] put it in my head about doing this. First, just writing songs, and then thinking, 'Well, what the hell, I don't need vocal proficiency. I could write songs to my own vocal limitations.'

"So I started to think, 'Rock 'n' roll!' When I did the shows with Patti, I saw that it could be done. It was incredible fun, and it was so intense and scary and beautiful at the same time. It was remarkable. What a feeling. It's *still* that way, you know. I think it's just a natural extension of my work, of the images. By making images just obscure enough to be made personal, I have the street imagery, but you have to have that kind of mythology built into it, because that's what kids understand. I don't like to deal with any subject matter straight out, you know. So, I'm pretty talked out."

He turned away silently to the wall while I dealt with the check.

"Henry Miller," he said. "Henry Miller's study of Rimbaud, which is really a study of Henry Miller, was the big factor for me going into rock—that was *it*. That whole thing about getting a heart quality out of work rather than just the intellectual quality. A good poet works on both. Miller spoke about the inner register and how a good poet has to affect virtual illiterates as well as affecting people through the intellect, and I figured so many poets are just writing for other poets today. It's all intellectual concrete minimal poetry. There's a school of poets in San Francisco called Language Poets. What the fuck does that mean?"

Chapter 9

Gluttony

The One-Page Dolly Parton Diet

August 25, 1985.

Dear Diary: Had lunch today with Dolly Parton in Beverly Hills. After all the times I've interviewed her, she says that now all she wants to talk about is food. Said she had developed a great diet. This is it:

"I love to eat. If I get to wanting something, whether it's spaghetti or whatever, I'm gonna eat it, regardless. But when I really want to lose a lot of weight, I do a variation of a low carbohydrate and high protein diet for five or six weeks. I go on like a zero carb diet for a week or two. I'll eat cheeses and eggs and meats, some salads, and mayonnaise and butter and all the things I like. You can't have bread and potatoes, but you can have a few vegetables. So I find that I can lose weight and still eat as much as I want. And it's not a real fast and you can have bacon and eggs and all that stuff. You can eat a ton of red meat, if you want to. The diet's just more boring than anything else. Like you can't have any fruit. After a couple of weeks, though, you can have a few berries, you know."

Saint Elvis

The first whisperings of a clandestine Elvis church service came out of Fort Wayne, Indiana. A group of paunchy, heavily sideburned, middle-aged men, the many rumors went, started having Elvis services once a

241

week. With an altar and all, but not too formal. Low Elvis, as it were.

Then, for more than a year, I started hearing serious rumors about an Elvis church in Manhattan. I heard the story of sightings from too many otherwise sobersided people to totally dismiss it as garbage: they had all heard of an Elvis church ceremony floating among various vacant storefronts on Manhattan's Lower East Side.

In both cases, the rumors remain tantalizing but impossible to confirm. And the more I explore the phenomenon of Elvis Alive the more I understand the Mystery: Nobody wants to be labeled an Elvis nut. No matter how innocent the connection. Millions of hard-core Elvis cases remain "in the closet" because their devotion to El might cause problems with the boss, wife, in-laws, school, job. Even so, it is obvious a dozen years after his death that Elvis touched a great many people more than even they at first realized.

Like many a grand Southern funeral, his was conducted on a larger-than-death scale: every flower in Memphis heaped up in memorial, every limousine within hundreds of miles pressed into service, tens upon thousands of weeping, prostrate mourners, the eyes of the world glued to the great spectacle. Elvis Presley's passing evoked many memories of illustrious funerals past: Huey Long crossing to glory over in Louisiana, Hank Williams taking his last ride down in Alabama, General Robert E. Lee giving up his last command in Virginia.

As a casual Elvis fan, I pretty much quit paying attention to him after he went into the Army. As a journalist, I kept up with him but had no idea what was really going on with his career until I went to his funeral. As a reporter, I've covered only two such occasions: JFK's and Elvis's funerals. Needless to say, there were many similarities. What most amazed me, however, was the emotional intensity present at each. In many ways, Elvis's laying-away was the more intense, especially because there was no protocol for the Elvis fans attending. At a President's funeral you know what you're supposed to and not supposed to do. At Elvis's, on the other hand, there was an undercurrent of such untapped . . . spirituality, if you will, that it was always unsettling and at times frightening. The potential was there for anything to happen. I had had no idea there were so many people, so fiercely devoted, who now felt such a devastating loss and emptiness.

In many ways, Elvis's death is best compared to Robert E. Lee's, both because of the cultural similarities as well as because of the extraordinary degree of public grief. Both Lee and Presley were identified by Southerners as ideal Southerners who were sullied or brought down by outside forces beyond their control. Both were deified as a result of their grand failures—which were caused by someone else. In Lee's case, the blame for Gettysburg was assigned to Longstreet. In Elvis's, it was the dope-doctor, Dr. Nick; it was the Judas bodyguards who exposed his pill-popping final years; it was pointy-headed Albert Goldman wallowing in Elvis's filth; it was anybody who brought down the noble Elvis. Elvis was martyred overnight. I can tell you, the silent intensity of feeling for the lost Elvis that day was so overwhelming among the crowds thronging Graceland that it could have levitated an unbeliever.

If you had to pick a day when Elvis started becoming a religion, that would be as good a choice as any. But it was really before. As longtime Elvis watcher and biographer Dave Marsh once told me, "It all depends on in whose mind Elvis became a religion. Remember, in the early days, Sam Phillips was running around comparing himself to John the Baptist and Elvis to Christ. And that was in '54 or so."

Patsy Guy Hammontree is an English professor at the University of Tennessee, in Knoxville. She also wrote the seminal Elvis reference book, *Elvis Presley: A Bio-Bibliography,* and has monitored Elvis hap-

penings for many years. She went to her first Elvis concert in 1972. "It was a religion back then," she says. "Forget saying that Elvis is becoming a religion now. It was one from the beginning. The first thing that struck me was that it was very much like a Baptist revival—without any of the sadness. People were weeping, but they were weeping for joy. They were joyous, I learned, because each one felt that Elvis was singing personally to them and only to them, directly to them. He was looking directly into their souls, they thought."

Yes, Elvis's passing brought back memories. But the one thing no one counted on at the time was that—unlike other famous dead Southerners—Elvis could not be counted on to remain dead. Either in the flesh or in the spirit. Amazingly, these dozen years after his alleged death, the hue and cry and glory and worship are not only *not* dying down, as the critics had predicted, they are increasing to the almost sacrilegious point of sainthood. For Elvis! There are literally thousands of otherwise partly sane citizens walking around thinking out loud that Elvis never croaked at all and is still walking among us, perhaps rearing back and passing an occasional miracle in between trips to Dunkin' Donuts and the Wal-Mart. Others—many others—are elevating Elvis to a hallowed spot somewhere just a tad below the Holy Trinity. Making him, that is to say, into a religion. As Hammontree points out, as years pass less and less is known about Elvis himself: The myth has quickly swallowed the man. Just how and why did things come to such a pass?

There were a number of reasons for Elvis's phenomenal popularity while he was alive, most of them self-evident. What took over with a fierce vengeance after he died, though, is a matter less easy to capture or chart. Still, it is impossible to deny that something far beyond the ordinary now informs the Elvis Mystique, something that has a genuine hold on millions of people. These are normal, workaday people of the kind you pass on the street every day without realizing they have a secret: they are Elvis worshipers. For most, it doesn't go beyond a very strong attachment to the man and his music: a collection of as many Elvis records as possible and the really important stuff beyond that, the personal Elvis icons like the ticket stubs from the Hilton show in Vegas, the Elvis scarf snatched out of the air almost from the master's hand, the ashtrays and place mats and other junk from the souvenir shops on Elvis Presley Boulevard across from Graceland itself.

Still others are more possessive, more obsessive. They're the ones with the Elvis rooms in their houses, those eerie shrines to the King. Entire rooms are turned over to spooky displays of Elvis *objets*: jars of pure Elvis dirt from the grounds of Graceland; rare photos (it's been estimated that at least a billion photos were taken of Elvis in concert during the last seven years of his life alone); snippets of His clothing; pieces of carpet from Graceland; a dried and pressed flower from his funeral; a scrap of aluminum foil that once blacked out his windows at the Hilton; Elvis busts and decanters; bootleg albums; souvenir programs from the Vegas shows; "Always Elvis" wine; Elvis dolls; an Elvis postage stamp from the Virgin Islands (prospects for a U.S. Elvis stamp dimmed somewhat after the stamp's champion—Congressman Ted Ray Miller—came under FBI scrutiny for alleged bribery). They vacation every year at Graceland. They listen to little but Elvis. They may have personalized Elvis plates on their vans. Some of them channel Elvis.

Then there are the really way-out cases, whose lives are virtually turned over to Elvis. They wear Elvis, think Elvis, eat and sleep Elvis, and maybe see him or hear from him occasionally. There's an unsettling documentary called *Mondo Elvis* that you should rent if you ever get the chance. It's a series of interviews with some extreme Elvis cases: twin teenage girls who are convinced Elvis was their father; a woman who abandoned her family to move to Memphis and be near El's spirit; and a truly dedicated Elvis impersonator who is acting as a true priest in carrying on the King's spirit. There are straight-faced Elvis fans in this film who predict that he will one day (in the not-so-distant future) be the first Protestant saint. Or should be.

From all accounts, his life-long interest in the spiritual began early in life and greatly intensified in his last years. Well, that's in accordance with his spiritual history. Especially since there are now frequent sightings of the King, along with the occasional miracle (shakily documented though they may be). For example, from a supermarket tabloid: "After she lost her sight saving her Elvis LPs from a fire in her home, Rosa D'Angelo was visited by the late idol's spirit and healed." There's even a whole book dedicated to "unusual psychic experiences surrounding the death of a superstar" (there are currently 155 books in print about Elvis). It's called *Elvis After Life* and contains several case studies of Elvis's activities since his alleged death. Why did Ruth Ann Bennett's Elvis records mysteriously melt just after Elvis died? Why did Arthur and Marian Parker's Elvis statue fall to the floor and crash? What exactly happened when Beverly Wilkins was temporarily "dead" and met Elvis?

Much of the supernatural and spiritual phenomena surrounding Elvis Presley in both death and life can be explained away in simple psychological terms: wishful thinking, psychosomatic effects of grief, anniversary reactions, photism, mass hysteria, and so on.

There was also, though not everyone realizes this, a strong spiritual attachment built up throughout his life. Elvis was certainly never comfortable with it, but the fact remains that there was a strong spiritual reaction to him from the first, and not just on the part of teenage girls. Those who saw his first appearance on "Louisiana Hayride" remarked on his phenomenal effect on women of all ages in the audience, an effect that went beyond any kind of reaction to the music or his raw sex appeal. Increasingly, members of his audience came to describe their initial reactions to Elvis in religious terms. And what they were talking about, more often than not, was the ecstasy of conversion, a fairly standardized religious experience. It was obviously something that went beyond the usual appeal of a charismatic leader. Critics and observers of the early Elvis phenomenon went so far as to compare his effect on audiences to that of Gandhi or Hitler. Or Jesus Christ.

Elvis's own image did not deviate from the holy: He loved his mother, he loved gospel music, he did not seem to sin, and he loved his fans. And he never forgot his roots. No more could be asked of a matinee idol. What's more, he himself seemed to become more spiritual, if not mystical, as the years went by. His hairdresser, Larry Geller, became his spiritual advisor and was apparently responsible for what books actually made it into Elvis's limited library over the years: Linda Goodman's *Sun Signs*, Gibran's *The Prophet*, Cheiro's *Book of Numbers*, *The Secret Doctrine* by Helena Blavatsky, books by Edgar Cayce, and so on. He also carried and read the Bible, and said that his favorite passage was I Corinthians 10:13.

Geller published a book called *The Truth About Elvis* in 1980 and followed it with a second book, *If I Can Dream: Elvis's Own Story*, in 1989. The big revelation in each book is Geller's claim that Elvis died of cancer. The same revelation also appeared in Jess Stern's 1982 book, *Elvis: His Spiritual Journey*, which was about Larry Geller and Elvis. It also contained the revelation that Elvis could cause clouds to move in the sky. According to Geller and Stern, Elvis began healing through the laying on of hands. One example: A man apparently having a heart attack was so startled to see Elvis come up and lay hands on that he forgot about his heart attack.

Televangelist Rex Humbard, who straightaway called up Vernon Presley and volunteered to deliver a eulogy the minute he heard that Elvis had passed, once confirmed Elvis's spirituality. He had gone to see Elvis perform in Las Vegas, went back to his dressing room after the show, and later said, "While Elvis and I talked, something supernatural happened—a light filled the room. We wept together. Elvis said to me, 'Mr. Humbard, this is the greatest Christmas gift I could have.' "

Humbard did not preach the funeral, although he did deliver a short, emotional eulogy. Reverend C. W. Bradley of the Wooddale Church of Christ did. Bradley was Vernon's pastor, and while he said he liked Elvis, he attributed no divine qualities to him.

Soon thereafter, however, the world at large began to get some inkling of the fanaticism with which enormous numbers of people worshiped Elvis. What struck me most at first was the stolid passivity of these people, who wanted nothing more than to stand at the gates of Graceland and weep. I watched in amazement as these same people literally stripped the grounds of Graceland Christian Church, next door to Graceland proper. They clawed at the very earth and denuded the shrubs and greenery, seeking something to carry away. Fans just assumed—incorrectly—that it was Elvis's church, and they treated it accordingly. Indigent fans, women pregnant with "Elvis's child," and just plain nutcases all showed up at the doors to "Elvis's church" expecting to be cared for. That poor church finally knuckled under and sold out to Graceland.

Many Memphians themselves were sick of the whole crazy business and wished it would just go away. Even today, Elvis plays better outside Tennessee than within. Not long ago at a charity auction in Nashville, for example, an Elvis shirt went for less than a Burt Reynolds jacket. Some folklorists who watch such things speculate that one reason for this is that Southerners find it harder to reconcile Elvis worship with their own church and religion. There is a preponderance of Northern, Midwestern, and Eastern fans in the fanatical crowd. Similarly, Catholics, with a tradition of icons and church ritual, seem to be more comfortable with the whole business of Elvis reverence. There's even a traveling passion play called *Elvis: A Musical Celebration,* with three "Elvii," as Elvis impersonators—effectively, Elvis priests—are called. When I saw it in Memphis last January, it was not doing the kind of business it had done in Dallas or Las Vegas, where it ran for two months. I've found better Elvis relics in Manhattan than in Memphis, among them a vial of Elvis's sweat ("His perspiration is your inspiration"), a black velvet Elvis painting, and a lapel button containing a bit of Elvis's hair. The nation's only all-Elvis radio station, WCVG, is in Cincinnati.

The man Colonel Parker once billed as "The Nation's Only Atomic Powered Singer" lives on in many ways. The fans' most cherished symbol, their cross, is the Elvis TCB ("Takin' Care of Business") emblem. There are traveling exhibits of Elvis relics. There are museums, such as the one in Pigeon Forge, Tennessee, where the pilgrims can view such icons as Elvis's X-rays and underwear. True believers have their own stations of the cross: Graceland; the tacky souvenir shops across from Graceland on Elvis Presley Boulevard; Elvis's plane, the Lisa Marie; Humes High School; the old Sun Records studio. Every August they make their pilgrimage.

The high holy days of Elvismania are officially known in Memphis as "Elvis International Tribute Week" but are derisively referred to by locals as "Dead Elvis Week." The third week of August encompasses Gladys and Elvis's death days, and the week is the highpoint of life for a true Elfan. Elvismania itself is too far-flung and too extensive to be catalogued comprehensively, but in this one week most of what goes on around Elvis can be glimpsed or experienced in Memphis. And what goes on is a splendiferous subculture at work. The motels up and down Elvis Presley Boulevard are booked solid for months in advance by the fan clubs and impersonators. Motel room windows are decorated competitively. There are candlelight vigils galore, an Elvis 5K Run, a Fan Appreciation Social, and more craziness than can be easily explained. The people who participate in these activities are otherwise normal people who just happen to feel that Elvis had a major impact on their lives that cannot be ignored. The rest of the year they may be in the closet, but come August holy week they're flaunting it in the streets of Memphis.

Actually, they are extremely well-behaved. And one thing they don't do is carry on in the media. They've been ridiculed so regularly that they just tune out reporters. Likewise, any mention of Elvis as a church makes them all very nervous, except for the nutcases. I was at Graceland on Elvis's birthday in January of this year and found that the messages on the floral offerings left at Elvis's grave had gotten more and more spiritual—to the point where Christ himself could have been the intended recipient of most of the displays. The Elfans I talked to, however, were unfailingly circumspect as they left the Meditation Gardens. They were there because they "loved Elvis," because he was a "great person and entertainer," because there was "nobody else like him," and because "he loved us."

Thanks to them, Graceland itself, and the Elvis estate in general, is doing much better than Elvis did when he was alive. It is a captive audience, after all. Elvis Presley Enterprises pulls in at least $5 million a year from over half a million visitors. Lisa Marie will inherit Graceland in 1993 on her twenty-fifth birthday and, apparently, will make no changes in this, the mother church of Elvis World.

I had the good fortune to last visit Graceland in the company of Jerry Lee Lewis. He was Elvis's biggest rival until his marriage to his thirteen-year-old cousin effectively caused him to be blacklisted by the music industry. He is no great Elvis fan—the last time he had been to Graceland, while Elvis was still alive, he had been arrested at the gate with a gun in his car. Even so, he had mellowed enough in the intervening years to consent to be the honored guest on a nationwide radio show broadcast live from Graceland. Jerry Lee was gracious enough on the show—surprisingly so, given his volatile nature. Later, though, he told me, "Yeah, they makin' all this damn money off damn Elvis Presley. I don't even know whether he's dead or not. I thought he was. I hoped he was, anyway. If that sumbitch comes back alive, I'm gonna kill myself."

High-Octane Lunches and Paul McCartney Biographies

Maybe it was the $24.95 steak that did it, or maybe it was the profusion of two-fisted, man-sized, drink-'em-up beef-tails that fueled our high-octane lunch which inclined me to agree to the editor's suggestion: "Do an unauthorized bio of Paul McCartney."

The last, and only, biography I had written was of the late Hank Williams, who had been certifiably dead since 1953. And McCartney was certainly not dead—no more so than he was during 1969's infamous "Paul Is Dead" media blitz. Writing about a dead person, I learned while crafting *Your Cheatin' Heart,* had many advantages, chief among them being that your subject no longer had the last word: You did.

But I was not completely plugged into the concept of an "unauthorized biography" of a living person, I discovered as I listened. (There is nothing like a free and expensive Manhattan lunch to get your attention.) "Unauthorized," said my editor, waving his fork, "means just that. If McCartney were to cooperate—he won't, we checked—he would have control. It would be sanitized. This way, you get the truth. Just go get it."

Well. It sounded great at lunch. Once the glow wore off—and the contract was signed—the enormity of the thing brought on nightmares. How do you reinvent the Beatles? Or at least a Beatle? The Beatles are such a part of the woof and warp of pop culture that everyone seems to know the myth. And that is what it has become: a myth so much bigger than life that little attention is paid the truth. Some Beatle myths and rumors are so intertwined with the skein of pop history as to be permanently woven: There is no way, for example, that I can convince my own niece that Linda Eastman (Paul's wife) is not an Eastman Kodak heiress ("Eastman" was once "Epstein").

So, I began by worrying a lot. My first few phone calls confirmed my worst fears. People I knew in the music business suddenly found it impossible to take—or return—my calls. Capitol Records said I could not possibly be allowed to see their file of McCartney and Beatles press releases without written permission from Paul. For press releases! Obviously, McCartney still has enormous clout in the music business. Even though he's not having the hits lately, he *is* the remaining Chief Beatle. Said to be worth in excess of $600 million (mostly due to publishing investments), he has sold more records since leaving the Beatles than the Beatles did.

So, the guy is not going to roll over and play dead. What to do? It was time to assess the situation and weigh assets against liabilities. In the plus department I had: years of experience in covering the music business for *Rolling Stone,* a fat address book, credibility, research skills, familiarity with Paul's music, a desire to write a book that no one had done before. On the negative side: Many of those in my fat address book suddenly weren't speaking.

Also on the plus side, I had a great deal of interview material with John Lennon that I had never used. I had first met John in 1974 when I moved to New York to run *Rolling Stone*'s New York bureau. He was estranged from Yoko at the time and took a liking to my secretary, often showing up unannounced at the office. We became friends, especially after I put *Rolling Stone*'s weight, such as it was, to work covering John's fight against being deported. After I was able to obtain and publish a secret memo to Attorney General John Mitchell that revealed the Nixon Administration's campaign to oust Lennon as a political radical, John warmed to me and we spent a great deal of time together. After he was killed in 1980, I sadly put away my Lennon file.

Years later, the notion of using his words and experiences to shape a profile of his ex-writing partner seemed somehow appropriate. And I decided I had to start somewhere. The best thing to do with a project like this, I long ago learned, is to read everything that has been written. With the Beatles, that was a daunting task. It took me months to go through all the English-language books, magazine articles, newspaper clippings, fanzines, and the like devoted to the Beatles in general and McCartney in particular. There are some 250 Beatle books. I found 175 of them.

The key to this, I soon discovered, is that with the Beatles, truth is a very relative thing. There is no one Beatles authority, no central source of absolute truth. There are many Beatle realities and everyone who ever came into contact with the Fab Four holds onto a different one. Even the Fabs themselves. Both John and Paul confessed, at one time or another, that, due to drugs, the Sixties for them were just a blur. No one around them kept a journal or any sort of sane record of what was going on. Everything they did has passed into fabledom: Your Beatle truth is whatever you believe.

Which presents quite a problem for your unauthorized biographer, unfortunately. How do you reconcile one truth with another when a fresh interview contradicts a dozen old ones? It became apparent that I would have to be the final arbiter: Who else was there? I spent one entire summer doing nothing but reading and re-reading those Beatle books, slowly establishing in the process what I felt was a reasonable reality.

Next, I started phase two of my domestic print review—all extant U.S. magazine and newspaper pieces on the Beatles and McCartney— gauging those realities against the books as I plowed through them. Then I plunged into the fanzines, the fanatics' privately printed publications about the Beatles and Paul. Who could have imagined that there was once a thriving fanzine devoted entirely to Jane Asher, the actress who was Paul's betrothed in the early Sixties? (His betrothed, that is, until she caught him in bed with an American groupie.)

Then I waded through thousands of pages of legal transcripts. The Beatles and their business associates have been highly litigious, yielding juicy depositions that don't ordinarily make it into print. These yielded some plums and confirmed some things I wasn't completely sure about. It also clarified the nature of Paul's split with John over who would manage the Beatles: John's friend Allen Klein or Paul's brother-in-law John Eastman.

Then I decided I was ready to tackle England. England turned out to be not terribly happy to see me, but that's the lot of the unauthorized biographer. I got some interviews I needed and didn't get others. All that time, most people who agreed to talk to me did so only if I promised not to use their names. McCartney's tendrils apparently extend deep down in the entertainment business. I found an ex-MPL executive who told funny stories of life on the McCartney farm: Animal-rights champion Linda would let insects drop into food on the table rather than allow them to be killed; Paul would have his chickens transported by private taxi from his London house to his Scottish farm; MPL employees would be summoned to the farm to Osterize oats and grain for the toothless elderly sheep (since Paul and Linda won't allow the sheep to be slaughtered, they live to doddering old ages).

Next, I moved on to the British Library's Newspaper Library at Colindale, which has virtually every issue of everything ever printed. Colindale opened up the past to me via such papers as the *South Liverpool Weekly News,* which had chronicled the obscure church fête where Paul first met John. The *Stoke-on-Trent Evening Sentinel* contained important Beatle and Paul news, as did the *Bootle Times* and a hundred other publications from around the world. For two weeks I commuted from London to Colindale, reading and ordering photocopies from *Melody*

Maker, the *Japan Times, New Musical Express,* the *London Times,* and so on.

Back in London, a friend mentioned that Beatle items were a big draw at the auctions. I went to Sotheby's and was pleased to learn that I could not only browse through their items currently up for bid but also through their past catalogs, which contained many previously obscure Beatle letters and drawings. Eldon E. Worrall & Co. in Liverpool also held many Beatle items.

Beatle and Paul gossip were rife in London. I knew a few writers there and they introduced me to others. All had a rare Paul story, mostly libelous. Surprisingly, some of those rumors had appeared in London's racy tabloids and had never been challenged by Paul. His few friends and relatives had written many of the pieces lambasting him as a cheap, conniving, drug-addled, insensitive, ungrateful wretch. On the other hand, some merely said that he had skipped both his mother and father's funerals. His stepmother charged that Paul had shamefully neglected his chronically ill father in his last painful years. Another said that he and Linda smoked joints like they were cigarettes and that Paul had once smuggled marijuana in his baby's clothing. That does not amount to absolute truth (although British libel laws are much stricter than ours), but I talked to London journalists who would confirm the essence of these stories—as long as I did not name them. There was more. Paul was obviously devoted to his wife, children, and animals. And he was almost completely responsible, it surprised me to learn, for the *Sgt. Pepper* and *Abbey Road* albums (Lennon had been too scrambled on LSD to assume his leadership role at the time). My view of Paul changed rapidly. At first he had been John's handmaid, a relationship that soon evolved into a close-knit writing partnership. That partnership eventually was dashed apart by both egos, but Paul was not the villain that John had been depicting him as over the years. *Both* John and Paul were the villains and neither would admit it.

Back in New York, I was approached by a shadowy figure who for years had been peddling Beatles' stuff. By that, I mean obviously stolen letters, files, and memorabilia. (There is a huge illegal traffic, mainly in Japan, where millionaire businessmen like to show off their framed John or Paul letter or drawing.) There are a couple of these guys in New York and London who have made a nice living off their larceny. This particular thief, whom I knew of before Yoko fired him for theft, was offering yet again the "full story" on the "Yoko Busts Paul" scenario. It's an old rumor to the effect that Paul's 1980 marijuana bust in Tokyo had been arranged by Japanese-born Yoko to get even for past infractions. "If you don't buy it," the thief told me, "I've got someone who will."

If the Tokyo story was finally going to see print, I figured I might as well try to get Yoko to finally respond. She did so and gave me a detailed rebuttal.

So I wrote the book, trying to balance the private Paul against the public Paul, trying to show what in his life had influenced his music. More people came forward for interviews—that is, if their names weren't used.

What surprised me was Yoko's decision to withhold her cooperation. She sent a note with a drawing of John, Yoko, and Sean: *Dear Chet, I cannot accommodate you. Have a nice life. Love, Yoko and Sean.* Yoko does, of course, have a contract with Knopf to write her own authorized book.

When I had finished, I found that much work lay ahead. Two Doubleday lawyers summoned me and presented a lengthy list of matters they felt warranted hard confirmation. There were a few things that had to be deleted because the lawyers felt the proof wasn't strong enough. With a straight face, one of them asked me to "please verify your assertion that Paul had his chickens sent to him in Scotland by taxi from London. Did the chickens ordinarily travel unaccompanied?" Well, I got to keep the chicken story but my source must remain anonymous.

Sunday Afternoon With Mick Jagger

Chop, chop, chop, chop, chop. Scrape. Chop, chop, chop, chop. Scrape. Chop. Pause. The brittle impact of a PAL single-edged razor blade slicing through a glittering pile of white powder and striking the small hand mirror upon which the pile gleams is the only sound in the room. Chop, chop. The chopper is very thorough. Determined to leave intact no powder chunks that might congest and thus foul up the internal passages eager to receive the shining white powder. Chop. The snowy crystals break apart into tiny billowy drifts. Chop. Scrape. The choppee scrapes the snowbanks into two thick lines and eyes them longingly, as one might let his gaze linger over the waiting, eager body of a lover. Then the choppee and scrapee hauls out a two-inch length of powder-encrusted transparent straw and inserts one end of it into the right nostril of his wide proboscis and the other end into a fat white line and—with a loud honk—proceeds to suck about sixty dollars of what I hope is lactose and Procaine into his sinus passages. He does not offer me any—

hey, no big deal, who wants the stuff?—as I sit watching. Then he tilts his head back to let all the luscious grains penetrate every cavity in his moneyed head. Then—and only then—does Mick Jagger look up at me, tap his nostril, smile his crooked grin that shows off the diamond in a front tooth, and speak. "You do smoke, don't you?" he asks in his most charming man-of-the-people voice.

"Depends—" I start to say and, without waiting for a reply, the most famous man in rock and roll reaches into a desk drawer and produces a Baggie of some green leafy special tobacco and a packet of rolling papers. He turns his attention to cleaning the special tobacco and discarding its peculiar "seeds" and assembling a homemade cigarette. I look around the room. I'm in no hurry to leave. It's about 4:00 on a balmy Sunday afternoon, April 7, 1979, here in Mick's apartment overlooking New York's Central Park. He was then living just up from John Lennon's aerie in the Dakota at 72nd. Mick's building was nothing special and his apartment wasn't either. His view was of the street and the trees across the street. And the noise level was considerable: A second-floor Manhattan apartment overlooking a major artery such as C.P.W. may as well be inside a ghetto-blaster. Still, it was airy, and roomy, and pleasant, and homey, as is any living space that was put together to live in comfortably, rather than to impress visitors. Why was I there that Sunday instead of staying in bed and drowsing through the six pounds or so that was the Sunday *New York Times?* I didn't know myself. I had written articles for years about the Rolling Stones. Not all of those articles had been what you might call "positive." I had, in fact, been thrown off the Stones' 1978 American tour, only the year before. I had, however, tried to write honestly about the band. Maybe, I pondered there in Mick's sunny sitting room that Sunday, honesty will earn me a Stones Gold Medal or something equally ludicrous. Mick, bent over, kept rolling his special cigarette.

I had gotten a call that morning from Jane Rose, who is the Stones' very effective interface with the real world. "Can you meet with Mick this afternoon?" she asked enigmatically. "Sure," I said. What do I have better to do? So I head up C.P.W., past John Lennon's gothic Dakota, and the doorman at 135 C.P.W. sends me right up to 2N. Up a circular marble staircase. Mick, in stockinged feet, jeans, and open-necked sport shirt, lets me in the door. "Can we go in here for a bit?" he asks, ushering me to a small living room overlooking C.P.W. The focus of the room is a Sony Trinitron sitting on the cardboard box it arrived in. Mick and I sit stiffly on a couch and run through the channels on the TV. Linda Ronstadt and Jerry Brown are off to Africa, we learn. "To rescue Idi Amin?" Mick asks sarcastically.

Since Keith Richards is about to play the Canadian benefit for the blind concert that was part and parcel of his sentence for being busted in Canada with a snootful of smack, I ask Mick if he will join Keith's New Barbarians group at the show to make it a full-blown Stones event. "Yeah," Mick sneers, "if we can find a way to mark the tickets to keep the 'blindies' from scalping them." We trade tasteless cripple jokes for a while.

Finally, the focus of Mick's delay arrives. Jade Jagger, radiant, comes in roller-skating across the wood parquet floor to hug her daddy. Just behind her is Jerry Hall, huge and gorgeous, out of breath from a quick shopping trip. She says she didn't have enough money to buy herself a pair of roller skates. "Why, they cost a hundred and fifty-seven dollars and I didn't have the money and I didn't have any checks left in my checkbook," she says in her charming, disarming Texas drawl, as she beams a sunshiny smile at Mick. He hugs her around the ass and grins. "They won't give you any credit cards, huh?"

Jerry and Jade leave to walk and skate in Central Park and Mick invites me into the corner sitting room. "There's nothing in the house," he apologizes. "What would you like?" He calls down to a deli for beer and soda to be sent up. While we wait, we exchange small talk. He wants to know what Dylan and Lennon are up to; I want to know what he's up to. Verbal sparring. Finally, the delivery boy comes, who of course recognizes Mick, to their mutual delight.

We settle down with cold bottles of Heineken and go through Mick's rituals of the razor blade and the rolling paper.

He licks down the seal on his fat special cigarette, lets it dry, fires it up, inhales what must be a lung-busting toke, and hands it to me.

"We want to go to China," he finally says, after exhaling a thick plume of smoke toward the open windows facing the park.

I am temporarily befuddled, whether from the apparently harmless funny cigarette or from this sudden, unexpected camaraderie with a rock 'n' roll giant with whom I have clashed before. I take a mind-clearing sip of beer and venture, "You want to go to China? So where do I fit in?"

Mick leans forward intently. "The Stones want to play China. We'll never get Russia. But the Chinese Government is interested." He smiles a smug smile. The Stones want everything, after all, but they have never gotten closer to penetrating the world of communism and corrupting as yet uncorruptible upright Communist youth than playing Warsaw, Poland, on April 13, 1967. China! What a virgin territory. Untold legions of rock and roll converts just waiting to be converted.

I mull that over as legions of ghetto-blaster-toting youths parade beneath Mick Jagger's windows. None of them are playing Stones songs. "Why me?" I finally venture, as Mick hands back the funny cigarette.

"The Chinese Government really doesn't know who the Stones are," he says with his crinkly grin, which is supposed to let you know that you are a favored Stones' insider. Big deal—if you think it is. "What we need," he continued, "is a concise, detailed history and description of the band to present to the Chinese Government. Something that explains to China why China *needs* us." The heavy emphasis on the word "needs" hangs heavier in the still air than does the thick smoke. "That's what we need written. Can you convince the Chinese Government that they *need* the Rolling Stones?"

Well—hell yes! Can you name me anything that would be more fun than trying to get the Stones into China? Than trying to match these misanthropic millionaire misogynist paragons of capitalism and decadence with the Chinese revolution? Amazing? I burst out laughing. Can't help myself. Mick is puzzled. The first thing I ask him actually surprises me because it is not a normal concern of mine. "Mick, there isn't enough electricity in China to run 'Jumping Jack Flash' outdoors." He looks relieved. "Oh well, then, we'll just take a jenny [generator]."

Okay. If you believe it'll work, I think. Aloud, I ask Mick where things stand with the Chinese. He becomes very serious. He had met, he says, with the Chinese ambassador-designate in Washington and the meeting had gone very well. A frank exchange of views and all that. The only problem was that the ambassador-designate was a little apprehensive that the Stones' presence might develop into a disruptive influence on Chinese young people heretofore unexposed to such influence. Mick said, though, that he felt he had won over the ambassador-designate. Who retained only one caveat: He needed a persuasive argument on paper to send to Peking regarding the worthy Rolling Stones and he needed it soonest. Fast.

"What exactly do you have in mind?" I ask Mick, after we get fresh beers. "Wal," he drawls in his fake Southern drawl with the crooked grin that is meant to be boyish charm (and which usually works), "can you tell China that they must have us?"

He is as serious as I have ever seen him be. Even so, neither of us— I think, anyway—feels that this is some kind of historic moment. We pass the funny cigarette and get some more beers.

"I can give it a whirl," I tell Mick in response to his question about China and that they "must have us."

"But," I say, "I can't sugarcoat you guys. You do have a checkered history [you do talk that way after smoking those things] and I don't think that the Chinese are naïve enough to think that they're getting the Trapp family."

Mick laughs exuberantly and gets up to fetch more beer. "I know that," he says when he returns. "Just haul out the good stuff about us. Quote the right lyrics. Explain why we are what we are." Chop, chop, chop.

We talk for a couple of hours about the benchmarks in the Stones' career, about the band's place in the history of American popular music (not British, interestingly), about the significance of the blues tradition, about the substantial constituency the Stones maintain worldwide, about the phenomenon of the continuing rock 'n' roll revolution in youth culture, and on and on. A stimulating discussion of pop culture and its role and impact and all that.

Then I look him straight in the eye and ask him the one question that I know I have to ask: "Mick, what about Altamont?"

The question hangs in the air like a huge dust mote on this sunny afternoon. A chunky disco beat from a ghetto-blaster down on the street dances through the open windows. Mick looks away and laughs nervously. Then he summons up his most charming and fetching smile and trains the 300-kilowatt look on me: "Why do you have to mention Altamont at all?"

I fall silent for a moment. Finally, I say, "It *is* a matter of history."

Mick grins. "Wal, no need to sensationalize it!"

We seesaw back and forth a while, both half-drunk and half-stoned, both spouting half-assed philosophy. I leave finally when Jerry and Jade come home.

I go home to try to tell my wife, "Guess what I did today, dear."

She is not impressed. But I do stay up for the next two nights writing one motherfucker of a defense paper for a renegade rock 'n' roll band that probably should not be allowed within a thousand miles of the Chinese border, much less hugged to the bosom of the continuing revolution. The Rolling Stones own total rights forever to this historic document (for which they paid me five hundred dollars), so I can't reprint it and you'll never read it. But the fucking Chinese swallowed it! They were going to let the Rolling Stones in! Going to let this insidious capitalistic deviationist agent of sloth and sin infect correct youth with the incorrect ways of Western poison. Here is an excerpt from the October 17, 1979, Starship Radio bulletin: "Stones to Tour China: The Rolling Stones are to tour China next spring. The invitation was extended to Mick Jagger as he chatted over a cup of tea with a Chinese ambassador in Washington. It's a remarkable breakthrough for the Stones, who have always been considered by Iron Curtain countries as symbols of Western decadence and a threat to Communist youth. Now it seems that China is eager to welcome them to build up an image of openness and liberalism."

Well. That's nothing compared to what I tried to whip up in that little Stones manifesto. Working-class heroes? You got them right here. Champions of the underdogs? Guess who. Who are the true revolutionaries in rock music? Not the Beatles. Guess who. Which rock group consistently attacks upper-class hypocrisy and decadence in Western society? I think you know. I even clinched the deal, I hear now, by celebrating the fact that Charlie Watts was the president of the North Wales Sheepdog Society. Actually, it was a fairly sober document that showed the Stones, warts and all (Altamont included), as the most Western of Western bands that the Chinese would appreciate. So I typed it up and sent it over to Jane Rose at Rolling Stones Records in Rockefeller Center and she had it translated into Chinese and fired it off to the ambassador-designate in Washington, who relayed it to Peking. And everyone sat back to see what would happen next. Keith Richards got his copy of the thing at his estate in Jamaica and he called me at home to tell me how much he appreciated it and, by the way, to ask what the Stones song was that I quoted from that was so democratic ("Salt of the Earth").

Peking was pleased, it seemed. Newspaper articles began appearing about the Stones' projected tour of China. Then Mick was invited back to Washington for a meeting with the ambassador-designate and other Chinese officials to discuss the realities of such a tour. Mick will not discuss what happened, but apparently the meeting was a mess and the Chinese were horrified by some of Mick's remarks. I heard from within the Stones camp that Mick gave the ambassador-designate rather a hard time and that they reached no meeting of the minds and that it developed that, rather than the Stones touring China next month, that it appeared that the Stones would tour China when, in fact, hell freezes over. The opinion within the Stones camp was that Mick blew it. Deliberately. Everyone close to the Stones knows that he does that now and then. What no one knows is why he possesses such a penchant for self-destruction, for so strong a sense of self-doubt that it amounts to nihilism.

Chapter 10

Envy

The Curse of the Brat People

Than Martin Scorsese, there is no greater rock 'n' roll film director. The fact that he'd done just one overt rock 'n' roll film only proves it. With *The Last Waltz* he got it right the first time. His close-to-the-bone documentary of the farewell performance by The Band—with its powerful cameos by friends like Bob Dylan, Neil Young, Van Morrison, and Joni Mitchell—was a shimmering triumph: the first time the movie camera really went for the throat of the rock stage experience and captured it.

Of course, he had already really made his mark with the toughest big-screen depictions of the raw and vital spirit of rebellion of rock 'n' roll in his red-line *Mean Streets* of 1973. 1976's *Taxi Driver* had predated music video's use of real images to reinforce music and vice versa. Since *The Last Waltz* in 1978, Scorsese has rejected scores of offers to do rock films or videos.

In late 1986, though, he agreed to do a Michael Jackson video, a project whose secrecy was rivaled only by that of the Manhattan Project. There were daily reports of sightings of Michael and Marty in the New York City subway system or in Harlem or wherever.

When it was finished, I went up to Scorsese's lofty offices in the Brill Building on Broadway to talk about it. He is, he claims, sworn to secrecy on the subject and chooses his words with the kind of extreme caution employed only by persons seeking to avoid the crippling litigation of the Jackson empire.

"The timing was right. I've been offered many videos. I haven't done anything with music since *Last Waltz,* which was in a way the beginning

of those video things. It was so simply done and was so beautiful. I enjoyed it so, I loved doing it. Why has there not been another like it? I don't know. Your guess is as good as mine. I have no idea. It was an experiment, you know. It started out as sixteen-millimeter archival footage. Then I said let's use thirty-five. It was the first time thirty-five was used on a stage like that, and seven cameras were used that way. When we saw the rushes, we knew it was quite extraordinary. It picked up something in the idea of concentrating only on the performance and not on the audience. You see all those looks on their faces and the relationships between themselves on the stage. I always said each song there is like a round in a prize fight, building and building in intensity."

He looks away, as he often does, one hand stroking his neatly trimmed goatee, the other on the knee of his neatly pressed designer jeans. The almost arid stillness of his dark, woody chambers suggests a dentist's office from the Thirties. This faintly clinical feeling is lent support by the No Smoking signs on the walls and the piles of antihistamine tablets on the desk: Scorsese is a lifelong asthma sufferer. A small, fluffy white dog—whose name I didn't catch—studies me suspiciously from the corner.

"So when *The Color of Money* was finished," he continues, "Quincy Jones calls up and talks about Michael Jackson. And one thing I like about Michael Jackson—he's not really rock and roll, it's performance, it's another thing entirely. I like his dancing. I think his moves—he's so unique, his moves, that it would really be a challenge to try to get it on film in traditional style, not quick cuts like an MTV. I should say 'indiscriminate' quick cutting. One thing led to another. I was making it difficult in the sense that I didn't think they would want to do the sort of thing I was interested in doing. And they were. So, we have a black-and-white section of the film, about eight minutes long, a nice long dramatic piece, and then the color section with the music and it's resolved again at the end."

I mention the rumors around town that the "dramatic" part of the video dealt with a recent incident in Harlem in which a young black man came home on vacation from his Ivy League school and was killed by a cop while allegedly taking part in a violent crime.

"Well," he says, looking out the window, "the problem is that we're not allowed to talk about it. Somehow, that story came out in a gossip column and so that's not exactly it, but I gotta be careful. I got Richard Price [the novelist whom Scorsese also had write the screenplay of *The Color of Money*] to write it. I said if they wanta do it, okay. We finally finished mixing it last night. It took longer to do than we thought. Michael really seemed to be enjoying himself. It took much longer than we thought, cost more than we thought, but I like it. It was just a good feeling to get back to music. I think to a certain extent, videos, rock videos, for the amount of effort I like to put into it, I do not necessarily get as much enjoyment out of it, so it's not really a feature. I don't know if I'll be doing that much. I may do one more with Michael. It's very simple, it's a very simple approach to it."

This is not always how Marty Scorsese has approached what seems to be a complicated cinematic career. He came in through the bathroom window, in a manner of speaking. Logically, there should have been no room for him in the Reaganesque vacuum chamber that modern American movie-making has become; no room for an intense, asthmatic, seminary dropout from New York's Little Italy with a burning celluloid vision of America that clearly was not bankable in Hollywood.

All you have to do, even now, is look at his history. He is still famous at New York University, where he studied film, for his *The Big Shave,* a six-minute film of a man actually shaving; razoring from an initial, cursory swipe at his chin whiskers and going on to the ultimate throat-clearing maneuver. Scorsese makes the movies that nobody else does. He's the clutch player, the guy with the eye for the play that everybody else on the field misses.

Look at his commercial history: *Mean Streets* (1973), *Alice Doesn't Live Here Anymore* (1975), *Taxi Driver* (1976), *New York, New York* (1977), *The Last Waltz* (1978), *Raging Bull* (1980), *The King of Comedy* (1983), *After Hours* (1985), and *The Color of Money* (1986). His attempt to film *The Last Temptation of Christ* has been repeatedly rejected by major studios. Of all his work, only *The Color of Money* could be considered a mainstream movie.

After *Taxi Driver* and the heady success it brought him, Marty moved to Los Angeles to be a big-time director and it didn't especially take. After *New York, New York* and *The Last Waltz* and *Raging Bull*, the word in Hollywood was that he was creatively played out for the moment and had quit movie-making.

"No, not *quit*," he says, looking out again toward Broadway. "I immediately said I wanted to direct another picture, I didn't care what it is. Then I started reading the scripts they gave me. They gave me a script right on the plane. I mean Jeff Katzenberg and [Michael] Eisner—who are now at Disney, who I made *The Color of Money* for—they're the guys who were at Paramount when they canceled *Last Temptation*. I mean, Barry Diller and Gulf and Western canceled, but Katzenberg and Eisner were still in charge too. They all had a hand in canceling. But we got along well, in a way, even though there was that problem. So when they went over to Disney and they wanted to do *The Color of Money*, I was kind of pleased.

"But back then, they gave me a script right away; they gave me *Witness* and I didn't want to do it. I started reading their scripts and I could have made a lot of money but I didn't like any of them, so instead I did this little one, *After Hours*, to in a way start again. Because in *After Hours* you have a situation where basically the central image is one man in the street at night. Nobody else. That's easily controllable. Easy with the high-speed film and the high-speed lenses. You have no extras. It's perfect to play with, perfect to play with the camera, too, to do some tracking."

Scorsese is also running some Hollywood development deals, he says, but managing to enlist Paul Newman was unexpected.

"It was my first experience with like a Hollywood star—as opposed to De Niro and the other guys, and De Niro and I were friends. We'd been making films and were very loose and we didn't realize what was happening to, you know, his [De Niro's] figure and the figure he became. But Newman was a big movie star, someone I'd seen when I was twelve years old in *Somebody Up There Likes Me* and *The Silver Chalice,* and it was a little hard for me to feel comfortable in the first few meetings. But I liked him, I liked his ideas and I liked him personally.

"So when I came up with the idea of switching—They had written some scripts into a version and I read that and the novel and felt it wasn't right and brought in Richard Price. I came up with an idea: I didn't believe that, according to the novel and according to the screenplay they had written, that Eddie Felson no longer played pool and no longer had anything to do with pool. He just put his tail between his legs and for twenty-five years he just ran a pool hall and the film opens with him, with the pool hall closing and him breaking up with his wife. I said I don't believe it, I just don't believe it, and I presented that idea to Newman. I said, I can't believe it in the sense that he was such a hustler that he would do *something,* and one of the things he would do would be survive, and if he survived the way he would do it is to become everything he hated, in spades. . . . He might not have the same obsessions, but he deals with the hustle . . . and puts young boys under his wing and he wants to make money. Well, this one particular kid [Tom Cruise] reminds him of himself and he feels he's gonna go on the road again with the kid and live vicariously through the kid. It's like it would be like me not making films anymore and finding a young filmmaker and producing one of his pictures and dying to get my hands in it and eventually the kid not directing and me taking over the direction of the picture. That's what happens and they cross roles. So what happens becomes Eddie's education rather than the kid's. And at the end of the movie he's just back where he should be: playing pool. Whether he wins or loses doesn't matter; it's really that he's back. Doesn't matter what age he's at. This is not one of those movies with the message that no matter how old you are you can do it. That's nonsense. I don't believe that.

"For example, in the first meeting that I had with Paul Newman, I asked him why if he doesn't win every race, why does he race?" Scorsese leans back in his chair for the first time and laughs. "He didn't have an answer! That's what the movie is about. He's just gotta race. He's gotta play pool, that's all."

After the success of *The Color of Money,* can he now do his own films as his own man in Hollywood?

"No. Now I can get to do more of *their* films, which I may want to do because I may just want to keep my hand in there and keep working. You learn something on every film. Hopefully, you don't unlearn. I don't know who the mainstream directors are now. I think Spielberg is mainstream. And Francis [Coppola] has always been mainstream, I think, no matter what he did, has always worked out mainstream in a terrific way. I don't know the others."

He turns sarcastic when asked if he wasn't indeed a certifiable, bankable director now.

"Oh, yeah! Absolutely! We didn't intend that, by the way. Don't forget that Paul Newman's previous picture was *Harry and Son*. Didn't do anything. And don't forget also that Tom Cruise—the picture he was in when we were shooting *Color* was *Legend*. A disaster. So it was luck to have a movie with two big movie stars. I just really tried to make the best picture I could with those people. Going in to make it, mainstream, no way. Remember, Fox owned the picture, again Barry Diller, who had canceled *Last Temptation of Christ* and went over to Fox, and they canceled *Hustler Two,* didn't care for it. Didn't want *Color of Money*. It bounced from studio to studio with Paul Newman and Tom Cruise and myself in it. Nobody would go near it. Disney finally picked it up on the basis that Newman and I would put up one-third of our salaries against the completion. So, it was just a movie, and it was my first commercial hit. So, now it's mainstream. Before we made it, it wasn't mainstream. Now it's mainstream!" He laughs. "So, now I'm considered a mainstream Hollywood director. Meaning, in Hollywood, they consider me someone whose films are 'too dark.' 'Too dark,' they always say. But now they say, oh, the sonuvabitch can do mainstream pictures. He always could do them but he wouldn't. Not when we wanted him to."

Scorsese is still most animated when asked about his cinematic tour de force, *Mean Streets*.

"It was the first video. That was the fun of it, that was really fun—the camera's flying down a bar and you hear Jimmy Roselli start and it cuts to the Aquatones, 'You' by the Aquatones, which is really how it is in real life, you know. You're in a bar and Tommy Dorsey is followed by Springsteen. *I* lived in a neighborhood where music was so important and where you would walk down the stairs of your tenement and from each house you would hear different kinds of music—opera, Spanish, whatever, swing of the Thirties and Forties, Django Reinhardt, Benny Goodman especially, Tom Dorsey, all that, and then late Fifties and early Sixties the Girl Groups and then the Phil Spector Sound, a very important period to me. *Mean Streets* takes place in 1960 to '63. 'Sixty-three really it takes place. And what happened was at that time I happened to see *Scorpio Rising* by Kenneth Anger. You see, the reason we couldn't use rock 'n' roll then, the way I wanted to use it—I was at NYU and at NYU they told us you have to get the clearances, you gotta get rights. We had no money. So we couldn't use it. And yet I saw *Scorpio Rising* and here this guy did it all, and I said this is ridiculous.

And he didn't ask for clearances. I'm sure. So we started using rock 'n' roll. *Who's That Knockin'* was the first film that really had rock and—I hate the term but it's doo-wop—but had that. I tried to structure it like a piece of music. In that you had three scenes repeating themselves over and over again. Each time like a motif. And each time they were repeated it was more intense until finally there's no more talking. There's guns. They're shooting each other.''

He is very proud now that he acted as record producer for the first time with *The Color of Money*.

"I had the real pleasure of tailor-making music to the picture. The only song we used of a record was the Bo-Deans, which I liked. But all the other stuff, I talked to Eric Clapton or Robbie Robertson talked to them. Said, we'll make it a little stronger, change the lyrics. Robbie and Eric re-wrote together. Then Robert Palmer came in and talked. And we actually gave them the footage to look at. I said to be careful because if you want your lyrics to comment on the scene, don't comment directly, have your lyrics be oblique and do it in this area where there's no dialogue. I loved it because I had all the different elements. Like I could bring up the guitar on Eric Clapton, I could put an echo on this. It was great. So, in a real sense, it was really the first album of one of my pictures. I really went to a lot of trouble with the music. I love Robbie Robertson's music at the beginning and the end, over the credits what you hear is just him moaning over the drum machine. It was just a cassette he sent me and now it's on seventy-millimeter.''

As for today's videos, Scorsese said he once tried but realized that watching all of MTV was too much.

"It's very hard because the images are so fast and would really give me a headache, and I love fast-moving, but these were too fast and were indiscriminate images. A lot of people doing them didn't really understand what they were doing and may have stumbled into a style. But then certain things emerge: the computer ones, the Talking Heads one, much of the Julien Temple stuff is great. 'Beat It' was a good one. There are others, too, I like. But I've stopped watching so much. My favorite from last year was for Robert Palmer's 'Addicted to Love.' The simplicity of it and the three colors, red and black and white, was just amazing. The cutting was excellent. I like Dire Straits and the computer ones, but watching them so much in a row, one begins to take away from the other. It's packaged like magazine covers now. It's like album covers instead of music.''

He admits that it would have been a video dream to direct the late, great Elvis.

"Oh, oh, it would've been something—just like what I did with Michael Jackson, which I can't tell you about. A straight dramatic picture. Stronger than *King Creole*, I can tell you that. Much stronger. I was thinking about that the other night. I tell you, Elvis had it all. He had it all, in his face, in his senses, in his whole persona. It would have been incredible to work with him."

Peter Allen Has It All

Peter Allen had barely settled into his chair at Bookbinders restaurant in Philadelphia and opened the menu when Mike the Waiter tapped him on the shoulder.

"You're Peter Allen, right?" Mike asked, and didn't wait for an answer. "You wrote that song 'You and Me' on Sinatra's *Trilogy* record, right? *Terrific* song."

And right there, Mike started singing it: "You and me, we wanted it all."

Heads turned and Peter Allen beamed. "You know you've made it when waiters in Philly know the words to your songs," he said.

He was joking, but he was right. At thirty-six, Peter Allen, songwriter and cabaret singer of the first order, is finally starting to sell some records and fill some halls after years of writing hits for other singers and playing to a small cult of his own. He was in Philadelphia to do two sold-out shows at the Walnut Street Theatre, coming on the high-kicking heels of three spectacular sold-out concerts with the Rockettes at Radio City Music Hall. Those were so well received that he's doing two more shows at the Music Hall on February 13 and 14.

"Okay, Mike," Allen said to Mike the Waiter, "cut out the singing already and bring us some drinks."

He drank a toast to his dining companions, who were his manager, Dee Anthony, a friend, Charles Suppon, and myself.

Anthony and Suppon in a way reflect the diversity of Allen's growing audience. Anthony is a barrel-chested take-charger who sparred with Jake LaMotta as a teenager, managed Tony Bennett and Jimmy Roselli in the Fifties, brought British supergroups like Traffic and Emerson, Lake and Palmer to the United States in the Sixties, and plucked Peter Frampton from Humble Pie in the Seventies and made him a superstar "like a moon shot." Suppon is a Coty Award–winning designer who—after the first time he saw Allen perform—took a charter busload of fashion muckamucks from Seventh Avenue over to see Allen at a show in Morristown, New Jersey.

Everybody, it seems, is suddenly coming on to Peter Allen. Mayor

Koch says he's his favorite entertainer. Olivia Newton-John, for whom Allen wrote the hit "I Honestly Love You," calls him every week to ask for more hit songs. Burt Bacharach called to ask him to write songs with him. After a show at Radio City, when he proved he could hoof it with the best of the Rockettes, they all bought gifts for him. He's not doing too badly for an itinerant Australian singer who bounced around the Village and SoHo for years without much real success.

"You know," he said as Mike brought him a bowl of lobster stew, "the first time I played Philly, in '75, I had about thirty people at the Bijou."

"Well, tonight," rasped Anthony, "you got thousands. You coulda filled the Academy. Next time here, you play the Academy."

"Yeah." A broad smile spread across Allen's angular face.

"But not too big," Anthony told him. "You know, all the critics said you made Radio City seem like a small room, intimate. You can't do that in the Garden. We got to go slow."

"Sure, Dee. Let's eat."

"Tell me, Peter," I said, "about the camel. I heard you had camel trouble."

"Oh, the camel story!" He laughed. "*Well.* At Radio City I wanted some kind of entrance for 'I Go to Rio' because I had already gone up and down on the elevator and you can only do that so many times. Well, they had three camels and a donkey left over from the Christmas Nativity scene. First they tried to give me the donkey. They said, '*Look,* it was good enough for Jesus, right?' I held out for a camel, George. But he wouldn't set foot onstage till he got paid. His agent, rather. We had to write a check out right there: $1,600 plus $128 in tax. Can you *believe* it?"

Earlier, while we were driving to a TV interview in a stretch Lincoln, a Peter Allen commercial came on the radio, and the breathless announcer called him "outrageous." Allen curled his lip in disdain and looked out at the strollers on Market Street, who returned his blank stare. "Oh, God," he said.

"How long is this show?" Allen asked the representative from KYW-TV, which was his next stop. "Ninety minutes," said the rep.

"Okay," Allen said slowly. " 'This Is Your Life,' huh? Ninety minutes live." It was eleven in the morning.

At KYW-TV they were hauling in wheelchair patients for the front rows at the "AM/PM" show, while Allen wandered back to the green room to find flowers, cards, and bottles of champagne. "This is just like an opening," he said in delight. He didn't seem to mind that he was about to have to do well over an hour of live TV.

Dee Anthony settled himself in a dressing room. "Peter's the complete professional," he said. "With him, I don't have to worry about anything. His work is his life, and his life is his work. Atlantic City is next. And then Vegas. Nothing too quick. But he's *ready*. It will happen. A matter of time." He sounded confident.

As well he might. Allen quit school in Australia when he was fourteen to sing full-time in pubs. He gigged around doing American rock 'n' roll and eventually formed a duo with Chris Bell. They called themselves Chris and Peter Allen, and they played throughout the Far East.

Judy Garland saw them perform in Hong Kong and summoned them to an audience. She pronounced her blessing on Allen and told him he should meet her teenage daughter, Liza, and had Peter and Chris fly to London to open a Judy Garland show at the Palladium. Peter was twenty and Liza was eighteen, and with Judy Garland's urging, they were wed. It was not a heaven-sent marriage. Both were trying to make it in show business, and Peter was growing weary of his duo with Chris.

"Everything hit the fan one day," he said. "With Liza, it had gotten to the point where we met only at airports, so one day we just said, 'Okay, this is it.' Chris had already said, 'Let's get a combo,' and I said, 'I think I'm gonna become a songwriter.' I went out that night with my sister, and we met David Steinberg, who said he had seen me sing on TV and thought I was wonderful. I was doing 'Mame' and 'The Impossible Dream,' and I'd never put anything of myself into the act. So I never thought of myself as a *contemporary*.

"Liza had a very good ear for contemporary people. She discovered Joni Mitchell, Harry Nilsson—no one else had ever heard of Randy Newman. So I started listening to all that, and I thought, 'Wait a minute—maybe there's something in there that I can do.' Liza convinced me to go into songwriting. She *made* me write songs. I said, 'What am I gonna write about?' She had just come back from making her first movie, with Albert Finney, and his son was named Simon. Liza said, 'I love the name Simon—write me a song called "Simon." ' So I made it up completely, and it's finally on the new album. And it's funny because it sounds like a very biographical song.

"Anyhow, the way I got to New York: David Steinberg told me, 'Pull some songs together and you can open for me at the Bitter End.' So there I was in the anti-pop culture of the Bitter End, owned one pair of jeans, lived down in the Village, having a fabulous time.

"I wrote a song for Neil Sedaka called 'The World Through a Tear,' which became a semi-hit because it started out with the words 'Grass is green, like I've never seen.' Everyone thought I'd written a drug song, and I'd never smoked a joint in my life."

*   *   *

At the Walnut Street Theatre, they were wearing black tie in the first row and throwing party streamers onto the stage. Allen's percussionist, José Rossy, started a thunderous drumroll on his kettledrum on the darkened stage. The rest of the six-piece band started the lead-in to "Don't Wish Too Hard." Back in his dressing room, Peter Allen put on his mirrored jacket and got ready to sprint out to the stage for the first show. "This is dirty work, but *someone* has to do it," he tossed over his shoulder.

Once he hit the stage, he was almost glowing with energy. After the first song, he stopped for a little monologue.

"Philly! It's been too long! It's been a wild year. Let me tell you about it. Radio City with the Rockettes! It was no easy task warming up those seventy-four legs every night. I found that I, a white Australian, had an R&B hit. Nancy called and wanted me to sing at the inaugural. I didn't go. Tom Snyder. He *likes* me. The straightest man in America. He wants to know in the worst way what bi-coastal means. Tom said my songs had double meanings. I was *shocked!* I never thought of that. What if I were a straight singer/songwriter?"

He jumped into "I Could Have Been a Sailor" and was already drawing standing ovations from parts of the crowd.

He worked hard, dancing, camping, doing the high kicks, jumping onto his piano, going nonstop for an hour and a half. After the second show, he sprawled exhausted in his dressing room and contemplated the cardboard containers of Chinese takeout food that would be both dinner and breakfast, at 3:00 A.M. "This is how I earn my living," he said. "Can you believe it?"

Did you really want to be Randy Newman? I asked Peter Allen. We were sitting in the back corner of the bar of one of Philadelphia's many Holiday Inns. ("I love that," he said. "No one can find me unless I let them. Do you know how many Holiday Inns there are in Philadelphia?") "Yeah," said Peter Allen as he downed half a Heineken. "Which I love, because I read an interview with Randy Newman where he said, 'When I think that people in America buy something like "I Honestly Love You," which is the sloppiest, most awful song I ever heard.' I laughed about that because he was my idol for so many years . . . and then the one song he singles out to hate is one of my songs." He laughed. "Poetic justice. I myself really didn't think that song could be a hit. So now I just shut up about my songs. If I didn't think 'Honestly' was a hit, then just forget about it. I don't care about hits. I do not have that lust for stardom, because I've seen so many people who were stars—and they ain't happy. So why should I want to be them?"

Well, I said, I didn't know, but the latest review of his show said that he wanted it all.

Allen became a bit testy. "*What* is *all?* If you're a carpenter, no one says, 'Will he be the Michelangelo of carpenters?' It's just in show business that unless you are the number one then you're a failure. My whole thing is that I don't want anyone to come to my show and say, 'He was good tonight, but I remember when . . .' I always want to shock the shit out of them. I always want to get better."

Well, I said, you've become comfortable with your role of being a camp counselor or gay blade or whatever.

"That was a categorization by the New York media. If you're not like anyone else, which I wasn't, because everyone else was a Sinatra clone or a flamboyant rock star—the fact was that I got up and did things that women normally do. I was out there singing about emotions that women usually sing about in intimate surroundings. And because I was at Reno Sweeney, the first people who said 'This is good' were from the Village or SoHo. They were the same people who went to Streisand or Bette Midler. The only difference was that I was a *guy*. So everyone said I had a gay cult following. So I was booked into the clubs on the so-called gay circuit. And I bombed so *badly*. The general gay audience did not take to me. I had a really interesting audience, but because I was a male and there were a lot of gays, the media said, 'Okay, gay show.'

"My audience is more female now. I think women spot in me something that they understand. I don't know really why they come, but I can spot that. If you look at my songs you'll realize that there's no male, no female."

That's true, I said, except for songs like "Bi-Coastal" with its boys on Broadway and—

Allen cut me off. "Oh, that's just me saying, 'So this is what you think of me? Okay then, I'll just put it right here and let you know.' It's an extension of what I said about bi-coastal on the 'Tomorrow' show. I said everyone in show biz is bi-coastal. It was just a snappy joke. Next thing, *New York* magazine has a piece on the new bi-coastals. I can't believe it!"

But, I said, he obviously has fun and is non-threatening with the songs.

"Oh, that's true. Mayor Koch is down in front laughing his ass off. Tom Snyder loves me. I'm talking about the straightest people in America. I think it's incredible that a boy can stand up and ask me what am I doing tonight on live TV. I think that's real healthy. Because that's what I'm actually saying. I mean, what's all this stuff where *People* magazine tries to come and take pictures of you in bed? Having breakfast with your dog? I said, *No!* There is such a thing as privacy.

"But by the same token, you should be able to joke about it. Doing just ballads all in a row is boring, but getting up and taking your clothes off and shaking maracas for an hour gets boring unless you play one against the other, and then it works. When I started out, I was regarded as *really* shocking, and then as decadent and cynical. And then all of a sudden it was just Peter up there taking off his clothes and let's have a good time. The press never knew what to write about me. While the critics were trying to figure out who I could possibly appeal to, there were all these nice fat housewives and their husbands coming in on the subway and just having the best time because they were being *entertained*. And I realized what it took to do that. I got the honesty from watching Judy Garland. Even when her voice was gone I watched her mind manipulating the audience every second. She knew what she was doing all the time. A huge ego."

In Peter Allen's case, is it ego or is it that he lives only to work?

"It's to work," he said seriously. "Everything I make I put back into my act. What else is there to spend it on?"

Chapter 11

Sloth

Dylan Meets the Durango Kid

Durango, Mexico—Fifteen nervous chickens that were buried up to their necks in dirt blinked in the bright Mexican sun and looked as unhappy as it is possible for chickens to look. They were arranged in a line on the parade ground of a crumbling adobe fort at the foot of the dark Sierra Madre near Durango. Chickens aren't given much credit for intelligence, but *these* chickens knew that something was about to happen. They caught a glimpse of a dapper young gunfighter—Billy the Kid—and his scruffy bandits lounging sixty feet away around a stone fountain.

The outlaws interrupted their whiskey-guzzling to taunt Billy to try his trigger finger on the hapless fowl. He slowly raised his Colt .44 and squeezed off three shots.

Crack! The head of the center chicken suddenly separated from its body in a whirl of blood and feathers. *Crack!* The head of the next chicken exploded straight upward, spraying technicolor blood across the parched ground. *Crack!* Another chicken head took off in a slow, lazy arc against the Kodachrome sky before coming to rest fifteen feet away. The outlaws laughed and Billy smiled. He was still Top Gun.

But before Billy and his boys could get back to their whiskey, three rifle shots shattered the silence and three more chickens became headless. Feathers were still drifting down as Billy whirled to confront Pat Garrett lowering a Winchester. "Hello, Billy," he rumbled.

"Cut!" snapped the short, gray man in a director's chair inscribed SAM PECKINPAH. This was Sam Peckinpah's latest film, *Pat Garrett and Billy the Kid*. It marks the first time he's dealt with the Old West since *The Wild Bunch*, and he had James Coburn as Garrett, Kris Kristofferson as Billy, and Bob Dylan—making his feature film debut—as Billy's mysterious sidekick "Alias."

Peckinpah had added the chicken scene to the script, branding the opening sequence as clearly one of his own. Rudy Wurlitzer, the novelist (*Quake, Flats, Nog,* and the script for *Two Lane Blacktop*) who wrote the *Billy* screenplay, sidled up to a visiting writer after the chicken scene and muttered, "That's Sam for you. I only had *one* chicken head in my script."

There could be no mistaking this set for John Wayne's Batjac location a few dusty miles back down Mex 45 toward Durango. For one thing, the Mexican government posted a nark here who, disguised as a swarthy *caballero,* wandered through the fort peering nearsightedly at everyone's cigarettes. For another, there was a discernible tension in the air, a sense that something terrible might happen any minute. Peckinpah was pushing and driving his cast and crew, and the strain was evident. The picture was said to be at least two weeks behind schedule and $1 million over budget.

Wurlitzer edged close and spoke *sotto voce* through his beard, "Hey, something heavy may happen." He turned to see if anyone overheard, and the sun sparkled on his gold earring. "The word's come down from the Cobra that if Sam doesn't get a full day of shooting today, he's fired. And he's behind, man. The Cobra—Jim Aubrey *himself*—is after him. If Sam goes, the cast walks and there goes the movie. Heavy?"

He gave a knowing glance and moved away as Gordon Carroll, the film's producer, walked up. Carroll, who could be perfectly cast as a Hollywood executive (tall, blond, tanned, slightly harried), watched preparations for closeups of another scene. The producer smiled a tight-lipped smile as Peckinpah exploded at a bumbling extra who strayed into camera range. "*Goddammit! Get outta* there!"

Rita Coolidge, who played a minor role (even more minor after she refused to do a nude scene), walked by and bumped her head on an earthen jug hanging from a tree. Carroll whispered, "The French critics will write that only Peckinpah could make her look stunned and cross-eyed at the first sight of Billy."

Carroll exited and Wurlitzer appeared from somewhere in his place. He continued his role as the Greek chorus of the set: "This scene is *the* most important. It's got to grab the audience. Sam wants it to be flashy so the audience will be into the picture without realizing how banal it is. Sam's really an old-fashioned director that way. That's Westerns, though, all banality. This scene here, man, wasn't in *my* script. There's *no* script left."

Then it's not a Wurlitzer? "It's a *Peckinpah*."

The writer, who had found Wurlitzer's original script tight and fast-paced and evocative of the legend (if not the fact) of Billy, had noticed lines and scenes being filmed daily that weren't in the script and inquired about those changes.

"Well." Wurlitzer turned his gaze inward. "Sam does the changes, mostly."

Dylan did his only scene of the day almost before anyone realized he was there. Scene 483, Take 4, found him seated on a stone wall, watching Kristofferson blasting away at cans and bottles. Dylan, responding to Peckinpah's cue, applauded by beating on a can with a stick.

The cast broke for lunch in a nearby tree-shaded courtyard of the fort, built for the Mexican army in the last century.

Dylan had taken a few bites of his steak when two young American hitchhikers, who had talked their way onto the set in hopes of getting work, sat down a table away and tried to cadge food from the cast. They began talking loudly. "What's happenin' with this movie, man? Is Dylan gonna sing or what, man? What's the story? Where is he, man?" Dylan bolted up and hurried to his camper. The two youths were banned from the set and publicist Larry Kaplan said it wasn't the first time such an incident had occurred.

"It's a complex situation," he said. "At first, you say 'Bob Dylan, the fucking *legend*.' And it takes a couple of weeks to get past that to the man underneath. He's really shy and withdrawn, and it's genuine. Reporters here have really spooked him. They follow him around and of course he won't talk to them, so they end up interviewing everyone else about him. It gets bad when you have reporters asking Mexican extras about Bob's kids."

After lunch, Kristofferson invited the writer to sit and sip cognac with actors Emelio Fernandez and Jorge Russek.

Kris, who had pleasantly surprised the cast with his portrayal of Billy, looked very close to what the script called for: youthful, but hard, highly charged with "erotic energy," with "very blue eyes" and "sensual lips." Russek offered him a slug of cognac, "for your throat, man."

"Thanks, you silver-tongued devil." Smacking his lips, Kristofferson turned to the writer. "Dylan was interested," he said, "interested in making movies and in Sam's stuff. I called him up and he said, um, there's a lot of heavies down there. I said, *shit,* you can get *paid* for *learnin'.* So he went and saw a couple of Sam's films and got really enthusiastic and decided to come down here, and he brought Sarah and the kids. He had already written the title song but he was still a little reluctant about acting. I said, hell, the only reason I got in was to learn about acting. He said, but then they got you on *film.* I said, shit, they got you on *record* anyway. Come on, we'll have a ball. I still feel guilty about sayin' that."

He laughed, shifted his weight in his canvas chair, and flipped a cigarette butt at a mud-encrusted pig that was rooting underfoot. "The first day we shot was also Bob's first day on camera. We had to be ridin' horses after these turkeys and he ropes 'em. Well, Bob hadn't ridden much and it was *hairy* riding, down in gullies and off through a river.

"And then we had to rope these damn *turkeys.* I couldn't do it but Bob did it all. I couldn't *believe* it. I've seen prints and he's got a presence on him like *Charlie Chaplin.* He's like a wild card that none of 'em knew they had. I think they just hired him for the name and all of a sudden you see him on screen and all eyes are on him. There's something about him that's magnetic. He doesn't even have to move. He's a *natural.*"

What about his role as Alias?

Kristofferson lowered his voice as Peckinpah called for silence for rehearsal. "Well, me and Rudy just got through writing a new scene for Bob. The sense is supposed to be that times are changin' and there's a push for me to get goin'. The way the scene was, the lines were embarrassin', like 'Hey, dude, hand me that apple,' but I was past complainin'. Rudy, who had to write it, hated it, and Dylan, man, it just *blew* his funk. So we changed it and now we gotta show it to Sam.

"The trouble is, man, Dylan ain't had a chance to *talk*. His speakin' lines have been a buncha stutterin' that really pissed me off. He's called Alias, and in every fuckin' scene the sonuvabitch is put in different wardrobe and he looks entirely different and *that* could be why he's called Alias. And that damn stutter thing—that could be as big a defense as his change of clothing. Who knows? *I* thought it was supposed to be like the fool in *Lear*. He sees it all, he knows the whole legend, and can see where it's all going. But we never relate as characters. We're always chasin' turkeys or some damn thing and don't even *look* at each other. But—the fucker's *fantastic* on film."

Assistant director Newt Arnold bellowed Kris's name for rehearsal and he stomped off, two-inch silver spurs jingling.

Peckinpah tried to get an interior scene in a bar going later in the day but it went badly. The hundred extras who lounged out of camera range kept chattering and he finally burst out of the bar, shouting and waving his arms: "Who *are* these *fucking people?* Get out, *get them out!* Everybody *out! Move, goddammit!*" The voice, like a bolt of thunder, did its job. People panicked and scattered in all directions, leaping fences, trampling each other, kicking pigs and dogs out of the way.

By late afternoon, things were worse, and it was time to ferry the press corps back to Durango. Wurlitzer, too, was preparing to leave.

"It's happening, man," Wurlitzer said. "Sam knows he's losing to Dylan. He's giving a screening of *The Getaway* in town tonight, but everybody wants to go to Mexico City with Dylan for his recording session because that's heavier. Sam'll be counting heads at that screening, and he also just called a six-thirty rehearsal for Monday morning because he knows we won't be back till after eight. But I don't care, man. I've got to get away from here for a while. See you at the airport."

Durango airport at 6:30 Saturday evening was a bleak study in gray stone and gray faces. The only plane on the only strip, a dented Aeroméxico 727, was warming up its engines for takeoff and there was a handful of worried Americans in the lobby. Coburn voiced the concern as he paced, brandy in hand, before the front windows. "Is the Big D coming?"

Wurlitzer the Pessimist wrung his hands. "*Christ*. If Bob decides not to come, this session'll *never* happen."

"Well," Coburn said, "the session is secondary to me. I just want to get out."

At the last possible moment, a car sped up and deposited a black-clad figure. Wurlitzer heaved a sigh of relief, but his smile flickered out as he found a new worry. "That plane, man. It don't look too good. What if it *went down?* Holly, Valens, the Big Bopper . . . think about it."

Dylan wasn't worried and got on the plane and went to sleep. A Jello-faced tourist reached over him, nudging him aside, to get Coburn's autograph.

CBS Discos studios, a gray fortress on the outskirts of Mexico City, had been alerted. A night crew was standing by for the American invasion. Dylan, Coburn, and Kristofferson—followed by Rita Coolidge, Kris's band, Gordon Carroll, the film's editor and sound man, and a visiting writer—swept by the security guards into an anteroom where a table sagged under the weight of food and drink.

"Sessions in Nashville ain't like this," said Kris between bites of turkey and cheese and a swig of whiskey. Dylan sat in a corner with a sandwich and a cup of vodka, while Coburn reached into the depths of his long coat and, grinning, withdrew a fat bomb of a Mexican joint. He took a puff that consumed a third of the bomb and leaned back, eyes closed, a contented man. "Adios, Bob," he waved as Dylan left for the studio.

The studio was a cavernous floodlighted red barn. There were two Mexican trumpet players in one corner playing off key. "Ask them," Dylan said, a half-grin playing on his lips, "if they know 'Help Me Make It Through the Night'?"

Kristofferson: "Now goddamn it, Bobby . . ."

"Well," Dylan said, "I want to use these guys on a song."

The trumpeters were not impressive, and Kris was impatient. "It ain't gonna work. Those cats don't know what he wants. If he'd let me tell 'em . . . fuck it, I ain't gonna run this thing."

Dylan had written two vocal tracks—the title song, "Billy," and "Holly," a lament for a man gunned down by Garrett—and several instrumentals and had recorded them earlier on a cassette unit at Peckinpah's house. After two months in Durango, he was obviously ready to record them properly, and he shed his straw hat and overcoat and strode briskly about the studio in white peasant shirt, Levis, boots, and metal-rim shades, moving mikes and setting up the board.

Coburn eased into the studio with another joint and a glass of red wine. He had a permanent Panavision smile. "Bob's so glad to be free," he said, "that he's *running* in here. He's been cooped up too long."

Dylan was ready shortly after 11:00 P.M. and started with "Billy." He gave it a long, languorous strumming introduction, overlaid with a lazy harmonic roll:

"There's guns across the river, tryin' to *ground you*/Lawman on your trail, like to *surround you*/Bounty hunters are dancin' all *around you*/Billy, they don't like you to be so free."

Except for the Tex-Mex riffs, the effect—especially the vocal—was pre-electric Dylan, recalling the *Another Side* era. He was singing hard and intensely, punching out the lines, as he ran through nine four-line verses, with an extended harmonica break after the sixth.

Kristofferson and Wurlitzer both reacted as if they'd been slapped in the face. Kris, gulping whiskey, snapped, "Ask him to do it in G!" Apparently this was not the same version Dylan had recorded at Peckinpah's. Wurlitzer was beside himself with wonder. "Hey man, do you dig what he's *doing?* He's *changed* the song. He's bein' perverse, man. See, he got fucked and now he's gonna do it *his* way."

Dylan called the writer aside. "Should I cut that? It seems *long.* Maybe I should cut a verse. I think I just might. Let's have a playback." He listened briefly, then called to the control room, "Let's do it again."

The second take was astounding. Dylan again did nine verses, but he changed two of them almost completely and dropped one of the original verses, replacing it with one that was improvised.

He bore down on the last line—"Billy, you're so far away from home"—and repeated it twice and then addressed the control room: "Keep that take and add this wild track to it: Corn. Beans. Succotash. Coffee. End of take." (Dylan, in one scene of the film, is required to stand against a wall and read the labels of canned goods.)

"See, man, what he's doin'," said Wurlitzer, "he's gettin' back at Sam. *Sure.* I don't know, man, if he's sayin' he's gonna quit the film or *what.*"

Dylan was extremely animated by then, sipping vodka straight and rushing to record. He threaded his way into "Will the Circle Be Unbroken" and was joined a third of the way through by Kris's band: Mike Utley laying gospel organ over Sammy Creason on drums, Stephen Bruton on electric guitar, and Terry Paul on bass. They started on instrumental tracks, Dylan leading the way with a galloping rhythm, paced by Bruton's electric lead that broke into what could only be called a turkey trot.

Dylan blended lyrics from the title song into it: "Don't it make you feel so *low down,* to be hunted by the man who was your friend." Then he slowed it to a halt. "Okay, that's called 'Turkey No. 2.' "

Next, he loped into a chunky, accelerating rhythm, trading off licks with Utley. Both were laughing and weaving and daring and challenging each other. Dylan and Terry Paul started a hypnotic "la la" lyric that grew more manic as they stood head to head and urged each other on.

They jammed for four minutes and then lurched to a stuttering finish. "Okayyy"—Dylan laughed and raised his cup—"we'll call this one . . . uhm, 'Billy Surrenders' or 'Speedball.' They're the same one. Hey, we need Sam here, to say what to *do*."

Wurlitzer gloomily appeared. "Sam *is* here, man. I feel him." He looked over his shoulder.

Coburn took his wine and joined the circle in the studio, which now included Kris and Rita on backup vocals. He sat before a mike to speak one of his lines, huskily: "Yeah, but I'm *alive*." Creason hit his drums a rifle shot, Bruton looped his staccato notes around Coburn's repeated line, and Dylan and Paul angled in on one mike, like streetcorner drunks, to harmonize on another "la laaaa" line.

Dylan was pleased with it. "What do we call that one, 'Turkey in the Straw'? Right. I got to put a lyric to that thing. *Forget* about the movie. Hey, Jim, this's just right for Billy coming out of Lincoln."

Coburn made a swooping motion. "Right! I can see it now, riding down through there and this music. *Yeeee-aaahhh!*"

Dylan unstrapped his guitar and came over to fetch a drink from a waiter, who had appeared at about three o'clock. Weren't there, Dylan was asked, some Doug Sahm riffs in that song?

"Oh yeah," Dylan replied. "We've learned a lot from each other. You should've been at those sessions with Doug in New York, the craziest things I've ever been in. They were the sessions to end all sessions. Oh—sometime you oughta ask the band about the times we had in Europe. Those are stories—I can't even get 'em out anymore."

Another drink and he rushed back to the microphone. "Here's another song, let's just call this 'Holly's Song.' " It was slow and gospelish, with simple lines: "Good-bye Holly, Holly good-bye. Your wife's gonna miss you, your baby's gonna cry."

Dylan, very much in command of the studio, called for his two Mexican trumpeters and showed them what he wanted for "Pecos Blues." He and Terry Paul sang "ah-ah-ahhh" lines over the tinny trumpets and a looping bass. The resulting sound suggested a Mexican whorehouse or a knock-down, pee-smelly dirt-floor bar. It was good, and Dylan nodded and smiled at the two beaming Mexicans, who had waited all night to play for two minutes.

Dylan went into the control room to hear the playback, and Coburn greeted him. "Fantastic, this is fucking *fantastic*. When it's matched with the film, it'll be beautiful. I hope they realize what they're getting here."

"Yeah?" Dylan looked at him.

Coburn gave him the full wide-screen Coburn treatment. *"Yeah."*

Dylan laughed. "Yeeahh."

Producer Carroll approached the Big D gingerly. About *that* song, he wondered, it seemed that it was different than it was on Sam's tape and he just wondered what *key* Dylan did it in.

"Same key," was the reply. Well, Carroll just thought that Sam's tape sounded *richer* and he wondered if Dylan would consider cutting it *another* way.

Dylan was edgy. "No, I can't even *hear* the song anymore. I guess it's what Sam wants. It's his movie. It's for the film."

Carroll persisted. "I don't understand the sense. What part of the film?" All of it, Dylan replied, all of it or none of it. He grew impatient. "You have two takes, you can have either of them."

Carroll backed down. "Want to hear them played back?"

Dylan, flatly. "I want to hear *everything* played back."

As Carroll turned, Dylan uttered one word: *"Hollywood."*

It was four in the morning, and he ordered another bourbon and sat, impassive behind his shades, as he listened to the tapes. Just after Kristofferson, Coburn, and Wurlitzer left to get some sleep before watching the Super Bowl, Dylan called for a new tape to be put on. "Let's," he said, "do 'Billy' again."

For the third take, he deleted his harmonica and added bass and drums and had Paul sing harmony. He cut it back to eight verses and the sound was bouncier and flashier.

But he didn't like the take and cut it again in G, just he and Paul singing over the guitar. He slowed it down and this version was eerie and mournful, almost dirge-like. Where earlier he had toyed with Billy, now he was pleading with him: "Billy, you're so *far* away from home."

He liked the take and turned to Carroll. "Right after this Garrett rides into town. Right?"

"Right," the producer said. "Right. That really is . . . *unbelievable.* Um. What do you think?"

"No," Dylan said. "I don't think. Usually. I don't think, I hold it all in and then . . . *act!"* He laughed. "I'm glad you were on the case, because I forgot all about that original."

Seven A.M. The Mexican technicians were rubbing their eyes sleepily and stepping around empty glasses and cigarette butts. As the others headed for the hotel, Dylan was wide awake and ready to return to Durango.

"I'm thinking about doing a show there," he said. "I'd like to. It's just a funky little hall. Real nice audience, though. They make a lot of noise. I'm kind of anxious to do it. I mean a *real* audience. I'm used to those audiences in the States, and they just come and *gawk* at you."

He found a last drink and last cigarette before leaving. "That song," he told the writer, "Rudy needed a song for the script. I wasn't doing anything. Rudy sent the script, and I read it and liked it and we got together and he needed a title song. And then I saw *The Wild Bunch* and *Straw Dogs* and *Cable Hogue* and liked them. The *best* one is *Ride the High Country*. Sam's really, like he's the last of a dying breed. They don't hire people like that to make movies anymore. So I wrote that song real quick and played it for Sam and he really liked it and asked me to be in the movie. I want now to *make* movies. I've never been this close to movies before. I'll make a hell of a movie after this."

Outlaws Willie and Waylon

Revolution and counterrevolution may seem to be the most unlikely topics ever to be associated with country music, but the tendency to rebel is ingrained in humans, it seems, and it certainly is imbedded in the persons most likely to be prominent in country music: white, Southern males of modest education, little or no formal music training, considerable ego, and virtually no sense of an enduring musical tradition. The history of country music is not a long one but neither is it especially tranquil.

Any conflict, though, was always carefully kept behind the scenes during country's first few decades. That was easily done because of the paternalistic nature of the country music structure, which was effectively run by a handful of men: the song publishers, the record company heads (who also controlled the producing of records), the Grand Ole Opry hierarchy, the few booking agents, and those who controlled the big country radio stations. The artists had virtually no say in anything (and, significantly, had no inkling whatsoever that they could ever have a say in anything approaching self-determination). Most evolution in country music came about from the top down, rather than the reverse, and came about for commercial, rather than artistic, reasons. (One distinction must be made here: Rebellion by country artists has inevitably been over lifestyle, for want of a better term, rather than over music. The classic example was Hank Williams, whose musical force could not be denied, but whose pathetic rebellion was rooted in the paranoia of an insular upbringing, alcohol, and drugs.)

Without going into great detail, even a casual reading of country music's history shows a cyclical pattern of action and reaction, based on commercial factors—on what the Nashville movers and shakers thought would sell. As a conservative business, country music may safely be said to have always preferred to follow, rather than to anticipate, trends. Rockabilly is a classic example. It was imposed upon Nashville by outside influences—from just down the road, in Memphis, at Sun Records—and could not be ignored after Elvis Presley's success. The country music industry initially tried to ignore it and keep selling honky-tonk music, deliberately disregarding the social forces behind the changes in musical tastes. But there was such a groundswell for the new music—particularly by artists—it became clear that it was a future that could not be swept away. RCA farsightedly signed Elvis and thereby guaranteed its commercial future.

At the time, the present and future titans of Nashville labored, with mixed successes, to make rockabilly work in the marketplace. Owen Bradley at Decca scored with Brenda Lee, but he completely misread and misunderstood Buddy Holly in a disastrous studio recording session in Nashville. Similarly, his studio work with Johnny Burnette's Rock 'n' Roll Trio was quickly forgotten. (Johnny Cash, who had been one of the great hopes at Sun Records, along with Elvis, later said that his rockabilly past was held against him by power shakers in Nashville, and Opry manager Jim Denny was one person he named.) At RCA, Chet Atkins, the wunderkind guitar picker who had worked with Hank Williams, now found himself in the studio trying to guide the likes of Presley and the Everly Brothers. And the reason is of course the reason why record companies exist: to sell records and make money.

As rockabilly waned and—not coincidentally—country moved closer to pop music, Bradley and Atkins brought forth what came to be known as the Nashville Sound. In another age, it might have been called "Lite Country." What it was was carefully formulated, inoffensive music designed to appeal to fans of pop music while still retaining enough of a country identity to make it on jukeboxes in the honky-tonks, even though the fiddles had been replaced by violins. With Bradley, the Sound peaked with his production of Patsy Cline ("Crazy," "I Fall to Pieces," "Sweet Dreams"). The Nashville Sound itself was more closely identified with Atkins and his best-known pickers: saxophonist Boots Randolph, pianist Floyd Cramer, and guitarists Hank Garland and Grady Martin (the latter would later join Willie Nelson's band). If you'd like one example, Jim Reeves's "He'll Have to Go" is perfect: country sentiments with a pop presentation. An airport lounge honky-tonk song.

The producer was truly king with the Nashville Sound in operation. He chose the songs, the pickers, the arrangements, the album cover, the strings and vocal backing used to "sweeten" the whole package. The singer was almost an afterthought. A lot of singers resented that, but there was nothing they could do about it. The record companies were selling records, not individual careers. In the past, country songs had crossed over to pop audiences mostly when covered by pop singers (as Tony Bennett did with Hank Williams's "Cold, Cold Heart"). Elvis changed all that, and the pop possibility became tantalizing.

It was into such a pop-country quagmire that a young generation of country singer-songwriters such as Willie Nelson and Waylon Jennings came in the Sixties. Nashville had tried to ignore the Beatles and all that they represented—the whole youth culture, pop culture, counterculture. Country music seemed fixed in a death frieze, epitomized by the Opry and its aging, rural, loyal-to-Roy Acuff audience on the one hand, and the younger, moved-to-the-city country blue-collar crowd that wasn't satisfied by Danny Davis & the Nashville Brass. The Nashville Sound had moved to middle-of-the-road music and lost whatever country identity it had had. Meanwhile, audiences were no longer isolated or segregated: even in rural areas, younger people listened to the latest Top Forty pop and rock hits, and, as they did so, they began to ask more of country music.

But Nashville wasn't listening. Albums were still recorded quickly on a nickel-and-dime budget and often featured a hit single surrounded by a lot of dross: country stage shows were often bare-bones affairs— music, but scarce else. For the artists, expectations were worse: sales of a hundred thousand for a record were wonderful (compare this with pop acts' frequent sales of over one million); bookings were still into the Crab Orchard circuit; and playing the Opry on Saturday night (for union scale) was still the ideal. It's easy to see in hindsight that there was a ceiling over Nashville: There was no notion that things could be bigger or better or even different. Country was a small-time game, played for small-time stakes. What sold was what was recorded, and what was recorded was what sold.

During this time (the Sixties going into the early Seventies) there were many factors that came to change country music drastically and forever. I would like to concentrate on one that was basically fostered by singers caught up in the Nashville Sound. There came to be a broad-based revolution spawned by the non-power brokers—the writers and singers—that was as much influenced by the Beatles as Bob Dylan, as much by the Vietnam War as by country star Johnny Cash (who had been a one-man phenomenon). It was called the "Outlaw" movement, a glib publicity term, but it came to represent a genuine watershed in country music history.

It sprang from a back-alley rendezvous in Nashville between kindred spirits who liked to stay up late and carouse around town before getting down to business with some music. But it came to represent a real determination by a handful of artists to bring country music into line with the rest of the music world—artistically as well as financially. By the time it ran its course, the Outlaw movement had changed the face of country music forever. The producer as king—that feudal notion was shattered. Country artists gained control over their own record sessions, their own booking, their record production, everything else related to their careers, including the right to make their own mistakes. It was a major shift in country music. It also brought country artists into the million-dollar stratosphere of pop and rock artists and also, of course, into their cocaine- and marijuana-laced decadence.

It's not often that one movement can coalesce around one event, but, conveniently, the whole Outlaw upheaval came to define itself by the release of one record album that was also the first platinum-selling (one million copies plus) albums in Nashville history.

The album—*Wanted! The Outlaws*—itself was not really anything spectacular, even by modest Nashville standards. RCA producer Jerry Bradley (Owen's son) conceded that, but knew he had hit upon what could become the biggest marketing coup of his life. For once, Nashville was selling a concept, rather than just peddling records. Bradley, in fact, said just that when he called me in 1975 to ask me to write liner notes for the *Outlaws* album. "I'll send you tapes on it," he told me, "but I'll bet you've heard most of it before. What I'm doing is putting Willie and Waylon and Tompall [with Waylon's wife, Jessi Colter] together as the Outlaws, because that's the way they are regarded here in town. This is a package, a total package that I'm looking to break outside the country market. That's why I'd like you to do the notes: You know the music and the musicians, but you're not a cheerleader like the writers here in town. You're definitely not considered part of the establishment."

Well, I had to admit that that was certainly true enough. One of Nashville's two daily newspapers had recently run a lengthy article attacking me for my views on the state of country music, in pieces published in *Rolling Stone* magazine. And I had received quite a bit of hate mail, most of it from Nashville. So, in a sense, I had to be flattered to be considered, even tangentially, an outlaw in Nashville.

Bradley, of course, had his own motives. Always in his father's shadow, he longed to make his mark in the industry. Even though he had nominally taken over RCA's Nashville reins from Chet Atkins, the latter's presence was still formidable within the company. And, with this album, Bradley was not going out on a limb so much as he was dealing with a relatively safe proposition. In all but name, the Outlaw business was pretty much in place and fairly successful long before the *Outlaws* album appeared, in 1976. The term itself had surfaced with Waylon's 1972 hit song and album of the same name, "Ladies Love Outlaws." The song, written by Lee Clayton, one of the junior Outlaws in Waylon's orbit, was intended, Clayton said, more or less tongue-in-cheek. But it quickly caught on as a sort of anthem.

And as far as the Outlaw business being a genuine rebellion against Nashville, it was at heart the inevitable revolt of sons against fathers. But even more so, it was a true declaration of independence by those involved. Willie had never been served well by the Nashville system and simply wanted to be left alone to pursue his musical visions. If he had to go to Texas to do so, so be it. (Ironically, a year before *Outlaws* was released, Willie went up to a little studio in Garland, Texas, with his band and recorded his true breakthrough album, *Red Headed Stranger*. When CBS Records' Billy Sherrill balked at releasing the sparsely arranged record, Willie won the test of wills.) Waylon had felt ill-served by the system for years, and rightly so. He mainly wanted a little freedom: to record with his road band and to record what songs he wanted to, when he wanted to, without a producer who had been assigned by Atkins, and especially where he wanted to. It was this last wish that led to his alignment with Tompall Glaser and the formation of Outlaw Headquarters at Hillbilly Central, Tompall's studio on Nineteenth Avenue South in Nashville. Under the terms of his RCA contract, Waylon was required to record at RCA if he was within two hundred miles of Nashville. Waylon had long chafed under RCA's heavy hand and had made his first move for independence in 1972 when Neil Reshen, his New York City manager (whom Waylon often referred to as his "mad dog on a leash"), discovered that, technically, RCA had not automatically picked up Waylon's option to re-sign with the company. Reshen soon had Columbia, Atlantic, Capitol, and Mercury wooing Waylon, to the great dismay of Chet Atkins and Jerry Bradley. After tense negotiations, RCA eventually re-signed Waylon, but gave him the greatest artistic freedom of any of its country artists. Atkins complained that his own contract with RCA held no such freedom. Waylon was pretty much left in control of his records—not something he really expected right away and certainly not something he was accustomed to. The freedom was also a muscle he himself would have to flex: RCA obviously was not going to spell out to him all the ways he could supplant what the label had been doing.

His music didn't change immediately, but his records did—especially the 1973 album that became the quintessential Outlaw work: *Honky Tonk Heroes*. It also set the formula for what became known as Outlaw music: sparsely accompanied and highly personal songs—a cowboy's diary set to a driving beat, as it were. This was Waylon Jennings working at full-bore, finally able to do what he wanted to, capturing his lusty, gritty vision. Nine of the ten songs on *Honky Tonk Heroes* were written by another Texas Outlaw, Billy Joe Shaver, a gifted poet who was determined to try Nashville because of his idols, Willie and Waylon. Billy Joe hitchhiked to Nashville on the back of a truck loaded with cantaloupes, naïve in his belief that such songs as "Black Rose"—about a black-white romance—could make it in Nashville. They did, although they could not have five years earlier or five years later. The Outlaw window was open, however briefly. Even though the credits say the album *Honky Tonk Heroes* was recorded at RCA, the bulk of it was cut at Tompall Glaser's Hillbilly Central studio, with Waylon and Tompall producing.

Of all the y-clept Outlaws, Tompall was the most outspoken in his reaction to the status quo in country music and in Nashville. He had come to Nashville via a circuitous route. He and brothers Jim and Chuck were from Nebraska and entered show business as a vocal group on Arthur Godfrey's "Talent Scouts" program and then backed Marty Robbins. The Glaser Brothers were brought to Nashville by the ubiquitous Owen Bradley. He signed them to Decca as a folk music act, as a sort of Kingston Trio clone. They were not clasped to Nashville's bosom—many thought they were Jewish or, even worse, Catholic (which they were). They left Decca for another parish, independent producer "Cowboy" Jack Clement, who founded Nashville's first independent studio and channeled the Glaser Brothers records to MGM, where they had modest hits. Clement came from Sun in Memphis, where he had produced Johnny Cash, to RCA, where he clearly did not fit in and did not last for very long. The Glasers themselves further antagonized the Nashville set by going against the grain and forming their own publishing company—something not done unless you were part of the hierarchy. They immediately succeeded by signing up John Hartford and thus acquiring the publishing rights to his "Gentle on My Mind," a song that for a time was probably performed somewhere in the world every sixty seconds. It further grated on some people's nerves that Hartford appeared to be a long-haired hippie.

Some of the Glasers' money went into a little state-of-the-art recording studio in a turn-of-the-century house on Nineteenth Avenue South, well off of Music Row. The brothers divorced as a musical act in 1972, and Tompall emerged as the nascent solo performer, cutting the introspective 1973 album *Charlie*. He also was the Glaser-in-residence at the comfortable studio, which quickly became known as Hillbilly Central, and which was a magnet for anyone in Nashville who was non-Nashville-establishment. It became, especially after dark, the clubhouse for the Outlaws, or those fancied to be one of their number. Waylon and Tompall, after a chance meeting, took a liking to each other. There are striking similarities: Both are strong individuals, loners, shy to the point of painfulness, distrustful of strangers, both had been burned in the music business, both were by nature trusting persons, and each held fierce and unwavering notions as to what their music ought to be. And especially what it ought not to be. And—perhaps most important of all—Waylon and Tompall were pinball nuts. They loved nothing better than to lean their lanky frames into a pinball machine and ride those flippers all night.

At the time, the area between Nineteenth Avenue and Vanderbilt University was a regular warren of cheap clubs, murky dives, hooch joints, raucous drive-ins, and beer-milk-bread convenience stores—each of which had at least one pinball machine. And these machines paid off. In real money. Waylon and Tompall sometimes would collect a couple of hundred bucks each for a few hours' work on the flippers.

I was privileged to spend more than a few nights on the pinball circuit with them, and I was to find that that was where they conducted a lot of their business—making decisions, meeting songwriters and being pitched songs and keeping up with who was writing what, doing a little songwriting themselves as they sent that little silver ball spinning. Their favorite joint was a dubious establishment called the Bump-Bump Room, and the Bump-Bump became—almost as much as Hillbilly Central—the nerve center of the Outlaw movement. An earlier generation had Tootsie's Orchid Lounge, next to the Opry. The Outlaws had the Bump-Bump Room (and they of course had no use for the Opry at all). They were, in effect, creating an alternative and parallel world distinct and separate from the Nashville establishment—no mean feat in a town as small as Nashville. In Hillbilly Central, Waylon finally found what he had not had at RCA's studios: a private outpost where he could come and go at any hour and do whatever he pleased, no questions asked. And he was surrounded by kindred folk. Very often, recording would not begin until Waylon and Tompall and whoever had cruised the pinball joints were ready to go to work. Then they would retire to Nineteenth, crack open the bottles of Black Jack, tune up the guitars and turn on the tape. It was an unregimented life they were seeking, one completely removed from the Nashville system, which actually was still patriarchal in nature, in which the producers and label heads, intentionally or not, treated the artists as dimwitted children or indentured servants. (Jennings still rankles over directives he received from RCA which began: "Dear Artist.") Glaser was even more vitriolic than Jennings, and his published comments about what he called a corrupt system seemed to guarantee that he would be frozen out by the system, which ultimately proved to be the case.

An astonishing thing was that, until Waylon in particular began to receive exposure in the rock press and success with rock audiences and became aware of how things were done in rock, the Outlaws—as well as most artists in Nashville—didn't realize that having artistic freedom in the recording studio was a given outside Nashville. You could record what you wanted and record it with your road band, you could pick the cover of your album, you could try to find a booking agent capable of putting you into places better than the blood-and-guts honky-tonks. You could pick a manager from Los Angeles or New York or anywhere else, and it could be someone who wasn't part of the tiny Nashville old-boy network. And—the biggest heresy—you could control your own publishing, which had always been Nashville's darkest little secret and of course was always where the real money was. You could even pick your own producer and not have to sign over half the publishing to him, which had been commonplace in Nashville. In short, that was the crux of the Outlaw movement: It had nothing to do with long hair or wearing black leather or smoking dope or any other such trivial sideshow issues. It was actually a fairly sober attempt at gaining self-determination and independence—not such a rare thing for creative people to seek. I can remember being touched by what I considered Waylon's naïveté when—after he started opening for such rock bands as the Grateful Dead—he was literally flabbergasted to learn that such groups could actually put riders into their contracts calling for specific food and drink to be served them in their dressing room. It was almost like watching a barefoot kid discover shoes.

For quite a while, the so-called Outlaws didn't really realize the power they were accruing and the impact they were making. Until their efforts translated into money—which is, after all, what the system really understands and appreciates—they were laboring in the wilderness, as it were. One of the most concrete and telling examples of their clout was an unprecedented concert presented as an alternative to the usual stuffy Disc Jockeys Convention in Nashville. The DJ convention was run by the major labels, with staid concerts and interview sessions and the like. But in 1973, Waylon decided to put on an independent show. Almost three thousand people jammed a ballroom at the Sheraton to see Troy Seals, Sammi Smith, Willie Nelson, and Waylon kick out all the jams in what was perhaps the one transcendent event of the whole Outlaw business. I was there, and the notes I took tell me that it was one of the most authoritative, self-confident musical evenings I have ever witnessed, that the music soared and the audience took off with it, and that in the early morning hours, as the show shut down, the heady, almost giddy feeling in the ballroom was contagious. There was a very real and spoken conviction that the old guard of country music was crumbling and the Huns were at the gate, starting to batter it down, and would not be denied. Their time had come.

What they did not yet have to effectuate real change in the Nashville music hierarchy was big record sales. Sales, anywhere in the music business, equaled money, and money equaled power. The more of everything, the better. Getting music writers from *Rolling Stone* to rave about an Outlaw concert at the Sheraton was one thing, but moving those albums out of the stores—that was the kicker, that would certify whether or not this little "movement" that Nashville seemed to have on its hands would amount to anything more than a temper tantrum being thrown by some talented, if immature, youngsters who had not yet learned the tribal ways. Jerry Bradley knew that. He knew, he thought, just how to fix all that with his big Concept Album.

What the album turned out to be was this: *Wanted! The Outlaws* had only Waylon's name on the spine (because he was the only one of the four Outlaws under contract to RCA at the time). Jerry Bradley decreed that there be a burnt-at-the-edges wanted-poster look to the cover of the thing, with Waylon's picture front and center, to be flanked by Willie, Tompall, and Jessi, with my liner notes on the back, in the form of a poster or broadside. The cuts on the record were unremarkable. Side one was made up of Waylon's "My Heroes Have Always Been Cowboys" and "Honky Tonk Heroes," Jessi's "I'm Looking for Blue Eyes" and "You Mean to Say," and "Suspicious Minds" by Waylon and Jessi. Side two opened with Willie and Waylon singing "Good Hearted Woman" and "Heaven or Hell," Willie's rendition of "Me and Paul" and "Yesterday's Wine." It ended with Tompall's "T for Texas" and "Put Another Log on the Fire." Not exactly a song lineup to draw the angels' hosannas. Yet, this *Outlaws* album was the first platinum album in country music history. There have been many answers advanced to explain that and, I suspect, the most nearly correct one is that the timing of the album was perfect. Two spectacular albums from 1975—Willie's *Red Headed Stranger* and Waylon's *Dreaming My Dreams*—primed the Outlaw audience. Had it been released even six months earlier or six months later, its impact might have been negligible. As it was, its fallout was considerable.

Outlaws was released on January 12, 1976, amid great hoopla by RCA. It soon crossed over to the pop charts, was certified gold by the beginning of April, and became country's first platinum-selling album by December. Country music was no longer just a singles market; it now was an album market and thus could rival the sales of rock releases. Willie and Waylon virtually became household names. Their albums began selling gold (500,000 copies) on their own strengths. They were invited to the White House by President Carter in 1978 (Willie and Jessi went; Waylon declined). Their names were more often in *Rolling Stone* than in *Music City News*. Jessi, who had never been overly ambitious and who had a new son at home, stayed in the background. Tompall Glaser, who had been between record labels at the time of the *Outlaws* release (and thus had no albums out to ride the *Outlaws* coattails) had a falling-out with Jennings. His solo career was static and he reunited with his brothers for a time.

Meanwhile, Outlaw-clone music inundated Nashville, and Willie and Waylon clones flooded the South and Southwest. In Texas, particularly, the Outlaw look became an everyday uniform, and that led right into the "Texas Chic" trend, which itself directly spawned the whole Urban Cowboy business. Willie and Waylon soon declared themselves sick of the Outlaw moniker, but they were more or less stuck with it. In 1978, Waylon felt moved to write and record the song "Don't You Think This Outlaw Bit's Done Got Out of Hand," and he doesn't write all that much.

The excesses performed in the name of Outlaw, by musicians and fans alike, were legion. A backlash was inevitable, especially after other performers began to see the amount of success (and money) that accrued to Willie and Waylon. Their records and concerts were scrutinized and criticized to a degree neither had thought possible. They were directly blamed for the basically sleazy Urban Cowboy craze that briefly touched country music. They were probably responsible for the New Traditionalists, who responded against the new commercialization of Urban Cowboyism (Nashville Sound as filtered through Gilley's in Pasadena, Texas, and then by the Eagles in California) by returning to a stripped-down, no-frills, back-to-the-basics hard-country music: white hat country, rescued by the likes of George Strait and Reba McEntire. It was not so different from what the Outlaws had started with, in their own revolt against Nashville Sound I. The fact that that revolt was effectively co-opted by commercial forces was not overlooked. (Even as the Outlaw surge was being effectively swamped by the excesses of Urban Cowboyism, Jerry Bradley was out there trying to conjure up an Outlaws II; but by then Waylon and Tompall had fallen out. What Bradley ended up with was the *Waylon and Willie* album in 1978. That was not a landmark record, in any sense.)

Oddly, what may have been the biggest legacy of the Outlaws was scarcely recognized. In effectively challenging and then shattering Nashville's feudal system, the Outlaw movement opened the doors of artistic freedom wide—perhaps a shade too wide for some. Country music (and its new pop audience and attendant prosperity) not only had made room now for a Joe Ely or a Rosanne Cash or a Ricky Skaggs, it also had room (too much, some said) for a Kenny Rogers.